"RIVETING . . .

Al Santoli's book truly captures the wisdom of George Santayana in his now famous phrase, 'Those who cannot remember the past are condemned to repeat it.' "

—Military

"LEADING THE WAY is a powerful account of how a small group of soldiers [of all branches of service] survived the horror and the pain of Vietnam to rebuild the American military. Al Santoli lets these fighting men tell their own story. They do so with authority, insight, and sensitivity."

—LALLY WEYMOUTH
Columnist
The Washington Post

"Worthy and timely."
—W. C. WESTMORELAND
General of the United States Army (Ret.)

"In a politically correct era, many people would like to put the lessons learned in Vietnam behind, and at a time when such lessons have renewed significance. Not Al Santoli."

—Leatherneck

Also by Al Santoli
Published by Ballantine Books:

EVERYTHING WE HAD
TO BEAR ANY BURDEN
NEW AMERICANS: AN ORAL HISTORY

LEADING THE WAY

How Vietnam Veterans Rebuilt
the U.S. Military:
An Oral History

Al Santoli

BALLANTINE BOOKS • NEW YORK

Copyright © 1993 by Al Santoli
Maps copyright © 1993 by Virginia Norey

All rights reserved under International and Pan-American Copyright Conventions. Published in the United States of America by Ballantine Books, a division of Random House, Inc., New York, and simultaneously in Canada by Random House of Canada Limited, Toronto.

Library of Congress Catalog Card Number: 93-70002

ISBN 0-345-38974-3

Manufactured in the United States of America

First Hardcover Edition: October 1993
First Mass Market Edition: November 1994

10 9 8 7 6 5 4 3 2 1

To Colonel James "Nick" Rowe:
His courage inspired all who knew him. A
warrior, writer and up-front leader. He
sacrificed his life so that others might
have freedom.

Human beings differ very little from one another;
but the ones who come out on top
are those who have trained in the hardest school.
—THUCYDIDES

To be a successful soldier you must know history . . .
weapons change, but men who use them change little at all.
—GENERAL GEORGE S. PATTON, JR.

The role of a leader
is to keep hope alive.
—MAJOR GENERAL BERNARD LOEFFKE

ACKNOWLEDGMENTS

This book would not have been possible without the vision and enthusiastic support of my editor at Ballantine, Pamela Strickler. My agent, Anne Sibbald, is always there for me. I am grateful to them. Walter Anderson, former Marine and editor-in-chief at *Parade*, permitted me for a decade to follow the development of the American military and to write a series of articles that strengthened my knowledge. My wife Phuong and daughters Christina and Julia provide the love that keeps balance in my life.

In the process of researching this book, I traveled to military bases and headquarters around the United States. This would not have been possible without the consent of the respective branches of the armed forces and the assistance of a large number of public affairs officers in the Pentagon and in bases in the field. Among those who opened key doors for me: in the Army, Colonel David "Rick" Kiernan, Colonel William Smullen, Lt. Colonel Larry Icenogle, Major Jesse Seigal, Major Barbara Goodno, Major John Marlin, Major Lewis Boone, Captain Bill Buckner, Sergeant Alex Gray, and Specialist Wendy Westlake; the Air Force, Colonel Don Black, Major Ron Fuchs, and Major Gail Hayes; the Marine Corps, Colonel Fred Peck, Major Nancy Laluntas, Major Rick DeSchaino, Chief Warrant Officer Eric Carlson, and Sergeant Renee Reyna; and the Navy, Lieutenant Mark Walker, Lieutenant Matt Brown.

Only half of the senior officers and sergeants whom I interviewed appear in this book. Those whose stories do not appear here provided valuable insight and are very much a part of this work of history.

CONTENTS

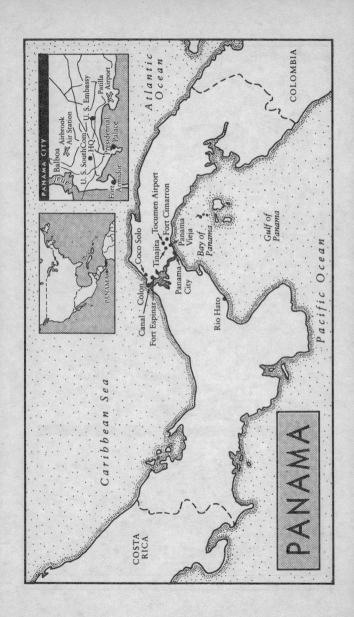

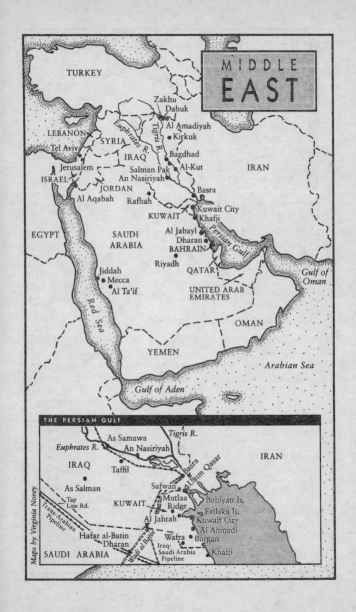

INTRODUCTION

This is the story of a small group of courageous and determined people. Against all odds, they helped to turn around a broken institution—the United States military—and to reinstill confidence among their ranks and in the eyes of the American people. These veterans recall, in their own words, how in the aftermath of bitter defeat, they overcame self-doubt as well as prejudice from their civilian peers. And above all else, how they developed qualities of leadership that were believed lacking in overall American society.

I am not a general or a professional soldier. However, I have been a young soldier covered in my own blood, lying in half-shock on a foreign battlefield. I have known the crushing feeling of being among those asked to put their lives on the line without having the support of our superiors, or the benefit of a coherent policy. That experience created a bond that unites most survivors of the Vietnam War. It motivated me to become a chronicler of men and women who have faced combat. And it inspired a core group of young officers and sergeants not to abandon a military community in shambles in the aftermath of Vietnam.

I started work on this project in the late spring of 1991, while the last large groups of U.S. ground troops, sailors, and airmen were returning from combat duty in the Persian Gulf after Desert Storm. For the next two years, as I conducted numerous interviews with men and women of all branches of service, U.S. forces were sent into Somalia, and a naval blockade and aerial patrols over Iraq continued, while the "drug war" in Latin America sputtered. And a debate raged over how to stop ethnic violence in the Balkans as the former Soviet Union was edging toward instability.

This dizzying turn of world events altered my original focus. I had intended to document a closure to the historical cycle that began with the introduction of U.S. ground forces to Vietnam in 1965, that reached its low point in the ill-fated 1980 hostage rescue attempt in Iran, and that ended triumphantly with the 1991 liberation of Kuwait.

But while the American public was celebrating joyous post–Desert Storm "Welcome Home" parades, a quiet sobriety was expressed by most senior military people I spoke with. And today, as the euphoria of victory fades, the greatest challenge that senior leaders face is to prevent their troops and young officers from resting on their laurels.

Domestic needs require that our military budget and manpower be scaled down. But instead of a "peace dividend," the post–Cold War era has rekindled age-old ethnic violence and regional instability. International economic competition has intensified. The scourge of drugs has spread. State-of-the-art weapons technologies are available on the open market. In many ways, the world has become a more unpredictable and explosive environment.

After the Gulf War, American forces immediately needed to continue training for whatever emergencies might occur next. However, the "draw down" of military budget and manpower is likely to require cutbacks in vital training time and resources, and may eventually curtail a Desert Storm-type ability to respond. Leadership, both in senior Pentagon management and in small field units, remains the intangible key to holding together a quality institution and saving lives in precarious situations.

My concern remains with the young American troops, who, unlike blocks on a war game board or characters in bloodless computer exercises, die easily. To be sure, there are important positive lessons to be learned from Desert Storm. However, there remains a chance that young soldiers or marines—overconfident from the ease of the victory over Iraq—may be sent into politically complex situations where battle lines are not clearly defined. Unlike in the desert of Kuwait, they may have to serve as peacekeepers in populated areas, perhaps under harsh conditions with harassment from violent forces and a questioning public at home. The use of overwhelming force may not be politically or morally feasible. Instead, leadership and discipline are critical. And lessons learned from

Vietnam—which many people would like to "put behind us"—have renewed significance.

During Desert Shield/Desert Storm, only around three percent of the active duty forces were Vietnam veterans. But they played the premier role in planning the operations and leading the forces into battle in the air, on land, and at sea. During the current RIF (reduction in force) a substantial number of them will leave active duty. Within five to ten years, practically all those who experienced the pain of Vietnam and the rebuilding years will be retired.

As we rush toward the future, there are lessons from those difficult days that should not be overlooked or cast aside. At stake are not only the lives of our young men and women who may be sent into harm's way. In this increasingly volatile world, the security of our nation may be jeopardized.

The fifty-six people you will meet in these pages—ranging from Joint Chiefs of Staff Chairman Colin Powell, Marine Corps Commandant Al Gray, Air Force Space Command General Chuck Horner to Navy SEAL Captain Timothy Holden, Army nurse Colonel Barbara Smith and Marine tank Master Sergeant James Graham—are all combat veterans. This should not be seen as a slight to the important role of those who work in the logistics and combat support branches. Any fighter will be the first to say that they could not succeed without those who provide the transport, maintenance, bullets, and beans. But as a former combat soldier, I best relate to those who do the fighting and bleeding, and who sometimes make split-second decisions that affect the lives of our sons and daughters under their command.

Besides the arduous trials of Vietnam and the intense planning for Desert Storm, the leaders in this book have collectively played a role in all major involvements of American military forces during the past five decades: These include the Pacific and European campaigns of World War II; the Korean War; the Cold War in Europe; the Cuban Missile Crisis; the fall of Iran and hostage rescue attempt; Lebanon; Grenada; Operation Just Cause in Panama, and Operation Provide Hope in Somalia. The through line that links all of these events and diverse leadership styles is that in all wars the combat experience has similar human traits.

Included as well are many valuable insights on the growing role of technology. Many new computerized weapons systems contributed to a quick resolution of the Gulf War. But technology by itself cannot guarantee success. Although Desert Storm was not a prolonged ground conflict, among the commanders I interviewed are a unique group who fought the Iraqis at close quarters. You will find that courage has many faces.

The book's five sections are organized in a chronological flow of events. Through personal stories, reflections and insights, you will get a glimpse into the minds and souls of individuals who have played key roles on the battlefield. Between Vietnam and the Gulf, each officer or sergeant had to struggle, not only to rebuild the system; he or she also had the very personal struggle to define his or her own goals and sense of purpose.

We veterans believe that our learning experiences from Vietnam and the rebuilding period must be remembered. These lessons can be critical in helping a new generation deal with difficult geopolitical challenges. They can provide guidance to successfully protect our national security and to fulfill international obligations. And more important, they can prevent our political and military policymakers from sliding into "another Vietnam" while dealing with complex political and military crises during this unpredictable period of history.

> —AL SANTOLI
> Falls Church, Virginia
> April 1993

PROLOGUE

APACHE MISSION

CHIEF WARRANT OFFICER 4
LOU HALL

Iraq 1991
Flight Lead
1st Battalion, 101st Aviation Regiment
101st Airborne Division

At 2:38 A.M. on January 17, 1991, a task force of eight American Apache attack helicopters fired the first shots of Desert Storm. Their objective, to destroy two early-warning radar sites, would open a radar-free corridor in the vast desert of southwest Iraq.

The pressure on the Apaches' two-man crews went far beyond their personal safety. Riding on the mission were the lives of the hundreds of allied air crews who were preparing to follow right behind the Apaches to bomb Scud missile sites and targets in the Baghdad area.

Chief Warrant Officer Lou Hall was the flight lead for Red Team, tasked with destroying one of the sites. Deceptively youthful at thirty-seven years old, except for his graying black hair, he was a veteran of heavy combat as a door gunner and helicopter crew chief in the closing stages of the Vietnam War.

I was the flight lead of Red Team on the first combat mission of the air war. Our objective was to open a hole in Iraq's forward defense radar. It was explained to us that we needed to have 100 percent success. If we missed even part of the Iraqi radar and communications equipment, it would tip off Iraq's entire air defense system and jet fighter bases that the air war was about to begin. Consequently a lot of allied pilots would be killed.

The plans and training for the strike had been tightly guarded and compartmentalized. Until twenty-four hours before the mission, my team had no idea where we were going.

3

Our destination—a 720-mile flight from our base in Saudi Arabia—was farther than anyone had ever gone before in a helicopter. We mounted an extra fuel tank on our aircraft because we needed "long legs." Setting up refueling areas in the desert was too risky.

We were chosen for the mission, in large part, because of the capabilities of our aircraft. The AH-64 Apache is the Ferrari of helicopter gunships. It weighs almost nine tons but can outmaneuver almost any aircraft. It can spin on a dime because of computer-enhanced flight controls. The crew is two people. The pilot usually flies from the back seat. The front seat is for the weapons system operator, who we call the "copilot gunner."

The Apache is capable of flying low-level at high speeds deep into enemy areas, under the cover of darkness. We can also hover at a stand-off distance and observe a target area while not being seen or heard. We are able to fly at night because of our night vision systems:

First, there is a FLIR [Forward Looking Infrared] television screen in both front and back seats, that gives amplified thermal pictures of the ground. Second, the pilot and copilot each have a see-through one-inch TV screen attached to their flight helmet, and placed over their right eye. That gives the pilot a "heads up" display of speed, altitude and direction. So he never has to look down into the cockpit. The display includes a thermal television image at night. We also had the copilot use night-vision goggles that are 2,000 to 3,500 more sensitive than the human eye.

Our amplified vision system gives us a phenomenal weapons range [up to eight kilometers, or five miles] day or night. We use pinpoint laser targeting for our Hellfire missiles that can beat any known armor. We also have 30mm cannons and rocket systems. If you go at night against people who don't have night vision optics, you can operate at a distance where they can't see or hear you when you open fire. All they can do is get blown away.

In training, our commander, Lt. Colonel Dick Cody, used sand tables to diagram the two radar sites that our task force would have to hit simultaneously. He said, "This is what we're going to do if we see this or that type of target." He instructed each of us on what specific building or vehicle to hit.

Even though he wouldn't tell us where we were going, everything was briefed to the minutest detail. Our "Task Force

Normandy" was divided into two teams of four Apaches: White Team and Red Team. Each team was to be guided by two Air Force special operations Pave Low helicopters, which have satellite navigation capability. I was the only combat veteran in my group.

The mission was scheduled to begin around midnight on January 16. We flew to our staging area in the Saudi desert and waited for the "Go" signal. A jeep drove by and said the code word to Colonel Cody.

We took off just before one A.M. I flew the lead gunship of Red Team, following the Air Force Pave Lows. Crossing into Iraq, with all of our lights off, it was pitch-dark. There was a muzzle flash from the ground as we flew past an Iraqi outpost, as somebody tried shooting at us. But I wasn't worried about it. They couldn't see us.

Flying in pitch-darkness over the desert at low level, the greatest danger in maneuvering is the optical illusion of not being able to tell up from down. The desert horizon is indistinguishable from the sky. So we rely on our forward-looking infrared system, that gives us imagery based on the heat differentials of any object. It can distinguish the difference between two small leaves. In the desert, rocks or vehicles have different temperatures than the sand.

As we flew, I kept my focus on navigating the aircraft, coordinating my left eye between scanning outside the aircraft and my TV screen, and my right eye reading the symbology on the "combiner" monocle and the FLIR.

In the front seat, my copilot was reading the target acquisitions and weapons system data on his FLIR screen. Scanning for potential threats, he was wearing night vision goggles that magnify ambient light outside of the aircraft. If his goggles picked up any reflections in the distance, he could magnify the object with the FLIR system. A person lighting a cigarette a mile away looks like he is shining a flashlight at you.

Flying to the target, I did feel nervous the whole time. It wasn't so much because I was going into combat. I'd been through that before. It was mostly because I knew how bad it would be for everyone that would follow us if we didn't accomplish the mission. I didn't want to mess up.

The day before, I went over the mission plans hundreds of times in my mind. I kept thinking back to a hillside in Vietnam. I was eighteen years old, flying in a medevac helicopter to rescue a bunch of wounded Korean allies. A Cobra gunship was shot down just prior to us going in. We flew onto that hill-side with mortars exploding around us. Shrapnel was bouncing off the aircraft.

I jumped out and ran to get the Koreans. One by one, I carried them to the aircraft and threw them in. After the last one, the aircraft was pulling off . . . shrapnel and bullets pounding us. I was later told that we took eighty-seven hits. I remember the aircraft spinning, seeing people being hit. I ended up spending three or four weeks in a hospital. And was awarded the Distinguished Flying Cross.

After that, I knew that I'd already been tested. I didn't worry as much as some other guys who had never seen combat. But I was a teenager and single in Vietnam. Now I'm married with kids. I hate to say this, because my wife will probably kill me. But that night in Iraq, I was totally concentrated on my mission. My kids are all taken care of. I had more insurance than I'll ever need. And the 101st's home base, Fort Campbell, Kentucky, is big on family support groups. If anything happened to me, my wife and kids would be well taken care of.

I had one single purpose. That was to take out the enemy radar site. Every fire support mission we fly has American lives at stake. But the opening air mission had a hell of a lot of lives depending on us.

The only other Vietnam veteran on the mission was an Air Force Pave Low guy named Tim Zarnowski. We talked with the other guys beforehand. And Colonel Cody warned about how nervous we would get and how important the mission was. We had to have everything clear in our minds.

Our target, the Iraqi radar site, was two groups of small buildings. They were not easy to find in the vast desert. We had been shown many satellite photos of the equipment. But we had never seen them on an FLIR screen. So we looked for silhouettes at different angles. We couldn't risk hitting a village or military outpost by mistake. If we engaged the wrong target, our mission would be blown. If Iraq's radar network was alerted, there would be no second chances. Within minutes, the Air Force was to open the air campaign.

We kept extreme radio silence. The Pave Lows led us to a staging area nine miles from the radar site. From there, our two Apache teams took off by ourselves toward our respective targets, around thirty miles apart. As we approached our battle station, we had to fly low and slow—down to 60 knots [69 mph]—to avoid radar detection. Because the faster you go, the more of a radar signal you create.

Each radar site's buildings and antennas were spread out and defended by missiles and antiaircraft cannons. Both teams had to coordinate our fire so that our aircrafts' munitions would destroy all targets at the exact same time. If we hit the sites at staggered sequence, some Iraqi would radio a warning to Baghdad.

In the pilot's seat, I can watch everything my weapons man does on my FLIR screen. Every Apache has the ability to paint a target with lasers. And we can assist each other. If another aircraft can't find a target, they can lock their weapons system onto another aircraft's beam.

At our predesignated battle stations, four kilometers from the radar sites, we hovered on line. On our screens we could see soldiers moving in the target areas. But they couldn't see or hear us. Our lasers locked on their radar and communication buildings.

At 2:37:50, both team leaders broke radio silence to signal his team, "Party at ten [seconds]." Each crew responded, "Tally." Everybody locked on their targets. We watched our clocks tick down ten seconds. At precisely 2:38 A.M. all eight Apaches released our missiles simultaneously.

My aircraft's Hellfires took down a power generator and two other primary targets. Then we fired rockets that fly a certain distance before the warhead opens up to drop bomblets. They explode, saturating the area with razor-sharp metal shards— what we call a "wall of steel."

As I came in, I had to quickly vary the rockets' computerized aiming systems. Because that particular rocket configuration had never been used before. After the first rockets were fired, I adjusted the aircraft toward our aiming points. And we hit everything that was targeted.

As we kept moving toward the radar site, we switched to our 30mm cannon, hosing the area with 650 grenades per minute. I heard over the radio that a few Iraqi surface-to-air missiles were being fired. I didn't pay attention. I was busy watching my weapons gunner on my video screen. Our total concentration was on taking out that site. Anything else was peripheral.

My copilot, Jerry Orsburn, was like a machine. We had practiced our firing sequence so many times that he worked from one target to the next, using one weapons system then another, with complete precision.

As we arrived at the preplanned break-off point, we came within range of Iraqi antiaircraft weapons.

I said, "Hey, Jerry, do you want to go or do you want to shoot some more?" He just kept shooting and coolly answered, "Yes, let's shoot some more." He wanted to make sure that there wasn't anything or anyone who could radio back to Baghdad. We felt that we'd rather die than fail the mission. There were too many American lives riding on our performance.

Within two or three minutes it was all over. Time to egress [return home]. We turned around and headed south toward Saudi. All of a sudden we saw waves of Air Force planes heading right over us. It was a good feeling.

I remembered Saddam Hussein ridiculing American resolve. I kept thinking, "Vietnam. . . . This time we're going to prove that we really can win."

And we knew that we had the support of the American people. That gave us 100 percent confidence: "This time we're going to win." We were determined not to mess up.

PART I

Points of Origin

BLOOD RIVER

REAR ADMIRAL
DAVID BILL

MEKONG DELTA, VIETNAM 1968–69
RIVERINE PATROL OFFICER
U.S. NAVY RIVER DIVISIONS 554 & 514

*The son of a career naval officer, David Bill grew up dreaming
of one day having his own ship command. That dream was realized in the Gulf War when he commanded the battleship USS
Wisconsin. Scholarly, in dark-rimmed glasses, he has the appearance of a high school principal or an executive of a For-
tune 500 company. In fact, commanding a 1,500 member crew
aboard a massive battleship requires a masterful fusion of
leadership and managerial skills. However, his most dangerous
and stressful mission may have been as a young lieutenant on
a riverboat in Vietnam, where he received the Bronze Star for
valor.*

After I came home from Desert Storm, I heard from a cousin
who lives in Sikeston, Missouri. He told a man who was organizing a Memorial Day observance, "I have a cousin who is
commander of a battleship." The guy said, "Wouldn't that be
wonderful if he could come." So I went.

As part of the ceremonies and parade, I gave a speech. We
went out to the graveyard and put a wreath on the grave of a
young Marine lance corporal who was killed in the desert. His
parents were there. That brought back memories of when I was
a young lieutenant on a riverboat in Vietnam.

I grew up in a Navy family. My Dad was a captain who had
eight ship commands. He was a dynamic guy who enjoyed being completely immersed in his work. I went to visit him on
at least three of his ships. At a very young age I made up my

mind that I wanted to go to the U.S. Naval Academy and pursue that life.

I graduated from the Academy in 1966. Going to Vietnam wasn't on my mind. My first assignment after graduation was shipboard on a destroyer, the USS *John King*. When the war heated up during the 1968 Tet Offensive, I asked for the Riverine Force in Vietnam. It only took two weeks to get orders.

It seemed that a lot of people went into the Navy during the war to get out of being drafted and put in a ground combat unit. But in the "brown water navy" we saw our share of close combat. We were especially vulnerable. In a thirty-three-foot fiberglass boat, we didn't have much protection.

The crews of four included: a forward .50-caliber machine gunner, an after gunner, an engineman/.30-caliber machine gunner, and a coxswain/boat petty officer. Most were volunteers. Every two to four boats had one Riverine Patrol Officer, who rotated among the boats. Usually a senior NCO [noncommissioned officer] like a 1st class petty officer or chief petty officer, was in charge of each riverboat. One of the lessons I quickly learned is that there are various reactions under pressure.

We operated from the area surrounding Saigon to the Cambodian border, in a place called the Grand Canal. Ironically, in our stateside training we were always told, "You should never go into a canal. You're a sitting duck."

Our mission was to stop the infiltration of Cambodia-based North Vietnamese forces into the Mekong Delta. Which they often did in riverboats called *sampans*. At first, we caught the NVA [North Vietnamese Army] and Viet Cong by surprise.

Advanced scouts of an NVA battalion infiltrated down the canal in small sampans, several miles ahead of the main group. An ambush was set up on the bank of the canal by a U.S. Army lieutenant and sergeant who were advising a South Vietnamese Popular Force unit. We came up the canal to support them.

When the shooting started, we fired flares to illuminate the canal while airplanes provided fire support. The next day, the airplanes found the NVA battalion hiding in the Plain of Reeds, just a few kilometers north. Allied reinforcements were called. In the subsequent battle, the whole NVA battalion was wiped out.

That incident, and other operations we were involved in, got the NVA's attention. All hell broke loose. They studied our movements and set ambushes for us. Our orders were to move up and down the canal, day and night—a dangerously predictable pattern. My patrol group was the first to be ambushed.

It was an absolutely pitch-black night. The section of the canal was not more than twenty feet wide. My boat was first in the column.

I walked up to the front of the boat with a starlight [night vision] scope to try to see where we were going. It was so dark, I couldn't see the banks. I walked back to the coxswain's [boat pilot's] flat. We hit a command-detonated mine . . . exploding right where I had been standing. Our forward gunner, a young Marine from California, was seriously wounded.

The power of the blast knocked me out. Ambushers opened fire from the riverbank. The coxswain, standing next to me, had a bullet penetrate his steel helmet and come out the other side, just grazing his head. The kid standing next to me got a bullet in the gut.

When I regained consciousness, I tried standing up. Water was up to my knees. The boat was sinking. The Communists kept firing on me. The only thing that saved us was that the fourth boat in our group was outside of the kill zone. They were able to maintain a steady volume of fire that broke up the ambush.

After the ambushers fled, the fourth boat came alongside mine. I was desperately tending to the wounded. The young Marine died in my arms. We tied our boats together and rammed mine into the bank to keep it from sinking. Medevac helicopters began arriving to evacuate the dead and wounded.

That incident started a series of attacks. The next night we lost another boat, and two patrol officers were killed. One of them has a ship named after him today. Gradually we learned to adapt our tactics. We set counterambushes along the trails the Communists used from the Cambodian border. Or along the streams that they traveled by sampan at night.

The immediate challenge I faced was to establish trust with the crews who worked for me. I needed to prove that I knew what the hell I was doing. As a young kid—twenty-three years old—I was making life and death decisions about when to shoot and when not to shoot. And how to carry out various combat missions. I adapted to my Riverine post with the spirit, "The other guys are trying to kill us. We'd better find a way to beat them."

ONE YEAR ROTATION

GENERAL ALFRED GRAY

DANANG/KHE SANH, VIETNAM 1964-65
COMMUNICATIONS ADVISOR
U.S. MARINES

General Al Gray revolutionized the Marine Corps as Comman-
dant from 1987 to 1991. In a distinguished forty-one-year ca-
reer, the barrel-chested, tobacco-chewing populist rose from a
private to four-star general. He grew up in a town on the New
Jersey shore during World War II. Gray was a college student
and ball player when he enlisted for three years at the outset
of the Korean War in 1950. His first combat experience was in
a recon unit, and in 1952 he was given a commission from ser-
geant to lieutenant. "I never decided to stay in the Corps," he
says, "I just never decided to get out."

I came home from Korea in 1954, a 1st lieutenant. I had commanded a mortar company in the 8th Marines. I was assigned
to Camp Lejeune, North Carolina, where all we did was train.
We had an occasional parade, like when General "Chesty"
Puller became division commander.

In 1955, all regular lieutenants had to go to supply school or
communications school because the Corps was shorthanded. I
had orders for Com School. I was brokenhearted because I
wanted to be an infantry officer.

I was going to the Personnel Office to register my protest.
As I walked past the Commandant's Office, a colonel came
out. He asked, "What are you doing here?" He had been my
battalion commander in the Korean War. I told him. He said,
"We can probably get that canceled if you don't want to go.
My advice is, don't ever turn down a school."

So I said, "Okay."

Around the time I graduated, 1,000 Marines were assigned
to Signal Intelligence for Europe. I packed my bags and made
plans for Germany. In our final briefing, we were told, "By the

way, the Commandant wants one unit to go to the Far East, as soon as possible. Lieutenant Gray, since you're single, you're going."

I spent two and a half years in Japan, and then went to Hawaii to form a radio battalion. I worked, in part, for the National Security Agency and Naval Security Group.

My first tour in Vietnam was in 1964, before the American buildup. I was doing signal intel with a mixed Vietnamese force. I had a South Vietnamese master sergeant who was an amazing guy. He had been commander of a machine-gun company in the Viet Minh [post-WWII anti-French resistance, dominated by Ho Chi Minh's Communists]. He was fed up with Communism, so he brought his company and weapons over to the South Vietnamese Republic side.

I had a young Vietnamese lieutenant, about twenty-four years old, who had been to the French officer's school in Saigon. There was an old guy who was a combat engineer. And a 2nd lieutenant forward observer who was very different— dark-skinned, never talked much. He was an ethnic Cambodian from the Mekong Delta. For security, I had Nungs, a tribe who considered themselves Chinese. They hated all Vietnamese, North or South. And everybody hated the Montagnard hill-tribe people.

In the town of Khe Sanh, we had some Montagnard people who were dying of intestinal worms. We had supply helicopters going back and forth to Dong Ha and Quang Tri. I damn near got shot by Vietnamese soldiers because I ordered these Montagnards to be transported for medical treatment.

Khe Sanh was near Laos, where most of the North Vietnamese infiltration came down the Ho Chi Minh Trail. In that northwest frontier we had a very active Viet Cong network, and a lot of North Vietnamese army activity.

We first went to Khe Sanh on a reconnaissance mission in a remote mountainous area. The Special Forces said that there wasn't any enemy activity up there. So I had a large Marine unit that was assigned to me stay back near the town. I went with local troops to recon the mountaintops and to set up our radio equipment.

We got trapped up there because the heavy monsoon cloud cover was too thick for helicopters to get in. We couldn't get resupplied. After eighteen days we were eating half-cups of rice a day, and a little bit of that goddamned paste in French cans.

Our little motley crew—I was the only American—walked out of those mountains to an ARVN [South Vietnamese Army] outpost on the Lao border. About halfway down, we stumbled into a Viet Cong command post. They heard us coming and set an ambush from the other side of a river.

We came upon a Viet Cong in the water, taking a bath. He grabbed for his carbine. I shot him before he could shoot me. The VC opened fire from across the river. I told my guys, "Let's get the hell out of here. Call for artillery support." Before we left, some of my troops stopped to fingerprint the dead VC, using litmus paper. Because that's how they got paid.

With help from artillery, we busted up the ambush. In the process we killed the Viet Cong company commander and captured all his papers and plans. That enabled us to destroy the local VC infrastructure for a long time to come.

After that, I remember going to Da Nang. I saw row after row of U.S. dump trucks and construction stuff. We were building a South Vietnamese army patterned after the American army. I said, "Why the hell don't we give these guys some light weapons and let them get out and protect the people?"

The real American buildup in Vietnam began in February to April 1965. I came back to Vietnam in October of that year, during the heyday of General William Westmoreland [Commander of U.S. forces in Vietnam]. An impressive guy. He would visit Da Nang and talk with everybody. But he was of the "big army" conceptual thought process.

One thing that some Pentagon people never understood is when you're a soldier—mainline or guerrilla—you get awfully good with what little you have. Our Marines got better and better when they were operating in the jungle every day, even if they didn't have the best equipment and logistic support. But what hurt us was the "one year rotation" policy. Just as a trooper was getting real smart, it was time for him to go home. Somebody brand-new replaced him, disrupting unit cohesion and effectiveness. And in the last weeks before rotation, people made tragic mistakes by being overly careful.

A NEW LIFE

COMMAND SERGEANT MAJOR
WILLIAM EARL MCCUNE

CENTRAL HIGHLANDS, VIETNAM 1966–67
RIFLEMAN
1ST CAVALRY DIVISION

I was born in Mississippi. My family was part of the big migration [of blacks] north to Chicago for freedom and all that. I was drafted in 1966, as I was about to turn twenty-five. I never intended to make the Army a career.

I was sent to Vietnam as a private in 1967. I didn't know what to expect. I was assigned to the 1st Cavalry Division at An Khe, in the Central Highlands.

For the first week I burned shit from the latrines with kerosene for the 1st sergeant. All of a sudden, they put me on a bird [helicopter] heading to the field. The company was in a firefight as I flew in. I was kicked out of the helicopter, landing in some kind of foxhole. The guy I landed next to seemed to know what he was doing. So I stuck with him. He said, "Follow what I do." That's all the training I got.

The company commander didn't know I was there for a week. We were in the midst of fighting, trying to evacuate dead bodies. Things didn't settle down for about seven days. I ended up walking point for the next six months with the guy I fell in the hole with. He took care of me and showed me the ropes.

My company commander was only a 1st lieutenant. He selected the best PFC or E4 [corporal or Spec. 4] to alert the company to anything that was in front of our position. The entire company depended on those one or two guys. An awful lot of responsibility was put on young soldiers. There wasn't any leadership training. My buddy learned how to walk point, how to identify booby traps and signs of enemy activity. That's what he taught me: How not to walk the company into an ambush.

I came out of my year in Vietnam a buck sergeant. Many guys like myself were dropped into stateside units without leadership training to prepare us for garrison duty. Fortunately, in the 2nd Armored Division I had an old platoon sergeant who taught me what the Army was all about. Six months later, my draft commitment was over. It was time for me to be discharged from military service. I walked out the front gate of Fort Hood, suitcase in hand.

I stopped at the east gate and turned around. I went back inside the base, across from the NCO Club, into the Reenlistment Office. I told the sergeant, "I don't want to go home. I want to reenlist in the Army." He said, "You'll have to stay right here." I said, "Fine."

I went home and told my wife about it. She was shocked. In Chicago, just two years earlier, I had been a street person. I didn't really work. But in the Army I enjoyed doing jobs well, and being in charge. It was a new life for me. I didn't want to go back to the streets.

ROLLING THUNDER

GENERAL CHARLES HORNER

KORAT, THAILAND 1965
FIGHTER PILOT
388TH TACTICAL FIGHTER WING

The early air campaign over North Vietnam, code-named "Rolling Thunder," was flown by some of the Air Force's most skilled but untested fighter pilots. Among those "volunteered" was a young captain from Iowa, Chuck Horner, who later gained prominence as a skilled tactician and Commanding General of the Central Command Air Forces during Operation Desert Storm.

I was one of the early Air Force people to fly combat missions over North Vietnam under a program called "Top Dog." I was flying F-105 fighters at Seymour Johnson Air Force Base in North Carolina in 1965, when people were needed for a new air wing being formed in Korat, Thailand.

I had been in the Air Force since 1958. When I came in, the only previous flying experience I had was in my senior year at the University of Iowa. I got fourteen rides in a 65-horsepower Aeronca Champ through the Air Force. It was a screening program where they gave students a chance to get a private flying license.

That was the final year of the Aviation Cadets. Like today, in the post–Cold War period, the entire U.S. military was cutting back after the Korean War. After I was commissioned, I went through Air Force flight school. They disqualified about half the class in primary training, and then about half the class in basic. If you made the least mistake, you washed out. I guess the system had bias against the cadets, who suffered over seventy-five percent attrition.

Flight training was excruciating. As I look back, what got me through is that I never doubted that I could do it. I seemed to have a natural flair for flying.

There were a lot of accidents in training back then. By the time I finished flying school and gunnery school, a two-year program, I saw four people killed. I remember sitting on a runway in an old T-33 propeller aircraft, waiting to take off. The airplane ahead of me takes off and crashes. Minutes later, the rescue helicopter flies by, with the legs of the dead pilot dangling out the door. Then the Tower says, "Okay, you're cleared for takeoff."

In the spring of 1965, I was on temporary duty in Orlando, Florida, and having dinner one evening. I got a telephone call, telling me, "You have to come home tonight." So I get in my F-105 and fly back to North Carolina. I got home and put my bags inside the front door. The next morning I was joined by another pilot. I didn't even have time to unpack my suitcase. We got on commercial air to San Francisco, where I was handed a duffel bag and sent down a supply line. They put in a helmet, a flak jacket, a rifle, a pistol . . . I said, "What's this for?" We had no idea where we were going.

We were flown to Korat Royal Air Force Base in Thailand. We stood on the dusty runway with our huge bags in the searing heat. We just stared at beautiful rolling hills and farmland.

Some engineers with plywood and screen wire were literally building a place for us to stay.

The "Top Dog" air wing we created was two squadrons of F-105s, flying missions each day over North Vietnam. A colonel named Bill Ritchie was brought in from the Pacific to be commander. He was an aviation pioneer. But we didn't know that.

We checked him out in an F-105, and guided him on a couple laps on the flight pattern. Then he took off on his first mission. I led the mission, with two ships behind him. He couldn't get hooked up on an airborne fuel tanker. So instead of doing reconnaissance, we went directly to our targets and back home, so he wouldn't run out of fuel.

That night at the bar we really gave Colonel Ritchie the red ass. Ironically, we found out later that he and a guy named Dave Schillings were the first pilots ever to cross an ocean by doing midair refueling. He never said a word about that while we razzed him. When we found that out, he became a real hero in our eyes.

The first bombing mission I went on was a big oil refinery at Vinh in North Vietnam. I was impressed that my experience was just like what the old guys said about World War II and Korea. When I came into the Air Force, my first squadron commander was a World War II veteran. And I always talked around bars with older guys. Even though the speed of aircraft change, combat is the same: the other guy is trying to kill you and you're trying to get the job done.

I flew forty-one combat missions as a Top Dog. In that early stage of the war, the air campaign over North Vietnam was called Rolling Thunder. We had strict Rules of Engagement created by Secretary of Defense Robert McNamara. Our route packages and targets were selected in Washington. And on the other hand, we did "road rec'y" [reconnaissance] where we'd fly over a segment of road and hit any military targets. It was an archaic way to do interdiction. Strategy was fragmented, objectives weren't clear.

For example, when our base ran out of bombs, we were told to go up and use our 20mm cannons to "intimidate" the North Vietnamese. We found that kind of ludicrous. Because we'd fly over Triple-A [antiaircraft artillery] sites, and they would open up at us. They were not intimidated.

It became more apparent that the air war planning was being done by people far away from the theater of operations who had no appreciation for the realities. I got the impression that a bunch of amateurs were running things.

For example, on July 26 and 27, 1965, was the first raids against North Vietnamese SAM [surface to air missile] sites. This was after an RF-4 had been shot down by a SAM. Before that, SAM sites were off-limits. We watched them being built and become operational, but were not permitted by Washington to take them out. If you think about that, it was ludicrous. But U.S. policymakers were trying to play a game with the Communists: "If we don't bomb your SAM site, then you don't shoot your SAMs at us." Well, give me a break. . . . That game didn't last very long.

So our orders were changed to bomb the SAM sites. They lined us up in our four airplanes . . . I will never forget this . . . First, we rolled into a valley in Laos. Then we continued low level up a river, like we were going to sneak up on them.

I heard on my radio, "Buick One is in the river." Meaning that one of the fighters from our Takli air base was shot down. So we get to the SAM site and it's like a North Vietnamese firepower display. We were flying right into a barrage of anti-aircraft fire. I watched a friend, Bob Purcell, drop his bombs, and pull up out of the clouds on fire, then crash.

The mission was just stupid. I couldn't believe it. We lost six airplanes that day. The tactics were being driven from Saigon, and I suspect they were coming from Washington. All they should've done was say, "Send a couple of jets to bomb the SAM sites." We could've done the job right.

It turned out, our photo reconnaissance showed that the target site was nothing but telephone poles on trucks. It was a trap.

Incidents like that caused troops in the field to lose confidence in their military leadership. If tactics don't make sense to a fighting guy, he'll still try to follow it because he's a military person. He wants to do what's right. But if you continue to give him things that don't make sense, he'll eventually say, "I've got to take the mission over." Especially when a lot of lives are at risk. For reasons like this, integrity was one of the first casualties of the Vietnam War.

PUSH ROD & BRUTE FORCE

MAJOR GENERAL
ROYAL MOORE, JR.

KANEOHE BAY, HAWAII 1958–62
AVIATOR
MARINE CORPS AIR STATION

I'm a product of the "push rod and brute force" period of aviation. Over the years, I developed an unconventional style of leadership in that I came from the enlisted ranks. That gave me a leg up on other officers, because I knew about every trick that my Marines could pull. I'd tell them, "Oh yeah, I've tried that one too. Guess what? It didn't work."

I joined the Marine Corps reserves in southern California in 1953 when I was seventeen, in the eleventh grade. I went through boot camp and joined a reserve unit in Los Alamitos. I began flying in 1956 in the old propeller-driven Corsair airplane.

My instructors began flying when pilots were still holding their airplanes together with chewing gum and Band-Aids. We still had fabric aircraft in some cases, and other aircraft right out of World War II.

We lost a lot of aircraft in those days. The first Marine Aircraft Group I was in lost thirteen or fourteen airplanes in six months: running off the end of runways, ploughing into the ground, flying into the jet stream and not being able to regain control . . . that's the way aviation technology was.

Those perilous conditions gave us a cavalier attitude. And we were allowed to get away with a lot of things. If any of my pilots today did half of the stunts that I pulled when I was a young aviator, I'd pull their wings. We rode motorcycles into Officers Clubs, threw guys into the pool, drove steamrollers into the pool, had live tigers in the club . . . You name it, we did it.

But kids don't do those kinds of things anymore. Thank

goodness. If we did that stuff today, the media would kill us. If our wives didn't kill us first.

A lot of my old retired buddies say, "Dammit, Royal, you flew under bridges, you flew flatheaded and hovered off the fantail of ships." They razz me, "You're just a hard-ass, Moore. Why don't you let your young guys do that?" I tell them, "The world has changed. My young people understand that."

THE GRADUATE

GENERAL RONALD YATES

CLARK AIR BASE, PHILIPPINES 1964–66
FIGHTER PILOT
509TH FIGHTER-INTERCEPTOR SQUADRON

In 1957 the Soviet Union shocked the world by successfully putting the first man-made satellite into earth orbit. Some U.S. military officials called it the "Pearl Harbor of the Technology War." In 1958 the U.S. Government followed with the launching of American satellites and creating the National Aeronautics and Space Administration (NASA). In May 1961 the first Soviet and American astronauts were launched into space. On May 25, President John F. Kennedy made a historic commitment before a joint session of Congress: to make space exploration among the highest national priorities. A generation of the most skilled and adventurous Navy, Marine, and Air Force test and fighter pilots began volunteering for the dangers and potential euphoria of space travel.

I graduated in the second-ever graduation class of the U.S. Air Force Academy in 1960. We thought we were laying the bedrock for a 200-year tradition. Because one could look at West Point and say, "This bedrock was laid two hundred years ago."

When I received my wings in 1961 at Webb Air Force Base in Texas, most of our instructors were Korean War fighter pilots. Fantastic role models. I can remember coming home one evening from a day at flight school. I had only been training for a few months. But I was overwhelmed with the feeling that I had found something that I could do really well. I had always been a good academic student, but not a great student. I was pretty good in almost all athletics, but not great in any one sport. But I knew that I could fly airplanes.

When I was about to graduate, I told my wife that I wanted to fly fighters. I can remember her saying, "Well, okay. But promise me one thing: that you will never be a test pilot." I replied, "That I can promise." Famous last words . . .

I chose to fly F-102 fighters because I thought that would help me to become an astronaut. I shared honors as a distinguished graduate of my flying class. In those days, the top graduates chose the F-100 "Supersabre" fighter bomber. I chose the F-102 "Delta Dagger" fighter-interceptor. I thought, "Why be a good pilot among a whole bunch of good guys?" I wanted to be a bigger fish in a smaller pond. That might get me noticed enough to be considered for astronaut training.

It worked. After about a year in my first squadron at Itazuke, Japan, people started saying, "Go to test pilot school. That's the first step to becoming an astronaut."

At the time, my squadron was starting to deploy on missions to a growing conflict in Indochina. I wasn't able to volunteer because I was one of only four junior lieutenants. But in 1964, I was offered the chance to transfer to the 509th Fighter-Interceptor Squadron in the Philippines. I knew the guys in that unit were flying to Vietnam. I thought, "That's incredible. I could get an Air Medal. That will put me ahead of my peers for astronaut selection."

I got to the 509th at Clark Air Base in June 1964. The Gulf of Tonkin incident happened in August. The war officially started. And, of course, everybody started coming over.

While at Clark, I was asked to get involved in developing some experimental war-fighting technology. This was a result of my technical Air Force Academy education. Ironically, engineering was not my first love or aptitude. In school, I had to work very hard at it. I made the academy Dean's List my junior and senior years. But while most subjects came easy to me, I spent almost 100 percent of my time studying for engineering classes.

At Clark, the first question my higher-ups asked was, "Can we use the F-102 for low level tactical strikes?" I went to the base library and found a book on trigonometric functions. I calculated the slight depression for a thirty-degree rocket pass.

The next thing I was asked, "Will you test the F-102's infrared air-to-air system for low level air-to-ground strikes against enemy camps?" To even attempt this in training was revolutionary.

On July 15, 1962, I led the first low-level tactical strike ever attempted by an F-102. We hunted for Viet Cong base-camp fires with our infrared devices. It was a very dangerous thing to do. Not only because we were vulnerable to ground fire. But because our only navigation aid in the airplane was not accurate enough for calculating our exact ground position.

Those airplanes didn't have computers. At night, flying low-level over forest and mountains, you had to know the terrain elevation at all times. I carried maps with terrain elevations written in each grid square. And I had to continuously check my range and bearing. When we reached the target area, we used our infrared to search for Viet Cong campfires to shoot at. Then we'd come in low and fast to shoot antipersonnel rockets.

We weren't very effective. The first thing you had to do was get the nose of the airplane down at least twenty degrees to direct the rockets on target. I had barely enough time to calculate my minimum altitude, to avoid a crash.

On one occasion, I shot my rockets and pulled up to come off target. I had miscalculated . . . All I could see was mountains around me. I thought, "Thank God," as I barely cleared the peaks.

After fifteen or twenty of these missions, I made another big mistake. We thought the Viet Cong were a lot less sophisticated than us. We had the feeling that they were some sort of savages wearing breechcloths. But they caught on to our new night tactics very quick.

I rolled in on a campfire and shot my rockets. All of a sudden, I thought the world had come to an end. The VC had set up an ambush. As soon as I released my rockets, everybody and his brother began shooting straight up in the air in my flight path. Fortunately, they only used small arms fire.

Because of the hazards, I never recommended that anyone join me and the other pilot testing these tactics in night rocket attacks. The infrared air-to-air missiles we fired weren't good for air-to-ground either. I shot a whole bunch of them—around 130. A good portion were what I called "sand seekers." But one morning before sunrise, I did blow up a large VC ammunition factory. It erupted in a huge fireball. An awesome sight.

The ARVN [South Vietnam Army] in the Delta reported a nuclear explosion. As I flew away, all kinds of debris was whizzing past my airplane at 3,000 to 4,000 feet.

I came away from those experiences with an attitude that all the equipment in an airplane ought to work. There were a lot of systems in an airplane created to help pilots. But they didn't work.

I didn't know anybody who trusted the automatic pilot control. There were times in combat when I needed both hands for weapons. But if I turned on the autopilot, I'd be flying along for a couple of minutes. All of a sudden, I'm taking a nosedive and scrambling to get the airplane back under control.

I returned from Vietnam in mid-1966 and was assigned to the Aerospace Research Pilot School at Edwards Air Force Base in California. The aircraft I test piloted was the rocket-powered NF-104 research plane. It had practically no wings and went to altitudes as high as 100,000 feet. I headed up the phase of the test-pilot school that involved flying lifting bodies, trying to find the right shapes for the space shuttle.

Arguably, the hardest part of the job was trying to explain to my wife about breaking my vow to not be a test pilot.

DEPENDENTS

SERGEANT MAJOR
JOSEPH CELESTINE

Danang, Vietnam 1965
Squad Leader
9th Marine Expeditionary Brigade

Hailing from St. Martinsville, a small semirural town in Louisiana, Joseph Celestine joined the Marine Corps at the beginning of the Civil Rights Movement. His goal was to earn the GI Bill.

After high school, in 1962 I went to the University of Southwest Louisiana. That was at the outset of the Civil Rights

Movement in the South. Most black students went to all-black schools. I chose an integrated school. But there were still problems.

Louisiana didn't deprive us blacks of an education. We were able to take college classes. But we couldn't participate in any sports or social activities. There weren't any black dorms because we weren't allowed to live on campus. We had to leave college premises right after class. You had to rent an apartment or live at home.

I would've preferred an all-black school like Southern University in Baton Rouge, where I could've played sports. My parents decided on the school for financial reasons—it was close to home.

I grew up in a little farm-type community. Although white kids went to separate schools, we still played together. Their parents, grandparents, and great-great-grandparents knew my parents and relatives for generations back. In some cases, my ancestors worked for their ancestors, as far back as you could go. So everyone was close.

I went to college with one of the white kids I grew up with. We took classes together. It was very frustrating, because at school the majority of kids could care less about racial differences. They didn't reflect any of the negative things that some adults were stirring up in the community. In fact, they went to great lengths to sneak me into the dorms at night, or invite me to some of the parties that blacks could go to without problems.

After one semester, I was dissatisfied with those policies. So, during Christmas break 1962 I joined the Marine Corps. I was eighteen. I would still be young when I finished my enlistment tour. I intended to use the GI Bill to attend the school of my choice.

I started boot camp in San Diego on January 17, 1963. After my infantry training at Camp Pendleton, I was assigned to the 1st Marine Division. In early 1964, prior to going to Okinawa, we started receiving classes on events in Indochina. We had no idea that we would go to Vietnam. We thought that these were newsreels being used for instruction.

During that fall, we were in Japan for cold weather training. The exercise was called off and we were sent back to Okinawa. Our ships were combat-loaded. We knew something was about to happen, but we weren't exactly sure what. We went back to sea to Thailand for jungle training. We heard rumors from the Thais that we would be going to Vietnam. We kept responding, "You're crazy. We're going to the Philippines."

We took off on schedule heading toward the Philippines. But we didn't land. A week later, the ship's captain came on the loudspeaker and told us, "The decision has been made by President Johnson. I've received orders to take you to Vietnam."

We got there in February 1965. They kept us off-coast for a month until various units arrived to form the 9th Marine Expeditionary Brigade [MEB]. I was a young NCO, a corporal. As a squad leader and sometimes section leader, I was in charge of people who I had gone through boot camp with.

The 9th MEB became the first Marine unit to make an amphibious landing into Vietnam after the President announced the involvement of U.S. conventional forces. A Marine battalion was already there to support and provide security for U.S. advisors.

We landed with helicopters firing into hills around the beachhead. We proceeded to march about five miles to take the high ground over Hill 327. The area later became the main Marine Corps base at Danang.

For the next three months, things were quiet. We went into villages doing first aid and helping out. It was very calm and pleasant. I was put in charge of a mortar section of fifteen people.

We could see the movement of North Vietnamese forces in the valleys. It was a time when they moved around freely. Both sides were building up for battle. They wouldn't shoot at us and we didn't shoot at them. We had all of these Rules of Engagement that prevented us from taking any offensive action.

In July, more aircraft began arriving. Things started to change. The North Vietnamese became more aggressive. One day we went into a little village that we normally went in, and got in a firefight. A chaplain's assistant got killed. From that time on, it escalated worse and worse.

I turned twenty-one in Vietnam, and was promoted to sergeant toward the end of my tour. As the war escalated, a large number of staff NCOs were commissioned as lieutenants. One of the problems I saw developing was in the staff NCO ranks, especially with E7s, company gunny [gunnery] sergeants. Most company gunnies hadn't been in the infantry for quite some time—as much as ten years. They were brought back because of the expansion of the Corps. They really weren't in physical shape to lead Marines in the tropical heat and mountainous terrain. So the Corps had to promote young sergeants up to fill these slots. This put a lot of pressure on young corporals and buck sergeants.

Before the war, corporals and sergeants would spend three to five years in rank, learning their profession. But the rapid promotion of junior NCOs during Vietnam denied them the expertise that the older generation had.

And we were short of Marines. So boot camp was shortened from twelve weeks to eight weeks. That shortened training remained until General Al Gray became Marine Corps commandant in 1987 and reinstituted Marine combat training.

I came home in December 1965 and got married in January. That June, I was working at the Weapons Training Battalion in San Diego as an instructor and range coach. I received orders to go back to Vietnam because of the shortage of mid-level NCOs there. I went to my commanding officer and reminded him that I had just come back and was newly married. So he called Marine Corps Headquarters and got me a six-month extension.

I met my wife, Mary, when we were both fifteen years old. I thought about getting married after I finished boot camp. But on a private or corporal's pay, I saw no way I could bring her to California. So I waited until after I made sergeant.

During my three tours of Vietnam, my wife coped pretty well. My oldest child, Jonathan, was born in September 1968. He was a year old when I left for my third tour of Vietnam. I took Mary and the baby back to Louisiana to stay with her folks during that tour. They gave her solid family support. That was important. I'm sure that if she was alone in California with the baby, she would've had problems.

During Vietnam there was no family support programs at all, except if you were fortunate enough to come from a large enough base where a lot of Marines were deployed from. Even then, the wives had to organize on their own. Because of the individual replacement system in Vietnam, there was no unit cohesion. Even if I had left Mary at Pendleton, she probably wouldn't have known anyone I was with in Vietnam—and most of the Marines were unmarried.

During those days, the Marine Corps frowned on young guys getting married. We had to get permission. The attitude was, "If the Corps wanted you to have a wife, they would have issued you one."

In my first outfit, there were only five married people around my age. I had one friend who got married. He was a PFC. I asked him, "How can you afford to take care of a wife and kid?" He said, "My wife is trying to get baby-sitting jobs." They were living mostly on baloney sandwiches and hot dogs. The Corps lost a lot of good people like my friend. He couldn't wait to get out, so that he could take care of his family.

Even when pay improved in 1967, it still wasn't good. A private went from $70 per month to $120. My second tour of Vietnam, with all the extra entitlements, came to around $500 a month. If my wife and child didn't have extended family, it would've been tough for them to get by.

BOOT CAMP

SERGEANT MAJOR DAVID SOMMERS

San Diego 1960
Recruit
Marine Recruit Depot

In February 1960, I turned seventeen and joined the Corps in March. I didn't know anything about making it a career. I just wanted to be a Marine Corps infantryman. I grew up outside of St. Louis, and was a junior at Bishop DuBourg High School. My grandmother had a farm in a place called Leesburg.

A recruit under eighteen needed parental permission. And my parents were not happy about me dropping out of school. I really worked on them. The selling point was the recruiting sergeant's promise, "You can finish high school in the Corps."

Back then it was common knowledge that Marines hadn't finished high school or college. Around half of my first platoon hadn't graduated from high school. We had guys who could hardly read. So we did a lot of "buddy" training, helping those guys who couldn't read all the instructions for the M-1 rifle.

We spent a lot of time training ourselves. When I tell that to drill instructors today, they cringe. After evening chow we'd come back to our Quonset huts. If we didn't have anything going on, we'd sit on our buckets in circles and quiz each other and work with the rifle. The drill instructor was at the other end of the hut, with two foot lockers piled like a desk.

At times I thought, "I'm never going to come out of boot camp alive." The old D.I.'s had a stone-hard dedication to training. Lessons that I learned from those drill instructors I still find valuable today. Things that aren't in books. I watched the willingness of the drill instructor, no matter how hard-core he was on the surface, to sit down with a kid and help him.

There's a difference between giving instruction and teaching. When you teach people, they retain it. For instance, anybody can read. But reading and understanding are two different things.

My drill instructors taught me discipline. I don't mean running around and yelling, "Aye aye, sir!" They taught me that discipline is self-motivation to study and perform when nobody is around to push you.

FIREFIGHT

COLONEL MICHAEL ANDREWS

Dau Tieng/Tay Ninh, Vietnam 1968–69
Platoon Leader
25th Infantry Division

Tall and lean, with a barely noticeable North Carolina accent after four years at West Point, Lieutenant Andrews was my infantry platoon leader in Vietnam. What made him unique—and somewhat controversial—was his idealistic commitment to keep his troops well-trained, in order to prevent needless casualties even in the unpredictable combat environment we faced on the Cambodian border.

We served together in both a "line" infantry company and

later in an all-volunteer, unconventional reconnaissance unit.
What earned him my respect was his openness to allow young
but combat-hardened soldiers to speak their minds. Although
he took the well-being of each of his troops very personally, he
never backed away from a dangerous mission.

The Gulf of Tonkin incident [which led to the introduction of
conventional U.S. forces in Vietnam] happened in 1964, my
sophomore year at West Point. For the next three years, the
specter of Vietnam overshadowed everything: our relationships
with women, our studies, our friendships.

It seemed that every instructor would begin every class by
saying, "If you don't pay attention to this class, you're going
to die in Vietnam." I went to Ranger School and to Leadership
classes. But it was all academic and theory.

The thing that impressed me most when I got to Vietnam
was that I looked into the faces and the eyes of the soldiers
who were there. I somehow thought that the soldiers of my
first unit would be seasoned, hardened troops who mechani-
cally knew how to do things. But they were young people who
were doing the best they could.

My first firefight was on September 19, 1968. I was ordered
to take my platoon across an open field and move into a
treeline. About halfway across, I knew something was wrong.
I turned and asked a young soldier who was carrying a machine gun to come forward. In the next couple of seconds an
ambush was sprung. The first round hit this boy in the head.
A boy on the other side of me was hit in the head, also.

The kid with the machine gun died instantly. The firefight
intensified and my soldiers did what we had to do. I went over
to the boy who was hit in the head. I was holding him. He was
crying. I could see the brains . . . the top of his head opened
up. He was delirious.

We were right in front of the VC machine gun and I was
trying to hold him down. He was thrashing around. I decided
that we better just get out of there. So I put his arm around my
neck and lifted him, trying to get him to safety. We drew fire.
He was hit again.

So I lay there with him for a while, just trying to hold him
down. During those few minutes he was crying and praying
. . . asking for God and Jesus . . . for his mother. At the end of
that stream, he asked for "Two-six." That was my radio call
sign.

After it was over, that boy, and the other boy that died, just devastated me. I carried the body back that night. I sat and looked at that boy, absolutely appalled that it happened. That was my turning point.

I began to look at my soldiers and ruminate about who was going to take care of them and train them. And I thought, "There will always be another time when we will be sending young people into desperate situations. The contribution I can make is to be there with them."

I had never intended to stay in the Army. I never thought about it. I went to West Point to get an education and improve myself. I didn't know anything about what officers did. But I could feel this almost horror of responsibility evolving.

Halfway through my Vietnam tour, I got married on R&R in Hawaii. I talked with my wife, Linda, about my realizations. I thought about myself being in danger. But I was more worried about the people I was responsible for. To see your young soldiers in danger or hurt . . . That's worse than being hit yourself.

CLASH OF CULTURES

LIEUTENANT COLONEL ANDREW GEMBARA

PHAN THIET, VIETNAM 1967–68
PSYOPS GROUP LEADER/PLATOON LEADER
1ST CAVALRY DIVISION/101ST AIRBORNE DIVISION

I was born in a Ukrainian family on the Lower East Side of Manhattan, a rough neighborhood. In 1966, I was working days at Nabisco and going to college at night. I couldn't afford to study full-time. And I always wanted to be a parachutist. So I asked for my draft number to be moved up.

After four months in the Army I saw that everyone was going to Vietnam with very little training. So I requested OCS [Officer Candidate School] and became an airborne infantry officer. And I volunteered for the Vietnamese language course.

In October 1967, I went off to war. I was assigned to the 2nd Psyop [Psychological Operations] Group in Nha Trang, on the central coast. I was able to get command of a field team with the 2nd Battalion of the 7th Cavalry, 1st Cavalry Division in Phan Thiet, farther down the coast. I had two teams. One was a loudspeaker team and the other was an audiovisual team on a jeep.

Some of my guys didn't have any training. And most of our equipment was used to show movies to U.S. troops on the base. Being young, dumb, and naive, I figured, "We need to get to work."

We had a bunch of 16mm films in Vietnamese about the government of South Vietnam. Other films spoke about the threat of the Viet Cong. Some of it was humorous and seemed to have some impact on villagers.

When I started taking my team out, the 1st Cav unit commander was reluctant. He thought that we were going to get ourselves killed. Looking back, I think he had a good argument. We went into remote areas that were controlled by the VC at one time or another. I usually traveled with two or three Americans and a couple of Vietnamese interpreters. We relied on the local Regional or Popular Forces [home guard] for security, especially if we were going overnight.

We weren't permitted to take our jeep on certain roads unless we were in a convoy. My fourth week in-country, I had to call a Chinook [giant helicopter] to lift my jeep out of what I thought was a road next to a rice paddy. We sunk. I asked a bunch of Vietnamese farmers to dig us out. I didn't know who the hell they were. If they were the bad guys, we would've been prisoners or dead. I took photos to remind myself how dumb I was.

I learned a lot of things that I will remember until I die. One is that we assume a lot about people until we get close to them. One night in a place called Tieng Giao, we used a big schoolyard next to a church to show a movie. I spoke with a French priest who spoke English. He told me, "There is a lot of VC in this area." They had an agreement. When the VC was in the area, they would bang on his door with the butt of their weapons. He wasn't to have any meetings with the people while they were around.

I'm convinced that at one time or another, our audience must have included some Viet Cong. They must have gotten a chuckle out of it. Or, they may have not bothered us because my Psyops people were very close to the people.

There was a switch in our area. The 1st Cavalry departed and the 3rd Battalion of the 506th Infantry, 101st Airborne Division, moved in. It was a green unit that just arrived in Vietnam. I thought, "Now is my chance to earn my spurs and be a platoon leader." I had some OCS classmates who were in some of the companies. So I joined the infantry.

It was amazing. On the same roads where people used to wave at my Psyop unit, my infantry company was getting shot at. We'd get stray sniper shots. Our point men would walk into booby traps. We were scared of everything ... anything that moved. Anyone with slanted eyes was the enemy.

I'd say to myself, "What the hell is going on? The same local people could've blown away my jeep hundreds of times." This contrast made me a believer in small advisory units working closely with local forces.

We had a situation where one of our sister companies went into a village on a "search and clear" operation. The VC in the area killed an officer in that company. They also killed a senior 1st sergeant, who had been the glue of that company. He was killed in a building where soldiers saw the VC run out the back door. There was an old lady inside.

I could see the hostility in these guys. They wanted to kill the lady. I stopped it. A year or two later, when I heard about My Lai, I was not surprised at all. I could see how in the heat of the moment, American kids could become something quite different.

Another thing that initially shocked me, but I fell into very easily, was the amount of cursing. In Psyops and working with villagers, I tried to use as much Vietnamese as I could. But with U.S. troops I used "fuck" more times and in more descriptive ways than I ever imagined. Cursing had become part of my normal language. That is common with line [combat] soldiers. You really do become part animal, with survival instincts.

Coming from Psyop, it hit me pretty hard that we were doing more to alienate the very people we were supposed to be protecting. I understood how our behavior could be used politically against us. Our mannerisms. And destruction caused by calling in artillery and air strikes into areas where we received one or two shots. Some of that is self-preservation. But we were destroying whatever community was there. I'll never forget an incident that reminded me that people of all cultures look out for themselves.

During the Tet Offensive, my infantry unit and Vietnamese regional forces were in Phan Thiet when the city was hit by a couple of Vietnamese communist companies. There was a napalm strike on the second largest *nuoc mam* [fermented fish sauce] factory in Vietnam. A very pungent odor permeated the area. I will never forget all the pandemonium of civilians running in all directions. I came across a scene that seemed surreal.

There was a field in front of a couple of sturdily built houses, napalm burning the fields. I'm walking with two of my guys. I see a Vietnamese fellow dressed in white peasant-type clothing, like pajamas. He's walking backward, away from the fire. He's blind. He could have easily been killed or injured.

We stopped some young people who were running from the opposite direction because they thought that the VC were on the road, and they were afraid of the firing going on. I asked them to take the old man with them. They refused. That was one of the few times I ever drew a weapon on civilians. I said, "If you don't take him, you're not going anywhere." They took him.

During the second wave of Tet attacks, in Phan Thiet the North Vietnamese Army took over half the city. My platoon was thrown into the battle to help clear some of the streets. Fighting house to house, we moved down an alley. I had three point people in front of me.

An NVA soldier backed out of a building. He was wearing a tan khaki uniform. He looked at us, just as surprised as we were. I don't know how many guys shot at him. He spun around and ran back in. I don't know if we missed him or the M-16 rounds went right through him.

As soon as that happened, we were trapped in the alley. We had grenades pitched on us. I lost two guys almost immediately—my radioman and a guy next to me. I was shot through the shoulder. We laid there a couple of hours, pinned down.

I ended up in a hospital in Japan with multiple injuries from gunshots and hand grenades. Half of my deltoid muscle was taken out. I was transferred to Valley Forge Hospital in Pennsylvania where I had physical therapy for my shoulder, which was locked. The doctors were concerned that I would have limited mobility. I had an eardrum taken out. And I had shrapnel in my eye. There was a lot of talk about me being medically discharged from the Army. At first my attitude was, "So what." But I started liking the military. I asked to be returned to duty.

I was promoted to captain. They said, "We'd like to send you back to Vietnam." I said, "Wait a minute, I still have two eye operations to go. I can only see out of one eye. In all fairness, I'd like to see about other possibilities." They said, "With your language abilities, how would you like to go to 10th Special Forces in Bad Tolz, Germany?"

I said, "Where do I sign?"

THE CIRCUS

COLONEL LAYTON DUNBAR

BONG SON, VIETNAM 1969–70
PLATOON LEADER
173RD AIRBORNE DIVISION

During Desert Storm, Colonel Layton Dunbar, a Tennessee native, was Commander of the Allied Psychological Operations campaign that played a significant role in convincing thousands of Iraqi troops to surrender. However, with a bemused smile, he remembers his first exposure to "Psyops" as a lieutenant in Vietnam.

To the ordinary infantryman in Vietnam, there didn't seem to be much of an emphasis on Psychological Operations. My platoon was in the middle of a valley, protecting a little village in a rice-growing region from Viet Cong and North Vietnamese soldiers and tax collectors. They had occupied it before we moved into the valley.

Personally, I did not feel prepared for the "pacification" mission. We were trained to "search and clear" and ambush the enemy. We came down from the hills after securing the area around the valley. Part of the mission was to install a Republic of South Vietnam government official. And, of course, we protected him, too.

He wound up being killed by some booby traps. So, I guess we failed in that part of the mission. But we did a lot of medical treatment of villagers, even though there were still some hostile people out there.

One night we got an assignment radioed in. We were instructed to assemble the villagers the next morning, because a team of Psychological Operations specialists were coming in.

We moved out very early the next morning, before first light, and sealed off the village. We ousted these poor villagers out of their homes—not really at gunpoint. But we were carrying our weapons and they weren't going to argue.

We couldn't speak their language. But we had a South Vietnamese army interpreter attached to our platoon. I have no idea where he was from. But he wasn't one of the locals. And he couldn't be with every soldier in the platoon as we went through the village. My soldiers gave commands in what few words they knew: "Move out. Go over there. Sit down and be quiet."

The villagers were assembled in a field, where they sat for several hours passively waiting for what was going to happen next. We had no idea what to tell them.

Eventually, a helicopter flew in. It covered everyone with the dust and dirt its propellers whipped up. Probably blew a couple of thatch roofs off people's houses. Off stepped this Psyop team. It was the first time I'd ever seen anything like that. It looked like a traveling circus.

A Vietnamese group piled off the helicopter with boxes and crates. They set up a small Honda generator, an amplifier, an electric guitar, and a microphone.

A fellow in skintight black pants and a silk shirt got up in front of the villagers and started haranguing them in Vietnamese. This went on for a while. Then they brought on the entertainment.

A female dressed very attractively belted out a couple of rock and roll songs, accompanied by a guy with an electric guitar. The villagers sat there expressionless, very glum, as if the troupe was speaking in a foreign language. Surrounded by GIs who had rousted them out early in the morning.

The show went on for a couple of hours. Finally—and I guess, thankfully—the Honda generator gave out. They brought the helicopter back in. Flew away. And we turned the villagers loose. I thought, "This Psyop stuff is really amazing."

Sixteen years later, in 1985, I got orders informing me that

I'd been chosen to command the 1st Psyop Battalion. I said, "What did I do wrong? Why me?"

RECON TEAM

COLONEL KENNETH BOWRA

A SHAU VALLEY, VIETNAM 1971-72
RECON A-TEAM LEADER
TASK FORCE 1, MACV-SOG

Army Special Forces, known by their unique "green berets," were initially intended for President John F. Kennedy's early-1960s' counterinsurgency campaigns in the Third World, and to act as behind-the-lines commandos in Europe in case of a Soviet invasion. The Special Forces are trained to operate among native peoples in self-contained twelve-man teams. Team members are fluent in foreign languages, and teams include experts in electronic communications, medicine, engineering, demolitions and weapons. In Vietnam their role was akin to "a Peace Corps with the ability to defend itself," to train rural and tribal peoples in self-defense, as well as community development and medical assistance. Specialized recon teams operated behind enemy lines to disrupt the flow of North Vietnamese weapons and reinforcements along the Ho Chi Minh Trail and other logistics areas.

By 1970, as American public discontent with the Vietnam War grew, the Special Forces' mission in Vietnam was radically reduced. Among the last special operations projects was MACV-SOG—Military Assistance Command, Vietnam-Studies and Observation Group—a highly secret unconventional warfare task force, involved in covert operations throughout Indochina.

I grew up in a very small town on Long Island, New York. It was a hometown of Memorial Day parades and Fourth of July cookouts. I left that in 1966 for an education at the Citadel, the military college of South Carolina. I received my Army commission in 1970, after graduation.

I immediately went to Fort Benning, Georgia, for infantry training and Airborne and Ranger schools. My initial assignment was to the 82nd Airborne Division at Fort Bragg, North Carolina. But I wanted to go to Vietnam. I was still very idealistic.

In late 1970, it was hard to get a Vietnam assignment because U.S. forces there were scaling down. I volunteered for Special Forces and MACV-SOG. Being a 1st lieutenant, the idea was for me to be a reconnaissance team leader.

At that time in SOG there was a cross section of veteran Special Forces people and newcomers. I trained and worked with senior sergeants. These were guys who had the language training and survival expertise.

When I got to my camp, Command and Control North [CCN] in Danang, the recon company had thirty teams. Each "1-0"—A-Team leader—was a senior NCO. The most junior grade was staff sergeant [E-6], who would've come into Special Forces in the mid-1960s. Most of them had previous tours in Vietnam. At any given time, we had no more than two officers assigned to those thirty teams. We were all team leaders together. We didn't wear any rank in that respect.

We usually had ten indigenous troops on our teams. My first team, RT [recon team] Idaho, was a Vietnamese team. I had one interpreter and an indigenous lieutenant who had been an NCO in the North Vietnamese Army. We trained them until they were able to act without Americans.

My second team was a Montagnard team. They were of the Bru tribe from the Mai Loc area, west of Quang Tri. Other Montagnard teams were of different tribes—Jarai, Sedang, Rhade, and Nung.

On missions, we would go to a forward launch site, such as Phu Bai, we'd be airlifted to the A Shau Valley, which was heavily occupied by the North Vietnamese Army. They utilized the heavy forest as good camouflage. They had heavy vehicles, Triple-A antiaircraft guns—very heavily fortified.

We'd insert in late afternoon. That gave us a couple hours of daylight to move as far away from the LZ [landing zone] as we could. We'd fishhook to ambush any NVA trackers who might be following us. Then move into our night position. We needed to put as much distance between us and the LZ as we could before darkness. So if we were being followed, we could lose them. We had sound suppressors for our weapons, depending on the mission.

Our means to communicate our mission status or any assistance needs or extraction was through an Air Force unit that supported us. In the A Shau, we had O-2 aircraft that flew out of Thailand. Our technique was that very early in the morning, at a predetermined time, the FAC [forward air controller] would fly within range of our radio. But not over us, to avoid undue attention to our position. As a team leader, when I heard the FAC, I'd get on the radio. I'd say one phrase like, "Good morning," or "Good day." He'd know that the team was alive and in position.

If we needed assistance, that FAC was our lifeline. There was no radio communication to American units, because we were beyond the range of any American field communication. The only units around us were North Vietnamese. And they could intercept our radio transmissions. So we had to maintain radio silence.

The NVA developed what they called "counter-recon" teams. They had personnel who had probably worked for a while with SOG, who had either been captured or had gone over. The NVA teams carried the same basic weapons load as ourselves. They knew our tactics. And they could track us and hold us up with a strong volume of fire until a conventional army unit could set up blocking positions, then push us into an area that was to their advantage. They loved to hit us at daylight, before our first contact with an FAC, to flush us out, then ambush us along the escape route.

I survived thanks to the NCOs who helped me. I pulled my first mission after being in-country about two months. I'd been out on some training missions at SOG "1-0" School. But those were against the VC, like going against the minor leagues. Up in I Corps were the professional North Vietnamese units.

My first objective was in the A Shau Valley [a remote area near the Laotian border] to go against the headquarters of a transportation regiment. NVA transport units had infantry companies attached to them. Not only that, the area had a limited number of possible helicopter landing zones. The NVA put a counter-recon team at every possible LZ in that sector.

Unknown to us, the NVA were building up strength for the coming 1972 Spring Offensive. SOG had lost two teams in that same area during the three previous weeks. No known survivors, bodies never recovered. The area was only six kilometers by six kilometers. But it was mountainous, heavily forested with a lot of enemy trail networks.

I briefed my team and we started our rehearsals, knowing up front that it was going to be bad. Word traveled fast in our recon company. A staff sergeant named Andre B. Smith had a lot of experience. He came up to me and said, "LT [Lieutenant], I don't want you to take this the wrong way. Maybe I should come with you on this mission. I won't take over your team. But I'd like to go with you."

I really knew that word had gotten out about the target when Sergeant 1st Class "Pappy" Wells came up to me. He had another A-Team that he worked with. He said, "Ken, I hear you've drawn a bad one." I said, "Yeah, Pappy. But Sergeant Frank Pulley and I are going to pull it off. And Andre is going to come with us, too."

Pappy said, "Well, look. My team is on stand down right now while our Rhade [tribesmen] are on home leave. I'd like to strap-hang with you on this mission."

I looked at him, and couldn't help but think, "God bless you." He knew damn well that we had just lost two teams in that area. And so did Andre Smith. They didn't have to get involved. I could have been "lost team number three." They didn't want that to happen.

I wouldn't believe anyone who says that they aren't scared when they launch on a mission. But with those veterans with me, I felt a hell of a lot better. We couldn't stop the entire North Vietnamese Army. But I had some guys with a lot of experience, who could be counted on when the going got tough. That mission was my baptism of fire.

We had two Huey "slicks" [transport helicopters] to carry my team in. But we had to back off for two consecutive days because our birds received enemy fire as they tried to set us down. On the third day we were able to insert. It was late in the afternoon. We were on a mountain ridge. After the slicks took off, there was absolutely dead silence. We thought we had made it.

Within yards, we found a trail network which had high grass bent over the trail, to make it invisible from the air. It was well-traveled. We even found telegraph poles.

We quickly moved out to the LZ area. My tail gunner, the last man in the file, passed a hand signal up the line that we were being tracked by an NVA team. And our point man spotted movement up ahead. We knew that we were trapped on that ridge.

I was in the front section of the column with the radio. We

sat down in the elephant grass to avoid being seen. I heard someone cough, probably ten meters off our flank. We were blocked.

We laid down and started pitching grenades in all directions. The NVA opened fire. We still couldn't see anybody. We got up and began withdrawing toward the LZ. It was the middle of the monsoon season. Rainstorm clouds were blowing in. Our extraction would be high adventure, if we could get out at all.

When the fire slackened, I radioed for extraction. A company of NVA was coming around the ridge line to try to cut us off. We returned fire as the helicopters came in. They had to pull back the first time because of the intense volume of fire. The pilot radioed to me that he had never seen such a heavy troop concentration that was moving in on us—from all directions. We could hear them coming up the ridge, but we couldn't see them.

The slick pilots called for fire support. Two Cobra gunships came overhead and saw the NVA unit bearing down on us. They opened up with their 40mm miniguns. Diving in, they came under very heavy NVA fire. But the Cobras kept on the NVA until running out of ammunition.

My radio call sign was "El Cid." They notified me, "El Cid, we've expended. We've pushed them back, we think, for a while. We'll try to get the slicks back for you. That's all we can do."

I said, "I appreciate that." And we loaded new magazines into our rifles and tried to tighten up our position.

When the Cobras took off, that was the loneliest feeling in the world. There was dead silence. The North Vietnamese were regrouping to make another assault . . . We just sat there and waited.

Around fifteen minutes later, I heard the high pitch of a Cobra. He came around behind us and called on the radio. He asked, "El Cid, are you still down there?" I said, "Affirmative." He said, "I couldn't leave you. I don't have any munitions left. And I don't have enough fuel to make it back to base. Maybe I can slow the NVA down by making some dry runs at them."

He went into a dive and made low tree top level passes right over the NVA. He succeeded in pushing them back. They didn't want to take any more 40mm. But he could only make a few of those passes. He radioed, "My fuel is too low. That's the best I can do. I'll try to make it back to refuel." I never found out what happened to him. I didn't even know his name.

It was becoming dusk, storm clouds were rolling in . . . it was our worst nightmare. We kept down in the elephant grass. I talked with Andre Smith and decided that all we could do was try to get out of the area. The slicks came overhead and dropped their sixty-foot rope ladders.

The NVA began charging the LZ. Myself and my Vietnamese team leader laid down a base of fire, while the others were hooking on to the ladders and were being pulled up. We killed a number of NVA right there, on the LZ. With more soldiers still charging forward, I snapped the rope ladder onto my web harness and was pulled up.

The NVA had strong antiaircraft capability, so we had to fly high. We were dangling beneath the aircraft, swinging from these rope ladders. It was the coldest I've ever been in my life. Getting rained on, my body cutting through the clouds. It was a great sensation just to be alive.

We hung from the rope ladders until we reached the refuel point, where the birds could safely set down. My team was pretty lucky to just have several wounded, and nobody lost or killed. It really was luck. But we had also trained very hard for the mission. Repeatedly going through the immediate action drills as a team is what saved us. Everyone knew what to do and didn't panic.

When we got back from missions, we would write up the "lessons learned" and in our after-action, post-mission brief we would discuss what was unique. That information was passed on to other teams, keeping everyone abreast of tactics changes of the enemy. For SOG teams, it was just a matter of time before we were hit on any given mission. Our company lost five teams out of thirty.

I operated in the northern quadrant for eight months. The Vietnamese team members I had were absolutely loyal. We got into some pretty rough situations together. On one mission, the North Vietnamese were yelling at us to surrender. The NVA knew the makeup of our teams. I asked my interpreter, "What did they say?" He replied, "They said, 'Give up the Americans and you can go free.' " He then continued to fire.

We'd come back from a mission, stand down. Then go up to a free-fire zone near Monkey Mountain, where we practiced our techniques and team coordination. We'd come back to our base and get a Warning Order for a mission.

Mission preparation involved studying the target, linking up with your FAC, and flying over the area for visual reconnaissance. Then developing film and analyzing it, and planning the extraction. If everything was working well, you'd have two weeks to train for the mission.

SOG was a classic cost-effective operation. With limited soldiers—only a couple of Americans per team—and using limited logistics resources, we tied up major enemy forces.

This had the opposite effect of large American units conducting "search and destroy" operations and setting up static fire bases. Those tactics wasted resources, human lives, and political capital. And gave the North Vietnamese the advantage to take the initiative on the level of fighting and creating American casualties.

BEWARE THE WEASELS

GENERAL CHARLES HORNER

Korat, Thailand 1967
388th Tactical Fighter Wing

After flying forty-one combat missions over North Vietnam in Operation Rolling Thunder in F-105s, Captain Charles Horner rotated back to the States as a flight instructor. He volunteered to return to Southeast Asia in a unit known as the "Wild Weasels." The Weasels flew fighter airplanes on some of the most dangerous missions of the war. Equipped with special electronic equipment and air-to-ground missiles, Weasels could home in on radar beams transmitted from enemy surface-to-air (SAM) missile sites.

Their mission was to precede bomber aircraft into a target area in order to bait SAM sites to turn on their radars. Then, attack the sites. The challenging mission attracted experienced fighter pilots, who volunteered to use their skills to protect fellow airmen over some of the most heavily defended areas of North Vietnam.

I came back to the States from Southeast Asia in January 1966, as an F-105 instructor at Nellis Air Force Base in Nevada. I was able to put behind my frustrations with the war tactics of the policymakers, because in the Air Force we deal with technology and equipment, and teaching pilots. Air Force people tend to be apolitical. There wasn't much discussion among guys who had already been to the war.

I hated being a flight instructor. When the chance came in May 1967 to go back to Southeast Asia as a "Wild Weasel," I volunteered. It was kind of funny: I found out about the position opening at nine-thirty in the morning and had orders cut by eleven A.M. That's how badly they needed Wild Weasels.

How did the Weasels get their name? Jack Donovan, Al Lamb, and Gary Willard went over in the first group of F-100 Wild Weasels. *Cavae bettorium*, or something like that, means "Beware of the weasel." The unit insignia was a weasel killing a snake. The snake being a SAM missile site.

The first attempt at counterradar was the F-100s that had an electronic box called APR-133 to home in on the radar of a SAM site. It was like a moth going toward a light. They lost a lot of aircraft. F-105s went with them to drop bombs on the site. But they had some initial victories. That was the first attempt to try to make the enemy's defenses pay a price for their operations.

The problem was that the F-100 didn't have the top speed or ruggedness. An F-105 can go supersonic by pointing its nose down. When it came time to exit a target area, the airplane could stream out. So the F-105 two-seat trainer was converted for the Weasels.

As a pilot, when the F-105 went supersonic, you wouldn't really feel it. If I ever was going against ground fire and I had my choice of any airplane, even now I would take an F-105. Because it is so rugged—you could have a wing blown off and it will keep on going. But it wouldn't turn worth a damn. For air-to-air combat, it would be the last airplane I would take.

Wild Weasel pilots were all volunteers. The Air Force wanted guys with flying experience in fighters, because it is a very dangerous and complex mission to maneuver against a ground target.

The Air Force needed the capability to bomb at night. So they taught our electronic warfare operators to do radar bombing with the F-105. They made some marginal modification for use of conventional bombs. We formed what we called Ryan's

Raiders. We'd fly some Weasel missions and we'd also fly single ship at night. We'd go to North Vietnam and hit airfields or munitions storage areas.

The North Vietnamese had searchlights at a place called Yen Bay. One night we were rolling in and they opened up with fifty or a hundred searchlights. All kinds of bullets were coming at us. So I started strafing searchlights.

I quickly discovered that wasn't very wise. Because in the pitch-dark, flying low, I had no idea where the ground was. So I asked the munitions people to put Sidewinder missiles on my aircraft. The next time we went out, after we hit a target north of Phu Khien airfield, I came up Thud Ridge at medium altitude. Near Yen Bay, I started circling at 15,000 feet. The searchlights all came on. I rolled in on a steep ninety-degree dive and fired a Sidewinder at them. My problem was how to pull out of my dive before hitting the ground.

Coming off the target, I thought, "That wasn't very smart." The next time I went back again with a Sidewinder and tried to get them to turn on the searchlights. They wouldn't do it.

Compared to today's aircraft, the technology we had in Vietnam was very rudimentary. Our bombing accuracy was horrible. The F-105 had an altimeter [altitude gauge], but not the infrared night-vision capability that our aircraft had in the Gulf War. If we had today's equipment in Vietnam, we could've saved a lot of pilots.

During my second Vietnam tour, I felt growing frustration that the war was dragging on. What especially bothered me was to come back home in 1965 or 1967 and people wondered where you'd been. Not that people spit on us, but they weren't involved in the war.

I had been killing people for America. I felt very badly about that, but I believed it had to be done. You'd been putting your life on the line. Then when you came home, it seemed that the American public wasn't behind you.

BOMBING HALTS

REAR ADMIRAL RILEY MIXSON

USS *ORISKANY* & USS *KITTY HAWK*, OFF VIETNAM
1969–71
NAVAL AVIATOR
ATTACK SQUADRON 195

*In May 1965, President Lyndon Johnson ordered the first of
what became a series of periodic bombing halts. The cease-
fires were intended to persuade Hanoi to begin serious peace
negotiations. However, the bombing halts became the epitome
of what aviators and infantrymen knew to be an inconsistent
war-fighting policy. Bombing halts allowed the North Vietnamese and Viet Cong to resupply and intensify their attacks
against American forces and their allies, and, in effect, convinced the North Vietnamese that if they pursued a war of attrition, a political victory was possible as American casualties
mounted.*

*The bitter experience of flying over North Vietnamese resup-
ply convoys during bombing halts made a lasting impression
on fighter pilots such as Riley Mixson, who later commanded
all U.S. aircraft-carrier forces in the Red Sea during Operation
Desert Storm.*

My first crisis participation was the 1962 Cuban Missile Crisis.
I was a young lieutenant on the Atlantic Coast, flying off the
last straight-decked aircraft carrier, the USS *Lake Champlain*.
I heard President Kennedy's speech on the severity of the Soviet missiles in Cuba. I thought there was a possibility of a major war.

Along with other carriers and ships that were sent down to
the waters around Cuba, we were involved in enforcing the
maritime quarantine. Taking photos of every ship that went
into and came out of Cuba. It was sort of like the Gulf War
embargo of Iraq. Our mission at sea was to make sure that any

ship that went into Cuba was empty. And that any ship that came out had missiles on it.

I couldn't see Vietnam on the horizon. I didn't think about political or geographical matters. I was just happy to be flying. I wasn't committed to a naval career. I was seriously considering the commercial airlines. What tipped the balance in my decision to stay was when the Navy chose me for postgraduate school to earn my master's degree. Vietnam began while I was in naval postgraduate school.

My first tour of Vietnam was flying A-4 Echoes aboard the aircraft carrier *Oriskany* in 1969. That was an eight-and-a-half-month deployment. We came back from that and transitioned as a squadron to A-7Es, brand new airplanes. We redeployed to Vietnam on the carrier *Kitty Hawk* from the fall of 1970 to July 1971.

Both deployments came after tactical bombing cutbacks. Every time we would have a little bit of success in Vietnam, President Johnson would restrict the bombing of North Vietnam. That prevented us from going after North Vietnamese logistics centers. Our missions were restricted to around the DMZ [demarcation of the two Vietnams] and into Laos, to stem the flow of enemy war supplies coming into South Vietnam.

Every time there was a bombing halt over the North, it enabled the North Vietnamese to intensify the shipment of weapons and soldiers to the South.

They moved many of their convoys through the forested mountains of Laos at night. We didn't have the kinds of night vision technology like we used in Desert Storm. So there was no way that we could stem the flow of supplies by attacking through the dense forests. It was very dangerous. But we tried anyway. As a result, we lost pilots who crashed into the sides of steep mountains.

I also flew escort for reconnaissance overflights of North Vietnam while there was no bombing allowed. We basically monitored the flow of supplies to the South and any kind of antiaircraft missile buildup.

In 1971, I participated in General John Lavelle's [Commander of the 7th Air Force and Chief of U.S. Air Operations in Vietnam] retaliatory strikes into North Vietnam, mostly against the heavy air defenses around Vinh. This was in retaliation for their abuse of the bombing halt by firing at our reconnaissance aircraft. The General eventually got fired over it because the strikes were not sanctioned by the White House.

The hallmark of that period was the lack of common sense in targeting packages and the restrictions being placed on the U.S. air campaign. At that point I was just a lieutenant commander. But in my mind, the targeting made no sense at all. Targets were selected in Washington, almost down to what types of ordnance we should use. You couldn't shoot at SAM sites, at one point in time, unless they shot at you first. You couldn't attack their resupply ships at a port if there was a third country [usually Soviet bloc or Chinese] ship in the area. Unlike Desert Storm, we were not permitted to systematically take down the air defenses. That cost us a lot of lives . . . and possibly the war.

Years later, going into Desert Storm, the common theme among all senior leaders who had been involved in Vietnam was, "We want to do this one right."

BUSHIDO CODE

MAJOR GENERAL JAMES DAY

PACIFIC CAMPAIGN 1943–45
RIFLEMAN
22ND MARINE REGIMENT

DMZ, VIETNAM 1966–67
BATTALION COMMANDER
1ST BATTALION, 9TH MARINE REGIMENT

Among Marines, few men are as respected as retired Major General Jim Day. In 1943 he enlisted as an infantryman in Oberlin, Missouri. At seventeen and eighteen years old, he participated in the Pacific Campaign of World War II and fought in the legendary battles of Guam and Okinawa.

While a senior sergeant, he was commissioned a lieutenant during the Korean War and was a platoon leader in the battles of the "Hook" and "Bunker Hill." And as a lieutenant colonel in Vietnam, he commanded a battalion known as the "Walking

*Dead" because of the fierce fighting they participated in along
the DMZ that divided North and South Vietnam. Wounded in
all three wars, he received a total of six Purple Hearts.*

You hear the argument, "It takes twenty years to become a
good officer or NCO." That's bullshit. I never heard that argument in World War II when the Marine Corps went from a little over 18,000 men to over 530,000 Marines in the field. No
one ever commented on the tremendous amount of enlisted
people who received commissions in that war.

In Vietnam, our kids had to learn overnight. Especially during heavy periods of fighting, like the Tet Offensive, a young
Marine might become a squad leader or even a platoon sergeant in six to nine months. Old-timers may have complained,
"You're making a kid into an NCO in seven months." But,
hell, those kids knew how to fight against a very determined
enemy.

In World War II, most NCOs were in their thirties and for-
ties. They came in after the war began in December 1941, and
earned their promotions through combat experience. I had one
sergeant who came in before 1941. He was killed in the Marshall Islands. But the rest of my sergeants enlisted in 1942, and
by 1943, when I arrived in the Pacific Theater, they were
NCOs.

The Japanese were committed to fight until they died. I
never saw a Japanese prisoner during 1943–44 in the Marshall
Islands, or Guam.

On Okinawa, our attack on Sugar Loaf Hill was probably
the costliest of all battles in the Pacific. We never saw a prisoner there. They would fight right until the end. In some battles, Japanese soldiers would fake surrender—with grenades or
explosives tied to their bodies—to lure Marines into their sui-
cidal kill zone. [During the fighting for Okinawa some 12,500
American troops were killed, and 11,000 Japanese.]

And they didn't believe in taking prisoners. From the time
we started our offensive at Guadalcanal, I never knew of a Marine being taken prisoner by the Japanese. If Marines were
caught, they were usually killed and strung on a wire.

I saw Japanese killed right in front of our fighting holes or
on top of their positions. A lot of them would fight hand-to-
hand if they ran out of ammunition. They would rush our position with bayonets. For the most part, they were sitting
ducks. On Okinawa, the last big battle in the Pacific, we took

around four prisoners—in eighty-two days of fighting. The Japanese were probably the hardest soldiers I ever fought against. They had that fighting spirit instilled in them.

I think the experience of being against an enemy who were so ruthless and totally unconcerned about their own well-being had a lasting impact on Marines. I think it made better soldiers of those people who stayed in uniform after the war. We had seen the absolute worst type of enemy an infantryman could face.

We not only fought them in daylight hours. We didn't get any respite. Their counterattacks and banzai suicide attacks would start right after dark. They were determined that nobody was going to take an inch of their land. They did everything they could to stop us. It's the ancient Bushido concept from samurai warrior days.

My experiences in the Pacific had a lasting impact on my development as an infantry officer. I learned that some things you need to learn well, you don't learn from the guys you're fighting with, but from the guys you are fighting against. It taught me that you can never count on an opponent to give up when he is hurt very badly. You can never believe for a moment that your air support and artillery and mortars have destroyed your opponent's positions, no matter how much fire you throw at him.

We saw similar tenacity in Vietnam. We would hit enemy positions with a large amount of napalm and big bombs. We'd go in afterwards, and those bastards were still dug in and willing to put up a fight.

The battalion I commanded in Vietnam operated in some very tough areas. We were told that we had taken more casualties than any other infantry battalion. I believe that was because of the area we operated in along the DMZ that divided North and South Vietnam. We didn't have any letup from North Vietnamese artillery across the DMZ. It was almost constant. And mine fields were laid out like carpets.

There was a constant infiltration of enemy forces from the Laotian border, who were protected by the political restrictions from Washington that prevented us from knocking out their reinforcement bases or supply lines. We would constantly be pushing them back, but they had a damned sanctuary across the border guaranteed by American politicians. So we had to take back the same areas over and over again. I don't think there was a guy, from private to general, who didn't have a stench in his mouth from the politics of the war.

MEDAL OF HONOR

COLONEL WESLEY FOX

DMZ, VIETNAM 1968–69
COMPANY COMMANDER
ALPHA COMPANY, 1ST BATTALION,
9TH MARINE REGIMENT

A year after James Day departed Vietnam, in the same 1st Battalion of the 9th Marine Regiment, nicknamed "the Walking Dead," a veteran 1st lieutenant, Wesley Fox, took command of Alpha Company. From a dirt-poor farm in the Blue Ridge mountains of Virginia, Fox, a high school dropout, began his career as a mud Marine in the Korean War. During the next sixteen years, he rose through the enlisted ranks, from squad leader to drill instructor to 1st sergeant.

As a result of one of the most heroic individual actions in Vietnam, Fox is among the few warriors in American history to be awarded the highest decoration for courage, the Congressional Medal of Honor.

In 1965–66, the Marine Corps began to swell in preparation for the Vietnam War. Some 5,000 staff NCOs were given commissions into the officer ranks. I was one of those. From a 1st sergeant I became an instant lieutenant. After sixteen years as a Marine, fourteen of those as an NCO, I knew something about leadership.

I didn't get to Vietnam until August 1967. The first year I was an advisor to the South Vietnamese marines. Then I extended my tour for another six months to work with American Marines. I took command of Alpha Company, 1st Battalion, 9th Marines, in a heavily contested area near the DMZ. Ominously, they were nicknamed the "Walking Dead."

The biggest difference between being an officer and an NCO at a company level is involvement. I was used to being personally involved with my Marines. As a company commander, I had a problem getting detached. I had to remind myself a few times to supervise the sergeants' work and not get overly involved.

I learned to know my people by going out with squad-sized ambushes. I found that they didn't know how to set up a good ambush. They would go into an assigned area, and get into a wagon-wheel formation. Half of them—or all of them—would go to sleep. So every chance, like when we got to provide security at Fire Base Vandergriff, I brought a group of my Marines together to practice assault and ambush techniques. Initially that drew a lot of resentment. They thought I was taking away from their rest time with training. They wanted to lay around and write letters and drink beer.

I gave classes by the numbers on how to set up an L-shaped ambush: how to place the machine gun, string out claymore mines, how to alternate watch and wake everyone if the enemy comes. I turned that company around by getting them to think the same way and coordinate together as a team.

This training paid dividends in the A Shau Valley on February 21 and 22, 1969, when we got into a fight with an entrenched North Vietnamese battalion. The enemy base camp was built near a small stream in triple canopy jungle. The foliage was so thick that you couldn't see more than two or three meters in front.

On the morning of the twenty-first, my 3rd platoon, led by Lieutenant Bill Christman, was on patrol into the valley. Suddenly they came under heavy fire. Their two point men were killed in the opening volley. Instead of panicking or wondering what to do next, the small platoon attempted to break contact with the much larger enemy force. But they wouldn't leave the area until they recovered the point Marines. If they had not learned to think the same way and knew what to expect of each other, I don't think they would have survived.

At that time I was with the rest of my company on top of a ridge line, in radio contact with 3rd platoon. Our mission was to hold defensive positions. And Bill Christman assured us that his platoon could break enemy contact. Our battalion commander, Lt. Colonel George Smith, realized that there was a heavy NVA force in the area. So he ordered my company to do a combat patrol into the same valley the following morning. The next day, a thick fog prevented us from starting our patrol until eleven A.M. Approaching our first checkpoint, my lead fire team came under fire from two fortified bunkers. We took out the bunkers, but it cost us one Marine dead and one wounded. My company took a break along a stream. I radioed to the battalion, in accordance with a prearranged plan, that they could send down a water detail. We held defensive positions until the detail arrived.

We started getting hit with 82mm mortars, exploding in the thick trees. Machine-gun fire opened up on the water detail. Some Marines in the detail fell wounded. I sent a squad to recover them, and organized my company to maneuver through the foliage to a better position to assault the NVA positions. We were at too close a distance to safely call for artillery support without getting ourselves hit. The enemy was between ourselves and the rest of our battalion on the right.

After we began the attack, a group of NVA were trying to outflank us and circle around behind us. Almost every member of my command group was hit, including myself.

[During our interview at his Command Office Marine Corps Officer Candidate School at Quantico, Colonel Fox was reluctant to continue his story. The following is taken from the written orders that were presented with the Medal of Honor.]

Although wounded, he continued to direct his company . . . calmly ordering an assault against the machine-gun and RPG (rocket propelled grenades) emplacement. He then crawled through the kill zone, with his radio, coordinating close aircraft support with the actions of his men. Advancing through heavy fire, he personally knocked out an enemy position. And when his executive officer fell mortally wounded, Captain Fox reorganized the company, directing his men to hurl grenades at the NVA, driving them into retreat. Wounded again in the final assault, Fox refused medical attention, to supervise setting up defensive positions. He waited until all of his dead and wounded marines were evacuated, before permitting himself to be flown out for medical treatment.

I was prepared for receiving the Medal of Honor by my battalion commander, George Smith, who is now a retired major general. He made a real push to get me the medal. My senior corpsman [medic] went to him with the story, and it was verified by a few platoon sergeants and others who all wrote statements.

At the time he submitted the paperwork, I was with my unit in the field. Colonel Smith called me back to his Command Post at Cam Lo. He said, "If you ever get the award. And I emphasize *if* . . ."

Two and a half years later, after I received the medal, he gave me a long lecture: "Now that you've received the medal, forget it. I had a close friend who got the medal in Korea who is now dead from alcohol. Actually, he killed himself. His career in the Corps was terminated when he was a lieutenant colonel because of his problems in not being able to handle the notoriety."

Colonel Smith's advice was well-taken. He went on to say, "Marines need to look up to you for what you can do. Not for what you have done."

Belonging to the Medal of Honor Society has been a real eye opener for me. There are 201 recipients still alive. I come to the realization each time that the group meets that those men could be a rifle company anywhere in the Marine Corps. Because among those men are the ten percent that are at the bottom who I don't want anything to do with, and I can't believe they are part of this group. There are also ten percent at the top who provide the leadership and guidance and the correctness of everything that honor stands for. And then there are the rest of us in between.

Those ten percent at the bottom, you might say, "What are those guys doing with the Medal of Honor?" Well, it's not because of who the individual is. But what he did on that one occasion.

THE THREE BEARS

COLONEL KENNETH BOWRA

Long Hai, Vietnam 1972
Instructor
U.S. Army Vietnam Individual Training Group

After eight months of special operations reconnaissance in MACV-SOG, I was about to rotate back to the States. But I heard about a project where Special Forces people were training army units of the Khmer [ethnic Cambodian] Republic. I didn't know anything about Cambodia. I was interviewed and considered for the job because I could speak French, the second language of Cambodia.

I was assigned to what was called the UITG Project—U.S. Army Vietnam Individual Training Group. The project began in 1971, based in Bien Hoa, to train the armed forces of the young Khmer Republic that was formed after Prince Sihanouk was overthrown. We were to train their infantry battalions. To equip them and give them the entire basic and advanced individual training. Then take them out on some combat operations in Vietnam. Build on the lessons learned, then send them back to Cambodia on their own.

All of this program was conducted inside of Vietnam. We were prohibited by U.S. law to do this in Cambodia. Our bottom line was to help Cambodian soldiers, who had a tough fight in their own country against both the North Vietnamese and the Khmer Rouge [Cambodian Communists]. I was assigned to one of the training camps, at Long Hai, on the eastern Vietnamese coast.

We conducted field operations in the Xuan Loc area or the Long Hai mountains to get the Cambodians some combat experience. We'd truck 512 troops into an area, divided into company sectors. We had a lot of contact with Viet Cong units. In the process, we were able to monitor the leadership of the Cambodian battalion and take charge when we had to. And we developed a close relationship with them.

I learned in combat that the choices we make we have to live with. There is an incident that I will never forget that happened when I was on a training mission with my Cambodians.

We were patrolling through a rice field and met an old man. He was very thin, dressed in peasant black, with a silver beard and droopy mustache. If there was a Ho Chi Minh look-alike contest that day, he would've won. His face was weathered, he wore a straw conical hat. He just stood in his field and watched 150 Cambodians and myself walking across. I went up to him with my Cambodian counterpart, who had no love for the Vietnamese.

I asked the old man if he spoke French. He replied in absolutely perfect Parisian French. I explained that we hoped not to do much damage to his crop and that we would move through the area rapidly. He followed politely with a barrage of questions: "Who are you? Where are you going to set up camp?" He kept getting more specific. I looked at him with a smile and he stopped. Without saying anything, there was no doubt in his mind that I was aware of what he was doing and who he was. The guy had probably been doing it since the early 1950s. I just smiled at him. And he kind of smiled back.

My Cambodians and I went across the field into a woods. We set up security. I was sitting there and looked at a tree that was broken over. On it was a pistol belt with pouches for a carbine rifle, with a rolled poncho and a first-aid pouch.

I looked at my Cambodian friend. He said, "That's not our gear." It was obvious that here was the old man's stash of equipment. We took it with us and moved on. We didn't bother to go back to the field to get him. I didn't feel that would affect the outcome of the war.

We proceeded out of the area. I took point, at the head of the company. It was "bad guy" country. We pitched camp, and after an uneventful night, we pushed on from first light all the way until around eleven A.M. The terrain was very flat with some hills in the distance, but it was heavy dense jungle. Cutting our way through it was pretty tiring. So I moved back about five places in the file and let some strong young Cambodians get in front.

We found a path in a Viet Cong base area, that we knew they wouldn't booby-trap. We started moving on it. We actually ran into an enemy squad. Our respective point men collided. The Viet Cong had a dog running with them who got mixed up in our column. It turned into a horrendous firefight.

We broke off contact with them, with fortunately no casualties among my people. We moved forward and set up an ambush position for the rest of the day.

A group of six figures in black pajamas approached our position. We were ready to trigger the ambush when I noticed that they didn't have weapons. I put down the clackers that we use to signal the start of an ambush. I began walking up the trail to stop the figures. As fate would have it, I had a Vietnamese army [ARVN] sergeant as translator. The six were all young women. They seemed to be coming back from a mission. They had no ID papers and wouldn't talk. They were playing hardball.

My Cambodians had no love for Vietnamese—North or South—after centuries of conflicts between the two nations and cultures. The ARVN sergeant said, "Yes, they're Viet Cong." The Cambodians said, "Let's just kill them now."

I tried to call for an aircraft to take them in for questioning. But I couldn't get an aircraft. And we were supposed to remain in the field for another couple of weeks. I looked at them. The ARVN sergeant didn't want any part of it. So I got all six women together. I said, "There are several options available."

I explained, "The Cambodian solution is to shoot you. That is unacceptable to me. The ARVN sergeant's solution is to tie you to a tree and leave you in the woods." I paused. Then I said, "I'm going to release you to go back to your camp. Tell your comrades what has occurred. We're going to be in the area. You won't know where. But if you do come down that trail again, it will be heavily ambushed. This is your one chance to get out." They looked in disbelief. I untied them and sent them on their way.

The next day, I went with one of my scouts in the direction that they came from. Just the two of us. We found the VC base camp, regimental size. It was a honeycomb of bunkers and underground tunnels. There were still clothes hanging on a line.

We crawled up pretty close and saw a few people walking around. I couldn't call in an air strike because we had no suitable communication equipment. We were out of range for artillery support. So we quietly observed their security positions, then went back to get the rest of our company.

We planned a good assault. The company moved up to the camp and got into attack formation, blocking off any escape routes. We moved forward and found that the VC regiment had moved out. We went in and began blowing up bunkers.

While we were doing this, I got a call on our radio, "An enemy element has just attacked a convoy. They were last seen moving toward your area."

Here we were destroying their bunkers. It was sort of like Goldilocks and the Three Bears. They outnumbered us by at least ten soldiers to one. So we expeditiously proceeded to move out.

Sometimes I think about those six women. If they survived the war, they probably tell the story today, just like I'm telling you. Saying, "You're not going to believe this, but one day we were out in the forest and a company of Cambodians captured us with this American lieutenant."

After all is said and done, I still think it was the right thing to do.

RED-HAIRED NURSE

COLONEL BARBARA SMITH

DANANG, VIETNAM 1970–71
INTENSIVE CARE NURSE
95TH EVACUATION HOSPITAL

In Vietnam I saw many forms of heroism. The Medical Corps was one of the only occupations open to women in the U.S. armed forces in Vietnam. Of some 11,000 military women who served in the combat zone, around 9,500 were nurses who served in MASH units and field hospitals. They were given an awesome responsibility to be the first healing contact for young soldiers who were torn up in combat. Most nurses arrived as young 2nd lieutenants fresh out of college, including Barbara Smith, a petite, red-haired twenty-two-year-old.

The Army paid my last two years of college at the University of South Carolina. And I said that I'd be a nurse for them for three years. If anybody said, "You'll make a career of this," I would've laughed.

I went to Vietnam in 1970, in my first full year of nursing. I wanted to go to Vietnam. And my chances were much greater by going into the Army than the Navy.

I was sent to the 95th Evacuation Hospital in Danang. A lot of our doctors were drafted. And the enlisted corpsmen were well-trained and an important help to us nurses. Our intensive care unit had eighteen beds and one nurse. Often at night it would just be myself and one or two corpsmen to care for all our patients.

I went to Vietnam a young 2nd lieutenant. Yes, I was a little scared. In Danang, our hospital treated American soldiers, Marines, Koreans, enemy prisoners, Vietnamese children and displaced civilians.

When I first got there, I met some nurses who were getting ready to rotate home who were very bitter. I thought, "Dear Lord, please don't let that happen to me." They were so down on life. I thought, "How ironic. They're letting something we disagree with—the war—tear them up inside. I can let this tear me apart, and go home really screwed up."

I realized, "These wounded soldiers want to go home just as much as me." I was determined to work harder for them.

After a month on the surgical ward, I was offered the ICU. I grabbed it, because excellent people worked there. Being around them boosted my confidence. In the intensive care ward we had traumatic amputees, head wounds, a lot of people on ventilators because of chest wounds.

I worked fourteen- to sixteen-hour shifts, depending on medical evacuation helicopters bringing in casualties. My intention was to work hard and play hard. Recently, I looked at the diary I kept and realized how little sleep a twenty-one- or twenty-two-year-old can get by on.

I wasn't worried about being promoted to captain. Because it seemed the higher rank you got, the more you were part of the bureaucracy. I didn't want that. I just wanted to take care of soldiers.

THE EASTER OFFENSIVE

LIEUTENANT GENERAL WALTER BOOMER

QUANG TRI PROVINCE, VIETNAM 1971–72
ADVISOR
MARINE ADVISORY UNIT

In early 1972, America's direct military involvement in Vietnam was rapidly coming to a conclusion. Practically no conventional infantry forces remained "in-country." Among the few U.S. ground combatants were a small group of Marine officers who served as advisors with their South Vietnamese counterparts. Among them was a young major, Walt Boomer, commissioned after graduating from the Duke University ROTC program.

As Easter week approached, the Paris Peace Talks were grinding toward a conclusion. To challenge American resolve and test the stamina of the South Vietnamese, the North Vietnamese Army launched a massive offensive across the DMZ and Laotian and Cambodian borders. Unlike the disastrous Tet Offensive, instead of relying on Maoist guerrilla and light infantry tactics, they utilized the Soviet doctrine of massive heavy artillery and armor-led assaults.

Overwhelmed by the initial onslaught, the American advisors struggled to stay alive. Eventually they guided a fierce counterattack aided by U.S. air support. Learning from their survival, the U.S. Marine advisors used the tactical lessons for years to come. Many went on to become senior commanders, including Lt. General Walt Boomer, Commander of Marine forces in Desert Storm.

When I returned in August 1971, American forces were drawn down to the point that all Marine line units were gone. Every Marine who went to Vietnam was a volunteer. I reported into Saigon to our Advisory Unit headquarters, and was assigned to the Vietnamese marines' 4th Battalion. We operated in I Corps, just below the DMZ.

In March 1972, my battalion was at a mountaintop outpost called Fire Support Base Sarge. It was the farthest western outpost, overlooking Route 9, near the Cam Lo River. We were seeing North Vietnamese units moving into our area from Laos. They were rolling in large truck convoys and becoming pretty blatant about stockpiling weapons and supplies. There was nobody out there to stop them. I had an uneasy feeling that something *big* was about to happen.

Myself and other American advisors were encouraging the South Vietnamese Army 3rd Division, under General Vu Van Giai, to go out in force to see what the North Vietnamese were up to. Perhaps to disrupt them. But we weren't able to convince him. The 3rd Division was newly formed, in part with deserters from other units, and sent out to this desolate mountain area.

Heavy monsoon rains prevented helicopters from flying in supplies. We were desperately low on food. So we split our battalion in two. I stayed at Fire Base Sarge with two infantry companies, a mortar platoon, and the battalion commander's headquarters' units. Captain Ray Smith went with the other half of the battalion around 1,000 meters north on Nui Ba Ho mountain.

On March 22–23, both Fire Base Sarge and Nui Ba Ho came under heavy artillery attacks. I suspected a big battle was coming our way. That happened on March 30, the Thursday before Easter. Three North Vietnamese divisions attacked across the DMZ into Quang Tri Province. Every South Vietnamese base in the area was hit simultaneously. Sarge and Nui Ba Ho were hit with a devastating artillery and rocket barrage, that slammed through our defensive structures. And infantry units of the NVA 308th Division moved into assault positions. Throughout the night there was no letup, with 82mm and 60mm mortars continuing to pound us. We were surrounded.

Storm clouds prevented Air Force gunships from providing us with fire support because the North Vietnamese were too close to our own position. With only a few hundred feet ceiling, the aircraft were afraid that they would hit friendly troops. So I risked exposure to artillery fire to signal with an infrared strobe light to mark our position. But the aircraft still couldn't see us. Low on fuel, they had to leave the area.

We braced ourselves for a ground assault. Around 75 percent of our north perimeter defenses were pulverized by the relentless incoming explosions. They just killed us with artillery and rocket fire. Then followed it with waves of ground forces. My Marines fought bravely to force them back.

After twenty-four hours, I received a radio message from Captain Smith that Nui Ba Ho was being overrun. My troops kept fighting, but my counterpart, Major De, and I knew that we couldn't hold Sarge much longer. Our mortar platoon helped to hold off the first waves of North Vietnamese. But by the second evening, every member of that platoon was either dead or wounded.

After midnight, with the NVA swarming through our defenses, Major De made the decision for whoever was still alive to escape from Sarge.

It became a desperate matter of pure survival. Close to half of our battalion was killed or wounded. Using the cover of smoke and darkness, we had to escape and evade in the jungle down the side of the mountain. It was not an organized "fighting" retreat. We had a lot of walking wounded with us. We struggled down the dense jungle undergrowth and jagged slope. We had no food, water, or medical aid for the wounded.

Everywhere we turned there were North Vietnamese units

hunting for us. They were above us and below us. So we tried to avoid a fight. I was the only American among several hundred Vietnamese.

After two days of running, on Easter Sunday, around nine o'clock in the morning, we were in six-foot-high elephant grass—almost out of the jungle. The NVA discovered us. We were surrounded and getting hit pretty hard.

At that point, my troops broke and ran. It was every guy for himself. The sad thing about it was that they left a large column of wounded.

I tried to stop them from running and turned around. In fact, I was yelling and shooting over their heads. The damn NVA heard me. I distinctly heard a North Vietnamese exclaim, "Co van, co van!" [American advisor!] I said, "Shit. It's time to get out of here."

I moved east as quickly as I could. I reached a small village near Fire Base Mai Loc, where I was surprised to find Captain Smith and Major De. The events of the past few days didn't seem real.

We finally regrouped across the river from Quang Tri fire base, a little to the northwest of the city. North Vietnamese units, supported by tanks, kept coming. They eventually overran Quang Tri city. But the South Vietnamese made a much stronger resistance than the NVA anticipated.

We fell back to the Cua Viet River and dug in for a last stand, and held our ground. That bought time for other South Vietnamese units to regroup and wage a fierce counterattack to take back Quang Tri.

The Easter Offensive was a product of the North Vietnamese having changed to commanders who were well-schooled in Soviet conventional tactics. That included saturation artillery fire and armor assaults.

The first time my people went up against tanks was at Fire Base Sarge. And at a simultaneous battle, Marine captain John Ripley and his South Vietnamese marine battalion were under a fierce tank attack from across the DMZ at the Dong Ha Bridge. The bridge was a passageway from North Vietnam into the South. Ripley and a U.S. Army advisor blew up the bridge by hand, almost by themselves. That, in itself, is an epic story.

My unit faced sporadic, smaller tank attacks—Soviet or Chinese built T-54 and T-55 models. We used a combination of weapons to stop one column of fifteen to twenty tanks. We used field artillery fire very effectively. Other units stopped tanks at short range with LAWs [shoulder-fired light antitank weapons]. We came away from that experience with the knowledge that once you overcome your initial fear, you certainly can fight tanks effectively.

After we fell back to Quang Tri, I went home on a long-scheduled two-week leave. My unit went down to Hue City to lick their wounds and get replacements and supplies. At that time, I said, "I can't do any more than I've done. So I'll go on leave and then come back."

In the States, I was called to Washington, which seemed surrealistic compared to the events I had just survived in the Vietnamese mountains. At the Pentagon, I was ushered into the office of the Secretary of Defense, Melvin Laird. I was scared to death. I thought, "What the hell am I doing in the Secretary of Defense's office?"

He asked, "What's your biggest problem?" I said, "Enemy artillery." He said, "People tell me it's tanks." I said, "We can handle that. But we can't turn off the artillery."

I remember him picking up the telephone. He called someone to ask about the Air Force. He put down the phone and said, "They tell me that they are taking care of the artillery." That was a lot of bullshit.

After two weeks, I went back to the same battalion in Vietnam. Our forces were dug in on the banks of the Cua Viet River, preparing for a classic set-piece battle. We were all that stood between the advancing NVA and Hue City. We stopped them. And with the help of U.S. air support, we began to push the North Vietnamese back.

PART II

Wilderness Years

REIGN OF TERROR

GENERAL ALFRED GRAY

CAMP LEJEUNE, NORTH CAROLINA 1971–73
BATTALION COMMANDER
2ND MARINE REGIMENT

Toward the end of the Vietnam War, despite bloated numbers of personnel and advances in technology, the American military was no longer the highly professional force that had gone into Southeast Asia. Discipline and morale had fallen apart in all branches, largely due to a lack of direction by senior leadership. However, a core group of dedicated officers and sergeants attempted to hold the system together by employing strict standards—which were sometimes scorned by their superiors.

After four tours and nearly five years in Vietnam, Al Gray returned to garrison duty in the States.

By 1970, we had a lot of people who did not deserve to wear the title "Marine." That was caused by high casualties, lowering our recruitment standards to balloon to twice our normal size, and the unpopularity of the war. And we lacked cohesion because of the individual rotation system in Vietnam.

That turned off a lot of good officers and staff NCOs. We lost a lot of good people. Let's say that you're a gunnery sergeant. You've been a Marine for fifteen, twenty years, you have been a good one. All of a sudden you have to play housemaid with a bunch of people who are like an undisciplined mob.

By "discipline problems," I'm not talking about people having a few more drinks than they should and getting into a little scrap. I'm talking about gang fights. And hundreds of hours spent on riot control.

I took command of 1st Battalion, 2nd Marine Regiment on June 22, 1971. I called formation and said, "Where the hell is B Company?" People said, "B Company is the discipline company." I said, "What the hell is the discipline company?" That's where all the bad guys in the battalion were sent. They said, "Nobody really goes over there." I said, "I'm going over there."

I went to the barracks and this great big black corporal says, "Who are you?" I said, "My name is Gray and I'm the new battalion commander. Who are you?" He said, "My name is Bowman. I'm in charge here. All these people do what I say."

I said, "You are a natural leader. People here listen to you. So you better have them out on the parade deck tomorrow morning at seven o'clock for me to inspect. Or you are not going to be in the Marine Corps by tomorrow night, nor are they."

I was not really authorized to do that. But the next morning they were present. I explained the rules. Bowman, believe it or not, never let me down. He was a natural leader in the black community. He knew that if they did anything wrong that I would hold him responsible. He'd be gone. And he didn't want to go back to the streets of Detroit.

We made eight landings and major exercises. Never had one little incident. Nobody hurt or killed. But I weeded a lot of people out. I was accused by my division commander of a "reign of terror."

One morning I had my sergeant major with me, the regiment commander, and the regiment sergeant major. I fell out my battalion—around 400 people showed. I said, "Where's the rest of them? Go get them." So they came flushing out of the barracks. I went and had an inspection. I busted guys in rank who hadn't shaved, or didn't do this or that. But, by God, they got the message.

When General Louis Wilson became Marine Corps Commandant, he brought in General Barrow and General McClellan to head Manpower and Manpower Policy. They set out to change the basic quality of people that came into the Corps. They said, "Enough is enough. We are going to get rid of these disciplinary problems." Somebody had to put their foot down.

In early 1973, I was still a lieutenant colonel. I left the 2nd Regiment to be the G3 [Operations and Planning Officer] of the division. The general in charge of force troops at MEF-LANT [Marine Expeditionary Force, Atlantic] was Brigadier General Bob Nicholas. I went to a conference at his office on all our unauthorized absences [AWOLs]. All the walls around his meeting room were covered with graphs and statistics.

That day we discovered that all of these people who were AWOL, all the troublemakers, very few were high school graduates. Out of that discovery emerged a theory: while it's not indicative of more intelligence—high schools being what they are—at least graduates have a sense of responsibility. Some parent or guardian encouraged them and they didn't quit. So that's where our focus went. We started a high school at the base. And we moved the recruiting emphasis out to the suburbs where a higher percentage of high school graduates are.

I attended the Army War College for a year. Then, in July 1974, I took command of the 4th Regiment at Camp Hansen in Okinawa. I had about 85,000 sailors and Marines. Around 55 percent did not have a high school diploma. It was unsafe for any Marine officer or enlisted man to walk around the camp alone. I cleaned it up with a very tough leadership program.

We had our share of bad people. Because, frankly, a lot of leaders didn't stand up and do something about it. You cannot be intimidated by racial confrontation or any other type of confrontation. That was rampant in the armed services during that period. There was an awesome drain on leadership to turn that around. I was out there every night breaking up fights. There were militant groups: white, black, and Hispanic. Too many senior people were looking the other way.

One of the reasons that I'm so adamantly against "careerism" is because too many leaders cared more about how they looked than how they worked. It's okay to want to get ahead—that's as apple pie as motherhood. But when a leader cares more about himself than the people he is privileged to lead, everyone is in trouble.

The way that the higher leadership in Washington planned the Vietnam War, a lot of people were taking advantage of the situation to advance their own careers. In the process, they were destroying the military institution. As a result, the war dragged on for years with 57,000 Americans dead, millions of people in Asia ended up living in tyranny. And the military needed riot control because we couldn't control our young people.

A factor in the breakdown in discipline in the Marine Corps was that many senior NCOs were given direct commissions in 1965–66. In turn, we had to make younger or not so good older people into staff NCOs. After the war, some of the commissioned guys reverted back to NCO. But they had missed six or seven years of important staff time. Many others retired or just got out. It was a hellish environment for good NCOs.

RESPECT

SERGEANT MAJOR JOSEPH CELESTINE

CAMP PENDLETON, CALIFORNIA 1992–93
BASE SERGEANT MAJOR

When I came into the Marine Corps, just before the Vietnam era, I saw very few officers when I was in boot camp. All of the training I received basically came from corporals and buck sergeants.

My staff NCOs didn't have much formal education. But they had a lot of good common sense. They encouraged young Marines to strive to do better, "Do as I say, not as I do."

I worked my butt off to be an NCO. Couldn't wait. Even though the NCOs didn't have much privileges, black, white, or Hispanic, they were respected. They lived with everyone in open squad bay, using lockers to form a wall, curtained off with a hand-painted sign that said, NCO QUARTERS.

When I was a young sergeant, NCOs had our own club. We had our own area in the mess hall. We felt that we were doing something very important and acted accordingly. If one NCO's personal behavior began to drop, two or three others would counsel him, "Hey, you're letting us all down."

Our leadership style was, "We should be feared and not loved." We made great effort to assure that fear. There was no doubt in a young Marine's mind that if he stepped out of line that he would probably get belted a few times. That was the way of the Corps.

I think that we have made great strides in our NCO training. Trust is important. You should lead by example. But there should also be an element of fear in a young Marine's mind that, "If I don't do this, there will be a consequence." An equal amount of reward and punishment.

Over the years, my wife and I often talk about raising our kids. I told her that even in raising kids, there needs to be some degree of fear. True, you let your kids know that you love them. But should they be tempted to do something wrong, it should be in the back of their minds, "Boy, if I do this, Dad and Mom are really going to do something." They're not exactly sure what Dad and Mom are going to do. And maybe Dad and Mom won't do very much at all. But there should be some degree of, "I don't want to do this. Because I don't want to face the consequences."

DRILL INSTRUCTOR

SERGEANT MAJOR DAVID SOMMERS

PARRIS ISLAND, SOUTH CAROLINA 1966–68, 1969–73
DRILL INSTRUCTOR & DRILL MASTER

When I came back to the States from my first Vietnam tour, I was a twenty-three-year-old buck sergeant. I was assigned to become a drill instructor.

Being a D.I. back then, you taught your recruit platoon practically all subjects. You marched them to some specialized classes, but you taught the rifle, grenade, first aid, history, and guard duty. And the subjects that you didn't teach, you were still responsible for making sure that your platoon knew them after they received formal instruction.

Because of the high casualties in Vietnam, the Corps was recruiting in large numbers. We called them "foxhole fillers." And we started getting people through the draft. This included a lower caliber of people through the "McNamara's 100,000 Project." I had kids in my platoon who were dropping out the first week to go to Language Orientation units. They had to learn basic English to make it through recruit training. They needed to learn "left, right, left" marching cadence, and words to identify their rifle's parts.

We dealt with a pretty rough crowd. I can remember standing on the parade deck in front of battalion headquarters. A police car pulled up, with two FBI agents who took a recruit from my platoon and hauled him away. The kid was wanted for murder in New York. That was not an isolated case.

I had a recruit try to kill me with a bayonet . . . cut my shirt. Another recruit attempted to club me with his rifle. He put a gash on the side of my eye. But I couldn't show any sign of fear or concern for my own safety. Because I would then lose the respect of the entire platoon. Not being physically large, I had to work twice as hard to maintain the image of authority.

We never had the luxury of an experienced D.I. team. We always had one or two new D.I.'s with an experienced sergeant. I often worked with just one junior D.I. to train 90 to 110 recruits. There was a tremendous amount of stress on drill instructors then. But we didn't hear the word "stress." I guess it wasn't invented yet.

I was single. So I worked continuously. I kept the trunk of my car packed, sometimes working two or three weeks straight without a break. I'd let my junior D.I.'s go home on weekends. And I'd look at the training calendar. If there was a weekend when nothing was scheduled, I'd say, "I'll see you on Monday." Then I'd be good to work for another two or three weeks until my platoon graduated.

At Parris Island we were so strapped for manpower that I often worked two platoons at one time. I'd have a platoon getting ready to graduate under one D.I. team, and I'd pick up a new platoon with another D.I. team. I'd always take advantage in the evening hours after I brought them back from chow. I marched the new platoon into the old platoon's squad bay or vice versa. The graduating recruits would tutor the new platoon. That was our saving grace.

TOP

SERGEANT MAJOR
WILLIAM BAINBRIDGE

PENTAGON 1975–79
SERGEANT MAJOR OF THE ARMY

The backbone of any military organization is its noncommissioned officers. The term "Top" for the most senior sergeant in a military unit is used with affection, respect, and sometimes fear. Sergeant Major of the Army Bill Bainbridge was the top sergeant of the entire Army during the troubled years immediately after the Vietnam War.

A wiry descendant of Illinois farmers and coal miners, during World War II he fought in the climactic Battle of the Bulge and survived six months as a prisoner of the Nazis. As Army Sergeant Major, "Top" Bainbridge became a key player in rebuilding the institution.

The school system for Army officers is 150 years old. But sergeants have never had a comparable training system for each level of their career. There's nothing wrong with smart sergeants. People used to say, "Sergeants don't need a classroom education." NCO schools were criticized for having a class on world affairs. But sergeants need to learn how to read the editorial page, as well as the sports page.

The first graduation class of the Sergeant Major Academy was in 1973. The need for a world affairs class was debated at a big conference at the Pentagon. General Creighton Abrams, the Army Chief of Staff, said, "When I was commander of MACV in Vietnam, I used to bring senior NCOs in on a Saturday or Sunday afternoon and have lunch with them. I learned a hell of a lot just listening to those people. I don't think it will hurt to have World Affairs as a subject at the academy."

A problem in Vietnam was that many senior sergeants had a limited knowledge of world affairs, and the troops had little idea about where they were. It would have been better if the

NCOs could have given the younger people information about what to expect of the local people and explain the overriding political events that effected battlefield policy.

The all-volunteer force began in 1973. The goal in those days was to recruit people with at least a high school diploma. We needed an NCO corps with enough education and knowledge to be able to communicate with the bright young people coming in.

The goal of the courses we created at the Sergeant Major Academy was for top NCOs to be able to talk with their commanders on the same level. As a result, in a recent graduating class at the academy, there were four people with doctorate degrees, twelve with master's degrees, and over a hundred bachelor's degrees. In contrast, in the first graduating class in 1973, out of 100 people, 80 percent had GEDs [high school equivalency diplomas].

During more than thirty-one years in the Army, I learned that you ought never give up the chance for a challenge. In 1972, I went from working for a four-star general who commanded the Army Pacific Command to working for a colonel at the Sergeant Major Academy, that was just forming at Fort Bliss, Texas. It didn't even have library shelves for textbooks. But I jumped at the chance to take that post.

I was able to use all of my experience from World War II, the Korean War era, and Vietnam, to help create a curriculum and pass it along to senior sergeants who hadn't been to where I had been. Teaching your professional skills is always beneficial. That gives you a chance to evaluate it as you are teaching.

We purposely set up the NCO education system so that at every level of their career, sergeants would have a chance to test their theories. After attending a school, they go back to their units and evaluate what leadership techniques really work.

After my time at the Sergeant Major Academy, I was chosen by Army Chief of Staff, General Frederick C. Weyand, to be Sergeant Major of the Army. I was asked to remain in that position by the new Army Chief of Staff, General Bernard Rogers. On one occasion, General Rogers asked me to give a speech to the senior class at West Point on the subject of leadership. I told those young lieutenants about how they needed to treat and use their sergeants.

I said, "You're going to your unit brand new. Your platoon sergeant will have been the leader maybe three or four years before you arrive. So don't go there and try to tell him what you're going to do with his platoon. He'll tell *you* when you're ready.

"But you can use that NCO as a teacher. You can talk with him openly, you can invite him to your house. You don't have to be afraid to be nice to him. That won't change his loyalty to you in the field. He's the catalyst between you and the troops. When he tells you the troops are yours, you'll be ready to take them."

HORATIUS

COLONEL MICHAEL ANDREWS

SCHWEINFURT, GERMANY 1969–71
CAVALRY TROOP LEADER
3RD INFANTRY DIVISION

The last time I saw Mike Andrews in Vietnam, we were both disillusioned by the seeming illogical tactics of the war. Our recon unit had nearly been left to die in an enemy base camp. He had just been married while on seven-day Rest and Relaxation in Hawaii, and he considered what to do when his West Point commitment was finished.

When I left Vietnam I was very disillusioned. I thought that perhaps I would leave the Army. Maybe join the Reserves. If there was a next war—God forbid—I would come back whenever soldiers were in combat. I had three years left on my military obligation.

In 1969, I was transferred to Germany. U.S. forces in Europe were understrength. So, as a captain, I was given a major's job as Brigade S3 [Operations and Plans officer]. I found myself working long and hard hours.

My wife, Linda, was second to the job. Because you could look across the German border into East Germany or Czechoslovakia and there was a growing threat. And we didn't have enough manpower or supplies.

I worked for three colonels, including John Wickham, who later became Chief of Staff of the Army, whom I grew to admire tremendously. They were like "Horatius* at the bridge." They never had enough time or resources. There were race riots and drug problems. So they worked long, hard hours to, at times, the detriment of their own families and to their own health. Everything they did was foreshadowed by the specter of a next war. Whether or not the American or German public cared or understood.

Eventually, I became a cavalry troop commander. We lived with a hostile Warsaw Pact force facing us every day. Every night before I went home, I'd ask my top sergeant and executive officer, "What if *it* happens tonight?" If something needed to be fixed, we did it right then.

We had unannounced alerts every month. I remember that my wife would lace my left boot while I laced my right boot, so I could get to my unit a little faster. I guess that sounds funny now. But I will never forget walking along the border with a German brigade commander. We looked across the border into East Germany: the barbed-wire fences, the guard dogs, and the menacing security forces with whom we had some unpleasant experiences.

I never thought we'd see the Berlin Wall go down in my lifetime. I strongly believe the reason that the Cold War ended without a shot being fired was because of the resoluteness of the forward deployed American forces. Important were such mundane activities as "road marching" up and down the German autobahn [highways] where Soviet spies saw disciplined units. They would report back to their headquarters, "It would not be wise to tangle with them." Year after year we deterred a conflict by showing determination and quality forces. At the time, it may have been something that not even we understood.

*An ancient warrior who saved Rome by single handedly holding off an invading army.

PRELUDE TO GENOCIDE

COLONEL KENNETH BOWRA

CAMBODIA 1974-75
TECHNICAL EXPERT
MILITARY EQUIPMENT DELIVERY TEAM

There is no greater case of the micromanaging by politicians of a U.S. war effort than the tragedy of Cambodia. After American combat forces withdrew from Vietnam 1973, the small neighboring nation of emerald rice fields and golden Buddhist pagodas was being overrun by the North Vietnamese Army and their fierce Cambodian Communist allies, the Khmer Rouge. Rather than strengthening the Cambodian armed forces, which was largely nonexistent before 1970, the U.S. Congress mandated severe restrictions on American military aid and advisors.

Only a handful of American soldiers were permitted by U.S. law to enter Cambodia in a noncombatant role.

In late 1972, after fourteen months of special operations and training Cambodians in Vietnam, I had to return to the States. The war was winding down and American troop strength was being reduced. Ten days after I was on home leave at my parents' home, I called up the Personnel Center and tried to get back to Southeast Asia. It was an obvious nonnegotiable. I was ordered to Fort Bragg, to a HALO [high-altitude, low-opening parachute] team. I was with it for eighteen months, eventually taking command of the team. The whole time, I was trying to get back to Cambodia.

Finally, in June 1974, the head of our infantry branch said, "Look, I can get you to Cambodia. You'll be assigned to the Military Equipment Delivery Team—MEDTC." I didn't know what he was talking about.

The Cambodian War has been called a "sideshow." It really wasn't given the full effort and full attention the Cambodian people deserved. We tried to assist the Khmer [ethnic Cambodians] to assist themselves. The earlier training we gave them in Vietnam was a minimal effort. They were seriously undercut by American politicians in the face of relentless attacks by tens of thousands of North Vietnamese forces. And the Khmer Rouge had heavy support from the Vietnamese Communists. How could the American Congress have overlooked that?

I had seen the dark side of the Khmer Rouge [also called KR] when some of my Cambodian friends took back the ancient capital of Oudong from them. We found hundreds of civilians and military that had been executed—throats cut, shot, beaten to death. Whoever they found, they executed.

Most of the Western media and "Cambodia watchers" thought that it was an isolated event. I tried to tell people, "No, it's not isolated. This is something that is real. And it's probably what we can expect from the Khmer Rouge if they take power."

In August 1974, the U.S. bombing ended. In Washington, it was depicted as "peace" and the "end of the war." But the war wasn't even close to ending. In fact, the North Vietnamese and Khmer Rouge were preparing a major escalation. The American disengagement had a direct negative impact on the survivability of our allies. And the future mass slaughter in Cambodia.

I was a captain, in the role of aide de camp to Brigadier General William Palmer, the chief of the MEDTC. A fierce war was going on all around us. But we were prohibited by U.S. law from inspecting Cambodian units. Our roster was strictly balanced on a daily basis. Only if an American left Cambodia could somebody else come in. Even if a temporary duty team was coming in, we had to send an equal number of people out of the country. The country was under siege and the government and military coming apart at the seams. Yet the American Congress prohibited U.S. military people stationed there from providing the assistance that was needed.

Everyone in the American embassy, from Ambassador John Gunther Dean down through the military attachés and MEDTC team gave everything they could under our restrictions. The noose was tightening around Phnom Penh. But we all believed that, "Maybe things will change." That we would get some additional foreign assistance aid.

A congressional delegation came. I won't mention any of their names. But I was very disappointed. These were our elected officials. And their priorities were not focused on reality. We explained the problems to them. And the ambassador and his staff all explained the desperate condition of the country. Some congresspeople were more concerned with going to Silver Street to buy souvenirs, rather than go to look at Cambodian soldiers dug in for a last stand, without shoes. They would have seen what few artillery rounds they had. Or talk with refugees and learn about Khmer Rouge atrocities in the countryside.

One or two of the congresspeople may have talked to refugees. But my memory is of a group who went to buy souvenirs or harangued us for violating the letter of the law for inspecting Cambodian military units. That was the Big Issue for them.

The last months in Phnom Penh, the KR used a lot of rockets and 105mm artillery. My driver, old Hang Ty, and I were in our jeep and saw rockets explode near one of the riverside parks in the city. We raced to the site and found several severely wounded folks. We had some first-aid dressings with us and did the best we could. While we were doing that another rocket whistled in and landed around ten meters from us. The concussion blew both of us over.

We stood up and shook our heads, our ears ringing from the blast. Old Ty had his Buddha chain in his mouth, which was the Cambodian custom when the going got tough. We loaded as many of the wounded as could fit in our jeep, and drove them to the hospital.

We were down at the Central Market on another occasion when a rocket slammed in. We tried to save an old man. He was hit in the head and the chest severely, I didn't even worry about the leg wounds. What was left of his face was hanging by shreds, like a Halloween mask. But he was still conscious. We tried to stop the bleeding. His wife was there expecting a miracle. He was too far gone. He died in my arms.

The Khmer Rouge escalated, hitting the city with indiscriminate rocket attacks. That became business as usual. It would've been a great prize for the gunners if they could hit Americans. One Saturday morning I was sitting in the embassy at an update briefing. Rockets sailed straight over the building. The rockets hit right across the street from us at an elementary school.

Everyone in the embassy was going into the bunkers, because the Khmer Rouge always followed up with more rockets. I was going in the other direction. General Palmer stopped me and said, "Where are you going?" I said, "Sir, it hit the school." We knew that people were hurt.

I ran across the street, toward probably half a dozen little kids . . . the oldest was seven, the youngest about three or four. Some were hit with head injuries, others had shrapnel entering through their back and protruding through their stomachs. There was no emergency service in town.

My old driver, Ty, was with me again. We carried the kids in our arms and filled up the jeep. We brought them to the hospital. But there was a lot of people who were hurt in the attack. So Ty and I worked on them in the hallway as best we could.

In late 1974, just before the Khmer Rouge launched their conquering "New Year Offensive," I had a series of mysterious incidents.

One night, my houseboy woke me up and said, "Captain, Khmer Rouge at gate." He was scared to death. His whole family was. So I went outside and met a man in the shadows. He said in French, "I have a group that would like to surrender." I said, "Let me put this through the embassy."

General Palmer told me, "Go out and see what this is about. We can't turn this down." So I went out, accompanied by old Hang Ty, who went everywhere with me. We had a handful of Khmer Republic soldiers as escorts. We drove south toward Kompong Spoe, about an hour, into an area controlled by the Khmer Rouge. We stopped at a preplanned landmark. The Khmer Rouge commander was waiting. He said, "We're going to send in a platoon first. Based on what happens to them is going to determine what happens with the rest of my company and force."

I agreed to his plan. The contact man said, "Fine. Let's go into my camp and we'll discuss the terms." This was a bit of a risk on my part. I had my embassy radio telephone. Old Hang Ty proceeded with me. As I was about to walk into the jungle, he turned to me and said, "Captain, I'm going to wait here." I didn't blame him. Our small group of government escort soldiers stayed with him on the highway.

The thought went through my mind, "How can I be sure that this isn't a trap to capture an American advisor?" But my gut instinct was that they were genuine.

When I got to the first outposts of the camp security, I was impressed by their defensive layout. It was the same as North Vietnamese, with concentric circles of defense. When the first soldier stood up, I didn't see his position until some light reflected off his ammunition vest.

We walked deeper into the jungle, past the security rings. We finally got into the center of the camp. It was a network of well-dug bunkers. I met with the commander. I asked, "Are you sure that you want to come with us?" He said, "Yes, if you can guarantee that we will be taken care of. And the government won't throw us in prison or worse. And that we'll be resettled and get some food and clothing."

I said, "Yes. I feel sure that we can guarantee that."

I called on my radio for FANK [Army of Khmer Republic] to meet us at a designated point, and disarm the Khmer Rouge. But I realized, "I can't carry all of these guys in our vehicle."

So, this Khmer Rouge platoon came walking out with me, fully armed with all their grenades and rifles. The Cambodian soldiers with my driver were shocked. We disarmed them. A truck came for them. I radioed back to the embassy to inform them we were coming. The next day I began the process with the Khmer Republic officials. We resettled them near Pochentong Airport, and started debriefing them. They went through the chronology of where they were from, what they had done, who was with what faction. No doubt that they were genuine. I gave all of my reports to the embassy.

We then had to battle with the bureaucracy to sustain these guys and to feed them. I remember the first day I found out that rice wasn't getting to them. So I bought big bags of rice with my own money and took care of them myself. Eventually the Khmer government took it up. But things changed . . .

My Khmer Rouge contact man came to my gate again. He said, "We have some Americans we would like to turn over to you." He explained that he had a certain amount of prisoners from Vietnam that he had gotten from a Vietnamese unit. The prisoners weren't in very good health and he was concerned about them.

He gave me enough specifics that I could pass on to my boss. And I asked for permission to continue to meet with them. My request was approved. They wanted to turn the Americans over. And of course wanted to be paid for it. We agreed upon a price in gold for each American.

I got the visit all lined up. I spoke to the Cambodian General Headquarters to make sure that no one would fire into that area. Because if we didn't get into the camp at a certain time, the prisoners were going to be handed over to another Khmer

Rouge unit that was very hard-core. This was our window of opportunity to get the prisoners out.

In late December 1974, I received embassy approval, and prepared to launch with a Khmer Republic helicopter. The night before our departure, in the middle of the night I received a knock at my gate. My houseboy hurried up to my bedroom. His eyes were as big as saucers. "Khmer Rouge are back. And they are furious."

The Khmer Rouge group wore pretty ragged civilian clothes. They didn't look like city dwellers. They were able to slip into the city despite the numerous Khmer Republican Army roadblocks. They obviously had contacts and a network.

I came down to the gate. My Khmer Rouge contact man looked very upset. He said, "I trusted you. I told you where we were going to meet you. The Khmer Republic air force brought in airplanes. They hit us with many air strikes. We have a lot of casualties.

"The American prisoners weren't hurt. But I don't know if we can deal anymore. I'll get back to you."

The next morning I went to my U.S. Air Force liaison man at MEDTC. We went to the Khmer Republic General Headquarters. We found out that the air strikes were exactly as the Khmer Rouge had said. It was obvious to me that the Cambodian air force used the information I had given about the prisoner extraction.

Was I chasing ghosts or "shadows"? I think that's how it was perceived in the U.S. Embassy. But it was still, "Hey, let this captain do his thing. We could come out winners on it." I don't think any U.S. official directed the Khmer air force to make the raid. I still believe that we had some American prisoners at that site.

After those events, my Khmer Rouge contact disappeared. He made one more contact about the prisoners, saying, "We'll try again. But I don't think it will work. Things are moving fast."

And they were. On New Year's Eve, the Khmer Communist's Final Offensive started. The capital city came under an intense rocket bombardment. The FANK units defending the city were hit hard. Looking across the river from Phnom Penh, you could see heavy fighting.

I was lucky that my boss let me visit units I had trained in Vietnam that were still in the field: the Para Brigade, the 48th Brigade, the 198th Battalion. My friends were still the leaders, but we lost a lot of people. The front line was in all directions from Phnom Penh. We were an enclave surrounded.

I tried to keep up with my normal duties. We started working out an evacuation plan, which became Operation Eagle Pull. We surveyed our LZs, figuring out how we were going to alert the community.

I went out to Svay Rieng on the Vietnam border, a few weeks before the country fell. In Vietnam, Danang and Nha Trang had fallen. It was an eerie sensation. The North Vietnamese main push toward Saigon cut right through Svay Rieng.

I went to the town's outskirts to visit defending units with Colonel Rod Pascal. Rod began checking bunkers and the mortar units, making sure their coordinates were locked in for protective fire. Cambodian units went on patrol trying to interdict the enemy, and promptly got hit real hard. The North Vietnamese commander got on the radio. He told the Cambodians, "Our objective is Saigon. If you continue to interfere we will annihilate you."

There was no American air support to help. Congress had ordered them out of Cambodia. That was the loneliest I ever felt.

I stood there, with everything in perspective . . . Vietnam was falling, our evacuation plan getting closer. There was kind of a lull. I looked up and saw a jet. My heart started beating fast. It was an American F-4 Phantom. For a split second, I thought, "Thank God, somebody has finally authorized U.S. close air support out here."

It wasn't my survivability I was worried about. Americans could go home. It's the local people who suffer the consequences. We'd gotten them somewhat up to their necks in this war.

This jet came over, very high, over the Tonle Sap River. As I looked up my heart raced. All the air in my body was let out at the same time. Because I realized immediately that it was a photo reconnaissance mission. That's all it was. I kept looking and hoping. But there was nothing coming behind it.

The American evacuation from Phnom Penh, Operation Eagle Pull, was on April 5. Until it came, I kept going out to check the youths I had trained in Vietnam.

On April 4, I visited some friends who were dug in across the city. After I got back into the city, they called on my radio and said, "Don't forget to come back tomorrow. We'd like to see you."

I got tears in my eyes. I knew damned well that there wasn't going to be a tomorrow, at least with the Americans. They said, "Come on, bring us that case of beer." I said, "Yeah. What kind do you want?" It hurt an awful lot.

I woke up the next morning. The Eagle Pull plan was in effect. We started the evacuation at first light. Around five A.M. was first call. The helicopters came in. U.S. Marines came off the helicopters and provided security on the LZs. Classified materials were burned in the embassy.

The effort was very well-organized. Not like in Saigon, a few weeks later, where there was chaos. Children from the school across the street were watching. The Khmer Rouge lobbed a few token rockets in.

My boss, General Palmer, said, "Ken, we've got to get the Ambassador out of here. You need to get him."

Ambassador John Gunther Dean was a refugee from Germany before World War II. He was commissioned in the U.S. Army. And in 1945 he helped to liberate his hometown.

I remember going up to Ambassador Dean and saying, "Mr. Ambassador, it's time to go." He didn't want to leave. But he didn't say anything. I took the flag from the embassy. We went up to the helicopter and I [planned to give] it to the Ambassador.

Just before getting the Ambassador onto his helicopter, I went up to the gate, to my driver. I said, "Ty, let's go. Don't worry about authorization." My houseboy had already said no. He didn't want to leave his parents.

Old Hang Ty stood next to my jeep. He had my map in his hands. He had an Uzi [submachine gun] and a box of Chicom grenades. He said, "No, *mon capitaine*." My French was never great. But his was worse. He whipped out my map and pointed to the mountains near Kompong Spoe. He said, "I'm going to stay out here and wait for you and the American Special Forces to come back."

I had tears in my eyes and got choked up. I said, "Ty, we're not coming back. It's over. Can't you see that?"

He said, "No. I know you. We've gone through a lot together. Your [Cambodian] soldiers are out there. You're not going to leave them. I'll wait for you. You'll be back."

I went ahead and loaded up the helicopters. We flew out over the river toward the coast. I get emotional when I remember looking down over the countryside, thinking about what Ty had said. I knew in my heart that it was all over.

A helicopter ship was waiting off the coast for the aircraft with the Cambodia Country team—including Ambassador Dean, General Palmer, myself. Before our helicopter landed, General Palmer said, "I think you'd better give the American flag to the Ambassador." I had it clutched in my hand.

When we landed on the ship, Ambassador Dean stepped off that helicopter and into history. Photographers captured that moment. The cover of *Newsweek* magazine showed him carrying that flag. Which I'll bet he still has to this day.

When I came back to the States, I was on assignment to the Officers Advanced Course. The Army didn't count my Special Forces time as prime-time leadership. They were wrong. Because as a 1st lieutenant I had an A-Team of twelve men. And also in Vietnam I had led a battalion of 512 Cambodians, who I advised, led and trained in combat. It took other American officers quite a long time in their career to get to the point where they took charge of 512 guys.

Deep down in my heart I kept believing that somehow we would help our Cambodians again. That was a remote hope. So I went down to the Advanced Course at Fort Benning, Georgia, for nine months. We learned Army Doctrine. Vietnam was never discussed once.

When I came to the course, I sat down to have a beer at the club with a couple of friends. They said, "Ken, you're not going to believe this. There is no reference to Vietnam in this entire course." We were being prepared to fight in Germany, at the Fulde Gap. We had Combined Arms training. New Doctrine was being developed. It was like Vietnam never happened.

BUFFALO HUNTER

LIEUTENANT COLONEL
ANDREW GEMBARA

SAIGON, VIETNAM 1972–75
ADVISOR
525TH & 500TH MILITARY INTELLIGENCE GROUPS

After being severely wounded during the Tet Offensive, Captain Andy Gembara was hospitalized in the States. After undergoing serious eye operations and months of physical therapy, he asked to return to active duty and was assigned to Europe.

When I learned of a possibility of joining Special Forces, I said, "Where do I sign?" First, I had to go back to jump school [parachute training] at Fort Benning to test my damaged right arm. I sweated that because I didn't have strength in the arm and the first two weeks of jump school requires a lot of pull-ups. I busted my ass. My left arm got incredibly strong because I had to compensate. I was very moved to get the Leadership Award at the end of my class.

In Special Forces, I eventually became an intelligence specialist. When I finished the Advanced Intelligence Course in July 1972, I asked for Vietnam. People thought I was crazy. There were a number of officers in the course who had never been to Vietnam, and had no intention of going.

When I arrived in Saigon in October, most American combat units were already gone. I was assigned to the 525th Military Intelligence Group at Tan Son Nhut Air Base. Everyone was expecting the Paris Peace Talks to result in a cease-fire.

What surprised the hell out of me was how badly our forces had degenerated. You have to understand that between 1965 and 1972 there were at least four or five different American armies in Vietnam. The army of 1965–67, during my first tour, was damned good. A lot of volunteers rather than draftees.

Even those who didn't want to be there saw it as a noble effort. By contrast, what I saw in 1972 was a shock. Mostly draftees, nobody wanted to be the last to die.

The Peace Accords were announced right after Christmas. Four or five of us spoke Vietnamese. We were asked if we would consider staying after the Accords were signed. About that time I was going through a divorce. So I said, "Yeah. If soldiering is what it's about, I'd just as well stay here."

I was happy to be assigned to Detachment K, part of the 500th Military Intelligence Group. I worked in civilian clothes, with the Vietnamese Military Security Service [MSS]. They were dirt poor. The concept of Vietnamization, where the Americans would support the Vietnamese to take over the war, was a crock of shit. For several months I was the only officer in Saigon doing any intel on the ground with the Vietnamese.

There was a bastard unit called Special Collection Detachment [SCD], Navy people who were the most aggressive guys I ever came across. They had detachments up and down the coast, working with Navy and Marines. They had junk boats.

I took them under my wing because they seemed abandoned. MSS could always make money, right or wrong, by extortion and stuff in the profits. They admitted that. But Navy SCD depended on the Navy to give them a budget. And they were at the bottom of the heap. I found supplies for them through the U.S. Defense Attaché's Office or my parent office in Bangkok. As a result, we had the best intelligence. We were able to recruit people who were working with the VC and NVA networks.

In Fall 1974, our mission was to document the violations of the cease-fire. That became almost a joke. Because violations were happening all the time. Another mission was to look for American POW/MIAs [prisoners of war/missing in action] to support a project run by the U.S. Joint Casualty Resolution Center. That quickly fell apart when the Communists shot an American captain just outside of Saigon.

There was a reward program for information on U.S. POW/MIAs. On one occasion, we had a Vietnamese lady come to us off of Canal 9 in the Delta. She had information on some Americans. It was a black and two whites. She had the names of the people. We went through the books and found that there were such guys missing. Significantly, she gave the description of a tattoo on one of the guys that most people didn't have.

We asked the Vietnamese to get her up to Saigon. They did.

We found out by Vietnamese questioning her that she was more than just a little knowledgeable. Her husband was one of the local VC guys. She was involved with this camp where the Americans were held. She brought them food by boat. We polygraphed her and she described the camp and everything.

In late 1974 to get U.S. forces in there to rescue these guys was not possible. We did intelligence reports on it. The Agency controlled something called Buffalo Hunter. Buffalo Hunters were aircraft that took photos and could do infrared. They were based at Nakhon Phanom Airforce Base in Thailand. We had requested Buffalo Hunter because this case was "Possible POWs," a high priority. They flew a mission over this denied area. It was heavily forested along the canal. They saw camp-fires at night just where this lady said they would be.

The sad part of it was we had the guys identified. One or two of them was from a Special Forces camp, who had been missing for some time. I was sure that these guys were real. They were right where she said they would be. This information went to JCRC. But it was too politically sensitive. No action was taken.

It's a ball buster to hear years later about, "No American prisoners were left behind." But we weren't permitted to do anything.

I saw a whole bunch of other reports during the last months in Vietnam. But that was the most vivid. That still haunts me.

SAIGON BURNING

GENERAL ALFRED GRAY

Saigon, Vietnam April 1975
Commander
Regimental Landing Team 4

In early April 1975 we were watching Saigon collapse from Okinawa. Two of us were designated to be Evacuation Security Force Commanders. The primary commander was Colonel Bachelor, and I was his alternate. We flew to Cambodia in February to assess the situation. We made recommendations for the departure of the American embassy staff and Cambodian employees.

That was a learning experience for the larger operation to evacuate Saigon. Our mission prepared to take anything from twenty-six stay-behind intelligence people to over a million people from Vung Tau beach. The U.S. Embassy had a horribly complex plan.

I said, "You've got to keep it simple. We'll fly out of Tan Son Nhut airfield." Everyone was supposed to come there. We divided the evacuation according to city wards. But on the last day, people panicked and went to the embassy. Whether they had all been informed was hard to say.

We flew into Saigon from the aircraft carriers *Hancock* and *Midway*. We touched down at Tan Son Nhut at 1400 on the afternoon of April 29. Unlike the embassy, which was in chaos, the airport evacuation was under control. The commander of our brigade, Colonel Dick Carey, came with me. We flew in on a Huey helicopter almost directly over North Vietnamese antiaircraft artillery batteries.

We began to get indications that things weren't so good at the embassy. A Marine major was ranking man at the embassy. He wasn't capable of being in charge of anything. So we sent a recon platoon to help out. Our communication between the airport and the embassy was not very good. So I wanted Colonel Carey back at the flagship where signal communications was better. He agreed, "We'll coordinate and direct the evacuation from the sea."

I didn't know until the next morning when I got back to ship that the Air Force helicopter took him to the wrong ship. And he used both of our smaller helicopters [that could fit on a rooftop] to carry out his aides. As a result, the airlift at the embassy was stalled.

I worried about how to get my people out of Tan Son Nhut. I had around 500 Marines on the ground.

At around ten o'clock that night we turned on all the radios at the Defense Attaché's compound at the airport. We were getting all these damned calls from Washington, "Hurry up. Hurry up." But nobody ever told us which Vietnamese should go and who shouldn't. I said, "We're not going to play God. We're taking everyone who wants to go. And we'll stay here until we're finished." We took out more than 8,000 people by helicopter that day.

The weather turned lousy—which was a blessing in disguise. North Vietnamese soldiers had overrun the outer perimeter around the airport and were firing at the helicopters. Fortunately, the overcast skies gave us some cover.

Little by little, we got thousands of nervous people organized into orderly lines, while North Vietnamese tanks were closing in. And they were firing artillery at us. They were trying to do some damage. The South Vietnamese Army was still fighting back. And my Marines prepared to take out North Vietnamese tanks if we had to.

I should've gone to the embassy and taken over. I knew the ambassador, I knew his aides. I could've said, "Get off your asses and get moving." But as commander, I belonged where the bulk of the operation was. And most of my people and the real threat was at the airport. In downtown Saigon there was chaos. But nobody was being shot at.

It was a horrible feeling, after spending a total of seven years in Vietnam, to watch it all collapse. I kept saying, "This doesn't have to happen. We could stop this offensive right in its tracks. Our air power can stop the North Vietnamese. There's still hope. This doesn't have to be."

The North Vietnamese had all of their forces exposed in flat open terrain. U.S. air strikes could have crippled them logistically. We could've knocked the hell out of them. In fact, we had a pretty powerful force on ships offshore. Aside from the air superiority, I had three battalion landing teams. My Marines could've blocked off Saigon, and stopped the offensive right there. We could've stopped it two weeks earlier when they were charging in from the highlands.

South Vietnamese forces within forty miles of Saigon fought pretty well at places like Xuan Loc and Long Binh. I think they could've stopped the North Vietnamese with some help. The NVA paused when the South Vietnamese air force used C-130s to drop fuel drums filled with explosives. They thought the B-52s were coming back. They were terror-struck.

The one thing that our policymakers should have known was that the North Vietnamese and Viet Cong could never take any major area in South Vietnam and hold it logistically. How would they be able to handle air strikes and counterattacks? But they had one thing going for them. They knew that the United States had lost the will to continue the war.

It just didn't seem real that South Vietnam was going to fall. After losing 57,000 American servicemen and -women, in the final stages it wasn't a military decision. It was all political.

The last day, as the country was collapsing, I listened to military radio and could still hear the South Vietnamese marines fighting up near Danang. The North Vietnamese had overrun Danang weeks before we started the evacuation. The marines went into the hills and were fighting back. Forty-three of their company commanders died while fighting in the hills. Great bravery.

About six P.M. some of my Marines came to me. They said, "We've got a real problem here. A South Vietnamese guy wants to come over the fence for evacuation." I went to the gate and here is this Vietnamese soldier. The Vietnamese MPs have their weapons pointed at him. He was trying to come inside the compound to be evacuated. He had worked in Intelligence. I went outside and he showed me an accommodation award for his work in the Intelligence section.

He said, "If my family and I don't get out of here, we're dead." The MPs let his family come through. But because the military still had orders to stay and fight, they were going to shoot him. When I stepped outside, they pointed their weapons at me. I stood between the MPs and this guy.

My Marines readied their weapons to take the MPs out. We had this stare down, or talk down, whatever you want to call it. I said, "We are taking out everybody who is authorized to go, everybody who wants to go. This man would be assassinated when the Communists get here. We're taking him with us."

The standoff went on for what seemed like an eternity. Probably two or three minutes. The ranking MP belted out an order, and these guys jumped into their jeep and drove off. And we took the man inside the gate. It was not the fault of the MPs. They had their orders. But I believed this guy was a special case.

We got the last people out of the airport. Around midnight, we destroyed all the files and computers at the U.S. Defense Attaché complex. We blew up General Creighton Abrams's house [Abrams was the last commander of U.S. forces in Vietnam]. Because I didn't want any North Vietnamese generals to live in General Abrams's quarters.

We set delayed action demolitions around the DAO headquarters and boarded our helicopters. We flew out. Heading south, about thirty-five kilometers over the Rung Sat mangrove swamps, and then twenty kilometers out to sea.

I just stood by the rear ramp and watched the flames burning from DAO headquarters that we had blown up. We still had worries about North Vietnamese antiaircraft missiles. So we really couldn't relax until we were over the water.

EXTENDED FAMILY

GENERAL CHARLES HORNER

WASHINGTON, D.C. 1975–76
GRADUATE STUDENT
NATIONAL WAR COLLEGE

After flying 111 combat missions during two tours as a "Top Dog" and "Wild Weasel" in Southeast Asia, Chuck Horner settled into a mid-career pattern as a staff officer at Air Force Headquarters at the Pentagon. During 1975, while Vietnam collapsed, he was attending the prestigious National War College in Washington.

After Saigon fell, I had a Vietnamese family of six live with my family. The head of the family is a wonderful lady named Chan. I knew her brother, an F-5 fighter pilot. As Vietnam was collapsing, Chan's husband's generals walked in and told him, "We're leaving the country. You're in charge of the army. Please surrender it to the Communists." So he stayed in Vietnam and was put into a "reeducation" camp. His sister came to live with me with her children.

Chan had a baby born in the refuge camp in Guam, so she is an American citizen. Her oldest daughter is one year older than my oldest daughter. Two sons that straddled my son's age. And the baby is a year younger than my youngest daughter. Her husband was imprisoned by the Communists. But Ba, the grandmother, escaped. They all lived in my house.

People said, "My God, how can you handle all of that?" It was easy. My wife and Chan are like sisters. They got along great. Chan is always embarrassed to speak English. I told Lingh, the oldest son, "Boy, let me tell you something. You've been screwed by life. Don't you get ideas about getting a car and a girlfriend and all of that. Your job is to get an education and to take care of your mother. Because your father may never come back."

Chan would cook for us. And I love Vietnamese food. I found out what it's like to live in the welfare society through them. They all qualified for Medicaid and for Food Stamps. They were worried because all of their papers and documents were left in Saigon. My wife would go to the commissary with these Food Stamps. One day the cashier looked at her and said, *"Food stamps?!"*

Chan could take a piece of beef as big as my fist and feed all of us. They are part of my family. Chan's youngest, who grew up in our house, can go from English to Vietnamese to English, it's all one language to her.

Chan's husband, Coung, had been a prisoner of war for more than a decade. Then he was sent back to Ho Chi Minh City, where he wasn't even permitted to work for five years. He finally came to the United States in 1990. His oldest boy graduated from the U.S. Naval Academy with a degree in nuclear engineering.

FIXING THE SYSTEM

GENERAL COLIN POWELL

SOUTH KOREA 1973–74
BATTALION COMMANDER
2ND INFANTRY DIVISION

In August 1973, Lt. Colonel Colin Powell arrived in Tongdu-chon, at an isolated outpost near the Demilitarized Zone that divides North and South Korea. An ROTC graduate of the City College of New York, he was a two-tour infantry veteran of Vietnam. In the next decade, Powell would make history as a soldier and statesman. He became the first African-American to serve in the White House as National Security Advisor. And later he was Chairman of the Joint Chiefs of Staff during the Persian Gulf War. In retrospect, he describes his tour as a bat-

talion commander in Korea as, "The best year of my life. Because it was the hardest."

I can't remember much of what happened in Vietnam in 1974–75. I was in Korea then. All of us were trying to get the war behind us. For those soldiers who had to return to Vietnam around 1972, it was very difficult. It is not fair or kind of me to say this, but at that point myself and others who were around me just wanted to get it over with.

The war wasn't going anywhere, we weren't winning. We were just losing guys. I was sorry that we couldn't bring out every Vietnamese friend who we wanted to bring out. But the war had to end. It all had to be left behind. It was not only Vietnam that was being lost. We had started to lose America.

In the Army, leadership studies coming out of the War College were saying that the system was busted. I knew a lot of good people who were saying, "I'm going back to civilian life." A lot of them did.

In Korea, we had terrible problems with discipline and morale. When I arrived, the battalion I was to command had huge drug problems, race riots, kids who couldn't read or write. I said, "This is unacceptable and we're going to fix it." And I was blessed to have a division commander, Major General Hank Emerson, nicknamed "Gunfighter," who is as gritty as the day is long. He understood what was needed. And he empowered us to do it.

It's hard to imagine why outrageous behavior was allowed to persist in the Army during that period. In the institution, we had kind of lost our bearings in what was right and what was wrong. And what was appropriate discipline and what wasn't. We had misused some of the psychological stuff that management theorists were pushing on us. We started to think that we were running some kind of democratic day camp: Generals sitting around coffeehouses talking to troops; troop councils reporting to battalion commanders about what they ought to do. It was a breakdown of the command structure. Like inmates had taken over the asylum.

In the 2nd Division, we reinstilled discipline with the attitude: "Let me explain to you. I'm in charge and you ain't." That's what the troops needed to hear.

General Emerson got rid of all the ineffective "junior officer councils" and "junior enlisted councils" and group gropers and tummy rubs. And we emphasized military discipline. We did it in a way that was based on understanding. We had classes on psychology and group dynamics. We had a lot of race relations training. And schools for the troops, such as English as a second language and basic literacy—lots of kids couldn't read or write. And we worked our soldiers so hard that they didn't have time to get into much trouble.

Another way we dealt with eliminating racial hate groups was by throwing out their leaders. We'd lock them up in jail for a day or two, then send them out on the next plane to the States and have their discharge papers waiting for them at Travis or McCord Air Base. We called it "the ant theory": Get rid of the ringleaders and the rest tend to go in a more acceptable direction.

General Emerson's support was key. Gunfighter just said, "Get rid of them." And he had the support of General Stillwell, the 8th Army commander, and General Hollingsworth, the Corps commander.

By my third day in command, I had put twenty-eight people in pretrial confinement. I cleaned out the bad apples. Guys who had threatened company commanders. One young thug tried to kill a provost marshal with a hair needle. I said, "That's it. You're out of here."

On a troop level, we suffered from some of the "shake and bake" NCOs [graduates of the "instant NCO" course] who hadn't been trained well enough or hadn't the necessary experience to be sergeants. And we had a lot of discontinuity in our NCO ranks: We might've had a lot of staff sergeants, but few buck sergeants or sergeants 1st class. And we were desperately short of officers. It was because of the long war in Vietnam and the draw down [reduction] of forces. A lot of people were getting out or not coming into the Army.

Korea was at the end of the manpower line. I ran my battalion on 33 percent officer strength for most of the year. Each company had, at best, a 1st lieutenant in command and maybe one other lieutenant. Many had been in the Army less than two years. So in effect, the battalion's two field-grade officers— myself and my executive—were helping command the companies. There was no time for our young officers to go to school. They learned on the job. The same with our NCOs. We learned "on the wing" as we went.

General Emerson made sure that his officers knew what they were there for: to lead troops and not worry about themselves. For instance, he refused to let battalion or brigade commanders have elaborate change-of-command ceremonies. He said, "It's a waste of troops' time to stand out in a field listening to goddamn colonels shooting their mouths off about each other."

And he wouldn't allow any of us senior officers to have medals. He said, "No goddamn field officer in this goddamn division is going to get a goddamn medal for doing your goddamn job." We didn't waste one piece of paper for award citations for field-grade officers. I thought that was terrific.

Finally, people said, "Gunfighter, we've got to change commands somehow." He said, "All right, I'll yield. You can have a change-of-command ceremony with the incoming and outgoing battalion commanders, the sergeant major, the color guard, four guidon bearers, and four company commanders. You can put them in regular formation. Only one thing . . . no troops. The troops can be invited to watch if they have nothing better to do. But they will not stand out there in formation." And that's the way we did it. No speeches. We would read the assumption order, pass the flag, and it was over. It took about thirty seconds.

When I left Korea in the fall of 1974, I handed over command of my battalion on a firing range. We cleared the firing line and walked down the back of the hill. Troops that were on the range that day were sitting in little groups. We didn't have the color guard present, we just had the battalion colors. My replacement was there to watch the firing exercise. When the range was clear and the flag came down, I took the colors and gave it to him. I said, "Well done," got in a helicopter and left. That was it. No medals, no ceremony. No waste of troops' time.

This was overdone, of course, and couldn't survive the Army tradition and institution as a whole. But I absolutely loved the selfless approach to command. It worked well in our part of Korea. It may not have worked well at Headquarters in Seoul or anywhere else. But through that technique and others like it, General Emerson made it clear to us: "Remember what the hell you're here for. The only thing you need to care about is taking care of your troops."

SNAKE EATERS

BRIGADIER GENERAL
DAVID BARATTO

FORT BRAGG, NORTH CAROLINA 1976–78
BATTALION COMMANDER
7TH SPECIAL FORCES GROUP

For all practical purposes, there were no Special Forces operations in Vietnam after 1972. And by 1976 it was extremely difficult for Special Forces to be deployed overseas. The leadership of the Army wanted to put all the messy counterguerrilla operations behind and focus on a European scenario.

I was put into the Armor Career Course. In the late 1970s, mechanized infantry was the mainstream. That's what the Army was going to be. So, as a West Point graduate with a good record, the Army purposely wanted to salvage my career.

Quite frankly, I did not want to go back to Special Forces because things were deteriorating. We went from eight Groups to four. It seemed the end was coming.

When I was informed that I was chosen to command a battalion, I was elated. Then I found out I was going to Special Forces. I said, "I just attended the Armor Career Program. And I just got my master's degree. Are you sure you really want me in a Special Forces battalion?"

In 1976, when I came to Fort Bragg to command the 1st Battalion of 7th Group, we were at 66 percent strength. Motivation was at an all-time low. People were lethargic and rebellious. Every day was a confrontation. I didn't have enough funding to provide transportation to the ranges. We had to walk. We didn't have enough money to buy parachutes.

I never really found out what our mission was. I didn't know whether to prepare to go to Korea to fight a war, which was a fairly frequent speculation in the newspapers at that time, whether we were going to the Middle East, or wherever. There was no training program except what I put together.

99

Much of the senior leadership of the Army never appreciated the role of Special Forces. There was no effort by the Army to get quality people into SF. Their attitude was, "If you want to be a snake eater, go to Special Forces and eat snakes. You can run around in the woods and jump out of airplanes. Have a good time. We don't want to be bothered with you."

It was shortsighted for planners to think that any future conflict would be exclusively related to a conventional battlefield in Europe. The Army reflected the civilian population's desire to wash their hands of the Vietnam experience.

As a battalion commander, I knew dedicated Special Forces old-timers who struggled with the deteriorating situation. They really tried. But there was a generation gap with the younger people. And they didn't have the Army's institutional support.

The lack of connection between senior leadership and the troops contributed to their attitude problem. Training didn't make sense to the soldiers because nobody told us what our mission was.

I remember going on a four-mile run with the battalion and almost having a mutiny. Their attitude was, "Hey, what are you trying to do? Make us the 82nd Airborne Division?"

When Special Forces was expanded in the middle to late 1960s, people were allowed in who wouldn't have qualified under original standards. Some of those people stayed in, while we were losing many of the highly motivated veterans. We had people coming in for all the wrong reasons. The "Rambos" who wanted the glory and to do their own thing. As a commander, I had both NCOs and younger officers tell me, "Sir, I can't work for you because you don't appreciate what I'm trying to do."

It wasn't limited to young officers. I relieved three company commanders in my battalion. Primarily for lying. Bold-faced lies. They told me they were doing one thing and they weren't doing anything at all.

During that low point in Special Forces, we were so paranoid about being dismantled and put out into the street that we tried by every means possible to demonstrate our abilities. But without a budget to train with, it became a charade. We might be able to fool visitors passing through, or even some VIPs. But we couldn't fool ourselves. I hardly had enough people willing to go out and endure hardship, and stay in the rain and weather and the elements to continue our mission . . . all the things we talk about in our Creed. We had lost our identity.

THE SWIMMER

CAPTAIN TIMOTHY HOLDEN

NORFOLK, VIRGINIA 1974–75
PLATOON COMMANDER
SEAL TEAM TWO

Descendants of the World War II "frogmen," Navy SEALs are an elite society of 1,600 Sea, Air, and Land commandos. Their task is to carry out secret missions underwater, on beaches or in harbors of enemy territory.

Their six months training is considered by many experts to be the most severe endurance test of any military organization. SEALs must excel in parachuting, scuba diving, underwater demolitions, sabotage, and silent reconnaissance techniques. Only one-third of all trainees who enter the training pass the qualification test.

Timothy Holden, a Naval Academy graduate, is of average height and build but a tenacious competitor. He entered Underwater Demolitions/SEAL training in 1973 after completing a tour off the coast of Vietnam aboard a frigate.

When I graduated from the U.S. Naval Academy in 1972, I chose Special Warfare as my field. But the deal was that I had to go aboard a frigate for a year first. I got aboard the USS *Bronstein* in July and deployed to Vietnam in August. We did gun-line operations and acted as guards for aircraft carriers during the intensified bombing of North Vietnam, which led to the signing of the Paris Accords.

I came back to the States in April 1973, after all U.S. combat forces were withdrawn from Vietnam. I entered SEAL training in June. I chose special operations because I felt that a surgical strike capability could make a difference.

I was a terrible swimmer. I struggled in every swimming test in Underwater Demolitions training. But except for pool drills, all swimming is done with fins—which makes everybody pretty equal. Speed isn't as important as endurance and comfortability in the water.

The SEAL community is very tight-knit because so few people are involved. The West Coast SEAL Team is assigned to PACCOM [Pacific Command] and CENTCOM [Central Command—the Persian Gulf]. The East Coast is LANTCOM [Atlantic Command], SOUTHCOM [Southern Command], and CINCEUR [Commander in Chief, Europe].

The SEAL teams were formed in 1962. Most of the people in my first team, SEAL Team Two, were all Vietnam veterans. They were a very different group than the young people coming in today. They had a "devil may care" attitude—a lot of drinking and partying. But the biggest impression that those combat veterans made on me was whenever we went into the field on training operations. I watched guys who were the biggest cutups. After they put on their "war paint," they were dead serious. No screwing around.

Guys with multiple combat tours used drinking and partying as a way of releasing tension. But now our profession has become more of a science in the way we train, prepare, and conduct our life-style.

The middle 1970s was a very strange time for us. A lot of cutbacks in military spending. Our ability to maintain the organization was pretty limited. I remember my first deployment: guys going out to buy their own backpacks and camping gear. The Command didn't have the money.

We deployed pretty much at no cost, living overseas out of our own pockets. But we couldn't do much about it. We were on our own in terms of defining missions. No one was asking us to perform particular missions or inviting us to exercises.

In the 1980s we began to define our missions better, getting written into naval exercises. That gave us the opportunity to show fleet commanders what we could do in carrier operations with strategic reconnaissance. We swim up the coastline to see what is there and mark land targets. Mine-clearing operations came later.

THE FALL OF IRAN

LIEUTENANT COLONEL ANDREW GEMBARA

IRAN 1975–79
U.S. SPECIAL FORCES

Following the defeat of South Vietnam, America's image as a moral and political leader was in seeming free-fall. In early 1979, the autocratic Shah of Iran, America's major military ally in the oil-rich Middle East, was overthrown by fundamentalist Shiite Muslim revolutionaries, led by the Ayatollah Khomeini. Turmoil in Iran set the stage for Iraq to emerge as a boisterous military power. And an era of increased terrorism and instability began in the Persian Gulf region.

After the evacuation from Saigon, I spent several months in Thailand. In early November 1975, I was posted to Iran. I was still a captain in special operations.

I spent more than two years in Iran on a "single thin" operation. It was "black" or undercover. I worked with Iranian Intelligence and their Special Forces Command in Tehran. I primarily helped them monitor their Eastern European [Soviet Union] neighbors and their Middle Eastern neighbors, the Iraqis.

There was a big threat of Soviet penetration following the U.S. debacle in Vietnam. I was involved in joint intelligence projects. Washington wanted our emphasis to be on intelligence. But I spent more productive time with the Iranian Special Forces, where I started to get a different picture of Iran's internal situation. And started reporting it back to Washington.

Other U.S. government agencies didn't want to hear anything negative regarding growing fundamentalist Muslim opposition. They didn't want any reporting about the growing instability. And there was a Catch-22:

There was supposedly an agreement between the Shah of Iran and the United States. The U.S. was not to conduct any intelligence operations in Iran. All of the operations that I was assigned were "passive" or overt intelligence. I wasn't being secretive. In dealing with my Iranian counterparts, when information came up, I would write in what we call "I.R.", or Intelligence Report.

People would call my reports "unique," "one of a kind." I don't know that anyone else was reporting these things. Still, I'd be getting my hand slapped for doing *internal* reporting. Why weren't people in other offices of the U.S. Embassy in Tehran not reporting this? Why didn't they have access to Iranian sources to know what was going on? Their interfaces with SAVAK [Iranian Intelligence] was very formal. They didn't go out into the field and move around.

I didn't wear an Army uniform. I had long hair and civilian clothes. We had an active terrorist threat. Uniformed military guys were killed in early 1975. We had several other military people targeted, including one of the people I later worked with in a little office in the embassy. I was very serious about paying attention to the terrorist threat. I changed cars periodically. I changed travel patterns. I changed dress.

The terrorist groups at that time were all local people. There were at least three groups: The Peoples' Strugglers, the Mujahideen, and a third group. Most of the members were young idealistic people, many of whom had been educated by the Shah's government and sent to schools in England and the United States during the anti–Vietnam War period. Almost any Iranian student who could make good grades and pass the tests could go overseas to get an excellent education. This was paid for, along with living stipends and other allowances, by the Shah. It was in countries outside of Iran that they were able to organize and receive political and insurgent training.

To some extent they were swept up in the radical chic trend on Western campuses that championed the Ho Chi Minhs and Che Guevaras. But there was an honest dislike of the Shah and/or the power structure that was under him. In some cases, it was people acting in the name of the Shah.

The Ayatollah Khomeini was always lurking. There were mullahs who opposed the Royal Family back in the 1950s when the Shah's father was in power. The mullahs had power usurped from them. They were determined to regain it. And they gave the people an alternative to believe in.

The Shah was not only a king, but he treated himself as a living god. This was intended to replace the influence of the religious leaders. Tehran had a lot of Western trappings and style. We in Special Forces felt that there was a greater ferment than the embassy was willing to admit. But even we had no idea how powerful the religious fervor was.

Coming from Vietnam into this situation was very frustrating. The U.S. had helped to lose that war by injecting large numbers of troops in 1965 without really thinking through how to strengthen the South Vietnamese government. In Iran, I also found a large amount of Americans. The difference from Vietnam was the Iranians were paying for it—top dollar.

The U.S. military didn't station combat units in Iran. Most Americans going there were civilian contract personnel with families. They had their own enclaves. They didn't venture out. They didn't understand the culture. All the same types of things you would think that we would've learned from Vietnam, we didn't.

I had friends with Bell Helicopter, which was very big in Iran. Often they scoured the United States for the cheapest labor they could find to bring over. In Isfahan, one of Iran's major cities, Bell employees ran their motorcycles through mosques. The "Ugly American" image was loud and clear. That spread more resentment.

The American role was half-assed with no long-term planning. We were very intent on getting as much petrol dollars as we could. Whatever the Iranian leadership wanted in terms of munitions and the latest weapons, they got. They were getting AWACs aircraft, the most sophisticated signal intelligence equipment, harpoon missiles . . . stuff that in many cases they had no idea about and no capacity to use. But we were selling it because they were paying.

This clash of technology and culture added to a deep schism caused by the large American presence. The Americans had to have their own life-style, had to have their cars, and refused to accept what was going on around them. That just added to the fire. Some of my Iranian friends commented on this, but in a very discreet way, because in some respects they are very similar to the Vietnamese. They express themselves in a very indirect manner, for fear of insulting you. They won't tell you, "You're a shithead," to your face. Instead, they will say, "Things around you smell."

Another irony, in Vietnam there had been the International Commission of Control and Supervision [ICCS] to supervise the 1973 Cease-Fire Agreement. A couple of those members were Iranian Intelligence/special operations people. I had a chance to work with them again in Iran.

I'll never forget talking with one of those guys, named Karush Tahlui, who was Chief of Staff of the Iranian J2 (Army Intelligence). He was also of the B'hai religious group that was greatly disliked by the mullahs.

Karush asked me if something like the fall of Saigon could happen in Iran. This was in late '75 or early '76. In my very naive way, I said, "Don't worry, that couldn't happen. Everyone here is happy. You have great wealth and the Shah is doing things." Little did I know that a couple years later Tahlui was one of the people who stayed behind. He was arrested and never seen again.

I did try to get his wife and kids out. But it was too late. The Iranian revolution in some ways was an offshoot of the Vietnam debacle. Jimmy Carter became President in 1977. He—with very good intentions—was very concerned about human rights. But the weakening of the Shah was probably speeded up by the demands of the Carter Administration, which were played up very widely in Iranian underground papers and illegal broadcasts.

When the revolution started in late 1978, I had been back in the U.S. about a year at Fort Bragg in the 5th Special Forces Group. I was asked to come back to Iran as part of a Special Forces team to retrieve some of the sensitive weapons that had been sold to the Iranians. We tried to get some hand receipts. This was Walt Disney–type thinking. The country was rocking.

I arrived in-country in January 1979, a week after the Shah left. Masses in the streets were crying for the return of the Ayatollah Khomeini, who was in France. Growing bands of armed people were roving the streets and crying out, "The Shah has left. Victory is here."

TIME DRAGS

COMMANDER DONALD MCSWAIN

PENSACOLA, FLORIDA 1975–76
NAVAL FLIGHT TRAINEE

The hallmark of the post-Vietnam reduction in American military power was a drastic reduction of America's naval forces. Once the predominant power on the world's oceans, by 1980 the Navy consisted of under 480 ships, many of them obsolete or in disrepair due to a lack of spare maintenance parts. The stress on undermanned U.S. Naval forces was intensified by a growing Soviet "blue water" surface and submarine fleet that aggressively made its presence felt on every strategic waterway. As a result of extended deployments at sea, low salaries, and a lackluster public image, many talented sailors and aviators chose to find civilian jobs.

I came into the Navy on May 18, 1975, two weeks after Vietnam fell. I had a Naval ROTC commission. I started college at the University of New Mexico with the intention to be a cartoonist. But in 1972, my draft number was 6. The Air Force had a two-year ROTC program that started in junior year. I needed something more immediate than that. So I signed up with Navy ROTC for the scholarship and to continue college. I changed my degree to both Geology and Geography.

My initial plan was to go into the NROTC, then when it came time to decide if you really were going to commit yourself to the Navy, I was going to step over and join the Air Force program. But at the time, the Air Force guys were given a sixty-day commission and then a "Thank You" discharge letter. They were put on the street because of the downsizing going on after Vietnam. I wanted to fly. So I stayed with the Navy.

In 1975 the training had changed. Along with the downsizing of squadrons, the oil crisis was beginning to take effect.

The OPEC nations banded together to drive up the cost of fuel. So I waited from May until October to get into Flight Training. The Navy began to train new pilots because of an exodus of experienced people to commercial airlines.

At the time, the flight simulator equipment was very crude. They were basically 1950s technology. At times we had to bail out of simulators because of electrical fires. New equipment wasn't delivered until 1978–79, with the arrival of upgraded A-6 and A-7 airplanes.

During the early part of my career, I had five cruises. Every one into the Indian Ocean. They were supposed to be six months long. When you get within forty-five days of that, you say, "It's just about over." Then they would give you an extension of a month or two.

The fuel crunch made it less fun to be there. If you're flying regularly or keeping active on a ship, you have something to look forward to. If you're not flying, time drags.

I had a number of friends who left the Navy during that period. Of the seventeen guys I received wings with, twelve stayed through their first tour. Since then, six have died in crashes. Today, just two of us are left in the Navy.

COUNTERMEASURES

CAPTAIN OLEG JANKOVIC

Whidbey Island Naval Air Station 1974–84
Electronic Warfare Aviator

Oleg Jankovic was born in a European refugee camp at the end of World War II. His parents were among the waves of thousands who had fled both Stalin and Hitler. After his father and stepfather perished in the postwar netherworld, Jankovic came to western Massachusetts at seven years old, speaking only Russian.

With dreams of becoming an aerospace engineer, he earned a naval ROTC scholarship to the University of Southern California. But the Vietnam War was raging. And in the memory of his stepfather, a decorated Soviet aviator who later fought in the partisan forces of British field marshal Alexander, Oleg volunteered to become a naval aviator and flew dangerous night reconnaissance missions in Southeast Asia.

After the Vietnam War, I spent ten years flying aboard aircraft carriers out of Whidbey Island Naval Air Station in Washington State. I flew in EA-6B electronic warfare fighters. During those ten years I spent a lot of time away from my family. We had cruises to the Mediterranean, the Pacific, and the Indian Ocean. Even when I was at a U.S. base, my work kept me away from home much of the time.

I was off the coast of Iran, in the Persian Gulf, south of the Straits of Hormuz, in January 1981 when the U.S. Embassy hostages were released. That was probably the toughest duty I've ever done. The cruise lasted 210 days, two hundred at sea. It felt like being dropped over a precipice at the end of the earth. From the time we mailed a letter, it took a month to get a reply from the States. By the time I received a response from my family, I forgot what I had originally written.

Back home, the nation was still in a negative post-Vietnam funk. Yet there we were, sitting in the Persian Gulf, very isolated. We knew if something happened to those American hostages, we were the ones who were going to have to respond. I was ready to fight, but certainly had no desire to lose my life. I was flying electronic countermeasures aircraft. In an air strike we usually go in first to negate enemy radar and antiaircraft missiles. With the Soviet Union on Iran's border, we couldn't rule out a conflict expanding to something more hideous.

After Iran released the hostages, we were going through the Suez Canal when the Israelis invaded Lebanon. We were ordered to remain there for thirty days before continuing home.

I remember the first day I got back home to Seattle following that cruise. I picked up a newspaper. The headline was an anti-Navy quote by a local religious leader. I had to put the paper down for a minute or two. I had just undergone a strenuous experience and witnessed the sacrifices of all those who were in the Gulf with me. That headline was extremely insulting.

My ten years at Whidbey Island were very difficult for my family. There was never a break. Following the Iran cruise, we were sent to the Mediterranean for nearly as long.

The separations put a lot of tension on my marriage. Susan and the kids stayed on the West Coast, away from her extended family, while I was gone. Oak Harbor on Whidbey Island is a very beautiful place to bring up a family. The problem was that I was never there. I can't blame the Navy for my marriage falling apart. But it didn't help my relationship with Susan any.

RODNEY DANGERFIELD

BRIGADIER GENERAL JOSEPH "KEITH" KELLOGG

UNIVERSITY OF KANSAS 1977–78
GRADUATE STUDENT

After Vietnam, until around 1980, the feeling was that we were trying to come out of a slump. But we didn't have the resources. Pay-wise, the military was hurting, which prevented us from retaining more quality people. Our equipment was old. The American public attitude was, "You guys have just lost a war. Why don't you go sit in a corner? You'll screw things up if we get you involved." So self-confidence wasn't there. It was being developed by a lot of us inside the system who were mad. We vowed, "We are going to work very hard to make this army good." But there were many long nights.

I went to the University of Kansas for my master's degree. At that campus I didn't feel any hostility toward me or my uniform. It was more like Rodney Dangerfield: there wasn't a lot of respect for the military as an institution. There were continual news stories about $650 hammers, crummy toilet seats, and cost overruns. And there were all the movies about crazed veterans.

While all this was going on we were training our tails off. We attracted a lot of good young people who worked very hard.

The turning started happening in late 1979, early 1980. The Iran hostage crisis helped to galvanize the American public's respect for our national security. And they realized our national vulnerability. In the Army, both soldiers and officers began to hold their heads higher. And we insulated ourselves.

We developed a value system. We said, "We don't care what society is doing. We aren't going to accept a drug problem, we will have urinalysis testing. And if people fail it, they're out. We know what type of people we need in here."

And we developed an unstated belief or credo, "It ain't going to happen again on my watch."

DESERT ONE

LIEUTENANT COLONEL ANDREW GEMBARA

FORT BRAGG, NORTH CAROLINA 1978–82
COMMANDER, INTELLIGENCE DETACHMENT
5TH SPECIAL FORCES GROUP

In November 1979, radical Iranian militants, with the blessing of Ayatollah Khomeini, overran the American embassy in Tehran, Iran, and took the embassy staff hostage. For more than one year the "Iranian Hostage Crisis" obsessed the American public and policymakers. Together with concern for the lives of the hostages, the humiliation and the threat of war jolted the nation out of a post-Vietnam funk.

In April 1980, a presidential-ordered secret military rescue operation was launched to free the hostages. It was a combined effort of Army, Marine Corps, and Air Force special operatives. "Desert One" was a landing strip in the Iranian desert that was to be used as the initial rendezvous point for Air Force and Marine aircraft.

The effort became an unmitigated disaster. "Operation Blue Light" never moved beyond Desert One. Equipment failure, stormy weather, lack of coordination between the joint forces, and faulty planning led to nine dead team members and international scorn. This was the low point of the post-Vietnam period. But "Desert One" also became a rallying cry to revamp the American military, especially its special operations capability.

Coming out of Vietnam, there was a desire by some people to revitalize Special Forces and special operations. There was an almost immediate response by conventional officers to say, "These are the same guys who in Vietnam were running around on their own. They were out of our control. They looked different than us. They didn't take orders from us."

During the heyday of Vietnam there were some six Special Forces Groups. But between 1980–82 the Special Forces was almost phased out of the Army. We were down to the 10th Group in Europe, 5th Group at Fort Bragg, and the 7th Group in Panama, which was reduced to two battalions.

Special operations had our biggest disaster in 1980 under Jimmy Carter, with the ill-fated Desert One rescue operation in Iran. That took almost eight to nine months to plan and put together. By the time it happened it was screwed up because too many people were involved. From the chain of command to the lengthy rehearsals, people were nervous.

A senior Iranian who consulted Colonel Charlie Beckwith, Commander of Delta Force [secret counterterrorist organization] for the raid, told the Carter Administration not to do it. They went ahead anyway. The guy's name was Sadi Rakni, a senior Iranian Special Forces colonel. He told them that the runway that they were looking to put in a C-130 airplane was highly used by smugglers.

As a result, a contributing factor to the mission's failure was a tanker truck that was smuggling oil was fired on by the rescue team and set on fire. Then a busload of people came by the runway that night.

I knew what was going on because I had come up to Washington and consulted with the Delta people. I volunteered my services because I had served in Iran. But they feared my presence on the mission would be a tip-off.

Among other things, a serious problem in Desert One was the lack of qualified special operations helicopter crews. Probably the best qualified at the time were the Air Force Special Operations Wing. But at the time, they were just starting to get their CH-54 helicopters. So a lousy decision was made to use Marine pilots who weren't trained in night operations.

SADNESS AND HOPE

BRIGADIER GENERAL
JAMES HILL

Fort Hood, Texas 1974–75
Company Commander
1st Cavalry Division

An important element of rebuilding the Army was the integration of the study of ethics and philosophy of leadership in Officer Training Courses. Many Vietnam combat veterans like James Hill developed a keen sense of personal introspection that made them more forthcoming with their soldiers. And more honest within themselves.

I've formed a philosophy, looking back to the time I came into the Army and looking into the future. I served with a pretty good draftee army in Vietnam in 1968. In my platoon in the 101st Airborne Division I had both a Ph.D. graduate and a kid who had never been to high school. A tremendous gap between those people. But as a leader, you could say, "You will." And for the most part, they obeyed. However, from the early 1970s until the last vestiges of the Carter era, I refer to that period as the "awful army."

An inspiration for me is a speech that the author Herman Wouk [*War and Remembrance*] gave at the Naval War College in 1980 called "Sadness and Hope." A magnificent speech that talks about selflessness. I've read it a hundred times. In recent years, when I became a battalion and then a brigade commander, during my first three days, I read this speech to my officers. I told them, "I want you to understand that this is how I perceive my life's calling." I emphasize, "In good times and bad times, selfless service is the cornerstone of our profession."

Being a college graduate, I didn't have to stay in the Army

113

after Vietnam. As a member of the 101st Airborne Division in Vietnam, I saw enough action that there was no doubt in my mind that I could do the job. There was nothing I needed to prove to myself. And the pay was lousy. In 1974 or '75 I signed the resignation papers. I'd had enough.

By coincidence, I had a conversation with Mrs. Schumaker, the wife of the division commander of the 1st Cavalry, where I was assigned then. She asked me what I was planning to do. I said, "I'm getting out of the Army." She said, "That is the worst mistake you'll make. You'll miss the challenge."

I looked around at all the young officers who were bailing out. Then I looked at the soldiers and the Army as an institution. I said to myself, "If I bail out, I'm leaving the soldiers to the assholes." I just couldn't do that. Even though I continually felt that I was beating my head against the wall.

PART III

Rebuilding

DRUG TESTS

REAR ADMIRAL DAVID BILL

USS *Coontz* 1979–81
Executive Officer

Following his tour with the riverine boats in Vietnam, David Bill spent four years in elite Navy schools. After completing Navy Postgraduate School, he attended Destroyer School and Nuclear Power Training. Surrounded by highly motivated young officers there, he was in for a rude awakening when he was reassigned.

In October 1973, I went to a two-year assignment on the frigate the *Talbot*, out of Norfolk. That clued me in to what was going on within the Navy. Social upheaval was transcending the boundary between the military and civilian world.

It was the first time I had been around any kind of drug abuse. In Vietnam, I didn't know what the word marijuana meant, because my riverboats were isolated out in the boondocks, away from large bases or cities or other places where drugs were available.

When I got back to the States I read a lot about the "drug culture" becoming a significant factor in society. So I was not completely naive about it. But I was appalled that the captain of the ship wasn't doing anything. I came forward to him and said, "Look, sir, we've got drug problems right here. We've got to do something about it."

For many of the older naval officers it was something new that they didn't know how to deal with. In this particular case, the captain was a brilliant man, who was more cut out to be an ambassador somewhere than the commander of a ship. He spoke two or three foreign languages. He went to Harvard for three years before he went to the Naval Academy. But he was not equipped to deal with the drug problem of our sailors.

I then spent three years ashore on various staff and education duties. I assumed my next ship assignment in mid-1979, as the executive officer of the destroyer *Coontz*. I arrived and found a list in my drawer. It had the names of at least a third of the crew who had used drugs or were using drugs with some regularity. One of my primary missions was to knock that off.

The Navy's urinalysis program was just getting started—surrounded with controversy. We applied the program in a clever sort of way. If you have everybody come test on the first Monday of every month, guess what? Nobody would use drugs for the week before that.

So we gave random tests, and often. We also cultivated shipmates who could finger ringleaders in selling drugs. These steps were instrumental in straightening out the problem. The institutional support was essential.

We kept the crew busy with an emphasis on training and readiness. With less ships in the Navy, the existing ships had to put in a lot more time on deployment. That caused a lot of turmoil for married officers and crew members.

And we didn't have a sufficient budget at the time, which caused some of the material conditions of the ship to decay. The high tempo of our training, fewer spare parts, and fewer numbers of bodies all took its toll. Some ships had worse problems than others. That all depended on the leadership.

GUARDIANS

COLONEL MICHAEL ANDREWS

WEST POINT, NEW YORK 1984–87
TACTICAL OFFICER
U.S. MILITARY ACADEMY

When I was on the staff at West Point in the mid-1980s, I talked to a friend who had graduated with me from the Academy almost twenty years earlier. He was a Signal Corps officer who was also on the teaching staff. During a backyard conversation he said in a very sheepish way, "I've never been in combat. I've never had a shot fired at me. I've always wondered how I would react. I feel inadequate as a leader not to have the experience. Not knowing how I would behave or how I would respond."

I was trying to make him feel better. So I said, "You're a hell of a smart guy, a technically competent officer. A student of the profession doesn't always have to experience something to know how to do it. You can become proficient by training hard. Generals Eisenhower and Bradley missed serving in World War One. But they were students of the profession between the wars. And in World War Two they provided valuable leadership."

The older I get, the more convinced I am that a great deal of time and effort must be spent with young cadets and lieutenants, reaffirming fundamental values. The most important role of a senior leader is to instill a sense of mission, purpose, and vision.

Our country demands uncompromising standards from its military leaders. And that's the way it should be. We give our military leaders our most precious commodity—our young people. We give them access to weapons with incredible destructive capability. They have to be unimpeachably ethical.

One of my favorite quotes is Plato in the *Republic* when he said that, "Nothing is more important than that the guardian's work be performed well." When I talk to my young officers, I call them the "Guardians of our country." They must know their business technically and tactically.

A long time ago, I came to the conclusion about my greatest hope for when my son, who is now an ROTC cadet in college, enters the Army. I would like him to be an honorable man, an ethical leader. In my order of priorities, even "technical and tactical proficiency" rate below that. The life and death decisions that a military officer may have to make require an ethically honest man.

HUMAN RELATIONS

SERGEANT MAJOR
JOSEPH CELESTINE

Danang, Vietnam 1969–70
Platoon Sergeant
3rd Battalion, 7th Marine Regiment

During the late 1960s, the racial breakdown was not only happening in the civilian community, but also in the military community. I call those days, "the bad times." Military personnel were joining various hate groups. Both white and black were separating from each other. In some places, they were holding hate meetings.

I was in a lot of combat during my three tours of Vietnam. I did not see racial problems in the field. But I saw that when we got back to the rear bases.

Being a leader is always a challenge. But during that era, we had major problems every day. We had guys in the rear bases who didn't want to work. The bad guys acted up in the rear areas where an illegal market was active and booze and dope was accessible. One way field units solved our problems was by leaving the bad guys in the rear.

During my third tour, I was a staff sergeant. We were having a lot of racial problems. In one particular company, a lot of blacks refused to go out to the field because they felt that they weren't being treated properly. At that time, the battalion commander chose me to be one of the black staff NCOs on a panel to deal with racial issues.

We held hearings for people who had grievances, to act as a sounding board. And we investigated certain allegations. We had a lot of group discussions to work out our differences. Personally my door was open at any hour to anyone who had a problem. Throughout the battalion, everyone knew who was on the panel and who they could trust.

There were few black officers at the time. But during the

course of the war, the number of black NCOs jumped sky high. Ironically, I went into the Marine Corps to get away from racial problems back home.

A lot of our problems were with people who had not volunteered to be Marines. Because of the casualties we were taking in the war, the Corps had to use the draft. Qualifying standards were lowered for draftees like those from the "McNamara's 100,000" group who would not ordinarily have qualified for any branch of service. Some of the people promoted to NCO also came from among the draftees. And those who caused much of the problem came from the McNamara's group. They just didn't want to be there—and shouldn't have been.

Back in the States there were a lot of race-related problems on Marine bases. The Marine Corps went full swing to deal with that by creating a Human Relations Institute in San Diego. They trained Marine instructors to set up human relations programs to deal with the tensions and racial problems throughout the Corps.

During the "bad times," the breakdown in discipline wasn't so much because of bad NCOs. The Marine Corps was looking for a new type of NCO who was more managerial—"task oriented." Who could herd people from one place to another, rather than be a teacher who emphasized a lot of discipline. For older NCOs who were dedicated to our jobs, that drove us crazy. Because we felt that we were not permitted to excel and do the things that we should be doing.

There wasn't the standardized NCO schooling system that we have today. Schools were available. But we couldn't afford to send promising young guys who should've gone. We needed them to help take care of problems in the units. So we sent the mediocre guys, who we felt that we couldn't rely on. In the long run, this hurt the promising NCOs who were denied the schooling.

And this hurt the Corps, because the mediocre guys had all the right schools in their records. That gave them a bureaucratic advantage over the hardworking NCOs when it came time for promotion. So the Corps lost a lot of good guys who didn't get the respect they deserved.

After Vietnam, the NCO education system was developed. Each Marine Corps base started their own NCO schools. Young Marines who had become NCOs in the Vietnam combat environment were able to develop professional skills. They were also sent to Troop Leader courses, and rounded off with an awareness of race relations. The human relations package was taught separately. That wasn't necessarily in the curriculum of the NCO schools. Rather, there was an emphasis on leadership traits with a "color blind" approach. If you really follow leadership principles, and are fair to all of your Marines, that should prevent racial problems.

On the West Coast, we had Marines from places like North Dakota, Idaho, and Utah who had never associated with blacks before. On the East Coast, at Camp Lejeune there had been racial confrontations that reflected attitudes in that part of the country. The West Coast civilian community was much more relaxed about those kinds of social issues.

The best approach the Marine Corps took to heal our racial problems was the "color blind" attitude in leadership training. We avoid emphasizing the differences between people. Instead, we teach that all Marines are part of a brotherhood.

MANEUVER TACTICS

GENERAL ALFRED GRAY

NATO NORFOLK, VIRGINIA 1976–78
COMMANDER
4TH MARINE AMPHIBIOUS BRIGADE

"Doctrine" is a military philosophy. After Vietnam, the American military moved away from planning for "counterinsurgency" against guerilla forces. The new emphasis was on the expansive conventional battlefields of Europe or the Middle East. It was believed that a reduced and outnumbered American military force would have to fight against Soviet-doctrine mechanized forces.

The Army and Air Force were developing a new battle plan to orchestrate ground force mobility while striking behind enemy lines with air power. It was called the "Air/Land Battle." And a small group of Marines were planning to "fight smart" by using a "Maneuver" doctrine.

I came back to the States in the fall of 1975, after completing follow-up reports on the evacuation of Phnom Penh and Saigon. It was a no-no to talk about Vietnam in the Army and Air Force. The Marine Corps adopted some of that attitude, too. There was a maxim, "Don't prepare for the last war. Prepare for the next one."

I was selected for brigadier general and was commander of both the Landing Force Training Command Atlantic and the 4th Marine Amphibious Brigade. The year before I took charge, the Marine Corps put an expeditionary unit in NATO. But they lacked mobility and took some criticism. My orders were, "Get that straightened out."

I began organizing, training, and equipping my forces for operating on the flanks of NATO against superior numbers of Soviet equipment and manpower. Our tactics included operating in fjords, creating a ski capability, and using sensors and infrared scopes for night fighting. I began experimenting with what eventually became known as "Maneuver" battle tactics.

The maneuver idea is not new. For example, when the 1st Marines were attacked at Yang Dang Po during the Korean War, the mission was to break out of there and get to the outskirts of Seoul. General Chesty Puller was the regional commander. Under him, a young captain found a point of no resistance and moved right through to Seoul. It happened to be Bob Barrow, who later became Commandant of the Marine Corps. He was practicing Maneuver Warfare whether he knew it or not.

I started using Maneuver tactics in Vietnam without naming it. In 1964 when I went up to the mountains around Khe Sanh, I took a small group of helicopters. We pretended to land on a mountaintop, then flew out at dusk and landed on our objective mountaintop.

The Maneuver process began to crystalize when I was with the 4th Amphibious Brigade. We began using those techniques in NATO exercises. For example, in one exercise we were encircled by the West German 7th Division. We had three mechanized task forces and a helicopter raid force. I sent multiple recon teams to probe German defense lines to find a weak spot. When that was discovered, the brigade charged through to successfully end the exercise.

I was then assigned to the Development Center at Quantico in 1978. We were assigned responsibility for Marine Corps organization, doctrine, tactics, techniques and hardware development. We were able to solidify more of our thoughts and start writing some papers on Maneuver.

It was greatly affected by the growth of Soviet forces to the point where we would be greatly outnumbered in a European conflict. But in Marine heritage we have always been outnumbered at the beginning of amphibious assaults.

Maneuver ideas are just as much, if not more applicable, in low intensity conflicts as they are in a tank battle. It involves the element of surprise of "being where they aren't," and "looking through the eyes of your opponent."

We did get some criticism, which has to be expected when you're trying to do something new. But there's nothing new about "leading from the front," or "trying to go where they aren't" and attacking the lines of enemy communications. Hell, that's in any version of the ancient Chinese general Sun Tzu. I started reading Sun Tzu when I was an NCO in the 1950s. I've reread him many times.

If a young NCO or lieutenant understands the commander's battlefield intent, they'll respond accordingly when they come up against uncertainty or an unexpected advantage. It's the young squad or platoon leaders that discover shifts on the battlefield first. They've got to be able to exploit a sudden opportunity.

REVOLUTION

COLONEL MICHAEL WYLY

QUANTICO, VIRGINIA 1979–81
HEAD, TACTICS DIVISION
MARINE AMPHIBIOUS WARFARE SCHOOL

Mike Wyly seems more like a soft-spoken college professor than a highly decorated fighting Marine. But as a tactics instructor at the Marine Corps Training Center at Quantico, he profoundly influenced the generation of young officers who fought in Operation Desert Storm, through his revolutionary Maneuver Doctrine theories.

In Vietnam I became aware of two Marine Corps. One stretched from Washington, all the way across the Pacific, to a palatial Command Post in Danang. The second Corps was somewhere out in the rice paddies. The two Corps got further and further apart.

For example, my rifle company hated to come in from the field because some rear area officer was going to report them for having muddy boots. I know of Silver Stars for valor that were given to people who were in a bunker on a telephone while rifle companies were out fighting. That caused tremendous resentment.

As the war drew down, fighting Marines left the ranks because they couldn't coexist with the bureaucratic Corps. They didn't fit in a peacetime situation. What was left was the non-fighters and a new breed that could bridge the gap between the two Corps—fighters who could coexist, even though they knew better.

When I got back to the States in 1971, after my second Vietnam tour as a rifle company commander, my way of thinking had changed. In 1974 I was an instructor at the Officers Basic School. That's when it really hit me. What my higher-ups were telling me to teach was not relevant to the real combat I had experienced. They forbade us to tell stories about Vietnam.

The other thing that bothered me was how regimented the teaching was: "This is what we want you to say, Major." A monkey could've taught the lesson plan. It was geared for the latter part of the Korean War, with static trench warfare. That was the origin of the ill-conceived tactics we took with us to Vietnam.

One of the first things I had realized under sustained combat was, "This isn't what they prepared us for. There aren't any static defense lines in Vietnam. There are no set battles."

At Basic School I got increasingly angry. The history teacher said, "Wyly, the best thing you can do for yourself is study history." And he helped me to enroll at a graduate school program at George Washington University.

The more I studied, my eyes opened. I realized, "Maybe a better way to prepare for war would be to read about battles throughout history." And I studied Russian. Because everybody was talking about fighting the Russians back then.

After I finished the graduate program, I went back to Quantico. In 1978, General Mick Trainor was my boss. I discovered that we had a similar concern about the Middle East wars of 1967 and 1973: whether U.S. forces could cope with the high tempo maneuver tactics that the Israelis were using. There was a real question as to how prepared we were for a modern battlefield.

The 1979 Soviet invasion of Afghanistan impressed us that we might be doing battle with them—possibly in the Persian Gulf region. Because of the Soviets' huge advantage in conventional forces, we needed to learn how to fight outnumbered and win.

That year, I composed an article for the *Marine Corps Gazette* magazine that challenged our tactics of attrition. At the same time I noticed that a congressional staffer, Bill Lind, was doing similar writing.

I called him up and said, "My name is Mike Wyly. You and I are against the same kind of tactics. I'm not sure what we're for. Let's talk." I liked him because he was honest. "I'm not sure either," he told me. "But I want to find out. The man I know who has done the most thinking along these lines is John Boyd, a retired Air Force colonel." He gave me Boyd's number and I called.

A small group of us began meeting informally in the evenings. Our "seminar" group included a few Army guys. Our attitude was, "The American military has serious tactical problems that nobody is going to correct if we don't."

In 1979, General Trainor assigned me to teach at the Amphibious Warfare School at Quantico, where we educate our Marine captains. I was promoted to Lieutenant Colonel. They had me teaching tactics again.

I made a personal decision: "I don't care if I ever get promoted again or not. I'm going to do this right. I'm not going to puppet the lesson plan. I'm going to teach whatever I think is best, because the Marine Corps is not going to give me a better way to do it. They can fire me, they can court-martial me. But I'm not going to teach it wrong again."

I inherited a teaching package of two-hour lesson plans from my predecessor. I saw in his outline: "Austerlitz: Offensive actions such as the French used." So I approached him, "It's an interesting battle. You really can't tell if Napoleon was on the offensive or defensive." It was clear that this instructor didn't know what happened at Austerlitz. I said, "You've been teaching this for three years. And you don't even know what happened?"

What I learned from the battle was that not only did Napoleon defeat two empires in that 1805 battle. But he put himself into his enemies' heads and figured out what they would do. He baited them with an apparent weak flank, tempting them to attack him. They fell for it. As soon as they made their move, he maneuvered his troops around them and attacked them from behind. In fact, he wrote to his wife, Josephine, in the elation of winning: "My Dear, I felt like I was commanding both armies."

Just like the North Vietnamese used to be good at doing to us. They'd send a small group to be seen by Marines who chased them in hot pursuit. The Marines thought, "We're going to get those guys." And, WHAM, they were ambushed by a larger Vietnamese force.

I taught the course in a way that I was comfortable with. Then, in 1980, the failure of the mission to rescue the hostages in Iran added to the post-Vietnam stigma that American military forces couldn't win anymore. That stimulated our ongoing seminar group to try to recall when we did things right. We had to go back three decades to the Inchon landing in Korea [under Army general Douglas MacArthur].

After meeting for a year, every Friday night, we conceptualized what became known as the "Maneuver Doctrine." None of us were involved to enhance our careers. We were involved because we cared. In fact, we risked our careers by being involved in this tactics debate. Our group included pilots, infantrymen, engineers . . . not all of whom had experience in Southeast Asia. However, Vietnam is only one war. If that is all you know, even if you were there for seven straight years, you have a limited picture of military history.

In my case, I'm such a believer in maneuver warfare because in Vietnam I saw that the methodical tactics I had been taught in Basic School failed to defeat the enemy and were very costly in terms of attrition on our own Marines. The "body count" game worked against us.

I became aware that even when we counted eighteen to twenty North Vietnamese soldiers dead after a battle and we only lost three Marines, that the NVA had won, because of the publicity that American casualties received back home. During my second tour, it was always in the back of my mind that, "Every Marine I lose contributes to losing the war."

We didn't have the authority to defeat the enemy by taking bold actions—sometimes without orders from higher command. An infantry force should be hungry to get behind the enemy to disrupt their battle line. In maneuver warfare, down to squad level, every Marine should know their role and look for opportunities. Even when you don't know which way the battle is going to go. That is very threatening to many senior officers. But I've seen lieutenants and sergeants adjust to this style quite well.

Among the ranks of colonel and above, before General Al Gray became Marine Corps commandant, there was a lot of fear to adopt maneuver warfare. Because for a colonel, it means the loss of control. Because lieutenants and corporals, rather than waiting for you to tell them what to do, are taking their own initiative. That is what we emphasize in Maneuver Doctrine. Junior officers and NCOs should know the commander's intent and the mission objective. With adequate training to develop teamwork, small units adjust to a given situation and figure out how to accomplish the mission. This is especially important on a nuclear/chemical/biological or smoke-covered battlefield where command and control is disrupted.

Part of maneuver warfare is reconnaissance-driven combat, where soldiers take action without orders. The commander isn't a Supreme Being sitting back at the command center. He needs to be up front, leading. Because even if he is fully informed, he can't do anything fast enough with the information. I don't care how much electronics or computer technology you give him.

In the fast-moving dynamics of battle, soldiers shouldn't have to wait for orders. I don't want you to read my thoughts as a commander. I want you to read the enemy's thoughts. Outmaneuver him. Whether you are on foot, in a tank or in an airplane, you must outthink that enemy.

Technology and mobility also made change necessary. Air, naval, and infantry weapons systems are continually smaller, more mobile, and more powerful.

In 1981 I began formulating this theory and teaching the ideas of maneuver warfare in my classes. There was an immediate division among students. Some were electrified by new ideas that encouraged them to think and have their own ideas. Others asked questions, "Why am I studying this if it's not going to get me promoted?"

My answer was, "You are studying this so that we can win the next war."

HONEST CRITICISM

GENERAL ALFRED GRAY

CAMP LEJEUNE, NORTH CAROLINA 1981–84
COMMANDING GENERAL
2ND MARINE DIVISION

In 1981, when General Al Gray became Commander of the 2nd Marine Division, he laid the groundwork for a profound change in Marine Corps battle doctrine.

When officers or staff NCOs joined my division, they had to spend an hour with the Commanding General. I would get a group of around fifty together and talk with them about the principles of the Maneuver thought process. The young people loved it.

I brought John Boyd, one of the Maneuver pioneers and a longtime student of Sun Tzu, to Camp Lejeune to speak to the division's officers.

A strong base was built among the young commanders, including some aviation and logistics people. We formed a Maneuver Warfare Board. They were former students of Colonel Mike Wyly and had read Bill Lind's writings. They had different levels of experience and came in with different approaches. Some of their ideas made sense, some of it did not. But I let them loose to debate and experiment, and instituted this process in the Carolina Marine Air/Ground Task Force. The Maneuver idea really began to catch on.

We developed a series of field exercises, where I'd always have some kind of surprise arranged. For example, one war game involved having the threat of an enemy mechanized force and airborne infantry. None of my Marines expected much. But I got together with a good friend of mine from the Army's 82nd Airborne Division and we dropped in a company of paratroopers right out of the blue.

We also initiated what I called Preplanning Exercises. We ran a lot of tabletop war games and then took it out to the field. I always attempted in training exercises to weave in air combat units as a maneuver element, as well as the logistics people. The idea is that when your combat forces are maneuvering, you don't want them to have to go back to a rear area to refuel. You want gasoline and other supplies up where you need to be. To coordinate that you need effective preplanning.

This Maneuver way of thinking is diametrically opposite of the "Zero Defects" mentality of the 1960s and '70s. When you have people who care more about looking good than being good, you can't win.

As part of my lecture to all my new staff NCOs and officers, I said, "You must allow people to learn from their mistakes. If you emphasize having a mistake-free environment, they can't grow and they won't learn."

Critiques are an important part of developing. After training exercises we would bring young corporals, sergeants and lieutenants into a meeting. They would tell their superiors what happened in their small units and how they saw events unfold. It's not important whether they quote you a "school" solution or go by the textbook. What matters is *why* they did something. What was their thought process?

We had some great sessions. I would take my rank off of my collar and sit in as an observer. A young corporal or sergeant would say, "The Captain said we ought to do this, but that wasn't right. Here's why . . ."

To develop your force's ability you need those types of honest critiques, where a corporal or lieutenant is not afraid to say something in front of a general. That doesn't mean lack of respect for superiors. Honest criticism is essential.

Some people paint a picture of me as a rough tough tobacco chewin' guy. But I've always been a pretty good listener to the opposition, people with other views. Even with stars on my collar, my attitude isn't, "You'd better learn this or else." My intention is to encourage people to use their minds to learn and grow.

Warfare, in many instances, is as much psychological as it is physical. The objective is to defeat the minds of your opponents.

THE GREEN LINE

MASTER SERGEANT
JAMES GRAHAM

LEBANON 1982–83
PLATOON SERGEANT
2ND TANK BATTALION, 8TH MARINE REGIMENT

The first overseas deployment to a combat zone for U.S. forces after Indochina was the killing ground of Lebanon, where a Christian-Muslim civil war was compounded by the spillover of the Israeli-Palestinian conflict. U.S. Marines deployed to Lebanon's war-torn capital included Vietnam veteran James Graham, who had returned to the Marine Corps after playing college football.

I was on a training operation in Germany in October 1982 when we were sent to Beirut. The civil war there was still very hot. And the Israelis had the city surrounded to trap Yasir Arafat and his Palestinian Liberation Organization [PLO], who were using the civilian population as a shield. Our mission was a show of force. We weren't supposed to be fighting anybody.

My platoon was in the first battalion that landed on the beach. There were bodies floating in the water. Everything in town, including schools, were shut down. Almost everybody we saw was carrying weapons, even kids. We became the first unit to occupy Beirut airport.

There was a section of town where the Israelis allowed a Lebanese militia to come in and murder a lot of Palestinians. That was two blocks from our operational area. We saw the results of the Israeli occupation—those were the floating bodies. And when it rained, mass graves were uncovered.

When we first went in, we all were pro-Israeli and believed all the media hype. But when we built a checkpoint outside the airport gate, Israeli soldiers began confronting American Marines. I was involved in the very first incident.

The Israelis were probing around our perimeter. They were acting like they were the kings of the Middle East and "whatever we say goes." They resented our Marines and the French forces. We established law and order: schools were reopened, the streets were passable. Substantially less people were carrying weapons. I think the Israelis were upset about that. So they were trying to make us look bad any way that they could . . . like bullying our defense lines.

We established a checkpoint around 500 meters outside the airport. A road, called the Green Line, was the main Israeli logistics line running through Beirut, around 1,500 meters from the airport. We set our checkpoint at a four-corners intersection, using two tanks, an amtrack, and some infantry people. Our job was to make sure that nobody except Marines could get to our airport perimeter.

One day, three Israeli armored personnel carriers came down the road. Myself and a couple of sentries went into the road to stop them. An Israeli lieutenant colonel got out of his vehicle and came forward, trying to intimidate us to let them through. We were being covered by tanks and TOW missiles. So they got back in their vehicles and drove away. We weren't trying to make anybody look bad. It was our mission, because of the terrorist threat, that nobody go through.

Well, a crowd of Lebanese people who watched this encounter began cheering. They had never seen anybody back the Israelis down. We were outside of a Pepsi factory. The people inside went ballistic, they were throwing free Pepsi to us. They wanted to show their appreciation.

The next day, the Israelis came back in force. A platoon-sized group with armored vehicles. This time our battalion commander was with us. We backed the Israelis down again. But two days later, the same lieutenant colonel that I had the encounter with tried another checkpoint. This time, a young Marine captain had to jump on the Israeli tank and point his pistol.

The way that happened, three Israeli tanks were chasing one Lebanese civilian, shooting their machine guns. The Lebanese ran into the Marine perimeter at a university campus, just outside the airport. Our Lima Company had that security. The Marine sentry ordered the Israelis to stop. Coincidentally, the company commander just happened to be out checking his posts. He asked the sentry, "What's going on?"

The Israeli commander said, "That man is a Palestinian soldier. We're going to take him." The Marine captain said, "He's just a farmer. He's in our perimeter. You're not going to take him." The Israeli said, "Okay, fine."

The captain started to guide the Israeli tanks back to the road. The first tank turned to follow him. But the second tank rammed the gate to chase the guy. The captain ran after the tank. He jumps onto it and pulls his pistol. He says, "Where do you think you're going?" The Israeli commander says, "After that guy." The Marine captain actually said, "Over my dead body."

Immediately after that happened, the captain was in hot water with the Marine chain of command. Because, heaven forbid, he pissed off an Israeli. Well, a couple days later President Reagan came on the news and said, "That Marine was great. We ought to give him a medal." All of a sudden, he was a hero. The greatest thing since sliced bread. At Camp Lejeune they had T-shirts made with the slogan, "Over my dead body."

All of us in Beirut below the rank of captain were determined not to take any shit from the Israelis. Initially, political people like the Ambassador were briefing our colonels, "You can't upset the Israelis." But after the President blessed the event, it all worked out.

We left Lebanon in February 1983, eight months before the Marine barracks was blown up. A lot of good things came out of our initial Beirut deployment. Institutionally, from the time U.S. forces withdrew from Vietnam—around ten years earlier—there hadn't been any sustained Marine Corps operations in a combat zone. Beirut got our people back into the mode that, "Things really do happen in the world."

It was inspiring to watch bunkers being built the same way they were in Vietnam. People got their adrenaline up and were starting to focus. The guys doing well were not the garrison Marines with spit-shined boots and starched cammies [camouflage fatigues]. What mattered was, "Can you take care of that machine gun? Can you take care of that tank?"

We were on the eastern side of the perimeter, on a gravel pit where the Israelis had their artillery set up. They had pulled about a mile or so further south. But we could see their tanks training every day.

On Christmas morning 1982, we were training either with

French Legionnaires or the Lebanese Christian army. We joked that, "The Christians and Muslims all got ammunition for Christmas." In America, kids get up and play with their new toys in the street. Well, all the Lebanese kids got up—junior high school age—and for about an hour and a half we watched all these firefights going on. Suddenly, it became like, "We used up all of our ammo. Let's go back home and have Christmas dinner."

During that period, the fighting was pretty routine. You could plan your day around it. They'd shoot each other up before they went to work in the morning, from 6:30 till 7:30 A.M. They used Nissan pickup trucks with .50-caliber machine guns mounted on a stand. Pull out of their garages and drive down the street shooting people up. Then turn around, get into their Mercedes, and go to work. Just as casual as that. The damnedest thing I've ever seen.

At lunchtime, they would be like, "We've got fifteen minutes before we go back. Let's have some action." They'd go out from 12:30 to 12:45 and fight for fifteen minutes. Come back to work, then go home, eat dinner and play with the kids. Then, "Ah, it's seven-thirty. Let's go out and shoot up some Christians."

I told my troops to keep their heads down. At first they thought it was kind of funny. But when rounds began impacting around them, they took it seriously. We were sniped at pretty regularly. Occasionally somebody would spray our bunkers with a .50-caliber. But we used to joke, "If they replaced the guys who are shooting at us, they might find somebody who can shoot better." So long as they were missing us, it wasn't a big issue.

A year later, when the Marine barracks in Beirut was blown up by Muslim terrorists, it sent shock waves through the Corps. There was never any doubt about the potential of the situation. The problem was that the Marines were kept there for too long.

When we landed there in 1982, we had permission to load the weapons in our tanks with ammunition. Our rules of engagement were: "If anyone points their weapon at you, you are authorized to engage them." In many cases, Israelis pointed their weapons at us, trying to intimidate us. We knew they weren't going to shoot, so we didn't engage them. That was a decision that young corporals made, using their heads. They could've started World War III if they used bad judgment. But our people were in control of themselves.

Colonel Stokes was our Marine Expeditionary Unit Commander. He didn't take any shit. He was there to protect us. At no time did he tie our hands from protecting ourselves. But as time went on, after we left, the politics shifted. The chain of command grew larger and larger. And the Marines had more restrictions that may have hampered their ability to protect themselves.

It became like Vietnam. Our Marines didn't have an offensive mission. And terrorists are very patient people. They had the time to sit there and watch us, learn our routines, and see our security maybe get a little weaker.

At first our presence was positive. My unit went home after four months feeling pretty good, because we went in there when people were killing each other in the streets, dead bodies all over the place. When we left, people were still fighting, but life had returned almost to normal.

Eight months later, when the barracks was blown up, all of us that had been there earlier were asking, "What are we still doing there? We're not accomplishing anything anymore." It was obvious that peace was not going to be struck. These people had been fighting for thousands of years.

THE BUCK STOPS HERE

GENERAL ALFRED GRAY

CAMP LEJEUNE, NORTH CAROLINA 1981–84
COMMANDING GENERAL
2ND MARINE DIVISION

U.S. involvement in Lebanon was terminated by a terrorist car-bombing of a Marine barracks. The toll was 241 lives—the single greatest loss of U.S. military lives since the Vietnam War had ended.

General Al Gray was commander of the division whose Marines were lost in the destroyed barracks. Based in North Car-

olina, he had no control over events on the ground in Lebanon, where a convoluted chain of command included diplomatic officials.

On October 24, 1983, the morning after the Beirut bombing, I stood with the replacements on the flight tarmac at Camp Lejeune, prepared to take responsibility.

I couldn't go to Beirut with the replacements because I had 241 bodies of my Marines who were killed in the bombing to get back to the States and bury. I had a responsibility to the families. Because it was a mass casualty situation, we coordinated notifying families through the division's Combat Operations Center.

I knew that the eyes of the world would be focused on the 2nd Marine Division. That morning, more than eighty members of the media arrived. The Pentagon kept sending me instructions, "No press interviews." I said, "You don't understand. I've got dish antennas outside of my Command Post. They're already here. We've got to talk with them. You're just going to have to hope that we do it right."

We galvanized a plan of action. We set up another command post across the street for casualty affairs. We briefed all the NCOs who had escort duty to accompany bodies to their hometowns for burial services. All the chaplains were briefed. Then we networked around the country through Marine Corps Reserve and Recruiting people.

I could not let my Marines feel sorry for themselves. They had to go forward. We were scheduled for an Inspector General visit that week. He called and said, "We're ready to cancel because of what happened." I said, "Don't. The 2nd Marine Division is ready for inspection."

As it was, the terrorists beat us that morning. But we had to go forward. My attitude was, "The buck stops here." I had to draw the line on chaos at the home base.

My wife Jan and I went to seventy-four funerals. We couldn't go to all of them because of the distance and time factor. Every year since, I've gone to memorial ceremonies. This was the first year that I've missed at Camp Lejeune since the bombing. Jan and I still touch base with a lot of the families.

After multiple combat tours, including Korea and Vietnam, there are friends who I lost that still stand out in my mind. I don't believe that is negative. Their memory doesn't disrupt me. In a way, they have helped me come to grip with my responsibility of Command.

GUNFIGHTERS

MAJOR GENERAL JAMES DAY

ARLINGTON, VIRGINIA 1982–84
DIRECTOR, TRAINING BRANCH
MARINE CORPS HEADQUARTERS

A veteran of World War II, Korea and Vietnam, Jim Day was the duty officer at Marine Corps Headquarters on the night of the Beirut bombing.

In the early 1980s, the "gunfighters"—generals who were combat veterans—were being phased out of the Marine Corps. Guys who had never really served in foxholes were getting the prime positions.

I served with many of the combat veterans, who were great Marines. Just because you're a "gunfighter" and good in the field doesn't mean that you're bad as a staff officer. If you have the basic intelligence to become a general, you're not dumb.

Of course, the Commandant wants people of his mold. If he's a staff man or a "great thinker," he may believe that some of his friends are better thinkers than other people who aren't his friends. There's no selection board for three-star generals. The Commandant says, "These are the people who I want to have three stars." And all the others have to retire.

One of the statements that came out during that time was, "Let's remember what Horatio—or some damned person—said thousands of years ago: Moral courage is harder to obtain and abide by than physical courage." That raised my temper. Because I don't think you can equate moral courage with physical courage. Physical courage is something a kid shows day in and day out when his life is on the line in combat. He knows that death is present. He just doesn't know when it will happen to him.

For a leader taking kids into that type of situation, his courage of *leadership by example* is what they will respect. Instead

137

of somebody giving them philosophy or an abstract pep talk. All they want is to come back home alive.

In perilous situations, Marines need to know that their leaders are with them and have their interests at heart. When I was a young Marine wounded badly, it was important to me to know that my company commander and other people in charge would get me assistance.

I was the Duty General at Marine Corps Headquarters in Washington the night of the Beirut bombing. The Duty General sleeps at home. I got a telephone call, "There's been a gigantic explosion in Beirut. We think we've lost seventy to eighty people." That was just the beginning . . . I could visualize these 241 Marines, sailors, and other people killed in that explosion . . . not having a goddamned chance.

I don't think you will find many professional military men that can understand why those kids were put in a position where we could give somebody the opportunity to kill them. I assumed that they were trying to protect the kids from the elements. But hell, the Marines are an infantry organization. They are supposed to be trained to live out in the elements.

It was just amazing that people at the top of the heap of the Marine Corps gave a talk from that building or from that area just a short time before the explosion, and didn't see anything wrong with having recon people and support people—cooks and bakers—living in that building. The people they were fighting were goddamned terrorists.

A lot of people were stunned. I don't recall a single battle in Vietnam where we lost 241 men. We couldn't understand it. Particularly senior officers who had been in infantry units when they were young. They just couldn't grasp what the hell had happened. Of course, it didn't hurt the careers of people who I think were at fault.

A problem after Vietnam and Beirut was that policymakers, both civilian and military, didn't take full responsibility. The buck was passed down the line to people in the field.

I heard that after Beirut there was a testimony before Congress where a very senior Pentagon Marine said that what happened in the field really wasn't his fault. I thought that was the most despicable goddamned thing that can ever be espoused. You can't put a sandbag between yourself and your commanders in the field when you are the Number One man.

GRENADA: A TURNING POINT

BRIGADIER GENERAL JAMES HILL

THE PENTAGON 1983
AIDE DE CAMP TO
THE ARMY CHIEF OF STAFF

Just two days after the Beirut bombing, in the predawn hours of October 25, 1983, a combined U.S. land, sea, and air task force invaded the tiny Caribbean island of Grenada to rescue American students and to suppress a violent coup. It was the first American offensive military action since the Vietnam War. Although there were a number of lapses in mission planning, intelligence, and joint service coordination and communication, the swift forty-eight-hour victory was a much needed confidence boost after a decade of military mishaps. And the operation provided much needed real-world experience for senior officers such as Major General Norman Schwarzkopf, and the Army's Advisor to the Operation Commander, Vice Admiral Joseph Metcalf.

In Vietnam, I had misgivings about the senior leadership that started with a micromanaging President who gave the military targets to bomb. That can only inhibit military leadership. A turning point was on October 25, 1983.

I was in the Secretary of Defense's Situation Room in the Pentagon on the morning of the Grenada invasion. I went in with the Chief of Staff of the Army at around four o'clock in the morning. I watched the J3 [Operations and Planning officer] react to an official from the Secretary's office.

The Situation Room is where all the intelligence feeds were coming in. The Defense official was picking up a telephone to call out. The Army J3 went over to the civilian and said, "Put the phone down. We're conducting a war here. It's been given to the military Joint Staff to run. It's not going to be conducted by [bureaucrats]. If you have a problem, go back to your office and work it out. But we've been instructed by the President and the Secretary of Defense to run the war."

The President showed a lot of courage to entrust the military. That was a very difficult time because we had just lost 241 Marines in the Beirut bombing. But he still let his Joint Chiefs run the Grenada invasion.

Off the coast of Grenada, General Norman Schwarzkopf was on the Command and Control ship. That experience set the stage for Desert Storm, by giving him and all the military leaders confidence. And it showed us that we had to work harder at joint service coordination.

1ST GROUP

BRIGADIER GENERAL DAVID BARATTO

Fort Lewis, Washington 1985–87
Commander
1st Special Forces Group

An indication that the U.S. military and political communities were coming out of the "Vietnam Syndrome" was the revitalized role of Special Forces. Especially significant was the rebuilding of the 1st Special Forces Group, whose area of operations covers Asia and the Pacific region.

David Baratto had left the Special Forces community in the late 1970s. He served in a variety of missions, including as a tactical officer at West Point, an advisor to a mechanized Nebraska National Guard brigade, and Chief of the Contingency Plans Branch in South Korea.

In 1985 I was assigned to build the 1st Special Forces Group at Fort Lewis, Washington. It had been decommissioned for ten or twelve years. My orders were classified. So when I arrived at Fort Lewis, nobody knew what I'd be doing.

I had been away from Special Forces for seven years. By

the 1980s the world was changed by the Iranian hostage crisis, the Soviet invasion of Afghanistan, revolutionary turmoil in Latin America, Cuban troops throughout Africa, Vietnam's invasion of Cambodia, instability in the Philippines, and the escalation of international terrorism.

These mostly unconventional conflicts around the world were unfeasible for conventional forces. The Iranian hostage crisis awoke people to the threat. And the failed Desert One mission to rescue the hostages in Iran highlighted the need to improve antiterrorist operations.

I arrived at Fort Lewis to create a special operations group for the Pacific with a deathly fear. I had no people, no equipment, I didn't know how to go about doing this. I was a long way from Fort Bragg, where people understood Special Forces. But, to my surprise, this post welcomed me with open arms. First, General Brandenburg called me and said, "If there's anything you need ... I've never put together a Special Forces Group either. Or, for that matter, organized a unit from scratch. You go up to North Port and look at the buildings. You identify what you think you need, and we'll do our best to help."

Special Forces Command had put out a levy that said, "1st Group is building up. 5th Group, you send X number of guys. 7th Group, you send X number."

I was concerned about the quality of the people I would get. In the early 1980s the Army had become more stringent on recruitment requirements. Most of the riffraff had already been run out of the Army, except for a sprinkling here and there. Most of the people in Special Forces were young and new to the special operations community.

I didn't have the authority to reject anyone. I had the challenge to find motivation techniques. The one thing I had going for me was that most of these people would be running from something: either their area of operations, or had been in a Group for too long. They were looking for an opportunity. So I tried to capitalize on that. Without criticizing their faults or shortfalls in training, I tried to develop a training program that would incorporate the philosophy I learned as a basic training commander: I accepted each guy for where he was and tried to bring him to a higher standard.

I knew that we were going to be a relatively inexperienced group. Because my soldiers were young, there was more opportunity to convince them about what their capabilities could be.

I didn't have nearly the budget I needed for language train-

ing and area studies. The first people I got into my command
were aviators, but I wasn't scheduled to receive helicopters for
a year and a half. The first trucks I got came from Alaska.
They were so worn that when you put your feet on the floor,
they went right through the floorboard. But those were physical problems that could be fixed. That didn't effect our motivation and trust and dedication and faith—the precious
commodities. Initially I pushed the physical aspects rather than
technical skills. I felt it important for them to measure their
physical improvement in a given period of time, as a confidence builder.

I required a quarterly set of physical requirements. Taking
the PT test every quarter and scoring 60 or above on every
event. We timed the four-mile run, with pull-ups in it. We
added a six-mile run, a ten-mile run. And then a twelve-mile
march with rucksacks. Every week we'd have a major competitive event. Rather than motivational problems, healthy competition developed between units to achieve the best scores or
times in each event. Even commanders were competing to establish their own records, visibly participating.

We were very conscious of the stigma that Special Forces
had. But there was a new kind of optimism. Enough time had
passed since the end of the Vietnam War. A new attitude of
pride was evolving.

Our Group assignment was Asia and the Pacific. We didn't
know exactly what. But at least we had a mission. I was determined to get a focus. So I made a journey through the Pacific
and touched base with commanders in Hawaii, the Philippines,
Korea, and Thailand. I just sort of fished around asking, "What
do you think we ought to be doing?"

We had a hell of a time getting into the annual Cobra Gold
exercise in Thailand. The U.S. Ambassador, Bill Brown, said,
"I don't want any Special Forces guys in here. You just stay
home." It was part of the image thing that we hadn't overcome
yet. But we had good relations with the Thai General Staff, including a couple of my West Point classmates. So at first we
just sent a couple of guys to monitor. They told the embassy's
military attaché, "We're not going to be intrusive. But allow us
to tell you what we have to offer. We could do some medical
exercises, whatever you want."

AD HOC GUERRILLAS

LIEUTENANT COLONEL
ANDREW GEMBARA

THE PENTAGON 1984–88
MILITARY ASSISTANT TO THE ASSISTANT SECRETARY OF
DEFENSE
FOR INTERNATIONAL SECURITY AFFAIRS.

*The "Desert One" debacle in Iran, and some gaps in planning
and coordination in Grenada, convinced authorities in the Defense Department of the need to have a unified Special Operations Command. This would better combine the unique skills
of Special Forces, SEALs, Air Force and Marine Corps special
operators.*

When Ronald Reagan was elected President, the people who
coordinated his military policy made noises about revitalizing
special operations. In 1983–84, we finally got a principal deputy at the Department of Defense for Special Operations, Noel
Koch—in addition to his being Deputy Assistant Secretary of
Defense for International Security Affairs. For the first time a
civilian official had military special operations as part of his
charter.

Noel had to get smart very fast. He put an Army colonel,
George McGovern, a West Point graduate and former 5th Special Forces Group commander, as an aide. But there was tremendous pressure from the conventional military, as well as
the civilian side, to not put much resources into special operations revitalization.

With the creation of this new guru for special operations,
other agencies feared that he might be given powers that had
been claimed by other people in the Pentagon, the State Department, and in other agencies. For that reason the support

and money weren't there. So an effort started to create legislation to give special operations a mandate.

I had just made lieutenant colonel, but was not on a fast promotion track because most of my assignments were in shitty Third World areas. Not *real* places, as far as the Army was concerned. In 1984 I was pulled from 5th Special Forces Group back to the Pentagon as the Military Assistant under Noel Koch.

One of our biggest problems through the years in Special Forces is that most of our people avoid Washington. They would rather be with special operations units overseas. Guys like myself are initially dragged to Washington. Once we're here, we learn how the power works, how political networks operate.

I got involved in a network to push for a special operations branch of the military. The effort included academics, sympathetic people in the media, and congressional staff. For example, Vaughn Forrest, an aide to Representative Bill McCollum, advised our ad hoc guerrilla campaign for legislation. Kris Kolesnik on Senator Charles Grassley's staff, and Bill Cowen, a former Marine who worked for Senator Warren Rudman, were very helpful.

What helped to pass the legislation in 1986 was that there wasn't an effective structure for special operations or counterterrorism. And there were the unauthorized operations of Ollie North, John Poindexter, and Richard Secord that became the Iran-Contra scandal. These problems showed the Congress a need for a special operations structure, and helped to gain support for our legislation. In October 1986, it was a near unanimous vote in the Senate, with one or two abstentions.

For the first time, there was a unified Special Operations Command [USSOCOM], headed by a four-star general, to coordinate Army, Navy, Air Force, and Marine Corps special operations units. We created an Assistant Secretary of Defense for Special Operations and Low Intensity Conflict. But attempts to create an office in the White House for a Special Assistant for Special Operations/Low Intensity Conflict were never filled.

The conventional military was still resisting. They countered by placing the Special Operations Command in Florida, far outside of Washington so they could not have an impact on decision making. A joke was made that, "If the Pentagon could put SOCOM any further south, they would put them in the water."

THE HUMAN DIMENSION

BRIGADIER GENERAL DAVID BARATTO

MacDill Air Force Base, Florida 1987–88
Director
Joint Studies and Analysis Group
U.S. Special Operations Command

When I was put on the Brigadier General list, it was a big surprise to everybody. Because few officers in special operations get higher than colonel. The greatest privilege I ever expected to see was commanding the 1st Special Forces Group.

That same year, in 1987, USSOCOM was created. The commander, General James Lindsay, requested that I go down to its headquarters at MacDill Air Force Base in Florida. He said, "I want you to help me develop an operational concept." The first thing I had to do was figure out what was expected of us in terms of the law and the charters that were granted to us. And where we fit in as an element of national power.

That was the first time I worked in a joint arena with Navy SEALs and Air Force special operations to develop a concept that would permit the independent special operations forces units to maintain their individual identity. Yet meld together on some sort of common ground.

At first some people thought that because of our surgical operations ability, that "direct action" was going to be Army Special Forces forte. The Navy SEALs are not so inclined to work with foreign nationals. They want to hit the beach, then pick out the target and get out.

It was quite a challenge to maintain the legacy that Special Forces has with some of the subtle talents like foreign languages and interpersonal skills. Those are difficult to quantify and transfer into a warrior image. On many occasions I was accused of "making statesmen rather than soldiers."

I believe it would be a shame to use Army Special Forces people who have multiple skills as strictly infantrymen on the battlefield. They have the ability to perform many subtle tasks and coalesce a variety of different efforts. The human dimension of what we do is the most important capability we've got.

CAMEL'S MILK

CHIEF WARRANT OFFICER 2 RICHARD BALWANZ

FORT CAMPBELL, KENTUCKY 1978-92
A-TEAM LEADER
5TH SPECIAL FORCES GROUP

I joined Special Forces as an enlisted man in 1978, during its low point. There was a stigma of being "snake eaters." And there were some people in Special Forces at the time who liked that kind of stigma attached to them. We had a lot of rowdy old-timers who probably wouldn't fit into today's Army.

Our commanders wanted us to wipe out the "snake eater" image. Discipline was steadily ingrained. In the 1970s we had people that came off the street and went directly into Special Forces. Now, volunteers must be mature sergeant E-5s, with maturity from conventional army experience.

I had seven years in the conventional army, in Vulcan air defense artillery. In Special Forces, I was retrained to be a medic. I learned how to perform minor surgery on wounds, and a lot of internal medicine. But the only time we practice our knowledge is overseas. My team was in Kenya, Africa, several years ago. Doctors there said, "Come on, get involved." So we provided a lot of rural medical assistance in villages.

I've spent the last twelve years on A-Teams. When we are away from home, we live at such close quarters that we sometimes fight with each other and then cry on each other's shoulders like a real family.

We don't change A-Teams very often. Enlisted guys stay three to five years or longer. As a warrant officer, I could stay on the same team until I was physically unable to perform. After a period of time, as you get older, your reflexes and your body control isn't quite the way it used to be. You rely upon experience. A twenty-mile run carrying a full rucksack is going to hurt like hell. But you know how to prepare—you fix your feet up, where younger guys get blisters.

The primary Special Forces mission is FID—foreign internal defense. I've done a whole lot of FID in the 5th Group. In the late 1970s, my group was oriented toward Greece. I learned the Greek language and traveled there annually as a part of NATO to field-train with the Greek army.

In the early 1980s we had just gotten familiar with the way the Greeks operate. All of a sudden, we were assigned to cover the Middle East and moved into desert warfare. I had to learn the Arabic language. One problem was that there was no standardized desert operations training. So we developed our own program. We had no idea that it would later be a big part of Operation Desert Storm.

These types of challenges is what has kept me in the Army. When I was younger, everything I did was devoted to my job. But as I've gotten older with a family—two children—my priorities have changed. Many times I've been away from home six to eight months. Because of the classified nature of my work, I can't always tell my wife where I am or what I'm doing.

Most of the guys on our A-Teams are married. It's always harder on the family than on the soldier, because they don't know how you're doing. They have to deal with all that worry and stress. For a marriage to survive, there has to be a whole lot of trust.

Maturity is essential for this type of work. The average age of a team member is around thirty-two years old. Experienced guys are more patient, not as hot-headed. It also requires a pretty strong stomach, especially in the Middle East, where you can't refuse when someone offers you the best thing they have to eat in their household.

In the Gulf War, my A-Team worked for the first several months right up on the Kuwaiti border doing surveillance of Iraqi forces. One of our Saudi counterparts was a prince. Of course, there are a lot of princes there. He had family in that area. So he took my team into the desert to visit his relatives who were Bedouin tribespeople.

A tent was set up and a big feast where they killed a camel. We sat in a circle and they passed around a steel bowl about three feet around that had camel's milk in it. We looked down—it was warm and there were gobs of gunk floating on top.

Most of my guys held their breath, took a little sip and passed it on. When they handed it to me, I thought, "I might get sick doing this." But I tilted the bowl up and chugged three, four, five big good gulps. Put the bowl down and rubbed my belly.

That did more to get me in with the Saudis than anything else the whole war. They liked that. They all came over to me. And when we'd go into the town of Khafji to meet with political people in the governor's headquarters, the first thing the prince would do was tell them about how I had drunk the camel's milk: "Yes, he's a good man. He drinks the camel's milk."

EL SALVADOR

SERGEANT MAJOR DUANE STONE

LATIN AMERICA 1982–92

ADVISOR

7TH SPECIAL FORCES GROUP

Sergeant Major Duane Stone was trained as a Special Forces medic. For much of the past ten years he and the 7th Group have operated in the midst of Latin America's violence, poverty, and despair. An especially rough assignment has been El Salvador. There, a small number of American advisors tried to curb human rights violations by professionalizing an autocratic military, while preventing the country from falling to Marxist guerrillas. The professional training was combined with pressure from the U.S. government for the removal of officers engaged in unlawful actions, such as the "Death Squads."

Combined with American political pressure, the U.S. military advisors' efforts made a difference. In 1981, Salvadoran death squads were killing 800 people a month. By 1988, political killings were down to 10 a month.

Sergeant Major Stone speaks in a slow midwestern twang and has an understated sense of humor.

I was a staff sergeant in the 82nd Airborne Division when I came into Special Forces in 1979. The Army was discouraging people from volunteering for Special Forces. You had to want it very badly. Seventh Group was at its low point when I arrived—there was talk of it being shut down.

To say that Special Forces was the "bastard child" of the Army was an understatement. We had trouble getting ammunition. We had trouble going places to train. In fact, the only way we could get transportation for training was to strap-hang with other units.

But we had excellent team sergeants who took their people into the North Carolina and Florida woods. We worked on reconnaissance and tracking techniques. Like on counterguerrilla or counternarcotics trafficking patrol.

During the mid-1980s the 7th Group picked up SOUTHCOM [Southern Command] as our primary region. That gave us two languages to train in, Spanish and Portuguese. I went to El Salvador in 1982 and 1984 on six-month mobile training teams. We deployed as an entire A-Team to do the training.

In countries like El Salvador and Honduras, the military leader of a Department [province] was like a warlord. He was a strong political figure and the law enforcer in the area. When we first arrived in Salvador, that was the case. The Department commanders were making their own treaties with the guerrillas: "You can have free access through my Department. Just leave my people alone."

In 1982, the country was near collapse. The FMLN [Farabundo Marti National Liberation Front, a coalition of Communist organizations] was operating in large company-sized units. They made an attack just before we arrived and destroyed about half the helicopters in the Salvadoran military. And they had a very strong infrastructure in the capital city. When we first arrived, they put threatening printed flyers under the doors of our hotel rooms at night.

Most of the Americans killed by the guerrillas in El Salvador were hit in the city. Marine embassy guards were ambushed while they sat at an outdoor café. A U.S. Navy advisor was ambushed in his car. Ironically, he was the person who gave us our briefing when we arrived in the city. He told us about safety precautions and things we shouldn't do.

In our Rules of Engagement, we had what was called "Force Protection Requirements." Among them was the "two man" rule: "All movement [travel] must be accomplished by two armed persons." This could mean a U.S. military person and a [Salvadoran] counterpart, as long as both were armed. In the U.S. MilGroup, if you had to go some place by yourself, you were assigned an armed driver, or an armed escort.

Other rules were: not to travel in predictable routes. For instance, we varied our routes to work each day. We had times that we were not to travel in certain areas of the city. And the majority of our cars had bulletproof windows, that we were to keep rolled up.

San Salvador is a beautiful city with an easy pace of life. That can give you a false sense of security. The guerrilla underground agents know who you are. They follow your daily routines and habits. The Navy advisor became too comfortable. He violated his own security rules, such as the "two man" rule. He was by himself. And the guerrillas knew his route and his movements, and took advantage of it. They waited in ambush for him. And his window was down—because the air-conditioning in his car was broken. He paid the price.

I worked primarily with local military at the training center at La Union, on the southeastern coast. The army had poor transport—limited helicopters, very few trained medics. And the NCO corps was nonexistent. They would rotate battalions in from around the country. We would give them basic training, advanced infantry training, and first aid. The course usually lasted around three months. The idea was for us to train enough Salvadoran cadre to be instructors so that we would no longer be needed. It took about two years for Salvadorans to be able to train their own soldiers.

La Union was not the safest area. It was directly on the rebel supply route from the Sandinistas in Nicaragua. At night, the Sandinistas would fly helicopters over the Gulf of Fonseca, to land weapons for the FMLN guerrillas. That was picked up on radar. The Salvadoran military had no intention to go out at night to interdict the shipments. That was tremendously frustrating.

In the early 1980s, FMLN had a series of radio broadcasts on "the lessons of Vietnam." They claimed that through sabotage and military campaigns they would erode the political will of American policymakers to support of the Salvadoran government. A key factor in that strategy was targeting Americans for assassination. Those of us in the MilGroup were a high priority on their target list. That was especially the case when I was down there right before the 1984 U.S. presidential election.

The guerrillas conducted probing sniper attacks against our camp in the La Union compound. And they laid mines or booby traps outside the main camp, in areas around our training ranges. As a precaution, before we would move out to the range, we'd send a patrol to clear the area. At that time we did not have mine detectors. But the mines weren't that sophisticated or hard to find—most were homemade with trip wires. If the troops weren't sharp about looking for the mines, they would find them the hard way. A couple of Salvadoran soldiers were lost to mines.

Later on, after I left La Union, the guerrillas launched a hard attack, targeting the American advisors' sleeping bunker with mortar fire. But I experienced probing attacks by snipers using small arms fire. That was a forewarning that they were targeting us. They even announced over their radio station that they were going to do it. That was psychological warfare—to show that the Salvadoran army couldn't stop them. They even went so far as to describe the vehicle that the American advisors were driving and give the license plate number. That shook up the MilGroup real fast. We got rid of that vehicle.

We had cleared back foliage quite a distance away from the camp. Usually in the middle of the night, when fewer of our people were on guard duty. The guerrillas would work their way into the open field and fire at the camp from a distance. That's why they weren't too accurate. Our people would return fire.

I remember one particular night, when we were fired on. We automatically went into our immediate action drills. We had mortar positions set up. We tried to get our counterparts to shoot some illumination rounds so we could put direct fire with the mortars. They didn't want to do that at all. And the older Salvadoran officers definitely wouldn't leave the camp until daybreak. To them, the term Quick Reaction Force meant "the next day."

The way we changed that was by focusing our training on new leaders. Not just the NCO corps, but young lieutenants. The leadership style of the old officer corps was, "I give orders. You jump." Most officers didn't have much military training. There was a military academy in San Salvador that was more of a social school. It covered how to act at formal ceremonies and public affairs. It didn't cover combat infantry skills.

One of the most difficult problems we had was that many senior officers did not like North Americans. We were a threat to their established authority. Especially because we were professionalizing the enlisted ranks. But by our using a little courtesy, language ability, and common sense, they gradually accepted our presence.

A mistake an advisor can make is to challenge a senior officer by telling him, "You need to go out and start doing more work." If a man is a major or a colonel in an old regime, he feels that it is his lieutenants' or captains' job to be out front. Not his. An American isn't going to change that. It's counterproductive to try. It's more effective to ingrain professionalism and good leadership in the young officers and NCOs.

When I first arrived, NCOs were chosen at the whim of a commander. It would usually be the guy who best shined the officer's boots and pressed his uniforms. We began to identify the quality soldiers and arrange for them to go to the NCO training we created.

Teaching marksmanship was a real challenge. Some of the recruits were half blind and didn't know it. None of them can afford eyeglasses. In large part it's due to lack of nutrition in their diets. To have a company of those raw conscripts on the firing range with loaded weapons was an exciting experience. [He laughs.]

The highest ranking officers I would deal with were company commanders. It was hard to train the soldiers because their attention span was short. But the campesinos [rural peasants] are hardworking people. There is no problem with their desire to work if they have proper nourishment and guidance. And if they believe that their leaders care about them.

Special Forces people were under the pressure of being part of only fifty-five American military people allowed by the U.S. Congress in the country at any given time. If the Salvadoran forces misbehaved and violated human rights, we would largely be held responsible. We are so sensitive to the issue that part of our program of instruction for new advisors includes human rights classes. Even with the best training, it's difficult to tell people whose family members have been killed or maimed by guerrillas how they should treat the enemy.

When we came to El Salvador in 1982–83, human rights abuses were rampant. We immediately tried to reduce the number of incidents by professionalizing the NCO corps in-country, while junior officers were brought to Fort Benning, Georgia, for intensive training. As those programs advanced, and a number of people were trained, incidents of human rights abuses went down dramatically.

What was largely unreported in the American press was that in most places the guerrillas operated, outside of a few strongholds, the local people didn't like them. Their campaign to disrupt the local economy included blowing up electric power lines and bridges, and planting land mines in fields where campesinos tried to scratch out a living. Before the Training Center was created in La Union, the guerrillas attacked the town. They did everything from rape and pillage, to take the priest out of his church and hang him.

During holidays, they would pull into a section of town and put up roadblocks to pull trucks and buses off to the side of the road and "tax" people. The rich didn't ride buses. The people the guerrillas forcibly took money from were campesinos who worked in the city. They were returning home with what little pay they earned.

La Union is a fishing village. We made a lot of friends in the community through civic action programs and buying food from them. The people came to like us. Some would come to us with warnings, "We have word that the guerrillas are coming back into the area. Don't come to the market until we tell you that it is safe." Their reasons were twofold. One, they didn't want to get blown up. And they cared enough about us, that they risked their own lives to warn us.

We kept a low profile. American advisors were restricted from going on combat operations. The only time we saw combat was if we were in the process of training troops and the guerrillas hit us.

In 1984, I saw the huge bridge that the guerrillas destroyed over the Rio Lampas River. It was a sophisticated job, not done by amateurs. I saw the massacred bodies of the local soldiers who were guarding the bridge. They were all shot with one bullet to the back of their heads. Their uniforms were stripped prior to execution. This was not an isolated incident.

If somebody has seen his fellow soldiers or family butchered, or has been wounded and left for dead, it's hard to stop him from committing human rights violations.

We teach a class on human rights in our training program. I'd ask, "If you capture prisoners what do you do?" One kid was really sharp. He said, "I'll segregate them. I'll secure them. I'll search them." I said, "Very good. Then what do you do?"

He said, "Then I'll kill them."

However, as the U.S. system and military advisors got deeper involved in the country, town mayors began picking up authority. Civilian government and the rule of law gradually became much more effective. The army leadership was harder to train than the basic troops. It takes a long time to get the unprofessional leadership out. They're established. It's not cut and dried, like: "He's corrupt, he's been illegal. Take steps to remove him." That's not the way it works. He may be corrupt and he may be illegal. But he may have ties with the government.

Regardless of the problems, we couldn't pull up stakes and not be involved. Lessons learned from Vietnam: We pulled up stakes and there was a bloodbath. It wasn't just in Vietnam. It covered the "killing fields" in Cambodia, and stretched into Laos. Some Americans put up a blind eye and pretended not to see the suffering. They didn't want to see the boat people or killing fields or the refugee camps that swelled to hundreds of thousands.

We shouldn't forget that unlike Asia, Latin America is on our doorstep. We can literally drive all the way down to Panama. If we handle it properly, we can bring about positive change. If we turn our back, whoever can wield the biggest sword becomes the warlord.

This was the picture of what military forces in El Salvador looked like in the early 1980s. However—I give credit to our MTTs [Mobile Training Teams]—by 1990, the Salvadorans built themselves into a very good modern military force with a solid NCO corps. This progress helped to bring the FMLN to the peace table. They realized that they could not win a military victory.

Working in Latin America isn't for everybody. I've had some good friends in Special Forces, who once they got south, really didn't like the conditions working with the campesinos. It wasn't what they expected. An awful lot of them transferred to Delta Force [top-secret counterterrorist unit] and have done quite well. Because Delta is primarily "direct action." And that is what they wanted to begin with.

Campesinos throughout Central America are tremendously friendly. For many years I was a Special Forces medic, which opened a lot of doors to me. Because I would become the medical authority in a province. And as long as Uncle Sam keeps providing the medicine, you can treat an awful lot of people who come from miles around to see you.

In Costa Rica, a farmer rode over the top of a mountain on his horse to tell me his wife was sick. I went back with him. It turned out to be a very minor illness. The next morning at sunup he was at my door with a big stack of tortillas about yea high. That was his way to thank me for my effort.

You've heard of war brides. We have a good percentage of Latina wives in our Group. It's a real pain for our guys to deal with Immigration red tape to get their wives into the country. When she gets here, she goes through additional stress. Because if she speaks English, it's usually not very good. And when her husband redeploys, she feels like she is stranded.

On many of our deployments we can't talk about where we're going or what we're doing. And we often can't write or use the telephone. We've lost some great young soldiers because they have a wife and kids they love, and they don't want to lose them. During a six-year period, I was deployed nine to eleven months out of every year.

My wife is from my hometown. We've been through a lot together in the twenty years we've been married. She's raised our kids pretty much by herself. I'd come home, change a few things, then I'd leave again. That's hard. Especially when kids reach adolescence and need Dad around.

My boy is now an eighteen-year-old senior in high school. He plays football and is on the wrestling team. When he was fourteen, he was six feet tall. Like a bull in a china closet. He was hard for his mama to handle, because I wasn't around. In that regard, it was a blessing when I was assigned to staff for a year. It made a difference with me being home. He settled down.

WARRIOR SPIRIT

GENERAL ALFRED GRAY

The Pentagon 1987–91
Commandant
U.S. Marine Corps

In mid-1987, James Webb, one of the most highly decorated Marines of the Vietnam era, was a surprise choice as Secretary of the Navy. At the time an internal battle was being waged for the soul of the Marine Corps. Commanders of the bureaucratic mold were in the process of retiring all the old "gunfighters." Highly decorated field commanders such as Major Generals James Day and Ernie Cheetham and Lt. General Al Gray were perceived as outsiders, unsuited for roles in the halls of higher management. However, the Secretary of the Navy has the authority to submit his own nominee for Marine Corps commandant to the Secretary of Defense. Webb shook up the established order with an unconventional choice of a "mud Marine."

When you are a Lieutenant General [three stars] you have to put in your retirement papers four months ahead of time, because Congress has to approve your retirement. And my retirement date was July 1, 1987. I submitted my retirement papers to Secretary of the Navy John Lehman in March. Fortunately, he purposely stuck them in his desk drawer.

James Webb replaced Lehman as Secretary in April. I didn't have an idea about what Lehman had done with my resignation papers. I kept busy in the field observing training exercises. I got a call from Webb on May 6. He said, "I need to talk to you. What are you doing tomorrow?" I had to go to Fort Meade to attend an awards ceremony. After the ceremony ended, I told my aide, "Let's skip the luncheon and go to the Pentagon. So we can see Mr. Webb as early as possible and get the hell out of there." I wanted to get back to Norfolk because there was this crisis in Haiti. My Marines were on standby.

We're driving toward the Pentagon, it's around one P.M. The phone rings. It was an Air Force general who worked for Secretary of Defense Casper Weinberger. He said, "Mr. Weinberger heard that you might be around town today. Can you get here by one-fifteen?" I said, "Okay."

Mr. Weinberger asked me, "What are the two or three things that the Corps really has to focus on?" I said, "Externally we have to mend our fences with Congress. We've got to mend any negative perception around the United States [from the Beirut bombing and Marine embassy guard spy scandal] and prove that we are what we're supposed to be. Internally, the Corps needs to focus on fighting readiness. And not get too big for our britches."

Then he asked my worldview about Europe, NATO, the Pacific. After that, I left and went down to see Jim Webb. We had the same type of conversation. I thought they were using me as a sounding board. I went back to Norfolk and out to sea.

At the time, my mother's health was going downhill. She was in a nursing home and didn't have long to live. I had to take care of her. And, in preparation for retirement, my wife and I had to find a house to live in. I didn't have much money because my mother's health bills were pretty expensive. So I started looking for a job. Still, I intended to soldier on until my last day in command.

On May 1, I was in the field and went into New River to get a pump for a helicopter. Jim Webb was en route to his swearing-in ceremony in Annapolis. He called me from his car phone. He said, "I just want you to know that you are going to be Commandant of the Marine Corps." I was shocked.

My Senate confirmation process went very swiftly. I got sworn in by Jim and Mr. Weinberger six hours before my mandatory retirement.

As you move up the ladder as a senior commander, and get responsibility for more and more people, and your tactical and strategic responsibilities are that much greater, there is a danger that you can get callous toward the troops. My wife, Jan, and I said, "We'll never let that happen." We vowed, "We'll never walk by a corporal without saying hello."

There is a special relationship between the Commandant and the parents or guardians who send their sons and daughters to be Marines. They expect you to take care of them. People can talk about "unified commands," or the fact that in the Gulf War General Schwarzkopf and Marine General Walt Boomer were in charge of the war effort. But the greater Marine Corps family expects the Commandant to make sure that everything is all right.

You deal with that with, hopefully, enough experience and a little wisdom that has crept in along the way. Plus the advice and thoughts of the people who you serve, like the Secretaries of Defense and Navy, and the Commander in Chief. But like the Maneuver process, you rely on instinct where you think you can influence matters.

With the types of communications equipment we have today, you can travel anywhere and still be in command. My radio operators traveled with me. In a briefcase I had a satellite radio. I could talk to any level of classification to any commander of any service, anyplace in the world. The communication system also has fax capability. I could write a letter on an airplane and send it immediately.

Institutionally, I felt very strongly that we had to return to the idea that every Marine is a fighter. Because in the types of conflicts we face today, there are no longer distinctions between front lines and rear areas.

In the early 1970s, because of economics and other pressures, we had to depart from a time-honored tradition in the Marine Corps where everybody went through an infantry training regiment. So among the first things I did as Commandant was to initiate "Basic Warrior Training."

SCHOOL OF HARD KNOCKS

SERGEANT MAJOR DAVID SOMMERS

THE PENTAGON 1987–91
MARINE CORPS SERGEANT MAJOR

General Al Gray chose Sergeant Major David Sommers to be his right-hand man on all enlisted Marine matters, not only because of his rock-solid loyalty, but because Sommers is not afraid to speak his mind to anyone about tough or controversial issues.

In June 1987 I had just arrived at Quantico to be the Director of the Staff NCO Academy. I was there only seven days when General Al Gray called late in the evening. He told me that I was going to be his Sergeant Major of the Marine Corps. I had a four-day transition.

I had served with General Gray when he was a brigadier. And he was my division commander during the Beirut period. From the start, General Gray made a comment to me, "Sergeant Major, we're going to take care of our people. And we're going to have fun doing it." When he said "take care of our people," he meant global training programs and revamping the structure.

Having James Webb as Secretary of the Navy helped. Because as a former Marine, he knew what it was like to be at the fighting hole level. Webb and Gray were a good team. After the Corps had gone through the Beirut tragedy, we were still struggling within ourselves. We needed to change directions. We needed to make things happen quickly.

In my opinion, we were recruiting quality people. But there was not the warrior spirit that we should've had in the Corps, from top to bottom. General Gray sparked that. I don't believe we intended to change Doctrine more than returning to the basic fundamental: "Every Marine is a rifleman."

The Corps always maintained that idea, but because of budget restraints, the Corps had to stop sending everybody through infantry training. General Gray required that additional time be added to recruit training and that everyone go through the School of Infantry.

We had been struggling with professional education for enlisted Marines for quite some time. The Corps was behind all the other services in enlisted education. Much of our professional education for staff NCOs was literally done in the "school of hard knocks." We learned from each other. And we learned from "staff calls" where a sergeant major would conduct classes.

Because of the groundwork of my predecessors, we established enlisted directors at the staff NCO academies. We were the last branch of service to come on line with that. We've opened more academies, but we've got a long way to go. We're able to get into more advanced training for staff NCOs because of training programs at lower ranks.

Staff NCOs and sergeants major shouldn't have an outside agenda. Our job is to make sure that the commander's programs work. And that was a handful under General Gray . . . we were moving fast.

I traveled extensively with the Commandant. Whenever he visited Marines, I was with him. When he went to an officers' function, I went off to do my own thing. Then, on the airplane, after a stop, we'd compare notes. The whole time, my agenda was to make sure that the programs the Commandant was putting into effect would work. If I found glitches within a program, I would be quick to tell him.

I would not only visit Marines on the division and air-wing level. I spent a lot of time with my battalion sergeants major—the guys at the fighting hole level. If there was a problem, I'd get the master gunnery sergeants together to discuss solutions.

I'd always ask the same question, "Does your superior know about the problem?" If not, I made them go back to brief their respective superiors, just so we all read from the same sheet of music. I didn't want any back-dooring going on. We lay it on the table.

I turned off a lot of hullabaloo, too. I'd be preparing to go somewhere, and they'd mail me an itinerary. I'd draw a big red X through the paper and send it back to them. I said, "We'll do whatever the resident battalion sergeant major recommends."

I agreed with General Gray's premise to give "warriors" a place in decision-making again. Within the Corps, I feel that the word "manager" should not be in any book we have. "Leader" covers it all. If you are a good leader, you will have those skills that the civilian community points to in a good manager.

General Gray brought in Marines with different talents and meshed them together. He kept all of his three-star generals involved and in decision-making. They all had a play in final decisions. And he allowed all Marines to have a voice in the future of the Corps.

We got tons of letters from everyone—privates to retired and active generals—with recommendations on how to do things better. When I received letters, I always sent them directly to the General. Before his staff got them, he would write a comment on the letter.

I was with the General one day when he went to Quantico to hang a medal on a lance corporal for an idea he submitted on an infrared system. Although he was a young enlisted man, he had a good idea. The General wanted all Marines to know that they had a play in what goes on in the Corps. If you were a Marine and had a good idea, General Gray wanted to hear it.

WHO GOES THERE?

MAJOR GENERAL
BERNARD LOEFFKE

PANAMA 1987–89
COMMANDING GENERAL
U.S. ARMY SOUTH

Major General Bernard Loeffke was Commanding General of U.S. Army South, the Army's headquarters in Panama, responsible for activities in Latin America. This headquarters contributed the Joint Task Force Panama during the period of hostility that led to Operation Just Cause. A soldier/diplomat, between 1959 and 1971 he served three combat tours in Vietnam as a Special Forces operative, an advisor to a Vietnamese paratroop unit, and commander of an American infantry battalion. After the war, in addition to White House duties, he served in the U.S. Embassy in Moscow as the Army Attaché, and as the U.S. Defense Attaché to China.

After General Manuel Noriega stole the 1988 presidential election, people were peacefully protesting in the street and getting beaten up. Noriega's "Dobermans"—the security thugs—were out in the streets twenty-four hours a day. I spent a year and a half watching Panamanians being brutalized by Noriega's Popular Defense Forces [PDF].

U.S. Military Headquarters was not in downtown Panama City. But I had 1,200 U.S. military families living downtown. During the riots, my wife and I made it a point at least three evenings a week to visit the riot areas. There was no electricity, no water in many of the apartments. Our visit was to reassure the military families. But when Noriega's forces became confrontational, we had to withdraw those families from their homes.

While I was a commanding general in Panama, leading up to Operation Just Cause, we had fifty-nine firefights with Noriega's people. We protected my soldiers by using deception. I learned the value of deception during my three years as Defense Attaché in China.

I thought I knew something about war, until I went to China and saw their deception techniques. I had already been in combat for four years, during three tours of Vietnam. And I had been Army Attaché in the Soviet Union. But when a Chinese general walks into a base, the first thing he looks for is the ways that his troops might deceive the enemy. Second, he looks at the camouflage.

Taking this into account, we designed our defensive setup in Panama. Noriega's forces would probe our defenses by firing at American checkpoints on roads. Their objective was to provoke us into firing back into civilian traffic. Their goal was to create a popular reaction against the American presence. So, we had to create very restrictive rules of engagement. It took incredible self-control not to respond.

We never had enough people, so I had to put a maintenance battalion on guard duty. One young female said, "General, how many times do I have to yell 'Halt' before I do something?"

That was a good question, because the PDF knew what our rules were—we didn't put a bullet in a rifle chamber unless we felt that bodily harm would be committed to our people. The procedure was to yell "Halt" in Spanish. If they continued forward, and you could identify that a person was armed, then you could chamber the round. Then you yelled, "Halt, or I will fire."

We knew that members of Noriega's Dignity Battalions were trained to infiltrate American bases. So we ordered deception to be integrated into our defensive tactics. Before our soldiers went out on guard duty, each one had to build a life-size mannequin. I ordered that the dummies be made fully visible, in case there was a sniper attack.

We put our people ten feet away from the dummy guard. Every forty-five minutes we moved the silhouette to give the illusion of movement. We had two dummies that were fired on. They saved the lives of the real guards.

One night I was the biggest "dummy," because I spoke to

one of these decoys for at least forty-five seconds. A signal unit had placed a dummy with a helmet and a rubber M-16 rifle. They rigged it like a puppet with an audio voice recorder. When I approached, the dummy came out of the dark. I heard, *"Halt!"* The "guard" pulled his weapon forward. I hear *"Who goes there?"* I identified myself. *"Advance and be recognized."* I was embarrassed and proud to find that the real guard was a signal sergeant who was pulling a cord in the shadows. He received the ingenuity award we gave each night to soldiers who built the most realistic decoy.

EL BRUJO: THE MAGICIAN

COLONEL LAYTON DUNBAR

PANAMA 1988–90
ARMY ATTACHÉ
U.S. EMBASSY

I first met Manuel Noriega in 1973 or '74. Back then he was a lieutenant colonel and the Panamanian Chief of Intelligence. He wrote a book about psychological operations and thought that he was an expert on it. He certainly tried to use his style of psyops on his own people, on American forces, and on the region.

After his 1989 electoral loss, he created and armed so-called "Dignity Battalions" to intimidate his democratic opposition. The battalions were nothing more than a bunch of thugs. He would move them into a more wealthy section of town to seize the neighborhood for a day. Just to make a point.

The harassment of U.S. military personnel was going on for many years. It increased greatly right before Operation Just Cause. It got out of hand with a U.S. Marine lieutenant being killed, and some rather cruel harassment of a Navy commander and his wife.

Dictators like Noriega or Saddam Hussein's primary use of psychological operations is using the Big Lie, total deceit and manipulation. That's exactly opposite of the way that U.S. Army Psyops people conduct ourselves.

Operation Just Cause began at 12:30 A.M. on December 20, 1989. The Army's 75th Ranger regiment and a Psyops loudspeaker team were parachuted on to Torrijos International Airport and the military garrison at Rio Jarra. Other loudspeaker teams were air-dropped under fire with the 82nd Airborne Division at Torrijos airfield. Loudspeaker teams offered the Panamanian military the option to surrender.

And Psyop loudspeaker teams were involved with the Army's 7th Infantry Division, as units tracked down Noriega's PDF and Dignity Battalion soldiers. The main concern was to warn innocent Panamanians who might get caught in a cross fire. Each infantry company involved had a two-man loudspeaker team attached. They broadcasted into neighborhoods before clearing clusters of buildings, to calm civilians and give them a chance to clear out. Without Psyops, the civilian casualty toll would have been much higher.

A radio station, the Voice of Liberty, was set up in mobile transmitters that went on the air as the first shots were fired. They broadcasted twenty-four hours a day for the first four days. It was estimated that most Panamanians who listened to the radio were tuned to the Voice of Liberty for information they could trust.

An Army Psyops unit took over a national television station, to show videos of ongoing military action. In commercials produced by Psyop broadcasters, Noriega's wealth and greed was juxtaposed against a backdrop of ordinary people's poverty and despair.

Other Psyop specialists printed leaflets and pamphlets. These included "Safe Conduct" passes for Noriega's soldiers who wished to surrender. At the site of a fierce firefight, our Marines dropped 20,000 of the Safe Conduct passes. The next morning, Psyop loudspeaker teams voiced the same message. The entire PDF battalion surrendered without firing another shot.

Noriega fled into a church. U.S. Army troops surrounded the building. A loudspeaker system was set up. What got the most media attention was the use of rock music to try to drive him to surrender.

I'm not exactly sure if that was thought up by a Psyops specialist or by the infantry people involved. I do know that the Psyop Commander still rues the day that it was filmed on CNN. After negotiations, Noriega did surrender. But now the public image of Psyops is rock music at 150 decibels.

CLEAR CUT OBJECTIVE

GENERAL COLIN POWELL

PENTAGON 1989–1993
CHAIRMAN
JOINT CHIEFS OF STAFF

In Panama, Operation Just Cause was not simply to remove Manuel Noriega. The clear-cut objective was the removal of the Panamanian government as it then existed, and the installation of the democratically elected government. That is a very important difference. Before the operation, we [the Joint Chiefs] made that clear in our advisory meetings with the Secretary of Defense and the President.

A lot of the reason for defining our objective in these terms came from my previous experience as the National Security Advisor [to President Ronald Reagan, 1987–89]. Watching Panama for those two years, it was clear that Noriega wasn't the ultimate problem. But the Panamanian Defense Force [PDF] was. We couldn't solve the problem just by getting rid of Noriega. He was a product of the PDF. And the PDF kept bringing up one thug after another. So if Noriega got hit by a bus, there were twelve other thugs in line waiting to take his place.

I told President Bush, "If you want democracy in Panama, it's not a matter of sending Noriega into retirement. If you ever have to use the armed forces of the United States to resolve this problem, our recommendation is that you select a political objective to remove the PDF." The political leadership said, "That sounds right." And we devised a military plan.

So, it wasn't that we used 26,000 troops to "take out Noriega." We used that many troops to take out the Panamanian military and to protect the installation of the democratically elected government.

PARACHUTE ASSAULT

COMMAND SERGEANT MAJOR
WILLIAM MCBRIDE

PANAMA 1989
DIVISION SERGEANT MAJOR
82ND AIRBORNE DIVISION

Sergeant Major McBride spent twenty-six out of his thirty-four years on active duty as a member of the 82nd Airborne, the last of the Army's legendary paratroop divisions. His seven years, 1984–91, as division sergeant major, may be a modern record for longevity. In the 82nd's parachute assault into Panama, at fifty-one years old, he jumped in the first wave of paratroopers.

The 82nd is the only active airborne division. In peacetime there is no other unit that exercises the courage that it takes to jump out of an airplane. It takes some balls to jump out of an airplane at 800 feet at night, loaded down like a pack mule. Not knowing what you're going to land on, or whether your chute will open.

Paratroopers do that routinely. They have to be able to control their emotions and their fear. They have to pay attention to minute detail. A guy is not going out the door of an aircraft unless he feels confident that his stuff is squared away. And confidence that his leaders are going to put him in the right place.

On December 20, 1989, during Operation Just Cause, I parachuted onto Panama's main airport to help set up the Division Assault CP [command post] on the main runway. I followed General James Johnson, the division commander, out of the airplane door.

We had three Assault Day objectives: One was Panama Viejo, which was the Panamanian cavalry and special opera-

166

tions forces base. One of our battalions was to take out Camp Cimmaron, the Panamanian Airborne School and all their training facilities. And the worst resistance was a hilltop called Tinajidas where our troops received heavy mortar and automatic weapons fire.

On D-Day we had four KIAs [killed] and more than 100 WIA [wounded]. Actually, more casualties than we had in the Persian Gulf War. More fighting, too. And our airplane trip from North Carolina was an adventure in itself.

We went into Panama on a nasty night. We departed from Pope Air Force Base, next to Fort Bragg, during an ice storm. We were due to leave in a twenty-aircraft formation. But ice was forming on the runway. They flew de-icers in from around the country trying to keep all the airplanes in flying condition. Because the planes kept icing up, we managed to get only eight aircraft off. That concerned everybody because the operation was to begin with Army Rangers attacking the military airfield at one A.M. Our mission was to arrive around 1:50 A.M. to knock out the lower half of the airfield—the Torrijos International Airport—and to reinforce the Rangers.

The first eight aircraft went into Panama over Torrijos Airport at 2:11 A.M. We came in over the coast forty-five seconds before reaching the airfield. All the lights at Torrijos had been knocked out by earlier fighting. It was dark as hell. I was standing in the airplane doorway behind the Commanding General. Despite the darkness, I could look down and see the difference between the ocean and the ground.

The Rangers were still fighting as we prepared to jump. We could see firefights taking place around the main airport terminal and the adjoining buildings.

Coming over Torrijos, our heavy platforms had been dropped five minutes before we came in. That included Sheridan armored vehicles, TOW missiles, and transport vehicles. The plan was to miss the runway, because they wanted it clear for subsequent aircraft landings. But they actually put the platforms too far off. They landed in swamps, with sixty percent outside of the airfield fence.

The platforms have small chemical lights. Before the aircrafts drop their loads, the crew breaks open the lights as an indicator to following aircraft where the parachutes land. When our airplane flew over the airfield, we saw the chemlights from the heavy drop.

I was on the lead aircraft that flew in at 500 feet. Each air-

craft after that was at intervals of fifty feet higher. It was a
safety factor—the Air Force didn't want to fly into any troops
jumping out of airplanes in front of them.

I rarely have any apprehension about jumping. But I was ap-
prehensive about jumping at 500 feet. Because I knew my reserve parachute couldn't be used if my main chute didn't open.

As soon as we jumped from the airplane I could see that we
were coming down to the right of the airfield. It took around
thirty seconds to reach the ground. We did not expect to land
in ten-foot-high elephant grass and swamp. There were approximately 105 soldiers in each aircraft, so we had around 850
people, most of whom were groping around in that swamp.

When I landed, I quickly got out of my parachute gear, recovered my equipment, and started moving toward the airfield.
The apprehension went away. I just focused on what I had to
do and started moving. We knew what direction we had to go,
but we couldn't see. It was darker than the dickens. The elephant grass was taller than us, and we were splashing in water.

There were explosions and a lot of shooting going on in the
northern portion of the International Airport. Some of our people landed at the juncture between the international and the
military airports, right in the middle of a firefight between the
Rangers and the PDF [Noriega's Popular Defense Forces].
What added to the confusion, an overdue civilian airliner
landed just before the Rangers jumped in there. Around 300 civilian passengers were in the terminal.

In the swamp, we didn't have any direct fire, but you didn't
have to be shot at to have your adrenaline flowing. Everybody
I came across had their weapons ready, challenging people
with the password. Some soldiers were misoriented and walking in the wrong direction. I knew we landed east of the airfield and I could hear the shooting and fighting and helicopters
flying around. So I moved in that direction.

My responsibility was to assist the Commanding General.
But we were separated when we jumped from the aircraft. I
tried looking for him but we couldn't find each other in the elephant grass. A guy could be twenty feet away and you
wouldn't know that he was there. And we were separated from
the General's two radio operators, his aide and his driver. Fortunately, we had preplanned the mission well. Everybody knew
where their battalion and company assembly area was on the
airfield.

The airfield was only about 250 to 300 meters away. But

cutting our way through the elephant grass, carrying the heavy loads on our backs—55 to 90 pounds of equipment—it took about an hour to get to the airfield. I was exhausted. I gathered up around twenty disoriented troops as I was working my way toward the airfield.

There was an eight- to ten-foot-high chain-link fence with barbed wire around the entire airfield. Most of our troops had to climb over that fence or cut their way through it. We all had wire cutters—our bayonets.

My Assault CP assembly area was at the southern tip of the airfield. The General and I linked up at the southern area, and we waited for his aide and driver. The aide finally came by, and he went out to find our command vehicle that was lost in the heavy drop.

The General and I walked about a hundred meters when a Signal Battalion vehicle drove by. I commandeered it. I told the Signal driver, "You are now driving for the Commanding General." And we climbed in. We drove down the runway where we met our G3 [Operations officer] had set up the Division Assault Command Post with his radio operators. We were around three-quarters of a mile from the international terminal. At that time, the General got together with the radio operators and started getting reports from the units. After daylight we moved our CP into an Eastern Airlines building, right next to the main terminal.

As division sergeant major, my responsibility was to take care of the Commanding General. I made it a practice to keep track of our casualties. We had some minor injuries from jumping into the swamp—like sprained ankles and broken bones.

I also checked on the medical facilities that we established at the airfield. I monitored all of our assembly reports. What made things difficult was that our vehicle, with all of our radios, was lost for two days in the swamp.

The 82nd had three critical air assault missions with helicopters that we were supposed to do before daylight. In the first wave, we had a mixed force on the ground. Portions of some units were without commanders who were on other aircrafts that hadn't taken off.

We were very anxious to get the air assaults started as soon as we could. We worked real hard at coordinating with Army aviation to establish pickup zones for the three battalions. In the meantime, the other twelve aircraft arrived as soon as they could get de-iced at Pope. Three planes arrived after four A.M., another couple planes arrived after five. The last load of troops didn't arrive until between eight and nine A.M.

After everybody got organized, we airlifted the battalions off to their objectives. [The first assault departed near seven A.M.] Doing them in daylight probably caused us casualties. The majority of our casualties resulted on the first day. After we sent the air assaults to their objectives, we had to send their vehicles loaded with supplies and equipment from the airfield to link up with the troops at their objectives. We used light tanks and MP [military police] gun jeeps as escorts. Every one of our convoys were hit with ambushes and sniper fire the first two days. We lost two KIAs in the convoys. We had around 130 people wounded during the operation. Most of those wounded resulted from the convoy operations.

In the air assaults, our 2nd Battalion/504th Infantry went into a place called Panama Viejo, a PDF cavalry base along the coast. They did an air assault right on the beach. And the 1st Battalion/504th was airlifted into a place called Tinajitas, where they had to take a PDF camp on top of a hill. They had two KIA from mortars and machine-gun fire. The General and I took off by helicopter to visit those units.

In retrospect, we later downplayed the initial air drop as a problem. But it took three or four days to recover all of our heavy gear from the swamp. We had to search the area and lift vehicles out with helicopters. But we didn't want to bad-mouth the Air Force. It was an intangible that happens in war. And they had to bust their butts to initially overcome severe problems from ice-storm conditions. They tried to do everything we asked for.

If we had to do it over again, we might have planned to drop everything on the runway. From the lessons learned from both Grenada and Panama, we will always parachute assault if we have that option.

For Grenada, our soldiers went in rigged to jump. But while they were en route, our commanding general got the word that the perimeter around the airfield was secure. So he decided not to jump. In fact, when their aircraft landed, they took some fire. The problem became the length of time it took to land and unload the airplanes. There is a limitation on how many aircraft you can fit on a runway.

The airfield could only fit two C-141s and five C-130s. It

took forever to unload everybody, taxi those airplanes around and move them out.

If those soldiers had jumped in, it would have taken seventy seconds to get the entire task force on the ground. That's why wherever we go from now on we will jump. There aren't a lot of airfields, particularly in Latin and South America, that can handle huge C-141 and C-5 transport airplanes. That's where our airborne division is valuable. We can put a lot of firepower on the ground very quickly.

Grenada also taught us the need for joint operations compatibility among the services. We had some bad problems with the Navy CINCLANT [Atlantic Command, in charge of the Grenada operation]. Navy staff planners didn't understand what Army units could do. And our airborne division could have exchanged some liaison people with the Army Rangers, but that didn't happen. The special operations community was paranoid about security. They didn't even want to talk with their own people. But the Army learned from Grenada the need to talk with each other; for units to exchange liaisons and be willing to do some planning ahead of time. That later paid off big in the Persian Gulf.

Panama was the first operation after the Joint Command was restructured through the Goldwater-Nichols [Congressional] legislation. In fact, Just Cause was the best joint operation I've seen. It wasn't on the scale of Desert Storm. But in many ways it was more complicated. We were engaging the enemy at much closer distances, in both urban and jungle terrain.

NIGHT FIGHTERS

BRIGADIER GENERAL
JOSEPH "KEITH" KELLOGG

PANAMA 1989
BRIGADE COMMANDER
TASK FORCE ATLANTIC, 7TH INFANTRY DIVISION

Operation Just Cause was the first real-world test for the 7th Infantry Division, the all-volunteer Army's light infantry specialists. Colonel Keith Kellogg, Commander of the brigade of the 7th—code-named Task Force Atlantic—sent to Panama, was one of the few Vietnam veterans involved.

When people say to me, "The Army did a really great job in Desert Storm," I respond, "You missed the earlier signal. Our performance in Panama showed what we are capable of doing."

I went to Panama for Operation Just Cause as commander of one of the assault brigades. The operation was divided into different task forces. Task Force Pacific was the 82nd Airborne. Task Force Red was the Rangers. Task Force Semper Fi was a Marine Corps battalion. Task Force Bayonet was the 193rd Infantry Brigade. And Task Force Atlantic was my brigade of the 7th Infantry Division.

We arrived in October 1989, a week after some of Noriega's security forces attempted a coup and failed. General Maxwell Thurman had just taken command of SOUTHCOM [U.S. Southern Command]. Within three weeks we were planning for Just Cause. The idea was for us to be ready in case another coup happened.

My task force was on the Atlantic Coast of Panama. We had responsibility for the city of Colon, the Gatun Locks, and Fort Espinar on the north end of the Panama Canal. A place called Renacer Prison held about 350 prisoners. They included mem-

172

bers of the failed October coup and political opposition parties. We pulled out some American prisoners, too.

In my brigade, the only combat veterans were the sergeants major and one or two other NCOs. For everybody else, from battalion commanders on down, it was their first time under fire.

The 7th Division's light infantry concept is to fight at night in urban terrain, in close-quarters battle. All Just Cause attacks were to commence at one A.M. in a coordinated operation. We chose the middle of the night to start the operation for a lot of reasons. First, we fight at night probably better than any other army in the world. Second, most people in the city would be asleep and not out in the streets, which would reduce civilian casualties.

The biggest fight we had was with a Panamanian naval infantry [marine] company at Coco Solo. Right next to the barracks was a garment factory/restaurant/nursery. In the nursery were kids whose mothers worked in the factory.

For this target, as with the city of Colon, I discussed with General Carl Stiner [XVIII Airborne Corps commander], "We've got to go at night. Because if we have to take this target down, there's too much of a chance of innocent people being hurt."

When we launched the attack, the nursery was empty and the factory was empty. But the restaurant was occupied by the family that lived there. What happened next is one of the great stories of fire discipline of the American soldier.

We used loudspeakers to give Noriega's troops the option to surrender. They fired back. We increased the fire and maneuvered on them. Some soldiers silently moved up to the target and went into the restaurant. The Chinese family—a large extended family—that owned the restaurant didn't hear us coming. We immediately seized control of them, passed them quickly through our lines and continued the assault.

In the ensuing firefight, not a single family member was hurt. The restaurant was a bit damaged, but the people were okay. For almost all of my guys, it was their first combat experience. This made it especially impressive that they had the discipline to hold back their fire until the family was safe.

We also had to go into the city of Colon, which is on a peninsula. It has a very narrow land neck to get into the city, with a two-lane highway. We thought that maybe Noriega might be there. So we cut the city off. We had helicopter gunships and other aircraft available. But we didn't want to use them, for fear of civilian casualties.

Colon is an old city built around the turn of the century. A lot of wooden and adobe buildings are very close together. There was the possibility for a very large fire sweeping through sections of town. I said, "We're not going to risk that. No tac air [jet fighter bombers]. We'll take it from the ground. We're good enough and smart enough to do it without using close air support." And we did. Literally, street by street.

The PDF had some snipers. But they got the hint real fast that our snipers were better than theirs. One of the places we had to take down in Colon was their FBI/Secret Service building. We went at it intensely. We called in a helicopter gunship, which was shot out of the sky, killing two pilots.

We called through a loudspeaker, "Come out. You're surrounded." They opened fire. So I called for direct fire from our 105mm artillery. They put five rounds into the building. That's when the PDF people said, "Can we talk about this?"

There were two commanders of Noriega's security forces named del Cid. One was the Military Zone 2 commander in Colon. The PDF soldiers had taken their uniforms off and melted into the city. But we had it surrounded and they couldn't get out. So, del Cid came out in civilian clothes, wanting to negotiate.

He pretended that he didn't speak English. But I knew he did. He said, "We're not going to negotiate." I said, "Here's the terms: Your forces come out now. Surrender now. Or we're going to come in and get you. There's no negotiations." He went back into the city and brought out 200 PDF soldiers.

Our Panama experience proved that, "You fight as you train." And we trained very hard. The combat came as rote. By six A.M.—five hours after H-Hour—we completed all targets.

CENTCOM

REAR ADMIRAL WILLIAM FOGARTY

MacDill Air Force Base and Middle East 1987–91
Director, Plans and Policy and Joint
[Naval] Task Force
U.S. Central Command

In 1980, President Jimmy Carter stated that the United States was prepared to use military force to protect "vital Western interests" in the Persian Gulf. This was due to the rise of radical Muslim fundamentalism, increasing terrorism, and the invasion of Afghanistan by Iran's neighbor, the Soviet Union. There was growing fear that the Soviets would try to sweep into Iran's southern oil fields, and move from there into the Arabian peninsula. And any limited U.S. response to hostilities by radicals in the region could quickly escalate into a superpower confrontation.

In response, the Pentagon formed the Rapid Deployment Force, consisting of the 1st Marine Division, the Army's 82nd Airborne Division, Navy and Air Force elements, and secret special operations projects, in order to quickly respond to any form of crisis in the Persian Gulf area.

The failure of the Desert One hostage rescue attempt led to the reorganization of the Rapid Deployment Force into the joint Central Command or CENTCOM. The command's area of responsibility covers Southwest Asia, the Horn of Africa, and the Persian Gulf.

I got involved in Middle East Operations in July 1987, in the heat of the [oil] "Tanker War" during the Iran-Iraq conflict. I was Commander of Amphibious Group Two in Norfolk, Virginia, when I got a call from the Chief of Naval Personnel on a Monday, telling me, "You are to report to Central Command at MacDill Air Force Base in Florida on Wednesday."

I had no academic expertise related to that part of the world.

My master's degree in International Relations focused mostly on the Soviet Union and China.

I reported to Central Command as their Director for Plans and Policy. CENTCOM's responsibility is the Persian Gulf region. There is an argument made that CENTCOM should also cover Israel, Syria, and Libya within a Theater umbrella. But policymakers opted not to assign that. Arab-Israeli matters were given to CINCEUROPE. So there is some interface between commanders.

During Desert Storm, the CINCCENTCOM [Commander in Chief of Central Command] General Norman Schwarzkopf, and CINCEUR General John Galvin, were able to work together well.

CENTCOM was one of the first truly joint operations. Interservice rivalries and lack of cooperation in the Rapid Deployment Force was evident in the failed 1980 Desert One hostage rescue attempt in Iran. The turning point in joint operations was the 1983 Grenada invasion. General Schwarzkopf was one of the commanders of that operation.

Previously, the Navy was in charge of operations like the Cuban Missile Crisis and Grenada. In Vietnam, we did our own thing. The Navy went through an evolutionary change in the way we do business during the Iran-Iraq War. First we had a Marine joint commander at CENTCOM in General Crisp, and then an Army commander in General Schwarzkopf. It took a while to get some of the old ideas and preconceived notions of "Navy only" changed, to effectively coordinate.

When I got to CENTCOM there were very few Navy people. It was mostly Army, Air Force, and Marine. There was no naval base near Tampa, Florida.

The United States interest in the Iran-Iraq War was a maritime operation. The Army and Marine leadership at CENTCOM didn't understand things like naval mine warfare and how ships operate and communicate. Just like I wouldn't understand armor warfare or field artillery.

The Navy was given a key role because of the sea lift involved. But the Marine Corps and the Army were the main players. The original objective was to prevent a Soviet land attack into Iran from going any farther. After the Soviet invasion of Afghanistan in 1979, there was a real fear that they would try to expand farther south, into the Gulf region.

The Navy's role in CENTCOM was originally envisioned to lift soldiers and Marines on rapid deployment. Other than that, the Navy didn't have an awful lot of tasks. Except for antimining and some escort roles.

In 1987, both Iran and Iraq were attacking shipping coming in and out of each country. Shortly after I arrived at CENTCOM, the decision was made to form a Joint [Naval] Task Force. Until then we had a naval command called the Middle East Task Force, with a relatively small staff. It was primarily a political/military operation.

The Joint Task Force was primarily Navy, with some Air Force AWAC early warning aircraft stationed in Saudi Arabia. We found a void in our attack helicopter capability. So some Army OH-58D helos were deployed on Navy ships. The OH-58D is a small gunship with night vision ability, .50-caliber machine gun, and Hellfire missiles. I have to admire Army aviation people. They did not have an easy job, adapting to living on ships and a totally new mission at sea.

We went into the Tanker War precariously, without many minesweepers. A decision had been made in Washington that the European allies should provide mine clearing for NATO, and we relied on the Japanese in the Pacific. That gave the budgetary naysayers all the ammunition they needed to claim that minesweeping ships were not a good option to spend money on.

With CENTCOM completely ensconced in the Iran-Iraq War, war plans for fighting the Soviets in Iran went to the back burner. Because while the Soviets were bogged down in Afghanistan, the Iran-Iraq War threatened international shipping. There were 150 to 200 merchant ships anchored outside the Gulf, primarily oil tankers, waiting for things to quiet down. And the insurance rates went so high that it became not profitable to carry oil. The shortfall would cause the price of oil to skyrocket.

The tanker companies feared their ships would be sunk and their employees killed. Because every day ships were being attacked inside the Gulf by small boats with rockets and grenade launchers. The Iranian navy would pull right up alongside tankers and shoot at the bridge area of the ships with rockets. Newspapers were filled with pictures of burning tankers.

Until then, none of the post–World War II naval technology or weapons systems had been tested in combat. Korea and Vietnam weren't really tests because we didn't have a navy against us, except for our brown-water riverine patrol crafts that had to deal with mines and ambushes from land.

The Joint Task Force gave us the capability to jointly plan not only defensive, but offensive operations. In April 1988, we attacked Iranian patrol boats in response to the USS *Roberts* hitting a mine. We did some pretty major damage to some of their oil platforms. This was a minor precursor to what followed after Iraq invaded Kuwait.

At CENTCOM, I not only directed the Navy's plans and policy, I traveled to the Gulf region several times, coordinating for all services. I was on the road around once a month with General Crisp and his successor, General Schwarzkopf. We looked at various plans and made sure that the region's leaders knew that we had the resolve to stay. That we weren't going to run away like we did in Beirut. This was an important issue to our allies.

I don't believe that the Iranians thought that we would stay the course once they started attacking tankers. They thought that they could force us out of the region by the threat of bloodshed. And later Saddam Hussein felt that we couldn't handle a potential "Vietnam" type of situation, where our military is deployed far from home and our young people being killed.

TOMORROW

MAJOR GENERAL JAMES DAY

CAMP PENDLETON, CALIFORNIA 1978–81
COMMANDING GENERAL
1ST MARINE DIVISION

I was the commander of the original Marine Corps division in the Rapid Deployment Force, now called CENTCOM. Everywhere I went, people would talk about the "awesome responsibility" of a division commander: You've got 20,000 people. They've all got problems every day. You're responsible if they live or die. And that responsibility causes a lot of stress.

Well, I'd like to walk those experts through one day of combat. And compare their description of a general's "awesome responsibility" with that of an infantry fire team or squad leader—usually a young nineteen-year-old corporal.

When I look back on my combat experience, the guy who holds it all together is that small unit leader. He starts out in the morning, making sure that his men have ammunition, water, and food. Makes sure that they know what the plan is on moving out. If they get into a firefight and any of them get wounded, he takes care of them and evacuates them. If any are dead, he makes sure their bodies are wrapped in a poncho. Gets ready to attack an enemy position, and after taking it, gets his people reorganized and tries to keep them together. And then takes another position, or two or three that day, until he accomplishes the mission.

He had orders from the platoon leader or sergeant. But he didn't have anyone telling him the best course to take. He had to do it himself. When night comes, he has to dig in and get back in the foxhole again, one more time. He may get two or three hours sleep, at most.

On the other hand, the division commander gets up in the morning at headquarters after having a good night's sleep between sheets or in a warm sleeping bag. Has a prepared meal. After breakfast, his aides come to brief him—usually eighteen to twenty people. They advise him on what to do or not to do.

Then, during daylight hours he probably goes to visit different units to find out how they are doing. During lunchtime another good meal. And another good meal at night, followed by a briefing. After that he hits the sack, knowing that nobody is going to come crawling over the side of his bed with a knife.

Stand these two people side by side and ask them what they would like more than anything in the world. The division commander is going to say, "I want to accomplish my mission with the minimum loss of personnel."

If you ask that young corporal or sergeant, he'll tell you, "Tomorrow. I'd like to see tomorrow."

PART IV

Desert Storm

INVASION

REAR ADMIRAL
WILLIAM FOGARTY

PERSIAN GULF 1989–91
COMMANDER
JOINT TASK FORCE MIDDLE EAST

On August 2, 1991, Iraq invaded and swiftly overran the small oil-rich nation of Kuwait. The senior U.S. military officer in the area, with thirty-three years in the Navy, was Rear Admiral William Fogarty.

I was watching very closely as Iraqi forces built up and moved south toward Kuwait. But April Glaspie [U.S. Ambassador to Iraq] met with Saddam Hussein, and Saddam told President Mubarak of Egypt and King Hussein of Jordan, "I'm not going to invade Kuwait." A lot of people thought he wouldn't.

I had seen Ambassador Glaspie in May 1990, when she came into Kuwait to do some shopping. At the time, Saddam was saying, "Let's get the U.S. forces out of the Gulf. We don't need them here." He was lambasting the U.S. because of a human rights report that was critical of Iraq. Ambassador Glaspie told me that she thought Saddam was "just saber rattling," and not a whole lot would come of it.

After talking with Glaspie, I spoke with some Kuwaitis. They advised me that we'd better be very careful: "Watch closely what goes on." At the time, I was the highest ranking American military officer in the area. As a prudent commander, I increased the readiness of our Gulf forces. I only had seven ships—cruisers and frigates—with some light Army helicopters. Two of the frigates were scheduled to return home. There were no U.S. ground forces or fighter aircraft in Saudi Arabia. There were only a few Marines on my staff.

On the night of the invasion, August 1, I got a call from

General Norman Schwarzkopf. He said something like, "They've crossed the border. We think they're heading toward the southern oil fields. Keep your ships in the Gulf. We've got a couple of aircraft carriers on the way to join you. Carry out your plans."

The carrier *Independence* was immediately deployed from the Pacific, and the carrier *Eisenhower* in the Mediterranean was coming to the Red Sea. My immediate concern was that Saddam would attack our ships with his airplanes that carried Exocet missiles. He showed a capability during the Iran-Iraq War to do that very easily. His air force flew all the way down to almost the Straits of Hormuz—doing midair refueling—to attack Iranian ships. My next greatest concern was the threat of terrorism.

Saddam still had our Vietnam and Beirut experiences on his mind. He thought that we would respond to minor incidents with a show of force. But that we wouldn't have the stomachs for a major or prolonged conflict on the ground.

WHERE'S KUWAIT?

COLONEL JOHN SYLVESTER

SAUDI ARABIA 1990–91
BRIGADE COMMANDER
TIGER BRIGADE, 2ND ARMORED DIVISION

Colonel John Sylvester is a tall, straight-talking Texan and among the Army's premier experts on armored warfare. His first combat experience was as a young lieutenant with the 11th Armored Cavalry Regiment in Vietnam.

By the end of the Cold War, after the Berlin Wall was dismantled, the 2nd Armored Division was in the process of being deactivated (retired). The division had earned its battle ribbons under General George Patton in World War II, and the 1st Brigade's nickname, Tiger Brigade, came from destroying a large number of German "Tiger" tanks.

When I took over the Tiger Brigade in October 1989, by coincidence I had just read a novel called *Sword Point*. It's not a particularly scholarly piece, but the writer tells a good yarn about a war in the Persian Gulf. It is fiction, but I made it a "you'd better read this" item for my troops.

I assigned the book because there was a prevailing philosophy at Fort Hood that if we went to war, it would be in Europe. And I believed that we could be called anywhere in the world. So I used the book as a discussion tool.

On August 3, 1990, the morning after Iraq invaded Kuwait, my brigade was training in the field, and preparing to go to the National Training Center in the California desert. I walked into my field TOC [tactical operations center]. My staff said, "Did you hear what happened in Kuwait?"

My attitude was, "Where's Kuwait?"

I walked into the office of my S2 [Intelligence officer]. He had already cleaned off an entire side of his wall. On a huge map of the Middle East, he was writing the Iraqi order of battle.

On the morning of August 8, I took emergency leave to Brownsville, Texas, where my mother was in hospital intensive care. The next day my troops came in from the field. At seven-thirty that night we got alerted for the Gulf. They called me up and said, "Kiss everybody good-bye. Come back now."

Although the 2nd Division was being phased out, we were assigned to become the 3rd Brigade of the 1st Cavalry Division. They didn't have time to wait for a Reserve or National Guard unit to round them out.

Within two weeks, our equipment was loaded on trains and en route to the ports of Houston and Beaumont. On September 26, my soldiers began to fly to the Gulf. I flew out on October 10 with one of my infantry battalions.

We had around twenty-five to thirty people in the brigade who had served in combat—all were senior NCOs. But no officer, except myself, was a veteran.

GOOD-BYE KISS

BRIGADIER GENERAL
JOSEPH "KEITH" KELLOGG

SAUDI ARABIA 1990–91
CHIEF OF STAFF
82ND AIRBORNE DIVISION

After returning home from Operation Just Cause in Panama, Colonel Keith Kellogg spent six months with his brigade before receiving new orders.

I changed command from my brigade of the 7th Infantry Division at Fort Ord, California, on August 8, 1990. I was to be Chief of Staff of the 82nd Airborne Division. On Monday, August 6, I got a call from the 82nd's headquarters at Fort Bragg, North Carolina. Colonel Mike Owens, the secretary of the General Staff, said, "Is your change of command still on Wednesday?" I asked, "What's going on?" He said, "We just alerted our heavy brigade for Saudi Arabia."

The next day I got another call on the secure line. This time, "The entire division has been alerted. Can you get here right away?"

So I turned over my command at eleven A.M. on the eighth, and immediately flew to Fort Bragg. I reported in at 2300 hours that evening. I was in Saudi Arabia a week later.

Through all that, my wife had to drive across the country. She was pregnant. Our other child had chicken pox. She had never driven across country before. And we have a rather overweight rottweiler dog. All in all, it was an adventure. She arrived in four days. I took off for Saudi three days later.

The night I left my family, it was raining in North Carolina. It was eleven o'clock. My kids couldn't keep awake. I kissed them good-bye in their sleep. And I walked out the door.

My wife later wrote: "To see you leave was so dreary . . .

You've been to Panama and other places. But this is the first time I was really scared that you would not come back."

When we arrived in August, it was a David and Goliath situation. Colonel Ron Rokosz's brigade of 2,500 soldiers were out by themselves on the Kuwait border, facing the entire Iraqi 3rd Armor Corps, backed by Republican Guards. It was flat scary.

The total numbers in the Theater were estimated at 180,000 Iraqis to 20,000 Americans. The entire 82nd Airborne only has 15,000 soldiers. Our job was to hold the ports and the airfields.

Every night I checked my protective mask, checked that our vehicles were full of gas, and made sure that my people knew what to do if there was trouble.

TARGETS

GENERAL CHARLES HORNER

Saudi Arabia 1990–91
Commanding General
Central Command Air Forces

On August 9, one week after the Iraqi invasion of Kuwait, General Chuck Horner was made commander of all U.S. forces in Saudi Arabia as the air, land and sea buildup was under way. He held that position for a critical few weeks until General Norman Schwarzkopf returned from Washington.

When Desert Shield first started, General Schwarzkopf, before he left me in Saudi Arabia, told me, "I'm going to talk with the people in Washington and have them start a targeting effort like the one you briefed me with last April." [Related to a CENTCOM war game based on Schwarzkopf's premise that Iraq posed a serious threat.]

A few days later, after the initial target sites were reviewed in Washington, the Chief of Staff of the Air Force called me. He said, "We are going to work in these targets at the request of General Schwarzkopf. But you are the approval authority."

The Pentagon remembered the stupidity of Vietnam, where

the President picked targets. President Bush and Defense Secretary Cheney were both very sensitive about not getting into the targeting business. My deputy, Buster Glosson took these targets and built an integrated air campaign in Riyadh. We kept Washington, through Schwarzkopf, fully informed about everything we did. They made all the decisions on anything that had to do with policy. Anything that had to do with military matters, we made the decisions.

I was ready to retire on the spot if there was any undue pressure on the campaign that might have endangered the lives of my people. It was implicit in everything we did. I think Schwarzkopf felt the same way but never said it. I know that General John Yeosock of the Army felt that way. I'm sure that General Walt Boomer [Marine Corps central commander] and Admiral Stan Arthur [Navy central commander] felt the same way.

The Chief of Staff of the Air Force and I talked every day. But under the Goldwater/Nichols legislation, he couldn't direct me to do anything. I wasn't in his chain of command. I worked for General Schwarzkopf.

The balance of joint command is that Schwarzkopf worked for the Joint Chiefs of Staff, and they advise the Secretary of Defense. General Colin Powell, the Chairman of the Joint Chiefs, invited Secretary Cheney to participate fully in all chains of command. Of course, there was frustration in Washington, because a lot of very capable people wanted to be part of the war. But it wasn't going to work that way. The war had to be fought in the Theater.

My personal staff included people I had previously worked with. Major General Buster Glosson previously worked for me when he was a young commander. John Corder and I had been in Vietnam together and at the Pentagon. And my regular 9th Air Force staff people included "true grit" kind of guys like Jim Crigger and Jeff Feinstein, an ace fighter pilot in Vietnam. He's worked with me for four years, exercising various scenarios for the Middle East.

The Army's Battlefield Coordination element I had worked with in Blue Flag training exercises. Saddam Hussein didn't realize that he was up against a team that had worked this scenario for four years, in my case. And even longer for other people. Unlike Korea, Vietnam, or even World War II, this wasn't a "pickup" ball club.

At CENTCOM, the original 1979 concern was a Russian invasion of Iran, to seize a warm water port. By the late 1980s, the Joint Chiefs of Staff reached the conclusion that Russia was not going to be a threat. They were bogged down in Afghanistan, and their empire was beginning to disintegrate. There was glasnost, perestroika. When General Schwarzkopf became CENTCOM commander, he said, "Guys, I know that you've been planning against the Russians. But that ain't going to happen. We have to prepare the command for other contingencies."

Well, the obvious contingency was that Iraq had emerged, after its war with Iran, as a powerful military force. Schwarzkopf said, "These guys could cause trouble." We looked for a what-if scenario of Iraq invading Kuwait and Saudi Arabia. In 1990, we planned a Command Post exercise to plan what we would do if this occurred. That's why in April 1990, in preparation for that exercise, I had drawn up a target plan. And presented my views to General Schwarzkopf.

We discussed using Patriot missiles to defend ports and airports. I talked with General John Yeosock about that. Yeosock and I had gone to the National War College together in 1976. We talked a lot about close air support. My point was, "When you get into desert warfare with armored forces, the Army doesn't know where it's going to be from day to day. How can they preplan their close air support needs?"

So I planned to keep airplanes over the battlefield twenty-four hours a day, diverting aircraft to useful targets on demand. I included a command and control system, so if a serious engagement occurred we could divert air support to them immediately. I called it "Push CAS" [close air support] because we always push the air support forward against interdiction targets or to support ground troops when they need it.

We prepared for this type of battlefield at our Tactical Air Control Center in Riyadh every day until the ground war started. The Marines do close air support in the same way.

THE STRIKE CELL

COMMANDER
DONALD MCSWAIN

Saudi Arabia 1990-91
Naval Aviation Strike Planner
Joint Forces Air Command

When Iraq invaded Kuwait, I had just finished a tour as a squadron operations officer aboard the aircraft carrier *Ranger*. On August 15, I was on Whidbey Island, Washington, working on the air wing staff.

We received a message from CINCPAC [Commander in Chief, Pacific] Fleet saying that they may be looking to send out a Strike Planner to a joint staff. Not many people thought that the Iraqi business would amount to much. But at nine A.M. on August 17, I was told, "You're leaving at 1700 this evening."

When I arrived at Riyadh, Saudi Arabia, it was total confusion. Hundreds of U.S. military people were already there, living in commercial hotels. All of us had "Secret" orders. We couldn't show them to anyone unless they had a need to know. My orders were to the "JFAC Staff."

I reported in to the U.S. section at the Saudi Ministry of Defense and Aviation. U.S. staffers looked at my orders and didn't understand what this "JFAC thing" was. They were a bunch of Army people from the CENTCOM staff. So they said, "Well, it's probably down that way with the Air Force guys."

I went three kilometers down the road to check in. It was mostly Arabs in the building. But I found out that there were some Air Force guys running around on the third floor. I went up there looking for the Chief of Staff or Lt. General Charles Horner. He had a lot on his mind. Saudi Arabia was on the verge of being invaded by Iraq, and he was trying to coordinate the air defenses.

He looked at my orders and I was directed down the road to work for Captain Bryant, who represented the Navy.

At the time, there were 165,000 Iraqi Republican Guards on the Kuwaiti-Saudi border. And only 11,000 U.S. Marines and soldiers in Saudi, who had no tanks or heavy weapons. The Saudi attitude was, "You Americans are a big world power. You come here and it should be all over in a matter of weeks."

Naval assets in the area were the aircraft carrier *Independence* battle group in the Gulf of Oman. They were staying on twenty-four-hours alert, with enough ordnance to sustain combat operations for three or four days. That was far more than the Air Force initially had.

If Iraq had crossed the border, our A-6s and F/A-18s have laser-guided bombs for tank killing. The F/A-18s need the A-6 to do the lasing for them. Or Navy SEALs or Army Special Forces do target spotting on the ground.

On August 23, the joint air planning effort started to come together. We had a very large briefing in Riyadh to discuss the way that air assets should be used. And to designate specific tasks and responsibilities for intelligence functions and target selection.

Initially, the Strike Cell area was Special Access. There was only thirty or forty people involved. During the first month we did mostly intelligence-related reaction to Iraqi movement along the Saudi border. We decided on their likely avenues of attack, which key bridges we should take out, and which lines of communication to hit to slow down their advance.

Our second set of plans was to provide for the evacuation of Riyadh. We were going to utilize 500 rental cars and set up two refueling points en route to the port of Jiddah on the Red Sea.

I was staying in the Sheraton hotel. On September 4, the Air Force moved out of their hotels to a complex called Escon Village. It was a high-rise apartment village built for the bedouins. It has condos and shopping centers and schools. A beautiful setup, all self-contained. Construction was not completed, so a lot of guys were staying in apartments without doors or without furniture. It was a royal pain to be stuck out there. And it was expensive.

Our admiral felt, "Let's find our own accommodations. Having nine thousand Americans in one area makes too inviting a target for terrorists." We learned something from the Beirut bombing and decided to spread out. He told our supply officer to scout around for a good deal.

The supply officer looked through want ads and classifieds in the newspaper and found that there were some openings in a Swedish compound. A lot of the families had moved out. So for us, life became pretty good.

We'd tease the Air Force guys by saying, "Yeah, there's a lot of Swedish ladies there. Olympic-size swimming pool and tennis courts. We have room service every night until ten P.M. Laundry service is every day, and they fold everything." We hated the thought of going back to the States [he laughs] because life there would be worse.

JFAC started with a makeshift Command and Control Center. The Saudis buy the best of everything. They had all these neat fancy weapons systems. But they had never been able to put them into full operational capability. It didn't take much work to put the computers on line.

If we had been in a country that lacked modern equipment, we would've been in trouble.

THE PRICE

LIEUTENANT GENERAL BUSTER GLOSSON

SAUDIA ARABIA 1990–91
DIRECTOR OF CAMPAIGN PLANS
CENTRAL COMMAND AIR FORCES &
COMMANDER, 14TH AIR DIVISION

At the outset of the American buildup in Saudi Arabia, the responsibility for coordinating the planning of a strategic air campaign was given to Major General Buster Glosson, forty-eight, an imposing no-nonsense North Carolinian. General Glosson, who had excelled as both a Vietnam-era fighter pilot and Pentagon political liaison under Secretary of Defense Richard Cheney, understood that he had to consider every military action with a view to its international political ramifications. In addition, he was Commander of the 14th Air Division, which included all Air Force bombers and fighter aircraft in Theater.

On August 16, I was on the USS *LaSalle* in the Persian Gulf when General Chuck Horner asked me to develop a joint offensive air campaign. He told me to move to Riyadh on the nineteenth. That provided me around forty-eight hours to jot down some thoughts. I reflected on some of my Vietnam experiences that I vowed, if ever given a senior command position, I would never relive. I also wanted to make sure that we had a very clear understanding of what we were trying to accomplish, what the bounds were, and to avoid false starts. But above all else, to be aggressive and willing to take risks to save lives.

There was no doubt in my mind that General Schwarzkopf and General Horner wanted a campaign totally devoid of interservice biases and rivalries. And I was obsessed with making sure that everything we did could be accomplished with the minimum loss of life. I never doubted the final outcome of the war. It was a matter of what price we would pay for it, in terms of the lives of fighter pilots and soldiers on the ground.

My last assignment before the Gulf War was at the Pentagon, as Deputy Assistant Secretary of Defense for Legislative Affairs. I had the opportunity to work with Secretary of Defense Dick Cheney. And in that legislative job, I had my first interface with General Colin Powell. This assignment served me well in the desert. Because any Joint Air Campaign plan had to be approved by both the Secretary of Defense and the Chairman of the Joint Chiefs of Staff.

I had known General Chuck Horner for ten years, and had previously worked for him as a wing commander. General Horner is the type of leader who has the toughness to encourage new tactics that could save lives. I believed that the impact of the air campaign on the Iraqi military and their infrastructure would be awesome. We both thought they would come unglued at the seams.

In September, most of the Air Force units were on the ground, and the Navy arrived off-coast. I visited every major flying organization and requested one or two representatives of those units to come to Riyadh and help plan the air campaign. Therefore, from the outset we had representatives from the Navy, Army, Marines, and Air Force in our planning group. They played an integral role. I kept individuals on two-week rotation so they could continue to fly. I wanted every air group to have a part in the planning.

We did have some different views. However, this was the first war with a fully integrated joint air campaign, with one joint commander. Additionally, our Coalition partners, such as the British and the Arabs, were involved in all aspects of the joint/combined air campaign.

Later on, when the air campaign was drafted, I had it shown to every major flying unit. I said, "You have forty-eight hours to make recommendations. Suggest any changes you want. But when you sign on the dotted line, it is now your part."

This approach was a result of my Vietnam experience, where I was a flight commander and flew missions daily. I was responsible for eight F-4 fighters with twelve front and back seaters—pilots and weapons officers. It wasn't a position to have a very broad view of the war. But broad enough for me to realize that we never had a clue, at the unit level, at what our overall effort was. That stymied initiative. You didn't feel the responsibility for the total success of the war.

I remember feeling that no one higher up cared enough to explain to us about what they were asking us fighter pilots to do. Or how we fit into the overall scheme.

In the Gulf, to make sure that no fighter pilot had those same feelings, I personally visited every fighter squadron in the 14th Air Division. We had over 600 airplanes and 1,400 crew members. I believed it was critical for them to know that the war would start in the next few days. I told the fighter pilots everything.

For instance, I had three different discussion sessions at Al Kharj, where we had the F-15Cs that flew air-to-air, the F-15Es who were air-to-ground, and F-16s that flew both air-to-air and air-to-ground. That was necessary, in order to personalize the mission for each squadron's unique role.

I wanted to share the total plan—its strengths and weaknesses—where they fit, what would happen if they succeeded, what would happen if they failed, and the synergistic impact created by the destruction of specific targets. I expressed my wish to see all of the pilots at similar meetings after the war ended. I even told them, "There is not a damn thing in Iraq worth you dying for until the first soldier or Marine crosses the border."

I have a deep-seated conviction that when you ask someone to risk dying for their country, you owe it to them to explain what they're dying for, and ensure that everyone understands how they fit into the larger picture. Not just be pawns.

Around the middle of February, approximately one week before the land campaign started, I sent the following message to every fighter wing. I made it mandatory reading for every fighter pilot before he flew his next mission:

". . . All of you heard me say earlier that 'Not one thing in Iraq is worth dying for,' and that was true. Sometime in the next week, there is going to be a lot worth dying for in Iraq. We call them American soldiers and marines. When I said I want a minimum loss of life, we cannot draw distinctions between Americans who die. If a marine dies or a soldier dies, it's the same to me as one of you dying. For that reason, there will be no restrictions placed on you by anyone. The individual fighter pilot or flight lead will decide what is necessary. That individual courage and ability of our flight leads and individual fighter pilots have always been and will continue to be our strength. God speed."

SCROUNGER'S PARADISE

CAPTAIN TIMOTHY HOLDEN

SAUDI ARABIA 1990–91
DEPUTY COMMANDER
NAVAL SPECIAL WARFARE TASK GROUP

Navy SEALs were the first American unit to deploy to the Persian Gulf region after the invasion of Kuwait. With a small number of special operators—not more than eighty men at any given time—they had a wide variety of missions that included rescuing downed pilots, training and in liaison with Saudi and Kuwaiti land and naval forces, counterterrorism, ordnance disposal of mines at sea, boarding suspicious cargo ships to enforce the maritime embargo of Iraq, as well as secret reconnaissance of Iraqi defenses on Kuwait beaches.

We got notified for Saudi Arabia on August 4 and rolled out on the tenth. As the first special operations unit to arrive, our mission was primarily defensive and CSAR—combat search and rescue of downed pilots at sea.

The Saudi Army was just south of the Kuwait border. If the Iraqis invaded, the Saudis had no communications and no ability to call in U.S. air strikes or naval gunfire. And General Schwarzkopf wanted some American eyes and ears up there to keep track of what was going on and find out how good these people really were. So we went to the border and set up the liaison work. Our headquarters was near Dahran airfield.

Initially, as deputy commander, I ran the staff, got everything organized. It was an absolutely crazy time. There was nothing built when we got there. Fortunately, an advance liaison group from SOCCENT [Central Command Special Operations] found a beach location for us. It was a scrounger's paradise. We had to find places to live, vehicles, food, water. And then worry about, "What are we going to do here?"

In our task group there was around 125 people. The final number was around 250 SEALs. We drew people from all the SEAL teams. Captain Ray Smith became the task group commander in Saudi Arabia.

I traveled fairly regularly to observe different outposts. But my main job was to keep the fires burning back at home base. I went back and forth a lot to King Fahad International Airport, where SOCCENT had its headquarters, about an hour drive from Dahran. There were no speed limits. [He laughs.] The command of SOCCENT was primarily Army. I had a number of discussions with SOCCENT Command to explain Naval Special Warfare capabilities and to define the types of missions we were trained to conduct.

I was backed up by Captain Ray Smith, the overall SEAL commander. He is not a big man, but is highly respected by his peers. He can perform physically as well as any troop. More important, in SOCCENT meetings, he was adamant that our missions were best suited for our capabilities. He would not compromise. The fact that we brought all of our people home alive is a tribute to his leadership. And he was supported by General Schwarzkopf, who did not permit unnecessary risks.

We had just come off the Just Cause operation in Panama where we had four SEALs killed while attacking an airfield. That created a lot of internal controversy in our community: whether a light infantry-type operation was suitable for our or-

Private James Day,
Okinawa 1945, 18 years old

Maj. General James Day,
1980, Commanding
General, 1st Marine
Division

General Charles Horner, 1991, Commanding General, U.S. Central Command Air Forces

Sergeant Major William Earl McCune, 1991, 2nd Armored Division

General Alfred Gray, 1991, Commandant U.S. Marine Corps

Commander Timothy Holden, 1991, Naval Special Warfare Task Unit Mike

Colonel Wesley Fox (center), Vietnam 1969, Commander Alpha Company, 1st Battalion 9th Marines

General Ronald Yates, 1984,
Program Director for the F-16 fighter aircraft

Colonel Michael Andrews
and family, 1991

Colonel Michael Andrews,
Vietnam 1968, 25th
Infantry Division

Colonel Barbara Smith, 1991,
Chief Nurse, Army Central Command

Lt. Colonel Richard Cody
(left), 1991, Battalion
Commander, 101st
Aviation Brigade

Colonel Kenneth
Bowra (left),
Vietnam 1972,
MACV-SOG, Recon
Team Leader

General Colin Powell, 1991,
Chairman, Joint Chiefs of Staff

Lt. General Walter Boomer,
Vietnam 1972, Advisor

Lt. General Walter Boomer,
New York City Ticker Tape
Parade, 1991, Commanding
General, U.S. Marines
Central Command

ganization. There was a tremendous amount of soul searching about Panama: Who was in charge? Who screwed it up? How could it happen? That was the backdrop to our deployment to the Gulf.

Captain Smith's criteria was: "We're going to do missions that make a difference in the war. We're not going to do missions just to keep busy. We're going to do missions with a high probability of success. And we're going to do missions where people have a good chance of coming back. No suicide operations."

TRIP WIRE

GENERAL CHARLES HORNER

SAUDI ARABIA 1990–91
COMMANDING GENERAL
CENTRAL COMMAND AIR FORCES

For close to a month during the initial stage of the buildup, before General Schwarzkopf arrived, I was the CINC [Commander in Chief] at CENTCOM in Riyadh. That was a very vulnerable period for U.S. forces. The initial air defense was the Saudis' F-15s. An aircraft carrier was steaming toward the Red Sea.

Within days, American F-16s and A-10s [both specialize in air-to-ground antiarmor warfare] arrived. That gave us a very credible way of limiting an Iraqi attack. The problem was that there was no fuel tanker support, so the aircraft could not stay up for very long. We couldn't have stopped an Iraqi attack. But we would've hit their fuel depots and supplies, so that the attack would run out of steam near the oil fields. That probably would have been Saddam's objective.

The Marines and the Army's 82nd Airborne were very mobile with TOW [antitank] missiles. They would have been overwhelmed by sheer numbers. But they could have done a fighting retreat, causing a lot of disruption. Our plan was to create an enclave near the coast at Dahran, like the Pusan perimeter in the Korean War.

It wasn't until late August when the 24th Infantry Division arrived with tanks that we felt ready. I briefed Defense Secretary Cheney at Jiddah. I said, "At this point, I think we can hold the line around Dahran." It was a case of figuring how far we would have to retreat.

It wasn't that we expected Saddam to push across the border, but we had to prepare for that. Each night, Army general John Yeosock, Admiral Grant Sharp, and I would sit down and review what had come into the Theater that day, and how we could use it. Fortunately, technology for a Tactical Air Control Center [TACC] arrived. We immediately put together an air exercise between my Air Force people, naval aviation, and the Saudis.

I had been with CENTCOM for four years. My long tenure—it's usually a two-year tour—proved invaluable. The head of the Saudi Air Force is a close friend. We developed trust over the years. I know how the Islamic forces operate and made sure that our people were informed. John Yeosock, the CENTCOM Army head, had spent a year in Saudi Arabia as an advisor to Crown Prince Abdullah and the National Guard. And Major General Don Kaufman, head of the U.S. Training Mission, had been in Saudi for a year and a half. So when we began building our forces, if we needed office space, rental cars or anything else, he knew who to see. That enabled us to set up a headquarters very quickly.

We had to deal with a lot of pressure in the early stages. We knew that a number of American ground troops along the border could be wiped off the map within hours.

No matter the pressure, I kept in mind that people were always looking to me as a commander. So I was very careful not to convey my internal stress or fatigue to the people around me. I always made a point of trying to look rested, no matter how tired. I always tried to smile. Not frivolous laughter, but keeping in good humor. I walked around with a smile, saying, "How you doing today? How's it going?" If I had doubts, I kept them to myself. I had a deputy, Colonel Tom Olson, who was my confidant. In private I had frank discussions with him.

The other thing I have is a fundamental belief in God. If you don't have that, you're lost. Because the responsibility is overwhelming, it's too much.

Something that hit me, and I'm sure it has hit other commanders: You go through all the war game exercises with little red boxes on plastic-covered maps, representing divisions and companies and squadrons and all that. But one day you are sitting in a war room, and those red markers represent 10,000 or 15,000 people, and your job is to wreak havoc on them. You come to an understanding that you may not be up to what is needed to do that kind of job.

At that time, you say to yourself, "I'm going to do the best I can. God is going to take care of the rest of it."

OCEAN OF SAND

COMMAND SERGEANT MAJOR ROBERT NICHOLS

SAUDI ARABIA 1990–91
COMMAND SERGEANT MAJOR
1ST BRIGADE, 101ST AIRBORNE DIVISION
(AIR ASSAULT)

Since the Army began, the role of the noncommissioned officers has been the cornerstone. Officers establish policies and give directions. And sergeants carry them out.

The role of NCOs and senior commissioned officers in peacetime is established and very solid. On the other hand, the role of senior NCOs in combat is not defined. It works off the abilities, personalities, and trust between the commander and his senior sergeants.

There are around 4,000 soldiers in a brigade. About one-third of them are NCOs. In our brigade, only twenty-five NCOs had been in combat, either Vietnam, Grenada or Panama. Fortunately, out of sixteen companies, all but two 1st sergeants had been in Vietnam.

When the Gulf War began, with all the buildup, the anxiety and excitement, very few people—the combat veterans—realized what could go wrong. The veterans sat down together to share our thoughts.

We discussed death. And the role that we would have if

things were going to shit. It's very difficult to look your people in the eye and realize that some of you may not come back.

A week before we left for war, Colonel Jim Hill, my brigade commander, and I talked to all the NCOs of the brigade, including our support soldiers. We gathered them in the division's museum. The conversation was very candid. We told them, "Prepare your wife, your mother and father, your children. Because the chance that you are not coming back is very strong." The soldiers' eyes got large. They were sitting on the edge of their seats. No one had ever spoken in those terms to them.

Myself, Colonel Hill, and all the experienced leaders planned for the worst. But we wanted our soldiers to have a positive mental attitude. Our support companies carried body bags on their trucks. Medics carried one or two body bags. We didn't have soldiers carry them.

I didn't even consider it. And if someone recommended it, I would yell at him, "I don't want our troops to think that they are not coming back."

I arrived in Saudi Arabia on September 9 with the lead element of the brigade. I was in the office with Colonel Hill when he got the call. He assigned all the sergeants major of the brigade to be the advance party. The initial supply aircraft could take only fifteen people. So the brigade's executive officer, the six sergeants major, and our drivers went.

My team arrived in Saudi with rucksacks on our backs, that's all. The major problem we faced was the logistics infrastructure didn't exist. Saudi Arabia is a barren plain, like a sea. I told my team, "This is going to be brigade base camp." The weather was above 100 degrees and it was miserable.

We couldn't set up tents right away because we needed drills for the hard ground. The area was a stopover place for pilgrims to Mecca [the holiest site in Islam, located in Saudi Arabia]. The ground was hard as rock. We could not pound a stake into the ground.

After we acquired drills, we would start work at around three o'clock in the morning, using flashlights. The predawn temperature was around 90 degrees. We'd drill until around midday, when the heat became so miserable that we couldn't work. We had no civilian construction people. There was only myself, my five battalion sergeants major and our six drivers. In two weeks, we fully prepared a camp for about 3,200 troops. We called it Camp Eagle II, after a 101st base camp in Vietnam.

The brigade stayed there in a defensive posture for a few weeks. We then deployed out to the desert as the Corps' covering force farthest north. Our brigade sector covered around forty miles between the Tap Line Road and Kuwait. For five months we literally lived in foxholes and bunkers. When the rainy season began, we rigged ponchos overhead for cover.

When the time for the ground attack drew near and General Schwarzkopf put his "Hail Mary" plan in motion, our brigade stayed in the northern sector to guard the Tap Line Road. That was very hard on morale. After Thanksgiving, we were given ten days to come back to Camp Eagle. Our soldiers went to the PX and got into the "junk food" syndrome.

We received newspapers that were usually a couple of weeks old. The *USA Today* and the European version of *Stars and Stripes* were very popular. We kept reading articles about hundreds of thousands of cookies that were being sent from the States. But where were *our* cookies?

All of a sudden, somebody opened a flood gate . . . The support of the American people was overwhelming. We had piles of boxes of cookies. School kids sent letters. I don't think there was a trooper who didn't have four or five pen pals—grade school classes or individuals.

During five months on the border, we learned a lot about ourselves. The constant training fostered strong bonding among people. And for men in their late thirties, who were at the middle stage of their lives, it gave us a chance to think, "If I survive, what am I going to do with the rest of it?"

UP FRONT

LIEUTENANT GENERAL
WALTER BOOMER

SAUDI ARABIA 1990–91
COMMANDING GENERAL
U.S. MARINES CENTRAL COMMAND
& 1ST MARINE EXPEDITIONARY FORCE

After surviving the 1972 Easter Offensive in Vietnam, Walt Boomer earned his way up the Marine Corps command ladder, graduating with honors from postgraduate academic courses and distinguishing himself in leadership roles. Included among those jobs were Chairman of the Department of Management at the U.S. Naval Academy, Commander of the Marine Security Guards who protect U.S. embassies worldwide, Director of Marine Corps Public Affairs, and a variety of combat commands. On August 15, he deployed to Saudi Arabia, tasked with ground combat.

The Gulf War was fought with Marine leadership up front. Which is the only place I believe that a leadership can fight from. I don't buy the argument that "because the battlefield has become more technical, the commander must stay back in his control room and manipulate from there."

I arrived in Saudi Arabia in August. I went to Riyadh to get a sense of how the CENTCOM staff were working. After ten days I accomplished that, and moved to Jubayl to be closer to front-line Marines. I was dual Commander of the CENTCOM Marine component, and also Commanding General of the Marine Expeditionary Force. I seldom returned to Riyadh.

I have a strong belief in what young Marines can achieve if they are properly led. It never ceases to amaze me. In the desert, they built bases and moved vast distances that you wouldn't think anyone would be able to do. And all they ask for in return is caring leadership. They are the first to know if you don't really care. And consequently, their performance will reflect that.

An important lesson of the Vietnam War was the lack of continuity of leadership. Most officers served three to six months with a unit and then transferred. Ever since, I have repeatedly stated, "We killed Marines as a result of changing leaders every six months." Because just as a commander got his feet on the ground and began to understand a little bit about the terrain and the enemy, the System moved him. For a very selfish reason: To give more officers exposure to command. That was an absolutely bullshit and immoral reason.

This is an emotional subject for me. If the war in the Gulf had gone on for a year, I would never have made a change in unit commanders unless a guy collapsed.

General Schwarzkopf had Marines on his Joint Staff, assigned to coordinate the larger picture rather than only Marine activities. And I sent seventy Marines to Riyadh to work with the CENTCOM staff as liaisons. They stayed in touch with my headquarters. And I rotated two-star generals, Jed Pearson and Norm Ehlert, to CENTCOM headquarters, to sit around the table at night to make sure that General Schwarzkopf heard my views.

A major lesson I learned from having been an advisor in Vietnam was how to deal with other cultures. The coalition approach was essential to our success. We simply couldn't ride roughshod over our Arab allies. We had to deal very carefully. And there were significant problems. In their culture they hold back from telling you their real feelings. Especially because Muslims consider Westerners to be "infidels." You will never be a part of their Brotherhood, no matter what you do.

I assigned Colonel John Admire to train the Arab Coalition forces. It was a matter of necessity. It was fortunate that he had previous experience in Vietnam as an advisor.

Almost all Marine infantry commanders in the Gulf had been advisors to the Vietnamese marines. As the years have gone by, this group has stayed in touch. And our friendships endure. This was an important factor in the teamwork among Marine leadership in the Gulf.

The intensity of the 1972 North Vietnamese Easter Offensive is something that none of us will ever forget. The tactical lessons from that stayed in our heads. We understood the importance of combined arms [coordination between land forces and close air support]. We knew that you could be hurt and outnumbered, and still deal with it without much assistance.

During the 1972 offensive, we had to fight against tanks. What I learned from those battles I carried into the Gulf: "An infantryman can deal with tanks." What you can't deal with is if you are outgunned by enemy artillery.

As a result of that experience, in the planning process for Desert Storm we concentrated on taking out enemy artillery. We knew that could be the biggest casualty producer. And artillery was a means to deliver chemical weapons, too.

LAWRENCE OF ARABIA

BRIGADIER GENERAL JOHN ADMIRE

SAUDI ARABIA 1990–91
REGIMENT COMMANDER
3RD MARINE REGIMENT, TASK FORCE TARO

I was one of the few Marines with previous experience in the danger zone of the Gulf. In 1988, during the Iran-Iraq War, I commanded MAGTF [Marine Air Ground Task Force] 3/88. We were aboard ship. But it familiarized me with the extreme temperatures of the area. The daily temperatures on the flight deck between ten A.M. and six P.M. was somewhere around 130 degrees.

We had some liberty and maintenance trips ashore in Saudi, Bahrain, and the UAE. They were tourist-type visits, but that gave us the opportunity to see some of the operations area. I had also been to Israel on three different occasions, and I had been to Egypt and Turkey.

My previous experience gave me credibility when briefing my Marines and sailors in Hawaii prior to our Desert Shield deployment. During my earlier cruise, I read and studied about Arab religion and culture. That turned out to be a benefit. I was able to pass that knowledge on to other Marines as we prepared physically and psychologically for what we would face.

The only people in my regiment with previous combat experience were the senior officers and NCOs. Very few Vietnam veterans. I would talk with people informally about lessons I had learned as an advisor in Vietnam. My primary advice was, "Treat the Arabs as you would like to be treated. Don't act like a godsend who is going to teach them everything they need to know."

I arrived in Saudi Arabia on August 26. My 4,000 Marines of the 3rd Regiment finished deploying from Hawaii by September 6. We linked up with our equipment at Jubayl port. Then we established a rear area base camp at Ra's al Gahr, south of Jubayl. It was a very remote coastal area. Occasionally we might see a bedouin tribesman. It's not like Lawrence of Arabia anymore. Modern bedouins have abandoned camels for pickup trucks.

During my second tour of Vietnam, I was an advisor with the Vietnamese Marine Corps. Back then I read the Lawrence of Arabia book, *The Seven Pillars of Wisdom*, which was the classic on how to be an advisor. It was phenomenal that twenty years later, a lot of those memories came back to me. They covered how to get along with foreign colleagues on a personal, as well as, professional basis.

Our 1st U.S. Marine Division commander, General Mike Myatt, the assistant commander, General Tom Draude, chief of staff Colonel John Stennick, and myself were all former advisors in Vietnam. We all recognized the benefits of working with Arab forces. My regiment was selected to do the cross-training with the Arab Coalition.

As former advisors, the senior division leadership knew that it was absolutely critical that the cross-training was mutually supportive. We gave classes in tactics, in weapons, and in maintenance. When we talked with the Saudis, we were very honest. We said, "You are the experts in the desert. Would you give us classes in desert navigation, tactics, and survival?"

They looked at us kind of amazed. Because the U.S. military has a reputation of being pretty good. For us to ask the Saudis for classes, boosted their self-esteem. Their chests puffed up a little and they were very proud that they were giving us instruction.

We were glad they did. Because when we first arrived in-country, I considered the desert to be our first and foremost enemy. It is a barren harsh existence: 120 degrees or more, complete absence of water. Nothing but sand as far as you can see. You could drive a hundred kilometers and see no one.

During the first week of October, because of the success we were having with the Saudi marines, we expanded our training to include the King Abdul Aziz Brigade of the Saudi National Guard. They are the king's elite troops. After the Iraqis overran Kuwait, they were deployed on the Kuwait border.

Other Arab Coalition forces included the Morrocans, Pakistanis, Bangladeshis, Qataris, and later, the Afghan Mujahideen. The American Marines knew that if we went into an offensive mode, that we needed to be familiar with that area. Task Force Taro, as my regiment was called, became the brother unit to the Saudis.

Beginning the first week in October, I rotated 150 to 200 Marines up north in shifts of eight to ten days to live and train with Saudi forces. We familiarized them with all of our support aircraft, because we didn't want them firing on our guys. We developed personal friendships, as well.

I got to know the Saudi brigade commander, Colonel Turki, and some of his battalion commanders. It reached the point, much like in Vietnam, where they invited us to their tents to share dinner with us. We sat around on rugs and cushions, family style, and ate rice and freshly slaughtered goat. As guests of honor, our hosts would pluck out the goats' eyes—which is a delicacy to them—and offer them to us. Somehow we would try to swallow it down.

I learned in my Vietnam advisory days that sometimes with a smile and pantomime you can communicate a hell of a lot. For example, on November 10, the Marine Corps birthday is celebrated. We flew the Marine band up to the Arab sector to visit our training units. We brought cake and a hot meal. We did it up in fine fashion. We invited all the local Saudi, Qatari, and Pakistani commanders to observe the ceremony and enjoy the hot meal. This helped to cement friendships and personal ties.

We continued the training program until the end of December, when we moved the whole task force up to the border. We were the only U.S. combat force positioned in an exclusive Arab sector. And we were the only Marine Corps helicopter-borne force. We deployed to a border airfield at al Mish'ab. If the Iraqis surprise-attacked across the border, we would fight alongside the Arab Coalition forces. With our parent command, the 1st Marine Division, eighty kilometers south, we were closer to the Iraqis than any U.S. force. That made the bonds between Task Force Taro and our Arab allies even stronger.

We had no armor to fight against Iraqi armor and mechanized forces. At best we had some Humvees with TOW anti-tank weapons. But the Saudis and Qataris had tanks. So through our cross-training we worked on "infantry versus tank" tactics. We'd dig in and have their tanks attack us from various angles. So my Marines would get a sense, day or night, of having armor bearing down.

We even had their armor roll over our defensive positions. So that my Marines would experience that psychological feeling of being overrun. We learned how to attack tanks from the rear, to know that we could survive.

We had helicopters, which the Saudis and Qataris didn't have. We invited their officers and NCOs to practice calling in fire support. And we had them participate in our heliborne operations, which was new to them. It was reciprocal, learning from each other. This continued to strengthen our bonds of friendship, as well as our professional skills. That paid off a hundred times over when the actual war started.

FRATERNITY

GENERAL CHARLES HORNER

Saudi Arabia 1990–91
Commanding General
Central Command Air Forces

I remember in Vietnam, American officials told the Vietnamese, "Okay, you little folks stand aside. We Americans are come to solve your problems, then we'll give you back your country."

In the Gulf, allied air commanders sat around the table with me as equals—it didn't matter how many airplanes they brought to the battle. We all listened to what each other had to say. The Arab air forces were relatively new to aerial warfare but they performed flawlessly.

I had previously worked with European air forces, but not specifically with their people who came into the war. I was sensitive to their concerns. I was concerned about the French, for example. They weren't NATO members, in the same sense as the British, for example. However, when the French arrived in Saudi, they came to me for help in bedding down. I went to see them after moving a bunch of Army helicopters off the ramp at Dahran to create space for housing them. However, they chose to put their forces at a place called Al Hassah, which is a terrible place—a lot of mud and flies. I felt a little peeved but didn't say anything. We had done a lot of work to prepare them a place where they would've had communications and food.

Later the French commander came to me and said, "It was a decision of the Minister of Defense [who opposed the war]. He didn't want French forces colocated with Americans." And that broke the commander's heart. After France got a new Minister of Defense, that problem went away. We colocated with the French fuel tankers at the International Airport in Riyadh. That was a great place to go because the French cooks shared our chow hall. The bread they baked was superb.

I made an effort to have all of the American and allied air units feel like they were a part of the process. The Navy and Marine Corps air people were integral. My headquarters was truly a combined operational headquarters. This type of teamwork is a lesson I learned in Vietnam.

The air campaign in Vietnam was divided into "route packages," because the Air Force and the Navy couldn't agree on a single commander. It was stupid. Rather than have a coordinated effort, we used geographic areas to separate our operations. I'll never forget flying toward my route package and looking down at a Communist resupply convoy. But we couldn't go after it because it was in the Navy's route package.

Early in the Gulf War, some people recommended that we use route packages. They were putting their own uniform in front of the flag. I was determined that we weren't going to have that.

You always have two wars going: one is budget rivalry in Washington, that promotes parochialism and competition. And you have the actual battlefield. In the Gulf we were blessed with commanders like Walt Boomer [Marines], Stan Arthur

[Navy] and John Yeosock [Army]—all of us had been through the trauma of Vietnam and trusted one another.

Sometimes people would come to me and complain, "The Marines are going to do this or that . . ." I would say with confidence, "Walt Boomer would never do anything behind my back."

One of the reasons that the war ended so quickly and with so few casualties is because of the lethality and flexibility of modern air power. But air power is only one part of a land, sea, and air campaign. The Navy's interdiction efforts proved very valuable, the Army and Marine ground campaign was vital to getting the Iraqis out of Kuwait. Still, I'm proud of the job air power accomplished. As General Colin Powell said, "In this one, Air gets the game ball."

CHOKE POINTS

REAR ADMIRAL WILLIAM FOGARTY

PERSIAN GULF 1990–91
COMMANDER OF INTERCEPT FORCE
MIDEASTFOR/JOINT TASK FORCE MIDDLE EAST

In an attempt to get Saddam Hussein to peacefully withdraw his forces from Kuwait, the United Nations imposed economic sanctions against Iraq. The key component of the sanctions was a maritime interdiction program enforced by multinational warships, commanded by U.S. Admiral William Fogarty.

The Maritime Interdiction Program covered both the Red Sea and the Gulf. Our objective was to prevent the Iraqis from making any money. And to prevent arms and supplies from reaching Saddam. In August we formed an intercept force of nine navies of some twenty countries. In early September we had a meeting to set up the procedures. I was the U.S. commander of the Intercept Force. Most of the countries deferred to us, because we had the majority of forces and had been there for a long time. We had meetings every two to three weeks with all the navies involved to coordinate where the ships would operate.

The area we covered was around 250,000 square miles. We couldn't cover that entire area. So we concentrated our forces at choke points where all sea traffic had to pass through. And we used aircraft to perform additional surveillance over a larger area.

My MIDEASTFOR [Middle East Force] staff was the coordinator for the interdiction forces. In the North Arabian Gulf and Red Sea, Admirals Marsh and Mixson concentrated primarily on the air strike aspect. They let their destroyer squadron commanders work directly with my staff for the intercept. That worked real well. They were in a listening mode to hear what was going on. If the squadron commander got into trouble, they would respond. We worked with both of those battle groups in the North Arabian Gulf and the Red Sea.

At MIDEASTFOR headquarters I had staff people assigned to monitor radio transmissions in each Intercept sector. We had a group in our staff called the MIF [Maritime Intercept Force] Watch, who did exactly that. So we knew what was going on in all sectors.

I couldn't micromanage every aspect of the intercept operation. I stayed aboard my flagship, the *LaSalle*, which served as my headquarters. We used a data transmission system called JOTS, which puts information on display like a television set. The radar information that was brought in came from ships' radar in different areas. And we would use manual plottings on a map in one of our big rooms to keep track of certain ships. And to better keep track of everyone, we updated ships' movements on a tote board.

In a sticky situation, like an Iraqi ship that didn't want to stop, we would micromanage from my command level. Because there could be some decisions that in worst-case scenarios would have to go all the way up to the President. But most of the time we had a heads-up when a ship was coming. We would discuss it with commanders on the scene.

More than 10,000 ships were intercepted through the end of Desert Storm. But only around 150 were actually boarded. We had pretty good intelligence to where there might be some problem cargo. Most shipmasters would stop. Not the Iraqis.

Because Iraqi shipmasters were told by their government that if they stopped, their families would be killed back home.

We would deal with that by informing them, "If you don't stop, we're going to board with a helicopter search team." We had some hairy moments, because we didn't know with the first few ships what would happen when our people got on board. Would our search teams be met with guys carrying guns and knives?

Once our people got on board, the Iraqi shipmaster was able to radio to Baghdad that they'd been overwhelmed. He was off the hook. He could say, "We tried to resist but we were overrun." Then the Iraqi crew would cooperate.

JORDAN OR BUST

COMMANDER RICHARD REASS

NORTHERN RED SEA 1990–91
DESTROYER SQUADRON COMMANDER/DIRECTOR
MARITIME INTERCEPTION OPERATIONS

During Desert Shield/Desert Storm I was commander of Destroyer Squadron 36 in the Red Sea. And I was also tasked to establish the Multinational Force and to direct the Maritime Interception Operation in the northern Red Sea. In September, to get the program started, we sat down and wrote rules and procedures that were eventually approved by the United Nations.

The three to five U.S. ships usually involved in the operation were tasked under me. We would rotate them back and forth to their aircraft carrier groups. We worked with Greek, French, and Spanish ships.

Each ship in our force was assigned a patrol sector. Any merchant ship coming in would be asked a series of questions: "Where are you coming from? Where are you going? What cargo are you carrying?" If a shipmaster said he was going to Aqaba, Jordan, we would ask him to halt. And a team would go aboard to inspect.

During the five months of Desert Shield, we found everything from surface-to-air missile systems to chemicals for nerve agents [weaponry], to motor propellents, tank parts, and munitions. Anything you can possibly think of.

The ship captains would say, "We're just bringing this to Jordan." Sometimes they would hide contraband—and call it "beans and rice." Our people had to do a thorough job not to overlook any crate.

As commander, I had to be at the scene of the operation to be effective and have what I call "situational awareness." To be able to look at the weather conditions, how many ships there are, where is the best place to position your forces.

As the coordinator of the American element of the interception operation, I was on twenty-four-hour duty call. My staff covered for me at times, when I needed rest. The guys knew when to call me and when to let me sleep.

There was no special time of day when merchant ships would try to run contraband cargo. A lot depended on Suez Canal traffic. They tried every trick imaginable.

At first, we'd call a ship up. The master would say, "I've got cargo bound for Iraq." We'd say, "Sorry, you can't pull in." They're businessmen. They're trying to make a buck. The Jordanian economy at Aqaba was based on trade with Iraq. Around 75 to 80 percent of the goods during the Iran-Iraq War came through Aqaba. The port has a high Palestinian pro-Iraq population. They realized, "We have to do something different or we'll be out of business."

Their first step was to not tell us the goods were bound for Iraq. We'd go aboard, look at the manifest. It would say "Iraq." And the ship would have to turn around.

So they started writing on the manifest that the cargo was going to Amman, Jordan. They didn't expect us to open the containers.

Then they started undercounting their cargo load. They'd say, "We have 240 containers on board going to Aqaba." We'd count 270. We'd ask, "What about the other thirty?" They'd say, "Those are just empty ones." "Well, which ones are empties?" "I don't know." We'd say, "Sorry, you can't come in."

Almost all international cargo ship manifests are in English, because English is the language of international commerce. The only time we needed somebody who could speak Arabic was when we caught a couple of ships coming out of Aqaba with stolen vehicles from Kuwait. They had a real chop shop going. The Iraqis were looting Kuwait. They drove all the cars into

Iraq and then to Jordan. You could get a new car for around ten percent of the list price. They would load them on ships and haul them out.

We had two Soviet ships lie to us. One was loaded with a surface-to-air missile system. The Soviet government denied it was there. But somebody in the Soviet government had to authorize the shipment. The problem was we couldn't tell whether it was the official government or the hard-line faction. We just turned the ship around. We wanted to confiscate the cargo. But we were only authorized to prohibit.

We stopped a million tons of shipping from reaching Iraq. That included a lot of chemicals and raw materials that would have kept their industrial base going. And after they fired their existing stock of surface-to-air missiles, we denied them any replacements.

CHIEF NURSE

COLONEL BARBARA SMITH

SAUDI ARABIA 1990–91
CHIEF NURSE
ARMY CENTRAL COMMAND

In Vietnam medical services in-country and offshore to service some 500,000 troops were built up over at least a five-year period. In contrast, medical services in Desert Storm for approximately the same number of troops was the first rapid deployment to a combat area.

Colonel Barbara Smith was named Chief Nurse of more than 2,000 Army nurses in the battle Theater. Although a noncombatant, she demonstrated selfless commitment to the soldiers by driving deep into the desert—often without security—to offer guidance to field hospitals and to inspect the hygiene of front-line troops.

When I was assigned to the Gulf, I kind of stepped back and took a deep breath. I never dreamed twenty years earlier as a young nurse in Vietnam that I would one day go to war as *THE* Army Central Command chief nurse. We had 2,300 Army nurses participate in Desert Shield/Desert Storm. Only around a third were active duty. The rest were Reserve and National Guard.

Until hospitals started coming in, I was the only Army nurse in Riyadh. Living conditions were awful for a while. Six hundred people were living under a big parking lot. At first I thought, "This is pretty safe." Then all the Scud missiles started coming in. I said, "Wait a minute."

As the buildup intensified, we had forty-four hospitals that I tried to visit by small truck. Because of the Arab restrictions on women, I couldn't just get into a car and go by myself. I had a wonderful traveling partner, Joe Fagan, the ARCENT psychiatrist. He and I became good buddies. I'd say, "Okay, Joe, we've got to visit a hospital." And we'd take off.

To a certain extent, young nurses in Saudi Arabia gravitated to the few Vietnam veterans like Ruth Cheney and me, because we had a certain credibility. Before I went to Saudi, I phoned one of my former chief nurses from Vietnam. It wasn't that she gave me specific advice. But when I was a lieutenant she made an impression because she made an effort to visit the wards. We knew that she cared about us because she was making the rounds. She always came across positive with the staff, using a "firm but gentle" approach. And her sense of humor kept us going, even during our down times.

My Vietnam experience gave me confidence in the desert. Above all, I went to Saudi knowing that I had already survived. You never feel like you're totally prepared. And you never get rid of all your anxiety. But I've learned to temper it.

The one thing I learned about myself in the Gulf, traveling around and visiting all the hospitals, was that I wanted to get back with the troops. At my level, that means getting back into a hospital. Staff jobs are important, but my expertise and love is being with people.

A challenge in some cases was the difficulty for Reserve or National Guard doctors to adjust to the confined environment of field hospitals. They came from a life-style on the outside which is fairly comfortable. Suddenly, they are living with twelve to sixteen people in a tent. You don't have control over your life anymore. And the situation changed on a daily basis as we created a medical system in the desert. Some people were frustrated with the lack of information, not knowing what to expect.

I believe in teamwork. I wanted my nurses to be part of

their hospital team. Most of my nurses demonstrated professionalism to do whatever needed to be done: fill sandbags, construct a field hospital, erect tents. Anything necessary to be part of the team.

A lesson learned is that it would be best for Reserve and National Guard physicians to train with their unit during peacetime. So if they are called up for an emergency situation, there will already be closeness and camaraderie built into the medical team.

Desert Storm was the first time that the rapid deployment of medical services was ever tested for 500,000 troops. We had to start from scratch with whatever supplies were available. People who worked in forward field hospitals learned a lot about being flexible. I had to laugh sometimes . . . in order to keep from crying.

At the outset we expected between 30,000 to 40,000 casualties, if chemicals were used. To use decontamination teams for the wounded would have been very challenging. The Army's Chemical Research and Development Command came to Saudi and trained 1,500 medical personnel in a two-and-a-half-day course on medical management of chemical casualties.

Our field hospitals are called DEPMEDS or Deployable Medical Systems. It is a temperature-controlled tent, modular, with portable frames. The floors are rubberized and it can be air-conditioned.

The DEPMEDS provide an excellent structure for patient care. But they are too heavy for transit. We've got to find a system that is more mobile for rapid deployment. The technology is available. Some Saudi units had flatbed trucks lined up as a floor, with a fold-out hospital constructed on top. This can be sealed in a chemical/biological battlefield. But how we'll obtain that system, I don't know. Because under present budgetary restrictions, the dollars aren't there.

A lot of Army medical care is now focused on the families. This is the first time ever that we've been tasked with the dual mission: "Not only will you take care of soldiers in wartime. There will be no degradation of health care in the States." I don't know that our system has the resources to do both well. The commitment has to come from the top. We shouldn't be satisfied to say, "Our soldiers have to do more with less." Our peacetime role is important. But our ultimate responsibility is to take care of soldiers in wartime.

Many of the cases we treated during Desert Shield were due

to sports injuries. And a lot of asthmatics, some people who never should have deployed because they weren't medically cleared. We did very well in preventive medicine, with a very small percentage of disease and nonbattle injury. We really forced troops to drink a lot of liquids and maintain good sanitation.

Traveling around to different bases, if I didn't see hand-washing facilities outside of latrines, I made it my responsibility to let someone know. My philosophy is, "Not doing the basics will cause you greater problems in the end." Usually the shortcomings would just be an oversight and easily corrected.

In hospitals that had really good morale, you could see that the leadership was taking good care of their people. A commander has got to make that a first priority. At a hospital the commander is the head doctor. In the old days, the chief nurse was not part of the command staff. If that wasn't there in writing, a lot of time when the commander held a staff meeting, the chief nurse would not be included. There's still some of that.

TOUGH LOVE

LIEUTENANT GENERAL J. BINFORD PEAY

Saudi Arabia 1990–91
Commanding General
101st Airborne Division (Air Assault)

The 101st Division, known as the "Screaming Eagles," no longer has paratroop status. However, it is the only helicopter assault infantry division in the American armed forces. The 101st's proud tradition dates back to its exploits during the "D-Day" liberation of Europe to some of the toughest battle campaigns of the Vietnam War.

When the 101st deployed to southwest Asia in 1990, the division took with it a philosophy of leadership embedded in the history of the Army. This philosophy served us well in peacetime and war. And it was summarized in five rules of leadership that I learned during my first command of an artillery battery, when I was a young captain in Vietnam:

1. Training in combat is a must. You've got to train every day. Even when you are almost in the middle of a combat period.

2. You need personal courage to fix things, even when people are tired, bored, and scared.

3. Ensure discipline, in a positive manner.

4. Ethics always.

5. Out-front leadership. I don't necessarily mean "leading from the point." But your soldiers must always feel your presence among them. That you are sharing their hardships and that you will be out front when events require that.

In Saudi Arabia, the five rules were emphasized again, to include rules of engagement. In combat, good commanders run a tighter ship than ever, so that you don't have your youngsters killed, wounded or injured unnecessarily.

The 101st spent six months in the desert just waiting and training. When people seem to be getting bored, you need to do something that will uphold discipline. We were fortunate that the 101st has a proud legacy. The division's command philosophy emphasized the unit's history. We would tell soldiers and officers, "If you want to be a Screaming Eagle, you have to walk like the great guys before you."

For six months in the desert, the division grew into a seasoned and cohesive team. We socialized together, we fought together, we trained hard together. We were a tough family, with tough standards. Some people call that "tough love."

In the desert, the 101st was stretched the distance of Nashville to New York City. The division fought over unheard-of distances. Great out-front leadership by all of our young and middle-grade officers made that happen. And the five leadership rules gave us a framework to work within. The feeling in the 101st was, "Okay, here are the rules. This is the way we do things in our division. We are a family. We all work together."

Among the lessons I learned from Vietnam: you've got to keep your soldiers informed. At every opportunity, our commanders would gather people around and talk about the situation. We also worked at that through battalion, brigade, and division newsletters.

SERGEANT MAJOR

COMMAND SERGEANT MAJOR WILLIAM EARL MCCUNE

SAUDI ARABIA 1990–91
BATTALION SERGEANT MAJOR
2ND ARMORED DIVISION

My soldiers had to learn to live in the desert twenty-four hours a day. We initially had a leadership problem when platoon leaders—young lieutenants and platoon sergeants—tried to live with their soldiers in the same living quarters. In that situation, leaders lose their identities and become "one of the boys." They lose some of their authority in the process.

My boss, the battalion commander, and I identified that problem after about a month. We moved the officers and platoon sergeants out and established separate tents.

For recreation, we established sports programs. We kept everyone busy with training and classes. We had to relearn land navigation. Because in the desert there were no terrain features. If there was a sandstorm, a road could be here today and gone tomorrow. At night there was total darkness where you couldn't see your hand in front of your face. Guys could walk across the road and be lost for two hours trying to get back where they were.

So we established reverse training cycles where we would train during daylight for a week. Then, the next week train in total darkness. Whether we got hit by the Iraqis night or day, we had to perform our rapid deployment role. So we developed reaction drills, waking up soldiers and making them man their tanks. Our guys had to learn the little things, like where to keep the flashlight.

If they crawled into the tank in total darkness, they would know where to reach for it. And when the driver or gunner sits down in their seats, they have to know where everything is. We did not have accidents because we taught standards. Like, "You cannot move fast at night in the desert."

I maintained strict standards. I didn't have one soldier in my battalion writing slogans on his helmet. I wouldn't let my soldiers go without haircuts, or let their mustaches grow wild, or not polish their boots. I told 1st sergeants, "You have barber kits. You will cut your soldiers' hair. You will make sure that they wash their clothes." And we didn't have a breakdown in discipline.

In Vietnam, few NCOs cared whether soldiers showered or brushed their teeth, or changed their socks. The only time we got a change of clothes was when the logistics helicopter would drop in. Cleanliness and hygiene of soldiers are an important part of maintaining discipline.

In the desert, soldiers had to learn how to take care of their bodies. There were long lines to use a few showers. And after showering you had to stroll a half mile back to where you were sleeping. It was especially awkward with female soldiers around.

We don't have females in my tank battalion. But in Saudi, female soldiers were in support units attached to my brigade. We were all sleeping in the same areas.

When the ground war started, we had to pass through the Iraqi mine field. We had female soldiers in support units in our column who were not supposed to be in a combat role. Yet they were.

FLASHBACK

LIEUTENANT COLONEL ROBERT WRIGHT

SAUDI ARABIA 1990–91
HISTORIAN
XVIII AIRBORNE CORPS

There aren't many Vietnam veterans left on active duty. Most of the younger soldiers' idea of Vietnam is a movie like *Platoon* or a TV show like "China Beach." As a result, we're starting to get a mythical stature. But there are times when the young guys have practical use for Vietnam veterans.

My driver in Saudi was six months old when I entered the Army in 1968. He had fun rubbing it in that I was "the Old Man." One night in Rafja we were sleeping in a tent with a bunch of drivers from Headquarters Company.

I was illegally in the tent. Because the sergeant major was very strict about segregating people by rank. But if I had gone where the officers were, I would've had to sleep in a sleeping bag on the floor. Being an ex-NCO myself, I just grabbed a cot and put my sleeping bag on it. I figured on staying there until I got caught.

My history team was working long hours. When we came into the tent, everybody else was already asleep.

I sleep quite soundly. But my guys got woken up at five A.M. by other people preparing for day shift. They got into a big argument, "Hey, be quiet. Show some consideration." But the day-shift people ignored them.

The next night we came in when the daytime folks were still awake. I didn't say anything. Took off my uniform. Stacked my web gear next to my bed. Pulled my pistol from its holster and climbed into my sleeping bag. I pretended to go to sleep.

My guys told the day people, "You see him get into his sleeping bag with his pistol?" They said, "Yeah."

"Well, he's a Vietnam veteran and he flashes back periodi-

220

cally. If you hear somebody scream in the middle of the night, *'Gooks in the wire,'* just dive on the floor and be quiet. We'll try to get the gun away from him." I just laid there, trying not to laugh too loudly.

The next day, my guys told me, "It worked great. They are terrified of you. This morning they were so quiet that we were able to sleep. Please don't blow it for us by telling them this is just a joke."

But as the ground war was about to begin, a lot of young soldiers came to us Vietnam vets and asked us, "What's going to happen? What's your advice to help me stay alive?"

FLOPPY HATS

COMMAND SERGEANT MAJOR WILLIAM MCBRIDE

SAUDI ARABIA 1990–91
DIVISION SERGEANT MAJOR
82ND AIRBORNE DIVISION

During the Gulf War, around 228,500 Reserves and National Guards were called to active duty, of whom 105,000 were sent to the war zone. They served in combat units, the medical corps, transport, supply, and a variety of support services and administrative positions. Although most of these men and women came to the Gulf ready to do their part, they often had to work extra hard to dispel the stigma of being "Weekend Warriors."

The 82nd Airborne built our own firing ranges out in the desert. We got the resources to build an entire mock city, so that we could train to fight in an urban environment. And our engineers built an Iraqi stronghold to scale. It was 1,400 meters across with all the obstacles the Iraqis use. Every one of our battalions went through there in very tough live-fire exercises.

We are affiliated with a lot of Reserve and National Guard

units. You've got to bless their hearts for being dedicated and sacrificing their time to help out. But I had some concerns whether they would be adequate to the task.

We had a number of those units attached to us in the desert. All in support or service roles. We had four National Guard truck companies who drove us into Iraq. They performed magnificently.

An MP [military police] company out of Florida did a fabulous job. I got with them the first day they arrived. They came in wearing floppy hats and little "Rambo" stuff. I talked to their 1st sergeant and company commander. I said, "This division doesn't wear floppy hats. Any time I see your people, I want to see them in all their equipment." I never had another problem with them the whole time they were there. Those MPs handled Iraqi prisoners.

And we had a postal unit attached to us who were mostly women. Most of our Reserve and National Guard units were doing jobs that they perform in civilian life. The MP company had regular policemen, the postal unit had people who worked in their hometown post offices. Truck drivers were the same.

I have a different concern for the combat units of the National Guard. The Army found that when they sent them to the National Training Center, they were not up to the task— through no fault of their own. Those types of units just don't have the time to get their soldiers physically fit and trained to go to war in a reasonably short period of time. The standard that the Army puts on Reservists and National Guard is the same as the active army. But there is no way that a combat unit can meet that with thirty-nine days a year of training.

TEAMWORK

COLONEL MICHAEL ANDREWS

FORT CARSON, COLORADO 1989–92
BRIGADE COMMANDER
4TH INFANTRY DIVISION

While waiting for his brigade to be called to duty in Desert Shield, Colonel Michael Andrews was assigned to head a training advisory team. Their job was to evaluate and prepare a National Guard armored brigade that was scheduled to join an active duty division on the front line in Saudi Arabia.

All through history, the real art of soldiering has been to synchronize different types of weapons systems at the right time and place.

In World War II, General Patton said, "It's not a question of shooting this or that weapon system. The problem is to synchronize them for decisive action." The speed of our tanks is around thirty-five miles an hour. You need clockwork timing to maneuver your forces.

During Desert Shield, I was tasked with being a training advisor to a National Guard armored brigade that was on standby for the Gulf. My job was to assist them in training exercises at Fort Hood, Texas, and make sure that they were combat ready.

Brigades need a high level of organization. It takes a lot of practice to coordinate all the operating systems: logistics, intelligence, aviation, air defense, artillery, and engineers. Some 4,000 soldiers and hundreds of vehicles must be synchronized as a team. That includes two battalions of 58 tanks each, and more than 500 vehicles in the task force.

In our Army Air/Land Battle Doctrine we emphasize a fluid fast-moving battlefield. To rapidly deploy a battalion or brigade that hasn't the benefit of extensive training endangers not only them, but soldiers in the adjacent units as well.

After I evaluated this Guard unit, a senior officer was upset that I wouldn't rate them 100 percent. But to take care of soldiers, you have to train them hard and be uncompromising on their performance standards.

Little mistakes get soldiers killed. I once saw a soldier killed because of the head space and timing gauge on a machine gun. Such a tiny thing caused the back plate to blow out. A metal shard hit the soldier's artery and he bled to death. A good commander has to hold his soldiers to such high standards that those types of little mistakes don't happen.

Some of the National Guard unit's senior people were upset that they weren't deployed to the Gulf right away. They thought they were ready on Day One. But the leaders at battalion and company level—who deal directly with the soldiers—were aware that they needed further preparation.

One day, during the training in Texas, I walked into the back doorway of a Bradley [armored personnel carrier]. It was rainy, muddy, cold. I'll never forget this. A young soldier was sitting there, a private, with his head between his knees. I looked at him for a moment, not saying anything. He looked at me. He knew that I was the training advisor. After a while, he said, "Sir, are you going to keep us alive?"

FAMILY SUPPORT

COLONEL JOHN SYLVESTER

SAUDI ARABIA 1990–91
BRIGADE COMMANDER
TIGER BRIGADE, 2ND ARMOR DIVISION

One of the success stories of the Gulf War was the family support network. That was one of the most important differences from our days in Vietnam. All of us went to Vietnam as individual replacements. We went to the Gulf in units. Therefore we had cohesive family groups and support structure. It was in place before we even went to war. It wasn't just the battalion and company commanders' wives who held the family networks together. It was also the wives of the sergeants who could be counted on.

I left an officer behind to be a liaison with the families. His wife had just left him about a month before we were alerted for the desert. He was suddenly a sole parent of a two-year-old child. He agonized. Finally, I said, "I want you to stay as my rear detachment guy."

He probably worked harder than any of us who went on the grand adventure in the desert. My wife tells me stories about him working all night long, day after day, on this problem and that problem. He would deal with taking kids to the hospital emergency room, working out bill-paying problems, and anything else that needed to be done. We had a sergeant like that in every single battalion. They should have gotten medals. Their lives were in just as much danger as ours—from irate wives.

We worked hard to try to keep in touch with the families. I made a weekly telephone call through the military radio-telephone system. The wives would get in a big theater and they'd put me on a PA system talking from the middle of the desert. And commanders of each battalion began sending back photos and videos. Any questions the wives had were answered by the following week.

On return I was accosted by some of the old World War II guys who said, "We never had any of this hubbub over our wives during World War Two." True, we didn't. That was because we weren't smart enough to recognize the need back then.

I don't know what the military divorce rate is vis-à-vis the rest of society. I don't think we've had a higher rate of divorce than any other segment of our society. In this brigade I've seen probably two or three officers split up after we got back from the Gulf. It's not to say that wouldn't have happened if we didn't go. There is usually the stress in a marriage: "You're going off to the field and leaving me and the kids to fend for ourselves. Now you're going off to war and I worried you could have been killed."

THE BOYS FROM SYRACUSE

LIEUTENANT COLONEL
DUANE CLAWSON

Saudi Arabia 1991
Flight Commander
138th Tactical Fighter Squadron,
174th Tactical Fighter Wing
Syracuse, New York Air National Guard

Duane Clawson, tall and lean with a neat-trimmed mustache, usually flies commercial passenger airplanes. A graduate of the U.S. Air Force Academy and a Vietnam fighter pilot, he left active duty in the middle of a promising career.

When we were called to the Gulf, we were the newest F-16 unit in the Air Force National Guard. New York State probably has the fourth or fifth largest air force in the world. Between the Guard and Reserve units in the state, we have every type of aircraft in the inventory, except strategic bombers. The C-5s and C-130 for transport, the F-4s for air defense, and F-16s for close air [to ground] support and air-to-air defense, as well as some sea rescue aircraft.

A strength of the Guard is that most of our pilots start out with active duty experience. We have four or five guys who were in the Navy or Marine Corps. And we have four or five guys that we sent to pilot training, who have never been with an active duty unit.

Somebody on active duty would look at my record and say, "This guy has been in the Air Force for twenty-seven years, and he's only a flight commander?" That's because the National Guard system is totally different than active duty. I left active duty as a captain in 1976, after eight years in the Air Force. At that time, in my A-7 unit I would've been a flight commander, if I wasn't a flight instructor.

But in the Guard, flight commanders are lieutenant colonels. On active duty, most fighter squadrons have approximately a 100 percent change of personnel every two or three years. In the Guard, in three years we have a twenty percent change. A strength of the Guard is that it's a very stable organization.

The main reason I left active duty was because I wanted to keep flying. At that time, nine of every ten field-grade officers were sitting behind a desk. I said, "No thanks."

I joined the National Guard in Syracuse and flew A-10s for eight years and the F-16 for the past two years. Both are single-seat airplanes. The difference is that the F-16 cruising speed is between 420 to 480 knots. That's about 200 knots difference in speed. The F-16 has advanced air-to-air radar that helps to discriminate who is in front of you in the air. You can see a commercial airliner at seventy or eighty miles away, and other fighters outside twenty miles.

The F-16A model has a conventional layout of individual control panels scattered around the cockpit, separate radio control, separate transponder control, separate INS, which gives you coordinates, latitude and longitude, anyplace you go. The weapons computer is underneath your armpit, and one of the radios is on your right side. But in the C model all of that is combined into one small compact control head, right in front of you. Everything you need to do in flight is hands-on. Weapons controls are on both the stick [right hand] and the throttle [left hand], and engine controls are on the throttle—so you don't have to move your hands.

The F-16 is the safest single-engine fighter the Air Force has ever had. But a two-engine airplane like the F-15 has a better peacetime survival rate because if you lose one engine, you can still fly the airplane home. You lose your engine in the F-16, you'd better have your parachute ready. However, in combat if an engine is hit by hostile fire it will explode, destroying the airplane. So two engines increase the risk to heat-seeking missiles.

We left Syracuse for Saudi Arabia on January 2, 1991. We got there after flying for fifteen hours. We had ten airborne refuelings en route. We arrived mid-afternoon. Everybody was dead on their rear.

We were told, "These are your squadron tents." We looked around. There were no cots, no chairs or tables, no facilities, no radios. Nothing. We had to totally build our squadron's living quarters and operations center.

The furniture we were given was the pressboard kits that you put together with screws. It's halfway decent, but we weren't supplied any screwdrivers. A couple guys brought their own tools. Once you got your hands on one, you used it until your hands were sore and raw. Because it might be hours before you would get another chance.

All together there were between 4,000 and 5,000 people living on the base, all in tents. We were the last fighter group to get in.

We spent the first week just building furniture and walls and desks, so that we could operate. Another problem was that our single-seat airplanes didn't have room for our mechanics. Eventually 700 people from Syracuse joined us in Saudi. By the time we got settled in, it was three days before the air war started.

BUYING TIME

GENERAL ALFRED GRAY

The Pentagon 1987–91
Commandant
U.S. Marine Corps

During the period leading into the Desert Storm, the intense debate on whether the Coalition should forcibly evict the Iraqi army from Kuwait also took place within the American military. The Marine Corps Commandant, General Al Gray, was among those who counseled a careful, deliberate approach.

During Desert Shield I didn't want two Marine Corps: those marines who were in the Gulf, and those who weren't. The sergeant major and I continued to make our trips to bases and recruiting stations. When we were in Okinawa, we spoke to a force that was preparing to go to Korea for an exercise. We explained to them why.

At the same time we had to evacuate the American embassy in Liberia [Africa] while the city was engulfed in civil war. And in the middle of Desert Storm, we had to send a rescue mission 460 miles to protect and evacuate U.S. and foreign citizens in Somalia.

In addition, we never had less than 4,000 Marines in the Philippines providing humanitarian assistance after the volcano and the flooding. We had 1,000 marines in South America on counternarcotics operations. And we ran a training exercise in Honduras because nobody else was able to do it.

There was hardly enough hours in a day to keep up with Marine Corps responsibilities. Fortunately, I've been blessed with a good metabolism. I've never needed a lot of sleep—I've mastered the "combat nap."

I could count on the perspective of my sergeant major and my aides. If there were simultaneous events going on, I chose generals who I trust to monitor activities that I could not attend.

If something important was going on in the Gulf, I'd drop into the Pentagon after dinner. I was always lucky that Watch officers and enlisted people on duty were never bothered while I was around. I tried not to ask a bunch of dumb questions. For example, we had Marine reservists who were in charge of targeting the key nuclear facilities in Iraq. I just stood in the background and they would show me what was going on.

Between August and December, the public debate raged as to whether our forces should be engaged in the Gulf. I could understand the views of people who opposed our military involvement in the Gulf. I was very strong, for example, on letting the sanctions take hold. In September and October, I was publicly saying on TV, "There's no rush."

What I was doing was emphasizing the need to buy time. U.S. forces weren't ready to fight in October. I told my people, "Be patient. Every day that we don't fight is another day to get better trained and acclimatized."

I knew that the Saudi weather would turn from extreme heat to extreme cold. I kept telling my logistics people, "Get the goddamned cold weather clothing over there." They thought I was crazy. It was like the experience I had in Vietnam in 1964. When the monsoon season started, we froze our ass off. I used to wrap Vietnamese newspapers around my feet for warmth.

When I returned from the Gulf in October 1990, I knew that time was on our side. We were shaping our forces. I told my Marines, "We're not at war with the Iraqi people. And we're not at war with that part of the Iraqi army that chooses not to follow Saddam. But we're at war with that guy [Saddam]. He's a murderer. We're here, not for oil alone. It's about people and long-term stability." So our young lance corporals knew why they were fighting.

When I went out to the region at the end of August, people were talking about troop rotation. I told my people, "We need to keep unit cohesion and continuity of training and readiness. Should the need arise to reinforce, we will double our force by the end of January." To have made that decision in early August was one of the best things we did.

DADS

REAR ADMIRAL RILEY MIXSON

Red Sea 1990–91
Carrier Battle Group Commander
USS *John F. Kennedy*

This war was unique for a number of reasons. One was that we had a lot of father/son or father/daughter teams serving in Desert Shield/Desert Storm. The Air Group commander, Mike Bowman on the USS *America*, had a daughter on a supply ship in the Persian Gulf. My son was on the front lines with the Marines. He was among the first ones through the mine fields and into the Kuwait City area. I would've liked to have been personally providing support for him.

There was a lot of concern among our senior military officers who had offspring in the war area. We would rather have been in harm's way ourselves. It's always all right for Dad to go out and fight the battle. But when your kids are out there, it puts a sobering perspective on the entire effort. It certainly did put extra pressure on me and my family.

With my own ship or my own carrier group, even if you don't have total control of the situation among the ground forces, at least you feel that you have the ability to influence what is happening in combat. But there is a lot of parental concern when you have no control over what would happen to one's child in another unit.

I cheered every time General Schwarzkopf decided to carry on the air war a while longer to soften up the Iraqi Republican Guards. I felt that was a courageous decision on General Schwarzkopf's part. Because there was pressure to get the ground forces involved. I supported his policy, as did all the other dads throughout the United States.

There were times, of course, during the planning and early stages of the air campaign, that I wished that I could've been flying missions with my pilots. Any aviator worth his salt wants to fly a mission. It's much harder to stay back than it is to go.

The way that feeling affected me was that I couldn't stay off the flight deck when my guys were getting ready to fly that first night. I made a point to talk to each one of them and wish them well.

RAKKASANS

COMMAND SERGEANT MAJOR JOSEPH GARRETT

SAUDI ARABIA 1991
BATTALION SERGEANT MAJOR
19TH COMBAT ENGINEER BATTALION

My son had been sitting in the desert since August with the 101st Airborne Division. On the first Sunday that my battalion camped in northern Saudi Arabia, February 14—ten days before the start of the ground war—I went looking for him among 500,000 American troops scattered across hundreds of miles.

There was only one road in the north, and the 101st was guarding it. I took off in my Humvee heading north. Around 150 miles later I found that Tap Line Road. As I drove through various camps, I looked at the soldiers' shoulder patches. I saw the 24th Division, the 18th Airborne Corps, the 82nd Airborne . . . Finally, I stopped and asked some people.

They said, "The 101st headquarters is about six miles on the right hand side of the road." Ironically, my boy was in the same

101st unit that I had served with in Vietnam—the 187th Rakkasans, whose emblem is a pagoda. All of a sudden I see a cardboard MRE [meals ready to eat] box propped on the road with that emblem and an arrow. So I turned off into the desert toward Iraq. After eighteen miles I found a battalion dug into foxholes.

I got out of my Humvee and started walking around. I walk up to another Humvee, looked back, and there's my boy reading a paperback book.

After all that trouble, I got to spend only about fifteen minutes with him. But I had to touch him. His Mom would've killed me if I hadn't at least found him before the ground war kicked off. We all knew that it would be happening soon.

D-DAY

GENERAL CHARLES HORNER

Saudi Arabia 1990–91
Commanding General
Central Command Air Forces

After months of concentrated planning, the air campaign of Operation Desert Storm began in the early morning hours of January 18, 1991. In the Air Tasking Orders there were many innovative tactics and post-Vietnam technologies to be flown by pilots who had never been tested in actual combat.

When the air war started, I sat in the TACC [Tactical Air Control Center at CENTCOM headquarters in Riyadh] feeling very badly. First, because we were embarking on taking human lives. And, I didn't know whether our technology would work. The test data showed that Stealth worked. But it had never been used in such numbers. But what bothered me most, I wondered that I might not have done enough to adequately prepare my people for what the enemy might do.

The plan for the first day and a half was set in concrete. It included striking targets in the Baghdad area, various airfields, and Iraq's land army in Kuwait. But the emphasis was on destroying nuclear and biological weapons sites, Scud missile sites, and Saddam's Command and Control, to isolate Baghdad from the battlefield. And to gain control of the air.

I had seen a high casualty rate in Vietnam. Going into this campaign, we honestly didn't know how many people we would lose. The problem was that we didn't have recent experience to test how good our electronic jamming equipment would work to neutralize the SAM [surface-to-air missile] sites.

We knew that Iraq had thousands of antiaircraft [Triple-A] guns. So I put all of our airplanes at medium altitude, to get them out of gun range. Iraq had a powerful, excellent air force. We didn't know how successful our strategy would be to gain control of the air.

The night before the air war started, Buster Glosson and I were sitting in the Command Post together. Buster said, "How many airplanes are we going to lose?" I wrote down the number 39 on a piece of paper, and handed it to Buster. By the end of the war our losses were forty-two.

You might think I knew what I was doing. In reality, when I wrote 39, I meant only for the U.S. Air Force, which constituted sixty percent of all U.S. airplanes. My full estimate would have been around sixty losses. I heard that other people briefed President Bush with an estimate of 175 lost aircraft, based on computer game planning.

The Iraqi air force was well-equipped and well-trained. They have Soviet MiG-29s and French Mirages. The Iraqi pilots I previously met were pretty good. They pulled off some fantastic missions in their war against Iran. But their weakness was central control. And they were tied to their ground control.

A key element of our overall strategy was to knock down Saddam's intercept aircraft before they could respond to our operations. During the first few days of the war, when the control of the air was being contested, Iraqi pilots would put on their gear, get into their airplanes, and be blown up before they could respond. That's because our F-15C fighters, with their "look down/shoot down" capability, were able to target and fire on them immediately after takeoff.

48 HOURS

LIEUTENANT GENERAL BUSTER GLOSSON

SAUDI ARABIA 1990–91
DIRECTOR OF CAMPAIGN PLANS
CENTRAL COMMAND AIR FORCES &
COMMANDER, 14TH AIR DIVISION

The first forty-eight hours of the air campaign, I'll never forget
. . . No sleep, anxiety over the unknown, and high tension best
describe those first couple of days.

Our Tactical Air Control Center—or TACC—in Riyadh had
a large screen that permitted us to watch the war in an overall
sense. We could not micromonitor every strike in every area.
So we had other command and control systems help with monitoring. AWAC airplanes were doing air-to-air coordination of
flight packages, and J-STARS coordinated the air-to-ground attacks.

Some strikes went into very high-threat environments. For
example, General Horner and I monitored the F-111s' attack
on Balad Southeast very closely. We knew how many airplanes
were involved, and our monitoring systems were able to tell us
if an airplane was shot down. We monitored a similar F-15E
attack on Scud sites in western Iraq. Our AWACs provided information relays back to the TACC center.

However, we didn't have the same capability to monitor the
Stealth F-117s that went over the Baghdad area. They maintained radio silence. We had to wait until they contacted
AWACs on their way out of Iraq. At twenty minutes before
H-Hour [opening of attack] F-117 bombers were one hundred
miles from Baghdad. At the same time, eight Army "Apache"
and four Air Force "Pave Low" helicopters were attacking two
forward radar sites near the Iraq-Saudi border. That would
open a radar-free corridor for F-15E bombers to go in undetected for an attack on Scud missile bases in western Iraq.

If the helicopters failed, there was a high probability that the Iraqis would pick up the F-15Es on radar and determine where they were going. Scuds would have been launched at Israel, antiaircraft systems throughout Iraq would have been alerted, and the first wave of non-Stealth Coalition airplanes would have been at risk.

TASK FORCE NORMANDY

LIEUTENANT COLONEL RICHARD CODY

SAUDI ARABIA 1990–91
BATTALION COMMANDER
1ST BATTALION, 101ST AVIATION BRIGADE
101ST AIRBORNE DIVISION (AIR ASSAULT)

Task Force Normandy was the mission name given to the two teams of AH-64 Apache attack helicopters that flew the first battle mission of Desert Storm. The mission name reflects the historical legacy of the 101st Division, among the first to make the D-Day Normandy landing in World War II.

The mission leader, Lieutenant Colonel Richard Cody, is called the "General Patton of Army aviation," although his personality is much more patient and tactful than the colorful Patton's. A 1972 West Point graduate, the six-foot aviator has spent much of his career adapting and test-flying special operations helicopters.

The greatest challenge in planning and organizing Task Force Normandy were the doubts that Colonel Cody's aviation superiors expressed that the Apache could perform in such a demanding long-distance role.

We were the first full-up "Apache" helicopter battalion in-country. Our primary mission was covering the small number of U.S. Marine and Army 82nd Airborne ground forces in "trip alert" on the Saudi-Kuwait border. We were to delay attacking Iraqi forces until heavy armor units could come in from U.S. and European bases.

There were thirty-five aircraft in my battalion, a relatively small but highly lethal force. The Iraqis had far more tanks than we had antitank missiles. We had 200 Hellfire [antitank] missiles in country. We didn't know what we would do after that.

We had trained for long-range navigation strikes, primarily for contingencies we had in the Caribbean Basin. The year prior to coming to Saudi, we experimented with deep strikes, using two 230-gallon fuel tanks. We used to take off from Fort Campbell, Kentucky at seven o'clock at night and attack by daylight in Georgia, nonstop. That's 600 miles.

I wanted my guys to get used to long distance flying while using night vision goggles and FLIR [forward looking infrared] technology, and carrying heavy fuel and munitions weight. This later proved significant in our first strike mission in Desert Storm.

In Saudi Arabia, during the planning of the air campaign, we were chosen to go a very long distance against two active adjacent radar sites in the Iraqi desert, to open the air war.

The mission came down from General Schwarzkopf to Colonel Jesse Johnson, [Commander of the CENTCOM Special Operations Command] on August 25, 1990. Only around eight people knew about it. It was classified, "Direct Action, Top Secret Mission." We were chosen because in the 101st Air Assault Division, our pilots live on the leading edge of technology and tactics. The advantage we have over jet airplanes like the F-15E "Strike Eagle" or F-117 "Stealth" bomber or the British "Tornado" is that we can slow our speed down to sixty knots and hover on line to precisely synchronize our fire. An extra challenge was that the Iraqi radar sites were mobile. They move them around quite a bit.

Their radar would pick up any "fast movers" [jet airplanes] because of the signal caused by their speed. You can't sneak them in. Even though the airplanes could have taken out the sites, the Iraqis would have time to relay to their headquarters that the allied air campaign had begun. Iraqi jet fighters and air defense SAM missile systems would have been activated, jeopardizing American and allied air crews. The planners of the air campaign wanted to utilize surprise to destroy Iraqi jet fighters on the ground, before they could scramble.

Each radar site was spread out over an area 2,000 meters with Tropo Scatter radar, two or three Squat Eye radar, and Flat Face and Spoon-Rest radar systems. There were at least two large communications vans, vans for ground control intercept and sundry other mobile buildings.

The mission task force, code-named Normandy, was eight Apaches and four Air Force MH-53J special operations Pave Low helicopters, under the command of Lt. Colonel Rich Comer, to guide us. The Pave Lows have Terrain-Following radar and a GPS [global positioning satellite] system that make them excellent flight leads at low altitude, high speed. They provided insurance that we got to the target area at the designated time. And they are capable of combat search and rescue in case any of our helicopters went down.

The two radar sites were thirty-five miles apart with overlapping radar systems. It was like a radar picket fence protecting the western corridor to Baghdad. My team of four Apaches and two Pave Lows, White Team, took one radar site. Red Team had the other. We were going to punch a hole in that picket fence.

I led two lives. As a cover for our mission training, we called our activities "search and rescue training." None of my staff or troops knew what was going on. At night, I'd go over to SOCCENT [Central Command Special Operations] headquarters to plan the mission with Colonel Jesse Johnson and his staff. After mid-October, my S2 [intelligence officer] Lieutenant Russ Stinger, assisted with the targeting and planning.

The radar site was in southern Iraq, along the air corridor that was the closest distance to Baghdad from Saudi Arabia. It wasn't very far across the border. But it was 750 miles from our 101st Division home base. We had to adapt our fuel tanks.

Normally on missions, Apaches will carry four Hellfire missiles on the outboard rails, nineteen rockets on the inboards, and about 1,000 rounds of 30mm. The fuel on board gives us two hours of flying time, traveling at 125 knots [160 mph]. The mission plan called for some hellacious distances. The jump-off point at al Jaouf, in western Saudi, was 600 miles from our home base. And there was no military presence or refueling base anywhere near there. So I decided to load an extra fuel tank. Because I wanted to fly the entire distance without refueling, hit the target, and not refuel until after we flew out.

Previously, I was not authorized by the Army to fly tactical combat missions with an extra fuel tank. Fortunately, at Fort

Campbell, when we received our orders to the desert, instinctively I looked at some of the distances across the desert and brought our extra tanks with us, anyway.

The Apache has external fuel tanks designed into the system. It has the proper plumbing to add an extra 230-gallon wing tank on. Not for combat speed, but to cruise, because it brings the aircraft weight up to 21,000 pounds.

When I received orders for the opening mission, I looked at using the extra tank. The problem of having two tanks was that I was downloading too much ammunition, which risked the effectiveness of our fire control computer. The solution we came up with was to balance the weight of the extra fuel tank with the number of rockets on the opposite side of the aircraft.

Our problem was getting an Air Worthiness release from higher headquarters at Aviation Systems Command. No one had ever gone into combat or fired with an extra fuel tank on. They gave me permission to fire Hellfire missiles, but not the rockets or 30mm cannons. They were worried that our maneuverability would be limited. And that sparks and debris from the rocket motor would blow up the fuel tank.

I told them that we would have the tank on one side with the Hellfires, that come out clean. We'd put the rockets on the other side. It took me three days of faxing letters, saying, "Trust me. We know what we're doing. I've personally test flown it myself. The aircraft will handle the weight. Please let us do it."

Some of my pilots were concerned that enemy small arms fire could explode the tank. I said, "Guys, with our FLIR system's magnification of images on our TV monitor, the Apache can see for miles. We can see and shoot farther than their weapons can reach. You're like a boxer with a multimile jab. If you're taking small arms fire, what are you doing in close?"

As commander, my main concern was mission accomplishment. I wasn't worried about my crews' capabilities. I had commanded the unit for a year, and we had done a lot of training against air defense systems. And I had great confidence in our crew chiefs, who had collectively produced the best Apache readiness rates in the Army.

However, I was uncomfortable with the possibility of a mechanical failure on any of the aircraft. Every helicopter has an Achilles heel, and an Apache is no different. There are some things that can go wrong, no matter how well you maintain it. And with eight of them flying in "Indian country," I was worried about that. The key to the mission was to stay synchronized. To destroy both radar sites at the exact same time.

Intelligence told us that the Iraqis had three Triple-A batteries at each radar site: ZPU-4 and S-60 guns. We knew that they couldn't touch us until we got within 2,000 meters.

My battle strategy was an orchestrated attack from longer distance with Hellfires, closing in with rockets and finishing up with 30mm. We practiced it over and over. My concern was that the Triple-A batteries might be moved out farther than what we expected.

As a commander, there are a couple types of stress I had to deal with. First, is the stress that you put on yourself. And, the stress your superiors put on you. My superiors, Division Commander General Binford Peay, and Brigade Commander Colonel Tom Garrett, were very supportive and very positive. They understood that I was juggling two separate missions—ground support for the division ground forces, and special operations. And Special Operations Commander Colonel Jesse Johnson never put me in an awkward situation.

The extra stress of this particular mission after picking the crews I wanted was to maintain cohesion in the unit. My pilots are highly competent, highly competitive people. I couldn't define to them exactly what the special mission was, but everybody knew it was going to be a unique challenge, and wanted to be involved.

I told them, "Guys, every one of you is capable of flying the mission. I will make the decision on who goes. But understand that beyond practicing for this mission, this battalion still has our division mission. I need a balanced team.

"I will make my selection. I don't want any of you guys to feel slighted. And those of you selected, don't walk around feeling that you are the greatest thing. Every one of you are wearing the team jersey, like offensive and defensive squads on a football team."

I always worry about losing people. The biggest stress I had on the mission was that I couldn't confide in anybody because it was secret. I drew up a plan, and for a long time scratched my head and questioned, "Is this the right way to go?" I did a lot of "what ifs." I laid out where we were going to refuel, how we were going to use the weapons, the fuel option—all in a vacuum. I couldn't bring in other people for feedback. So I worried whether I made the right decisions or not.

How did I handle the stress? I played basketball with my

troops every day. And I had battalion formations every other day, where company commanders inspected their troops. Then I circled the battalion. We discussed rumors and exchanged information. I'd dispel rumors and told them what I knew. That let off a little steam and kept our heads straight. My troops did not hesitate to give me feedback. Believe me, they were very candid. Throughout the XVIII Airborne Corps, a point was made for everyone to fully understand the game plan, and the next higher level of command's intent. The troops knew that. And that makes a big difference in morale.

I had two orders in my "Direct Action Operations Order" from Colonel Jesse Johnson. They were clear and concise: "H-minus 22 [minutes]: Attack. Destroy."

And my rules of engagement for Task Force Normandy were very simple: "Conduct a direct action to destroy that radar site." I told my people, "Everything at that site must come down."

As we made our final preparations for the mission, Colonel Johnson spoke to my pilots. He didn't tell them everything. He said, "You will probably start the war." But didn't spell out all the particulars.

On January 15, when we got to al Jaouf, I pulled out the target folders and laid out the real deal. That didn't surprise them very much. These are pretty smart kids. They'd been hypothesizing. Especially during December exercises when I tightened the task standards: "Guys, that wasn't good enough. You missed by ten seconds. I want it perfect." Still, they had no idea that we would fire the first shots of the war.

I didn't have to impress upon them how important the mission was. I showed them Iraq's nationwide air defense system that the two forward radar sites were tied into . . . and the estimated U.S. aircraft losses if we failed.

We were on the flight line before midnight and took off at one A.M. on January 17. Crossing over the border, some Iraqi border posts fired some small arms and launched a shoulder-fired missile. But I don't think they saw us.

Led by the Air Force Pave Lows, we flew near ground level. Around nine miles from our targets, they dropped chemical lights to identify our "release point." At that time, Red Team and White Team locked on our computerized target acquisition systems. By the time we traveled to our battle position, we were ready to open fire.

The Iraqi radar picked us up. But they couldn't discriminate us from the ground clutter. With the magnification of our TV monitors, we saw soldiers running around outside the radar sites. Our radar system indicated that they were searching for us. But they couldn't identify us to pass target information to their higher headquarters.

We got in position, on line. Looking at our FLIR screens, everyone knew precisely which building or piece of equipment they were to hit. We slowed down, methodically moving on line together.

The code word, "Party in ten," was given. Pilots painted their lasers on targets, and counted to ten before we simultaneously opened fire. My gunner, Brian Stewmon, put two missiles right on target.

With my naked eye I watched three and a half minutes of bedlam. People on the ground never knew what hit them. Explosions across the entire target area. Big flash BANGS. Missiles hitting incessantly. We moved forward peppering the place with rockets. Then hosed the area down with 30mm high-explosive incendiary rounds.

My pilots remained calm. Most were twenty-five- or twenty-six-year-old kids who had never been in combat before: "Roger. I've got my target." "Okay." "Next target." No screaming or yelling or swearing. I took some small arms fire when we broke off from the radar site, but those soldiers were finished off by my wing man. Both bases were taken down in three to four minutes. Then we were done.

As we pulled out of the target area, I saw Air Force F-15E fast movers coming overhead to the left and right of me. We were cheering them on, "Go get 'em!"

AIR WING COMMAND

BRIGADIER GENERAL
TOM LENNON

SAUDI ARABIA 1990–91
WING COMMANDER
48TH TACTICAL FIGHTER WING

I led my air wing off to war on the first night of Desert Storm. We launched 56 of our F-111s in the second wave, and hit our targets—hardened aircraft silos, munition storage depots and Saddam's command and control—around one hour after the war started. I took the deepest target.

I had 66 F-111F [fighter bombers] and 20 EF-111 [electronic radar jamming] aircraft, around 250 crew members. Out of that group, only six had combat experience in Vietnam. A couple guys had been in Panama, and two on the Libya raid. All together, including maintenance and support people, there were 3,200 people under my command.

Before the opening missions, I spoke about combat with my people. I had three pieces of advice for them, "The biggest threat is the ground. The next largest threat is the lack of fuel. And the third, is the enemy defenses. In that order."

I made sure that my people had trained in the desert as they would fight. For five months we practiced our most difficult bomb delivery: a night strike at 200 feet altitude, doing a 90 degree manual turn at around 650 knots (750 mph). We go straight up to 500 to 1,500 feet, then back down to 200 feet, using our terrain-following radars.

It's actually much safer to fly above the Triple-A. But early on, not knowing how much ECM [electronic counter-measure] support we'd have going in with us to jam their radar, we didn't have much choice but to go in low. The first night of the war, that tactic—flying Auto TF [terrain following] at 200 feet or lower—is what saved some of my pilots who went against

All Asseliem base, on the outskirts of Kuwait City. Without the training, they would not have been able to do it.

My target was north of Baghdad. It was amazing the amount of munitions they threw at us. Some was shot in a blanket over the target area. Other fire was aimed directly at the aircraft. When the sky is all lit up from airbursts, the gunners probably could see our airplanes. And that first night they still had some radar-guided antiaircraft systems. I had some radar-guided Triple-A coming at me. No doubt about it. I could see it bursting around my aircraft.

And we had three Rolands and an SA2 missile fired at us during our bomb delivery approach. We saw the missile coming off the rail [launcher]. We dropped our aluminum chaff and maneuvered. That threw it off in another direction.

Day One of the war, everyone was able to handle the fear. It was in the subsequent days that some people were less able to handle it. That is only normal. My philosophy was not to preach about the fear aspect. Because every individual handles it differently.

My Command group watched everyone closely, I had a flight surgeon in the Mission Planning room. If a pilot looked over-tired or stressed out, or was having a problem sleeping, we'd have his squadron commander or operations officer pull him aside. Take him off the flying schedule, if necessary, to get a little rest.

It's not wise to have someone who is not performing to the best of their ability flying missions. Because he will jeopardize someone else's life.

Even though I had a lot of past combat experience, I still felt the stress. Anyone who says that they don't have fear when someone is shooting at them, is a damned liar or a fool. It's not about whether you have fear, but how you handle that fear in combat.

Two or three weeks into the air campaign, the amount of ground fire depended on where you went. We took down Iraqi airfields where we put twenty-four airplanes over the field in twenty minutes, making two passes each. We took out every hardened shelter on the airfield, the hardened command posts, the hardened fuel dumps and a couple of munitions storage areas—all with direct hits.

That's partly due to the skill and training of the pilots, and to the quality of the munitions. To have a 75 to 85 percent target killed per bomb is phenomenal. In Vietnam we were lucky to get 5 percent. That is our advantage today of using laser-guided systems and infrared GBU-15s.

We dropped GBU-15s from between six to eighteen miles away from a target. In Vietnam, flying F-4 "Phantoms," we dropped the "dumb" bombs from 6,000 to 10,000 feet directly over a target. In the later stages of that war, we did begin to drop some precision-guided munitions. I was involved in dropping around fifteen TV-guided bombs that were in the development stage.

We had so many more planes shot down over Vietnam than in Desert Storm, not so much because of technology, but also because of employment concepts, altitudes and tactics. We did an awful lot of daytime operations in Southeast Asia. In the Gulf, from my perspective, the F-111's greatest advantage was the night. The airplane has unique PAVE-TAC pods that allows us to see clearly at night and deliver precision-guided munitions.

In Vietnam we were not permitted from the outset to systematically roll back the North Vietnamese air defense system. Where, in the Gulf, General Glosson and the rest of us spent five months planning to achieve that in the first three days of the air war. We went in with overwhelming force and basically took out Saddam's electronic eyes and ears. We isolated his army on the battlefield, and started waging a war of attrition on them. That was the contribution of the first week. By the second week, his airplanes were not getting up. We were not allowed to do that in Vietnam.

The hardest decision I had as a commander, was prior to the war starting when predicted pilot losses were at 15 to 19 percent. When it came time for the first raids, I made the decision to put my best people against the most difficult targets. Even though some of these people were my very best friends. I knew that if the computer prediction was correct, they could have been lost.

I chose the Mission Commanders for each strike package. The tougher the target, the more talented the individual I put in the lead. I didn't care what rank the guy was. It had nothing to do with whether they were married or had kids. Or how many sorties they had already flown. It was based on maturity and leadership ability: How much guts did he have to face the hard issues on the ground, as well as, in the air?

When I flew in Southeast Asia, I did lose some friends. That wasn't really a factor in my decisions in the Gulf. You have to be able to store those kinds of memories away. If you start to dwell on those types of things, that's when you can go off the deep end. When it comes time to make the hard decisions, you have to appoint the people who you feel can bring their guys back alive.

FIREWORKS

LIEUTENANT GENERAL BUSTER GLOSSON

SAUDI ARABIA 1990–91
DIRECTOR OF CAMPAIGN PLANS
CENTRAL COMMAND AIR FORCES &
COMMANDER, 14TH AIR DIVISION

I think it was Churchill who said, "The most exhilarating thing in the world is to be shot at and missed." When a pilot gets to the other side of his target, that's how he feels.

On the first night of the air war, what we saw on television was a tremendous amount of antiaircraft fire directed at our pilots. A lot of young fighter pilots became veterans very fast. I talked quite extensively with the young fighter pilots that flew in and around Baghdad. I asked F-117 Stealth pilots, "Tell me exactly what you saw."

They quite candidly would admit that there were occasions, especially in the first missions when they were thirty seconds from their bomb releases, that all of their instincts were saying "you will not make it through" the intense antiaircraft fire.

The same impulses were true for people flying F-111s, F-15Es, A-6s and GR-1s attacking the airfields and industrial base targets. The one thing about those F-117 pilots that I'm proudest of, we never had a bomb run aborted because of hostile fire. Their training made the difference. But it also takes plain guts.

The reason I kept talking with them was to make sure we were executing the air war smartly. We continuously adjusted attack profiles. Iraqi Triple-A fire was set to burst at certain altitudes. So I kept very close track on where the Triple-A was exploding. For example, the first night the Triple-A was primarily exploding between 7,000 to 9,000 feet and again at 15,000 to 18,000 feet. But our airplanes weren't at those altitudes.

Approximately three days later, the Iraqis figured that out and changed their burst altitudes. However, we stayed ahead of them. We'd go in at a certain altitude for one or two nights and then change radically. We did not give them predictable targets. Also, as a result of our stealth technology, the Iraqis fired their Triple-A weapons at aircraft noise, not a visual or radar target.

General Horner and I tried to save our pilots' lives by taking prudent action. Most daytime raids were in areas far enough from Baghdad where the antiaircraft threat wasn't as high. We attacked the fixed SAM sites with raids before we did anything else.

The very first morning, as the sun came up, we had the Air National Guard F-16s from Syracuse, New York, and McIntyre Air Base in South Carolina, and Marine Corps F/A-18s—more than forty airplanes—go against nothing but fixed SAM sites in the Kuwait area. The air defense forces supporting the Iraq ground army never recovered.

800-POUND GORILLAS

LIEUTENANT COLONEL DUANE CLAWSON

Saudi Arabia 1990–91
Flight Commander
138th Tactical Fighter Squadron,
174th Tactical Fighter Wing
Syracuse, New York Air National Guard

The F-16 was designed to be the most agile fighter plane in the world. In Desert Storm the F-16s were used in a variety of day and night roles, including radar suppression, where pilots could utilize the airplane's thrust and agility to outmaneuver SAM missiles. After SAM sites were sufficiently suppressed in Kuwait and Iraq, the F-16s were assigned as tank killers. They could fly high above the battlefield at high speed, beyond the reach of air defense artillery on the ground and shoulder-fired missiles.

There were more combat-experienced pilots at our air base in two squadrons of National Guard than probably anywhere else in Saudi Arabia. But most of our combat experience from Vietnam did not apply, because the Rules of Engagement had changed.

The decision to call off a mission was given to the flight leaders. On that first day, it was mine. Earlier, when General Glosson briefed us, he said, "Fight smart. There's nothing worth dying for." We took that to heart. We operated that way until the ground war started. And none of my guys died.

That was very different than my experience in Vietnam. During the first four months of 1971, my air wing lost eleven airplanes. Because of ground fire—just small arms and automatic weapons. Trees.

During the Lam Son 710 operation into Laos, we lost a lieutenant who had been in-country for three weeks. He was flying an F-100, going after North Vietnamese tanks. They were down in a valley between mountain peaks. He had Mark-82 munitions where you had to fly low into the enemy.

He acted like any lieutenant does straight out of training with no experience. He lined up his target, made a little bit of correction this way and that way. He flew in a straight line. Everybody on the ground said, "Ha, ha, I can hit this guy." And they hammered him, straight into the ground.

Because of incidents like that, to counter pilots' lack of combat experience, the Air Force instituted the "Red Flag" training exercise at Nellis Air Force Base in Nevada. During Vietnam, people found out that half of our losses occurred during pilots' first ten missions. So Red Flag training was created to replicate a combat environment. It put a guy under combat stress, but with nobody shooting real munitions at him. By giving a guy his first ten stressful missions in that environment, it doubles his chances of survival in war. The casualties you prevent are like doubling the number of pilots and airplanes you will have available. In effect, doubling the size of your air force.

In Desert Storm, the first few days of the war we were assigned primarily against radar and SAM missile sites. The anti-SAM assignment was totally new to us. We had not trained for that.

In a single-seat airplane, a pilot has to rely on his own skill. I wouldn't say that it caused me to have butterflies in my stomach. It felt more like buzzards. [He laughs.]

All of our training in the States was to prepare for close air support of ground troops. We usually flew in two ship formations. A four-ship formation was the largest. But if you are going after SAM sites, you need to take an "800-pound gorilla," like a sixteen-ship formation.

We remembered our Air Force briefing, "You won't do anything over here that you haven't done before." That became a joke. Because almost everything we were asked to do we had never done before. We had two days to prepare.

We held a squadron meeting every evening after dinner. Everybody would sit together and we'd talk about tactics. We had a couple of guys who had prepared for anti-SAM missions when they were on active duty. They gave the rest of us some pointers.

On the first day of the air war, I led the afternoon mission. We drove toward the border, still in the clouds. That caused me some concern. Because you can't defend yourself against a radar-guided missile if you can't see it. On the radar indicator inside the airplane, all you can see is that the ground defense has his radar on and he is tracking you.

The indicator tells you the direction of the radar. So you look in that direction and try to find the missile coming through the clouds. When you see a missile is coming at you from a distance, you head toward it. At the last instant, you turn. You will be out of its range by the time the missile turns around and recalculates.

But if you can't see it, and do a 180-degree turn, you may put yourself in jeopardy. Because it travels much faster than you, and you are directly in its path. Or, you may maneuver directly into its range without knowing it.

The Flight Commander is an administrative position in the squadron. On a mission, the Flight Lead is the guy responsible for that flight, whether it be two or four ships. Besides being a flight leader, as mission commander I was responsible for all twelve to sixteen airplanes.

The flight leader role is not like some other types of command where a leader can watch from a distance. With [jet] fighters, the leader is up front. By the nature of the game, you have to be. But you keep track of where your other people are by radio communicating. You keep track when somebody is going in on a SAM site, then jettisoning their bomb load and egressing [leaving].

Going against radar sites, we carried Mark-84 bombs. They are 2,000-pound bombs, around ten feet long, with radar fuses. They explode five to ten feet in the air, with a destruction radius a couple hundred feet.

We'd roll in from 25,000 to 27,000 feet. We'd stay as high as we could above the antiaircraft threat. We can tell the computer in the airplane exactly where the target is, and it will compute the weapons delivery for you. It's not as accurate as a laser-guided bomb. But SAM-6 sites are not pinpoint targets. They cover a large area, with a radar system and all the missile launchers arranged in a circular fashion, several hundred feet across. All we try to do is put the bombs in that area, to knock out the missiles and their radar vans.

In our initial missions of the war, we saw a lot of ground fire. As my wing man came off a target I would look over. There were all these little popcorn balls or white puffs following behind him. It dawned on me as I was pulling off target that they were behind me, too.

As mission commander, I was also in charge of preplanning and coordinating with the Wild Weasels airplanes, to make sure that they were on target to give us electronic countermeasures protection. There were not enough Wild Weasels to cover every strike because of the massive numbers of sorties. Every ten minutes, there was a strike going on, around the clock.

WILD WEASELS

COLONEL GENE "NEAL" PATTON

BAHRAIN 1990–91
DEPUTY COMMANDER FOR OPERATIONS
35TH TACTICAL FIGHTER WING

*Probably the most revered Vietnam-era aircraft participating in
Desert Storm was the F-4 "Phantom" that was adapted to fly
"Wild Weasel" missions against SAM radar and missile air-
defense systems. The original F-4 came into service in 1958 as
a flight interceptor of enemy aircraft. In 1978 the F4-E had its
gun and ammunition bay removed from the aircraft and replaced by electronic radar receiving gear, and gradually added
fifty-two antennas to the exterior of the aircraft. This led to the
Weasel's APR-47 electronics system, which tells pilots where
they are in relation to radar sites on the ground.*

*Colonel "Neal" Patton, forty-six, joined the Air Force in
1967 after graduating from Texas A&M University. "Like many
other Air Force officers of my vintage," he says, "the draft
was breathing down our necks. So we said: Why don't we join
the Air Force?"*

*He earned his flying wings as an F-4 pilot in 1968. How-
ever, in Vietnam he flew some 380 combat missions in an 0-1
airplane in a ground support role for infantry. In 1975 he returned to the F-4 as a flight commander in Japan, and since
then he has spent much of his career flying in the aircraft.*

Today's "Wild Weasels" are two seat F-4G "Phantom" fighters. The pilot sits in the front seat and an electronic warfare officer is in the back seat. Our mission is the lethal suppression
of enemy SAM and radar-guided Triple-A air defense systems.

All through the Gulf War we escorted strike packages made
up of F-111s, F-16s, B-52s or F-15Es. We would be the first
airplanes in the target area, between the bombers and enemy
defenses. We covered the area while they bombed, and stayed

until the package was out of danger. Then followed out behind them.

We didn't carry iron bombs. We only carried radar-seeking HARMs [high speed antiradiation missiles]. Because our job is to get in close so that enemy radars come up, then fire a HARM to put them down. The HARMs' accurate guidance capability could allow us to stay outside of the threat area. But we often can't do that. Because if we are outside of their range, air defense radars will remain off.

The F4-G has antennas all over its body. When enemy radars look at us, our antennas collect information about them. They cycle it through our APR-47 computer, the heart of the system, which figures out the threat and feeds the data to the HARM.

The HARM's rocket motor is faster than most SAM systems. Theoretically, if we shot at each other at the same time, the HARM would destroy the radar before his missile got to you.

The HARM has its own intelligence system. If it's in flight and the targeted radar turns off, the missile scans for other sites. It can flex—change in flight—to a new target.

Another device we carry on our airplane is a jamming pod, which can jam specific radars that look at us. But part of the jeopardy for the Weasels is spending so much time on target. We are vulnerable to small arms fire and Triple-A, just like everybody else. We had trained a great deal for the Soviet threat. That meant going in at low altitude, pop up to deliver your ordnance, then come back out. But in the Middle East, the air campaign was very successful in turning off the Iraqi Early Warning and central Command and Control system. So we had to go in relatively close where a lot of their smaller guns are more accurate.

Just about all allied airplane losses were from Triple-A fire. The British Tornados took a terrific thumping initially because they came in at low altitude. To destroy airfield runways, they dropped a combination of bomblets and mines and delayed ordnance. The Iraqis would put up a blanket of gunfire, and the Brits flew through it like the "Charge of the Light Brigade." They only had twelve Tornados. They lost three or four.

Before the air war, I talked with my younger pilots a lot. My big bitch to them was, "The SAMs aren't going to hurt you. It's the guns that can kill you." I'm not sure they believed me—until after Day One.

I was the night-shift Flight Leader, responsible for either two or four airplanes. You need peripheral vision of the other aircraft while flying your own airplane. That is why training and practice are so important. It's like running a pass pattern on a football team. After a number of practices, the plays are run on timing. The Flight Lead is responsible for navigating to the target. Your wing man is responsible for covering your six o'clock. And you are responsible for covering his.

There are times, due to ground fire or enemy aircraft threat, that your flight formation gets spread out all over the sky. Particularly at night, when we flew with our lights off. Going into a target area, we adopted a snakelike formation, using our radars and timing, and watching the geographic flow. We jinked around to avoid antiaircraft fire, going as fast as we can. We tried to keep at 500 to 600 knots, depending on the wind. The key to success is never slow down.

When a SAM is fired at us, we do a series of maneuvers. Many look like barrel rolls, as we roll toward the approaching missile, where its beam has a lower kill probability. Then we maneuver around and release our chaff and flares to decoy it.

We were able to put most of their SAM sites down during the first three days of the war. There was a lull for about two weeks. And then they came back up again. They had repaired some and had gotten replacement systems installed. Fortunately none of our people were hit. The F-4 is a pretty rugged airplane. I remember in Vietnam seeing lots of them with holes shot in them.

We tried to work around the weather. I flew through thunderstorms—which is forbidden in peacetime—with lightning all over the place. The moisture and static electricity could really screw up our radios. But we had to be on station on time to protect the strike airplanes. One of the greatest dangers flying in bad weather at night was tanker rendezvous. The only airplane we lost happened that way.

In Desert Storm, we didn't see anything that we hadn't confronted in training. That helped the younger guys to maintain their composure. Everybody talks about the "cosmic weaponry and great machinery" we used. That's only part of the story. The larger part is the skill of the people who flew the airplanes, and the support people who did the maintenance and kept the airplanes flying.

In the Wild Weasels, only myself and my wing commander had previously flown in combat. I don't want to downplay the skill of our younger guys, but I don't think the personality of the fighter pilot has changed between Vietnam and today. If there is any change at all, it is how well-trained our young people are.

In Vietnam, pilots flew one mission per day. In the air campaign over North Vietnam there was a morning mission and an afternoon mission. That was it. We did very little at night. You flew your sortie, came back, and there wasn't any mission until the next day or two. There were a lot of places to let off steam. You could get a drink and find female companionship. But that did not exist in the Gulf. Maybe to our benefit.

I don't know if not having a beer had any noticeable effect on my guys. A friend of mine, who is a history buff, came up to me one day and said, "You know, we're probably the only military force in the history of the world who has gone to war celibate and sober. This does not look good." [He laughs.]

In fact, we had a few places in Bahrain to get beers. But we didn't have time for that. Our guys put in twelve- to fourteen-hour workdays. Got home, did our after-action briefing, and collapsed. And we had these Scud alerts. So we were shaking guys out of bed. Seven days a week, you were either planning for a sortie, flying a sortie, doing a little bit of debrief, or sleeping.

Weasels flew twenty-four-hour operations, anywhere that strike packages went. In the initial stages of the war, we flew all over the place. But as the war went on, we concentrated more on the Kuwait Theater. We called ourselves "Weasel Police," over areas that were being hit with continual strikes. We just roved over an area for a period of time—thirty to forty-five minutes—with several TOTs [times on target] to work.

I was Deputy Commander for Operations of the Wing. We would get our air tasking orders [ATO] for the next day from Riyadh late at night. We would pass them along to our Mission Planning Cell. I had four lieutenant colonels who took twelve-hour cycles. They would break down the ATO and give assignments to squadrons.

We rotated senior people through the Planning Cell. Every third day, they would get a chance to fly. And we had younger guys take a day off from flying to help.

About three to four hours before takeoff, pilots who were flying a particular mission would come to the cell to collect their information. If necessary, they would make a last minute phone call to the strikers they were going to protect. Then they would talk about target area tactics for the mission.

This briefing usually took thirty minutes to an hour. You briefed what you were going to do: how you were going to divide up the target area threat. Who was going to shoot what. What your target area tactics were going to be. What was your fallback plan in case somebody aborted.

Then you go in and get all your personal flight equipment on: We wore a "G-suit," a survival vest with a pistol, extra water, maps, radios, and a mini-survival kit; a torso harness with life preservers on it. The torso harness is for the parachute that is kept in the airplane. You just buckle into it. You then get your helmet, your bag, and all the paperwork you carry with you: your map, radio frequency cards, classified code cards that apply to that twenty-four-hour period. A gas mask. And it was cold, so we wore a jacket.

You went outside and got into your airplane. Everybody taxied off together and took off. We went immediately to a fuel tanker. Within thirty to forty-five minutes we were in-flight refueling over northern Saudi Arabia.

Each type of airplane in the Theater had a different series of radio call signs. The tankers all had fish names like Perch or Trout. The AWACs were Bulldog. The strikers were Hammer, Anvil, Nail, and things like that. The F-16s were birds. And the Weasels' call signs were brand names of beers. Like Coors, Löwenbräu, Blatz, and Bud. I'm from Texas, so I had brand names like Lone Star and Pearl.

After the first day, everybody wanted the Weasels in their area. Every striker was always happy to hear a beer call sign. It was kind of a joke. You'd hear strikers ask: "Are there any beer call signs up?" Or they'd be trying to talk to the AWACs to find out where the Weasels were.

One of the first sorties I had, I heard a guy in a B-52 hollering over the radio, "Are the Weasels on time? Are the Weasels on time?" Finally, he had to pause for a breath. I got on the radio and said, "Yes, the Weasels are on time." He responded, "Ahh . . ." A sigh of relief.

RESPONSIBILITY

LIEUTENANT GENERAL BUSTER GLOSSON

Saudi Arabia 1990–91
Director of Campaign Plans
Central Command Air Forces &
Commander, 14th Air Division

After the first night, General Horner and I went on opposite schedules. I would walk to my quarters—about a hundred yards from the Black Hole [the planning office]—around seven A.M. I would set the alarm clock to wake up at around one P.M. I didn't always sleep for five hours. Sometimes I would be called for some reason. General Horner would get to bed from one A.M. until around six A.M. He would come in just as I was leaving, so we had some overlap.

I wouldn't say that we alone "shared responsibility." He had a vice-commander and a director of operations. But no other person understood the air campaign to the depth that he and I did. How all the pieces fit together.

About two weeks before the ground war started I told General Horner that I wanted to try "Killer Scouts" with two F-16s at targets on a high/low scenario like the Fast FACs [forward air controllers] in Vietnam that we had worked with. He said, "I can't see how the Fast FACs are going to bring us very much benefit. But if that's what you want to do, go ahead."

F-16s were sent on "killer scout" missions over designated areas where they would spot targets and identify Iraqi army positions. They were very helpful in systematically destroying that army. We sent two or four fighter pilots over a fifteen miles square every day until there was no ground threat there. After a couple days they became very familiar with every little sand dune in that fifteen miles square.

During Week Four I asked General Horner if I could send my A-10s deeper. I had been keeping them around thirty miles of the Saudi border. General Horner said, "I'm not sure they can handle the environment." I said, "We've beaten down the first thirty miles. We should try to beat down the second echelon of the Republican Guard. Only the A-10s can do that to the degree I want it done. The F-16s are working that problem, and doing it very well. But it will take another two weeks with F-16s. I can do it in a week by using both."

He said, "I have some misgiving about that. But if you want to do it, go ahead." So the next day we sent ten A-10s over the Iraqi Medina Division. In four hours, I lost two A-10 aircraft and four were shot all to pieces. I considered this a personal loss. The other four came back without too many bullet holes. We never sent them more than thirty miles north of the Iraqi border again.

The problem for the A-10s was they can't survive in a sustained high-threat combat environment. Of the two aircraft hit by heat-seeking missiles, one got shot down at 11,000 feet, the other at 9,000.

Heat-seeking missiles aren't a threat to the F-16s at that altitude. I thought we had beaten the Iraqis down enough that the remaining heat-seeking missiles were not that significant. We were obviously wrong. We pulled the A-10s back and put in more F-16s and FA-18s to beat the Republican Guards down. We continued to use the F-15Es and F-111s at night.

I was trying to have the intensity and level of destruction of the Iraqi units consistent twenty-four hours a day. We were really effective at night. During the day we were successful against resupply and from a psychological standpoint. But we weren't destroying as much armor as I wanted.

NIGHT SQUADRON

LIEUTENANT COLONEL RICHARD MCDOW

SAUDI ARABIA 1990–91
SQUADRON COMMANDER
355TH TACTICAL FIGHTER SQUADRON,
354TH TACTICAL FIGHTER
WING

Lieutenant Colonel Rick McDow was the only former prisoner of war from Vietnam involved in a combat role in the Gulf War. A young lieutenant when he was shot down over North Vietnam, he returned from captivity in 1973. Then McDow, raised in the small town of Columbiana, Alabama, went on to attend elite Air Force schools, including the Command and Staff College and the Fighter Weapons Instructor Course.

Within two weeks of Iraq's invasion of Kuwait, McDow's 355th Tactical Fighter Squadron of A-10 "Warthogs" were on the ground in Saudi Arabia. The greatest conventional military threat from the Iraqis was their superiority in armored vehicles and artillery. The A-10s mission during the air campaign was to bring those weapons numbers down with relentless twenty-four-hour attack missions.

The A-10 is hand-flown like an old-time airplane, whose mission is to protect U.S. ground forces. The Air Force designed the A-10 using the lessons learned from Vietnam. We needed an airplane with the ability to loiter over a battle area and withstand heavy small arms fire. It had to be very maneuverable to avoid ground fire.

The A-10's survivability was enhanced with armor plating called a "titanium bathtub" that protects the pilot from the waist down. If you take a hit on the side or bottom of the airplane with a 37mm munition (or lesser caliber), the titanium prevents it from penetrating the cockpit.

We carry a couple of Maverick antiarmor missiles on the wings, and a 30mm minigun built into the airplane. All you can see of the gun is the barrel sticking out of the nose. But it actually extends all the way back to a drum that can carry around 1,000 rounds of armor-piercing bullets.

How can we maneuver while carrying so much weight? Very carefully. [He laughs.] Although it looks heavy and awkward because of its structure, the airplane itself is very lightweight. Without munitions it can put on a dandy aerial acrobatics show.

There is only one seat in the airplane. The pilot handles all of his own weapons systems. We don't have autopilot. You have to constantly fly hands-on or you will roll off course and start falling or climbing when you shouldn't.

The pilot has to do his own navigation. We have an Inertial Navigation system that steers us to coordinates. But we don't have backup navigation technology like Ground Mapping radar on a computer screen.

Instead, we hand-carry maps that we spend a lot of time preparing. We cover them with plastic to make sure that they don't tear. We write on it with a grease pencil to mark where we want to go and make circles around targets. It was a hell of a thing to fly over the desert where you don't have many geographic landmarks to navigate by. And my squadron flew at night. We didn't have much ground reference at all.

Some guys ask to fly A-10s because of our low-level ground attack mission. More pilots ask to fly F-15s or F-16s because they are faster, and are perceived as more fighter aircraft than the A-10 "Warthog." But guys that grow up in the A-10 pride ourselves on our piloting abilities. If you get in a tight situation in an F-15 or F-16, you just put the throttle on "afterburner" and speed will solve your problems. In the A-10 we don't have the power to do that.

A few weeks after we arrived in Saudi Arabia, our wing commander, Colonel Robert Haden, came to me. The air-war plan was built around fighting a twenty-four hour around-the-clock war. There weren't enough F-111s or LANTIRN-equipped F-16s to prosecute the war at night. The solution: include a night A-10 squadron. I volunteered for the mission.

The A-10 was designed to be a primarily daytime aircraft. It had very little high-tech delivery capability. We do not have an infrared night vision system. But I believed that flying at night has its advantages in combat.

I wasn't concerned about enemy radar systems, which you can predetermine and plot on your map. The most dangerous threat were visually aimed handheld weapons. There were a half-million Iraqis with rifles. One out of 100 might have shoulder-fired heat-seeking missiles. But you fly at night with your lights off. They can't see you. So their small arms are neutralized.

Out of sixty-five people in my squadron, I was the only pilot with combat experience. I was concerned about flying missions before we were ready. During Vietnam, there were a lot of very good pilots with a lot of combat flying hours who got shot down. It was not a question of their skill. Most of our flying was done in daylight. And most losses were to small arms and visually aimed Triple-A. We used low-level tactics that exposed us to ground fire.

And, our political leaders did not design a war with definite goals. Air power was used as a continual "harassing action" against the enemy. And a cardinal rule is: if you do not destroy his ability to wage war, you intensify his will to fight. As a consequence, you suffer losses that could have been prevented.

I was shot down on June 27, 1972, my 141st mission. I was over western Vietnam, attempting a search and rescue of a downed pilot when my airplane was hit by an air-to-air missile from an MiG-21. Captured toward the end of U.S. involvement in the war, I was younger than most other prisoners. I had just made 1st lieutenant en route to Vietnam. I was held prisoner for nine months and three days, in the Hanoi area.

I took lessons from my Vietnam experience that I used as a squadron commander in the Gulf. I wanted to provide a precise focus for my guys on their mission. Because I think in Vietnam that some guys were shot down by not doing the mission that they were tasked. For example, fighter escorts were assigned to protect a strike package while hitting a target, then get the hell out. But some people got into trouble by diverting from their mission to kill some MiGs. That is what I wanted to prevent my guys from doing over Iraq.

I told my squadron, "We're going to be flying at night." Some people thought I was crazy. It was extremely hazardous. And the desert is an unforgiving environment.

We started training in September when there was no moon. There were a few twinkling stars in about half of the sky. And there was nothing on the ground except for a few twinkling lights from bedouin camps. So in maneuvering, we had no visual reference to know up from down.

When you cannot see with your eyeballs, the motion of an airplane may deceive you. Due to the physical effects of the body while maneuvering the airplane, your mind can become disoriented due to the effects of gravity. You might think that you are climbing when you are descending, or in a left turn when you are in a right turn.

We had a couple of severe cases of disorientation. The pilot had to struggle to knock it off and say, "Okay, I'm going to concentrate on the instruments. I'm going home to land this airplane."

Within a few nights, the moon started coming out. That made it significantly easier. And as U.S. forces continued to arrive and build camps, there were more lights on the desert floor.

I adapted a mixture of things from flying night sorties in an F-4 "Phantom" in Vietnam. Like using flares: there are two kinds of flares. One type is illumination flares that light under a small parachute. They burn for about five minutes and allow you to see the ground. The other type of flares are called "logs." They have little parachutes. When they hit the ground, they glow for about thirty minutes to mark targets.

We adapted our infrared Maverick antiarmor missiles as our FLIR [forward-looking infrared] system. It wasn't designed to be used that way. But, except for dropping flares, that was all we had available to search for night targets. The Iraqi military positions would be blacked out. And they were dug in. Some tanks were buried up to their turret. With our FLIR we could sometimes see the heat of the tank through the dirt covering. We could tell when we hit a tank because of secondary explosions.

Normally, we drop our bombs from around 8,000 feet up, and shoot our 30mm Gatling gun during a 45-degree dive. When we find our target, we roll in from a mile away, making a diving pass over or near the target at forty-five degrees—often exposed to enemy ground fire.

Enemy anitaircraft fire is easier to see at night. Because of the tracer bullets, it's very obvious within a half second to determine whether the fire is a threat to you. If they come close, we maneuver to get out of their range.

I went on the first night combat mission and flew a total of thirty-eight sorties in the forty-two days of the air campaign.

The Kuwait coast was very heavily defended. Triple-A fire blanketed the sky. We put six airplanes up there before we had a successful pass across the target. My instructions were, "Don't do anything stupid. You won't help anybody by getting shot down."

We had remarkable success destroying a lot of targets without taking any losses. I didn't want anyone to get overconfident or careless. Every day, every conversation, we would focus on the mission. We would try to determine why we were being successful. We didn't want to leave it to just pure luck.

In combat, the risk of dying is always there. I did not enjoy going back into combat. It did scare me. Especially some of the targets we went after. I knew that if we took a hit, we were twenty to thirty minutes flying time behind enemy lines. Those thoughts of having been a prisoner in Vietnam did cross my mind. But once I stepped into my airplane, I stayed too busy to worry about that.

I knew that going back into combat would be tough on my wife. We got married in college, before I came into the Air Force. She had to endure the period I spent as a prisoner of war in Vietnam.

Although combat wasn't a certainty until January 17, for the families the pressure was on since August, because of media commentaries of how tough the Iraqis were. My wife is a strong woman and understands the limits of the news media. But it was worrisome for her, just the same. I was concerned about my two teenage daughters. I knew it worried them.

I was more worried about the squadron than for myself. When you take forty pilots into a war, even a six-week war, the odds of bringing everyone home are not very good. I had commanded the squadron for a year and a half before the war started. I was very close with everyone. The pressure on me was that I knew their wives and their girlfriends. I knew their kids. We had five or six guys with pregnant wives. There was more than one occasion when I reminded myself that I did not want to have to write any condolence letters or make telephone calls.

Our first support of ground troops was on January 29, during the Khafji battle. We had no prewarning that the Iraqis would make a move. Around eleven P.M., a number of airplanes were diverted to the battle by the Airborne Command and Control Center.

I was the second airplane on site at Khafji with my wing man, dropping flares to search for Iraqi vehicles. We could see the shooting below us. But the Marine FAC [forward air controller] couldn't determine which end of the tracers were the good guys. So, instead of risking dropping ordnance on our own people, we stayed in the area for forty-five minutes dropping illumination flares. I think our presence convinced the Iraqis to disperse.

There was a lot of additional movement of Iraqi trucks filled with soldiers and supplies coming down the roads. So we spent the rest of the night going after those vehicles. My squadron is credited with destroying twenty to thirty Iraqi tanks during a five- to six-hour period.

Throughout the war we flew significantly underpowered because of the weight of our munitions. And flying heavy degraded our maneuverability. Going into the target with a lot of ordnance on board, we were hard-pressed to fly at 220 knots. We don't like being that slow. But because of the high numbers of Iraqi armor and artillery that we had to go after, carrying a heavy munitions load was our trade-off. Each pilot's biggest measure of protection was his wing man, who would orbit up high watching as his partner dove toward a target. In a more vulnerable climb, he would warn by radio if there was a SAM launch.

You don't "John Wayne" a war. You don't strap an airplane to your butt and fly up there saying, "Okay, what would the Duke do right now?" That mentality gets people killed.

When the ground war started, there was rain, heavy cloud cover, and dense smoke in Kuwait from the oil fires. It was very difficult to see the ground. It was not easy to tell friendly forces from the bad guys, because the battlefield was rapidly changing. Sometimes even the people we had radio contact with on the ground didn't have an idea where the friendlies had moved.

We tried a lot of techniques to identify friendly forces. But I don't think you will ever come up with a scenario— especially with the speed of today's armored vehicles—where you can eliminate fratricide 100 percent. However, we are trying very hard to do that. One incident is unacceptable to us. Even if there is no fault, it doesn't make it acceptable.

Fortunately, allied armored vehicles were moving fast and

encountering very little resistance. They didn't need much close air support. So most of our support to the army, once they started moving, was taking out Iraqis far in front of them. Generally, we didn't work any closer than five to eight kilometers. My squadron alone flew 1,500 combat sorties. But only around fifty sorties were in support of ground units.

There was talk before Desert Storm about the A-10 being retired. Fast-movers like the F-16 can go a long way, drop down and make only one pass over a target, because they have accurate munitions-delivery systems. But with their speed they burn more gas. They can't hang around a battlefield for thirty to forty-five minutes the way that we do sometimes. In a ground war scenario, that could make the difference in saving a lot of U.S. infantry people.

KHAFJI

BRIGADIER GENERAL JOHN ADMIRE

SAUDI ARABIA 1990–91
REGIMENT COMMANDER
3RD MARINE REGIMENT, TASK FORCE TARO

On the night of January 29, 1991, Iraqi armored units made a surprise attack from Kuwait into Saudi Arabia. The main target was the coastal city of Khafji and the oil industry in the nearby area. The probe was an attempt by Saddam Hussein to intimidate and test the willpower of the allies, particularly the Arab Coalition, to resist what was perceived to be the most battle-hardened army in the region.

Ra's Al Khafji is a fairly large city by Saudi standards. It is located on the coast and has an oil refinery nearby, an oil tank farm, and water desalinization plant. It was so close to the Kuwait border that the Iraqis could easily fire rockets. So the civilian population evacuated.

In that area, the Iraqis had six to eight times more artillery and four to six times more armor than we had. So we set up a defensive line south of the city, with a twenty-kilometer buffer zone. Air power was our fundamental weapon that could do the most damage. We designed our defense of Khafji to be a trap. Sure as hell, the Iraqis fell for it.

On the night of January 29, Iraqi armored vehicles crossed into Saudi Arabia near Al Wafra. Our 1st LAV [light armored vehicle] Battalion beat back that incursion. And just before midnight, a reinforced Iraqi battalion came across near Khafji with their tank turrets turned backwards, pretending to surrender. They had two divisions north of the border poised to follow.

U.S. Navy SEAL teams and Marine force recon were doing reconnaissance along the coast. In the city of Khafji I had two six-man recon teams. When the Iraqis attacked, while the SEAL teams fell back through our lines, I preferred that my teams remain in place to collect intelligence, and to act as spotters for air strikes. We had an extraction planned for them. But they made the decision that they would stay. Corporal Ingram was the leader.

The teams occupied two different rooftops in the southern portion of the city. They radio-reported to their recon platoon commander, Lieutenant Bukowski, who worked in my COC [Combat Operations Center]. And I reported their information directly to Division.

There was a concern at higher headquarters about their safety, and how they had allowed themselves to be put in that position. I told higher headquarters, "Let's don't quibble at this point over the rightness or wrongness of the decision. Let's just take full tactical advantage of their reports from the city. And let's proceed with planning for their safe extraction by means of the Coalition counterattack."

One of our main concerns was that the Iraqi thrust into Khafji might be a diversion to pull us up the coast, to the border. Our intelligence people estimated that their main objective was Al Mish'ab, thirty miles down the coast, which had an oil refinery and military airfield. So I had to keep my attention on a lot of different areas. My regiment covered a twenty to thirty kilometer arc. We had our maneuver battalions in Mish'ab, while some elements moved up to the Khafji area.

That night, I met along the coastal road with Saudi colonel Turki, and Major Omani of Qatar. We discussed our options.

There were a number of reasons to counterattack as quickly as we could before other Iraqi forces came forward. For tactical and political reasons, I preferred to use air strikes. My Arab counterparts and I had a frank conversation. I explained that my two recon teams were in the city. I said, "I believe that my teams can operate for thirty-six to forty-eight hours before they are jeopardized by the Iraqis."

The courage of those young Marines had an impact. Colonel Turki listened quietly. Then, in my opinion, he said the two most important words of the war . . . "We attack."

Until Colonel Turk spoke those two words, the Iraqis were considered by the Arab Coalition to be giants, ten feet tall. The Iraqis were the most hardened, disciplined forces in the region, primarily because of their eight-year war with Iran. Plus, they were the fourth largest army in the world.

Meanwhile, the Saudis had never been in a major battle in modern times. Certainly, not with today's sophisticated weapons. The Qataris had never deployed from their own sovereign borders, much less an actual combat operation. But they took it upon themselves to take on the Iraqis. We didn't do a lot of planning. We just drew it out in the sand and went for it.

I emphasized that the Arab force would do the main attack. My Marines would support them from the air, with artillery, and our TOW rockets, our .50-caliber machine guns, our security elements . . . anything they needed. But I wanted the Arab Coalition forces to lead the main attack. I briefed my division commander, General Mike Myatt, that I felt this would be best.

That was one of the most difficult decisions I had ever made, because most commanders wait an entire military career for an opportunity to conduct a major counterattack. I had all the confidence in the world in my Marines. It was an opportunity for us to validate six months of arduous training in the desert.

But I felt that if we had tried to take charge, all of a sudden, it would be like Vietnam. Where the Americans come in and do it all, and the home forces get the idea that they have a secondary role. I wanted the Arabs to get the credit. It was an important psychological statement.

We thought that particular Iraqi unit was pretty good. Our recon teams in the city supported this by saying, "These are good-looking troops. They have spit-shined boots and pressed uniforms." They wore classy berets.

At first, the Coalition conducted a probing attack. Our recon elements in the city radioed to us where the Iraqis were shifting their forces to react to our movement. We pulled back. Then the Arab forces led a forceful counterattack. Within six to twelve hours, we destroyed 93 Iraqi armor and mechanized vehicles. We captured more than 600 prisoners, including a brigadier general and five colonels.

Most of the Iraqi reinforcement vehicles north of the city were destroyed by Marine air and Air Force A-10 Warthogs. The fighting in the city was a courageous tactical victory for the Arab forces. But it was a strategic victory for the U.S.

Khafji was a watershed for three reasons: First, the morale and confidence of the Arab forces went sky high. They had defeated the veteran Iraqis rather soundly. After it was over, we were coming out south of the city. All of a sudden, every single vehicle had the Saudi flag flying. All the crews were flashing the old traditional V for Victory hand sign. They were pumped up.

Second, it was our evaluation that the Iraqis had no resolve or determination for a toe-to-toe slugfest with a determined opponent. If you hit them fast and hard, they'd quit early. There were some good firefights in the city. But the Arab Coalition hit them harder and faster.

We briefed General Mike Myatt and gave our opinion that we would have prisoners of war in large numbers. As a result, General Myatt made the decision to assign units with the mission of collecting and processing prisoners of war, once the ground war began. We knew that mobility, maneuver, and momentum were going to be essential for allied success. If we had to stop to round up prisoners, that would impede the success by slowing down our offensive.

Third, and most important, after Khafji the Saudis, Qataris, and other Arab Coalition forces requested, if not demanded, to be equal partners when the attack came.

Up to that point, the planning by Americans—including CENTCOM—was that the Marines attack north, primarily along the coastal road. We would have the eastern portion of Kuwait. The U.S. Army would have the western portion and attack through the desert to take on the Iraqi Republican Guards. The Arab Coalition were going to be the reserve forces, simply to follow behind U.S. and European forces.

But after their success at Khafji, Prince Khalid said, "We want to be equal partners. If U.S. forces are going to attack, we want to attack north, too. If the Marines are going to breach the Iraqi barrier, we want to breach the barrier." They volunteered to attack along the coastal road.

We Marines thought that would be ideal because we always had an eye on shifting west for our attack. If we tried to attack all across the Kuwait border, we would be spread too thin. Now that the Saudis and other Arab forces wanted to attack along the coast, we were free to shift west. There we had a straight shot to Kuwait International Airport without having to go through oil fields or built-up areas. We could slice through the Iraqis rapidly.

More importantly, that freed the U.S. Army to shift even farther west and do what General Schwarzkopf later called the "Hail Mary" or "End Around" flanking of Iraqi forces.

EXTREME VIOLENCE

GENERAL CHARLES HORNER

SAUDI ARABIA 1990–91
COMMANDING GENERAL
CENTRAL COMMAND AIR FORCES

There was a fair amount of innovation in the Desert Storm air campaign. But I did not want operational weapons testing. I only permitted two untried systems into the Theater. One was Joint Stars [joint service tactical airborne radar system]. It proved helpful, as a backup airborne Command and Control for my ground-based TACC. It worked to great effect.

The other was two 6,000-pound penetrating bombs we used against hardened Iraqi bunkers. One didn't fuse, but the other worked perfectly. The developers took artillery barrels, put a steel plug in their noses, then filled them with explosives. We used them during the last days of the war to penetrate vast depths of reinforced concrete on the "Taji One" control bunker, north of Baghdad. That was a primary command and communications center for the Iraqi military.

A laser kit on the bomb guided it right through the concrete reinforcement. When the bombs were loaded on the airplanes to fly to Iraq, they were still hot from the factory process.

We fought the air war unrelentingly, and always tried to keep integrity in our reporting. All of the senior military were set against a campaign like in Vietnam where we used bombing halts. The enemy took advantage of those type of things to resupply and prepare for future offensives. That prolonged the suffering and ultimately worked against us.

As to honesty, one of my wing commanders called up and said, "We shot down two Iraqi airplanes inside Iran. We were chasing them and we went by the border. We didn't realize we were by the border."

In their debriefing, we checked and found that they had been about twenty miles inside Iran. So I called General Schwarzkopf. He relayed the information on to Washington. I said, "It was a mistake. I'm not going to do anything to the pilots." He agreed with that 100 percent. Integrity was kept intact that way. My guys had confidence to tell me. In Vietnam they would've never told.

After this happened, I was waiting for somebody in Washington to come up with the idea that we need to stop pursuing Iraqi aircraft into Iran and therefore we should give them a buffer zone—a ten- or twenty-miles cushion in Iraq where we couldn't fly near Iran. That would cost American lives. I was determined that if I got orders to do that, and I couldn't convince my superiors otherwise, I was prepared to quit. I would have retired.

There are important issues a commander must take a stand on. But the political pressure never came. And the Iranians sort of put out the word to [their] air defense, "If an American airplane comes on our side of the border, don't get too upset about it, he's probably chasing some Iraqis."

We made every effort to keep to a minimum the number of casualties, both civilian and military. For example, we didn't use cluster bombs over large areas. Instead, we used laser-guided bombs against tanks. The enemy knew this. And as soon as they could park their tank, they got away from it. With every target, we looked at how to limit the loss of life. We gave priority to destroy the Iraqi weapons systems that would cause allied loss of lives.

There are some fundamental political/military principles: you should use military force only as a last resort to stop grave injustice. To take a life is a serious issue. You must have a moral basis for military action. President Bush defined the objectives of Desert Storm very carefully so that they were obtainable. They made sense, and there was the support of international law.

I don't know any military man who loves combat. It is something that you learn to hate. You hate it because it's wasteful. I actually feel a sense of immorality in the taking of life. Nevertheless, in the Gulf, it had to be done. But I lost a good friend. My former executive officer died in an F-15. That hurts deeply.

Some people asked when we attacked retreating Iraqi forces near Basrah, wasn't that "extreme violence." They missed the point. War is extreme violence. And the way to halt the suffering is to get the war over as quickly and decisively as you possibly can.

THE NUMBERS GAME

COMMANDER DONALD MCSWAIN

SAUDI ARABIA 1990–91
NAVAL AVIATION STRIKE PLANNER
JOINT FORCES AIR COMMAND

In the TACC [Tactical Air Command Center] where General Horner sat side by side with his Saudi counterpart, there were hundreds of telephones and a fairly big computer system. A screen picture was too broad to make out details. We'd see blips moving around and somebody would say, "That's your F-15E strike." Or, "This is your A-6 strike over here." To keep track of our naval air people we followed the ATO [air tasking order], looking for a bunch of blips coming from the Red Sea or Persian Gulf.

The first night, my personal responsibility was targeting. I worked on the master attack plan that was formulated into the ATO. We had written it two days before the war started. The next morning we started working on the plan for Day Three. We tried to find out if anyone had to abort because of weather or had trouble finding their target. Had we miscalculated the threat? Had any airplanes been wiped out?

During the course of the campaign we had to adapt to targets from day to day as BDA [bomb damage assessments] and the weather reports came in. Forecasting the weather was real tough because the only decent reporting area we had was in Incirlik, Turkey. That was very far away. We had a pretty good facility in Israel. But there was no way to connect Israel with anything in Saudi Arabia. If you wanted to call Haifa, Israel, the Muslim operator was not going to connect you.

There were differences in philosophy among the services. Going after an airfield, the Marine Corps, the Brits, and the Navy would go in with one initial air strike. We'd hit the runway, hit different buildings and the hangars. We told the Air Force, "We want to hit this same airfield every three or four hours for two days." They'd say, "You can't do that. We've got all these other targets to hit."

The Air Force wanted to hit a much broader area and selection of targets, rather than hitting the same target over and over. They wanted to take a little bit of the bad news to everybody in Iraq. We felt that is counterproductive, because it enables them to repair a lot of the slight damage throughout the country.

Putting holes in an airfield's concrete is useful. But you need to go back and blow up a few trucks and forklifts, too, so they won't be able to do repairs.

The way that we advocate to take down a target is to hit the entire area around the airfield first. Take out the Triple-A batteries. Then bring the strike package in. A lot of Triple-A guns are portable. So today's reconnaissance photograph may not indicate where they will be tomorrow. Going in with dozens of airplanes makes people on the ground keep their heads down. That helps low-flying bombers to survive.

The same with bridge destruction. It is not enough to destroy a bridge tonight and then wait for a BDA to get back to you three days later. It's better to hit the thing with two or three strikes in a row and get a fairly good assurance that even if I never get a photo of it, I know that it is destroyed.

A lot of encouraging news comes from pilots' reports. But you've got to take those with a grain of salt. Because when you drop a bomb and look back, you see your target engulfed in a big fireball. That looks great. You say, "I really nailed that guy." But that doesn't mean a lot. Because the cloud of smoke may have overshadowed what you didn't hit on the target.

Some pilots used their infrared system to confirm bomb

damage. They'd show a tank on their infrared system. The bomb would impact, and the infrared camera is very sensitive to heat and light. You see a big huge blast around the target. The Air Force would say, "Okay, that's a hit."

We had some footage of an F-16 dropping 2,000-pound bombs right alongside a moving T-72 tank. It actually lifted up the tank and displaced it by about twenty feet. That's awesome . . . But the tank kept going.

The pilot would've reported, "I nailed that thing." But his own video showed the tank moving away. So it's a terribly inexact science to go by a pilot's report.

The Navy was saying, "If you see a displaced tank turret, consider that a kill." That may be extreme BDA. But the Navy was making careful reports like: seventeen tanks killed, fourteen probable, and six possible. That drove the Air Force guys nuts. They would say, "Can't you do better than that?"

They were required to have 100 tanks killed per night. So they'd report, "We killed 104 tanks tonight." The next night, "106," then "109." They never had like an 88-tank day. I never trusted that way of counting. Especially when you saw the videos.

I guess a way to fix that would be to have more RPVs [remotely piloted vehicles] to fly over the battlefield day and night to give "real time" BDA. We need something fairly simple and inexpensive to get better intelligence.

BATTLESHIP COMMAND

REAR ADMIRAL DAVID BILL

PERSIAN GULF 1990–91
BATTLESHIP COMMANDER
USS *WISCONSIN*

A long way from the small riverine patrols he led as a lieutenant in Vietnam, in the Persian Gulf David Bill was assigned command of a massive battleship. Staging off the coast of Kuwait, the USS Wisconsin *conducted fire missions in support of*

allied ground forces. Its massive guns fire five-foot-long,
2,000-pound artillery shells that have a range of up to twenty-
three miles.

Commanding a battleship is exhilarating. Under way at sea,
you are fully responsible for a billion dollars' worth of equipment and developing the pride and expertise of 1,600 sailors to
run the ship. It is a small city unto itself. The sense of belonging within the crew of the ship is very special. It's a tight-knit
camaraderie comparable to an infantry outfit, where you have
to rely on your buddy. Teamwork is what gets the job done. In
combat that is certainly the case.

I took command of the battleship *Wisconsin* in the Gulf in
September 1990. I knew we would have to fight at some point.
So it was a very focused situation.

I took over for a good friend of mine. Of course, he wanted
to stay. And I was anxious to get in the saddle, because I knew
the shooting was probably going to start. I needed to organize
the ship and be ready to fight in my own way. My predecessor
had drilled the crew well and they were prepared. But each
commanding officer has a different approach.

I had a couple of previous deployments into the Gulf area.
And I had lived in the Middle East for a year when I was nine
years old, in Bahrain. So I was more familiar than most Americans with the area. I could count to ten in Arabic. [He laughs.]

When I first arrived, the mission of the *Wisconsin* was to
provide firepower as a deterrence to Saddam Hussein. To make
the Iraqis think twice about venturing further south into Saudi
Arabia. If they did, our guns would significantly respond.

The explosive shells for our sixteen-inch guns weigh 2,000
pounds each. The armor-piercing shells can penetrate thirty-
two feet of concrete. They make a humungous bang.

I needed time to get comfortable with my crew, and vice
versa. There is no way that a leader can be successful without
having the trust and confidence of his men. Establishing that
you are sincerely concerned about the best interest of your
people is absolutely the key. It's not enough to be a "good
guy." You have to also set standards. And also, make the tough
decisions to maintain good order and discipline.

As commander, responsible for 1,600 crew members, you
can't micromanage every little thing. I was blessed with an
outstanding group of senior NCOs. On my ship, the senior

NCO, the command master chief [equivalent to command sergeant major], has access to me at any time on any issue.

During Desert Shield, I would get up at six o'clock each morning. I had breakfast by six-fifteen and read my message traffic. Then the XO would come in and I would do a personnel inspection around seven A.M I would keep a full schedule through the eight P.M. evening meeting. Some nights we had refueling or were conducting night combat exercises. The captain's position is on the bridge. It was an intense schedule. But we had one goal: Get battle-ready.

The key is to develop that sense of pride down at the troop level. The captain sets the mood. If the captain enjoys his work, the people who work for you will be influenced. Every member of that organization needs to understand that he is a part of that team and has important responsibilities to perform. Your men will take pride in being a part of a team effort. When it all comes together and works properly, there's nothing like it.

I don't know many other organizations that match the intensity of going to sea and living together in a very confined space for up to eight months. It's twenty-four hours a day. You don't go home on the weekend.

It is not much fun leaving my wife and children behind for eight months. I have a twelve-year-old son and ten-year-old daughter. It's important to spend some time and energy to help them grow up.

I married a lady who I knew was strong enough to be able to handle the unpredictable military life-style. I made sure that she knew what she would be getting into. Maria is not from a Navy family. In fact, she came from a completely different background. But she feels the same sense of responsibility that I do in the leadership position of a commanding officer. The other wives love her because she is a warm, approachable person. And she takes an active role to assure that the wives are part of the community.

During Desert Shield, we stayed busy refueling and doing minor repair work for other ships. We picked up and took care of a downed pilot. We did gunnery practice and training. And we were continually studying the evolving tactical picture, keeping abreast of military intelligence. During Desert Shield it was analyzed by my staff and discussed at the regular morning briefings.

My primary concern was the threat of mines. Because Iraqi

mines broke loose from their moorings and drifted into international water in the Gulf. You could be hit by a mine anywhere. We had to maintain constant vigilance.

The second threat were Iraq's air-launched missiles. These could be fired by their Mirage jets, and they had some super helicopters that carried the Exocet missile. Two Iraqi aircraft were shot down just as they were flying over the Gulf. If the Iraqis had flown their large number of Mirages, the Exocets would have been a significant threat.

A mine may have knocked some of our electronic equipment temporarily off line, and we may have sprung some leaks. But the brilliance of a battleship is that it would not impair our mission capability. Even if you lost a pump or a generator, by design strategy, the backup systems on the ship are more than adequate. The battleship is the most formidable type of ship ever built. And the most survivable.

In a battle group, an Aegis cruiser is the most capable antiaircraft ship. The Aegis system has a big display screen that can show you the whole air picture. We exchange information between ships electronically.

The *Wisconsin* has a poor man's Aegis display system. It allowed us to project sensor information from radars and from other ships onto a screen on the wall. I sat in a position where I could see that information and listen to the radio to focus on the tactical situation.

The opening night of the air war, our job was to orchestrate the entire Tomahawk TLAM [Tomahawk Land Attack (cruise) Missile] fire mission. We put missile-launching ships in position and arranged for backup fire missions. It was the first time that the Tomahawks had ever been used in combat. There may have been someone aboard our ship who previously had fired a TLAM in training, but I don't think so. There was a reasonable amount of anticipation about whether these things would really work.

The first night of the war, I stood on deck and watched the first-ever Tomahawk fire mission. The TLAMs were fired as a prelude to the F-117 Stealth airplane attacks on Iraq. It was very gratifying to see the other ships synchronize firing with us, the missiles taking off and streaking through the sky.

The *Wisconsin*'s Tomahawks were preprogrammed for targets in Baghdad. It was apparent from live television that the missiles were extraordinarily effective. All the lights in Baghdad went out as they hit their targets: the power system,

Saddam's Command and Control facilities, and weapons production plants.

While my ship was assigned TLAM Strike Command, our sister battleship, the *Missouri*, was tasked as the Gunfire Support Coordinator. The range of our sixteen-inch guns is in excess of twenty miles.

After the Desert Storm air campaign started, we did gunfire support off the coast of Saudi Arabia and Kuwait. We went there after the Iraqis attacked across the border at Khafji on January 29. We helped with the mop-up operation. Then we used our ship's RPVs [remotely piloted (aircraft) vehicles] to look for Iraqi artillery positions in southern Kuwait.

We had a detachment of five RPVs, launched and recovered aboard the battleship. They launch from a stationary rocket-assisted takeoff. They fly over the target area for around four hours with a day and night video camera. They show us real-time pictures on a TV monitor aboard ship of what is going on. They are radio-controlled, so we can fly them wherever we choose. And we can focus the camera. If we see something interesting, they can orbit around it. Battlefield surveillance took on a new meaning.

I couldn't help but think, "Wouldn't this be nice to have when I was doing the riverine patrols in Vietnam." The beauty about an RPV is that you can fly them into harm's way. If they get shot down, there are no casualties.

The biggest target we hit was a command and control center and coastal watch complex. The Iraqis had a complex of buildings and trenches and radio transmitters that were well-concealed. We only became aware that they were there because our RPV spotted people milling around. We fired fifty rounds from sixteen-inch guns, effectively destroying the complex.

The RPVs again informed us of Iraqi activity in a marina, where small boats were staging raids into Saudi Arabia. It was a small area, around 75 meters by 100 meters. Our sixteen-inch gun was our only weapon that could reach them. We were able to put a lot of shells into that area with devastating effect.

For the ground offensive our fire support areas were off the coast of Kuwait City, within range of Faylakah Island. The *Missouri* was tasked to shoot a lot of rounds at Faylakah and onto the beach at Kuwait City. It was part of a diversion plan to pin down a large number of Iraqi troops, who expected an amphibious invasion. That prevented them from moving south to oppose U.S. ground forces.

We supported Coalition forces as they advanced north along
the coast to Kuwait City. We had calls for fire missions from
them when they ran into resistance. We had naval ANGLICO
[air and seaborne fire support] people with the Saudis. They
spotted targets and radioed the coordinates to us. A minute
later we had a sixteen-inch round winging on its way.

That was a great morale boost for Coalition troops on the
ground. Their enthusiasm rose dramatically when they understood that they had us on call. After the first fire support mission, which had devastating effect, the Saudi commander took
the radio from the ANGLICO. He thanked us and said, "I wish
we had a battleship in the Saudi navy."

MINESWEEPERS

CAPTAIN BRUCE MCEWEN

Arabian Gulf/Persian Gulf 1990–91
Amphibious Assault Ship Commander
USS *Tripoli*

If you are an aviator, and aspire to eventually take command
of an aircraft carrier, you must first have "deep draft," a major
command at sea. A "deep draft" is a ship of at least 600 feet
(two football fields) in length with a draft in excess of twenty-
five feet. I was the executive officer aboard the carrier USS *Independence* from July 1989 until I was assigned to a "deep
draft" command in April 1990.

I was assigned to command an LPH [helicopter landing plat-
form] amphibious assault ship, the USS *Tripoli*. It carried a
complement of twenty-four helicopters, around 1,500 Marines,
and 700 ship's company [crew]. A crowded ship when you put
everybody on board. It's like a small floating city. We were
given the minesweeping mission during Desert Storm.

We deployed to the Persian Gulf from San Diego on December 1, 1990, as part of a thirteen-ship amphibious task
force. The largest such deployment since the Korean War.
When we reached Masira, an island off Oman, we were reas-

signed as the support ship for the mine countermeasures group.

I off-loaded all but 275 of my Marines. We proceeded to Abu Dhabi on the Arabian Gulf to onload six MH-53E mine-sweeping helicopters. As well as four Marine Corps Cobra attack helicopters to provide an armed escort. The pilots were all reservists from Atlanta. The MH-53 is so large that six was all that we could handle. The entire hangar bay is filled with their minesweeping equipment.

We conducted some training with both British Royal Navy mine countermeasures ships. Then we were ordered north into the Persian Gulf on February 12 to commence mine-clearing operations.

I had never received any mine-clearing training. But my XO had been a former commanding officer of a mine-clearing squadron. The ship's company had conducted some mine-clearing training the year before, so I had a wealth of experience on the ship.

Our role was to be the support base for the helicopters and all their equipment. I also provided command and control for the U.S. mine countermeasures group. I served as a logistics base for all of the U.S. minesweepers. I refueled and replenished them in the north Arabian Gulf. I served as a logistics hub for all the surface ships in the area. And we handled all the mail.

We coordinated our mission with the British ships. The tactical employment of the surface minesweeping ships was under the control of the British, and the aircraft were under U.S. control. And the overall control of the mission was under U.S. command. We had a very friendly relationship. The Brits demonstrated time and again that they would do anything to support us. Their minesweepers are around the same size as ours. But more modern and less susceptible to magnetic signatures that trigger mines.

Once our helicopters spot a mine, Navy EOD [explosive ordnance disposal] divers jump out of helicopters and wrestle with those beauties. They attach explosive charges with detonating cords. Then they get back into the helicopters and trigger the explosive charge.

We used to shoot at floating mines from our ship with small-caliber weapons, to try to set them off. But we found that only about thirty percent of the time would we get a detonation. The other seventy percent simply put a hole in the mine's casing. It would fill with water. And instead of detonating, it became a submerged floating mine. That's even more dangerous, because they are harder to see. So we relied exclusively on EOD divers to detonate mines.

There are other techniques to detonate mines. Remotely piloted vehicles [RPVs] on some of the minesweeping ships can do that without human involvement. They place a charge beside the mine and detonate it. The helicopters can also influence "magnetic" mines and cause them to detonate by magnetic devices they tow behind their flight path.

The Iraqis also used "bottom" mines that detonate on the sea floor. The explosion causes a giant air bubble. The ship rises up off the water. It comes back down hard and the impact breaks the keel of the ship.

The dangerous area where the Iraqis laid mines was in the north Arabian Gulf to protect the coast of Kuwait against amphibious assault. They put approximately 1,200 mines in the water. It turned out to be an intensive operation, further out to sea than we had anticipated.

The mines were probably laid prior to our arrival. The Iraqis planted mines in layers. We could visibly spot them. Floating mines were discovered all over the Arabian Gulf. But no ship hit one. Perhaps the grace of God entered, too. There were some very close calls where lookouts spotted mines at the very last moment. Disaster was averted by a matter of inches.

Patrol ships in the area had lookouts on their bows with night vision devices and binoculars. Our ships didn't have sonar that is capable of detecting mines. Most U.S. ships aren't really equipped with any mine detection capability. A ship moving at twenty to thirty knots has no warning time at all.

On the night of January 17, when the air war started, we heard that the Iraqis had targeted our mine countermeasures group with Silkworm missiles. They had the capability and range to fire chemical weapons. So we moved randomly to confuse their targeting systems on the coast of Kuwait. And, if need be, to maneuver or outrun chemical munitions vapors.

We trained for an emergency four times each week, one hour a day. I didn't overdo it. Just enough to keep the crew's attention. We trained on a number of occasions with our chemical suits. Every crew member knew how to decontaminate. How to don their gas masks in less than nine seconds. And we did innovative exercises.

During movie call [showing motion pictures] at night, we'd

interrupt the movie and have a "damage control minute." Or we'd have a five minute lecture or reminders about how to don a piece of protective equipment, or how to administer chemical or nerve gas antidote. The crew paid attention. There were no complaints.

We were sobered by an experience that happened during our transit to the Middle East. Just before Christmas, we lost a helicopter at sea. Everybody reflected on that. While saddened, they realized, "We're not immortal. Death is around the corner if we don't take care of one another." That tragedy brought the ship together. Everybody looked out for each other.

As flag ship for the minesweeping group, we were in front of seven ships. We kept the lead because we had greater height to spot floating mines. Our initial objective was to clear a channel to get battleships in. So that they could rain their sixteen-inch guns on the coast of Kuwait. After we cleared that area, we were to expand a path for amphibious ships to maneuver in.

By February 18, a week before G-Day [start of the ground war], we had declared the area "mine-free." Our objective was to go to an area short of where mines were planted to do exploratory operations, to ensure that the Iraqis hadn't planted mines further out to sea. If that was the case, the next morning I would be on my way to a location fifteen miles further west, off the coast of Kuwait. That phase would be to clear a huge area for amphibious ships to carry Marines for a possible assault.

We'd been up until about 2:30 A.M. watching an air raid take place on the Kuwait coast. And we were observing for anything on the water that might be visible. We'd operated in that area for two days.

At 4:30 A.M. I was in my "at sea" cabin, which is about ten feet behind the bridge. I was sitting on my sofa mulling over our mission, thinking about the next day's operations.

Suddenly, a BANG was followed by a tremendous shudder down the keel. The rigid structures of the ship shook like a dog shaking water off his back. It was immediately apparent to me what was happening. We had hit a mine.

As soon as the shock wore off, the alarm sounded. All crew members went to their duty stations. We had already set watertight boundaries [to seal leak areas] as a normal precaution.

The first task was to determine the extent of the damage and then do shoring. If we had a weakened ship structure, we had to reinforce it. The crew worked together like an Amish barn-raising. Sailors were cutting two-by-fours to brace bulkheads weakened by the blast and all that water pressure. There was nothing we could do to patch a sixteen-by-twenty-foot hole.

My initial fear was that I'd lost my mine lookouts on the bow. Those sailors were reported as missing. I was convinced that they were blown over the side of the ship, as well as convinced that I would have a large number of casualties. I anxiously waited for damage and casualty reports to come in.

In that type of emergency, my station is on the bridge to coordinate the effort. I needed to stay there, and trust that my subordinates are trained to do their jobs. It was my decision to anchor until we had a clear path. If we struck another mine, the ship clearly would have been lost.

There was a big hole on the side of our ship. Our immediate concerns were of fire and secondary explosions. We weren't sure if we could control the flooding. My crew immediately proceeded to their stations and went into action. There was never a panicked moment. I told the people to maintain a calm professional attitude. A lot of people told me afterward, "Those words gave the crew confidence that you were not panicked and the ship was in good hands."

People made sure that their shipmates where out of their compartments, made sure that people put their protective equipment on correctly. If someone was injured or overcome by fumes, they were immediately cared for.

The ship was compartmentalized. So we secured the first intact compartment to establish a watertight boundary. Then, a second watertight boundary as a backup. Because if we lost both of them, we'd lose the ship.

The greatest danger of a ship fire is the smoke and the fumes. That has killed more people than all the flames combined. We have always had electric fans that are said to be "spark-proof." But I preferred not to have an electric device in the forward part of the ship. Electric equipment shorts out, and sparks fly as electrical devices are flooded. You just don't know what will happen when sparks hit the fumes.

We were very fortunate to have a "ram fan" installed two weeks before we deployed. The fans are driven by floodwater to get rid of exhaust and high explosive vapors in the front part of a ship. They push the exhaust up, over the hangar bay and off the side of the ship.

I went down to the blast area later on to have a look and

give encouragement to my sailors. I can't express how pleased I was when I heard, "Captain, we have no serious injuries."

Some crew members suffered minor injuries. A half-dozen people were overcome by fumes. They were treated on board and went back to duty.

At daylight, divers jumped overboard to investigate the damage. That's when we discovered that we had struck a submerged mine. That made our position more frightening. We were in a mine field.

The minesweepers started discovering more mines in our vicinity. Our immediate task was to keep our ship from drifting into another mine.

We had hit a 320-pound "contact" mine, held by a cable or moor to an anchor on the water bottom. They are very easy to detonate, and are set at various depths. The one we hit was about fifteen feet below the waterline. Invisible to the ship's lookouts.

We had a twenty-five- to thirty-foot hole. It was just a matter of luck that none of my crew was hurt. The mine blew up my fuel tanks and paint storage areas. Those fumes were atomized throughout the forward part of the ship. A single spark or fire could've set off an explosion.

Eventually we were able to get emergency power. We cautiously went into a clear area and anchored, allowing minesweepers to determine a safe path. It was dangerous for our 600-foot ship to be following the smaller minesweepers. If they discovered a mine at seventy-five yards, they would come to a stop rather quickly. A 600-foot ship at three or four knots does not stop. It was a challenge trying to back an engine in order to avoid ramming a minesweeper that was trying to protect us.

After we had an idea of the amount of damage, there was almost a groundswell from the crew: "Let's get our aircraft flying. Let's not permit Saddam to kick us out with a cheap shot. We've got a mission to accomplish to show people what we're all about."

Our helicopters were up flying minesweeping operations that same day; even while we were doing damage assessments and securing the ship, in the middle of the minefield.

I routinely tried to have a talk with the ship's company. The day after the strike, I tried to keep everyone informed. It was difficult because our internal communications system was knocked out until later in the day. But one of my journalists discovered that the on-board television system was still working.

He brought a video camera to the bridge and filmed me addressing the crew. And they could watch me via the video. Late in the day we got a live camera on the bridge. Any time I wanted to talk, we simply turned the camera on and the ship's company would watch the video screens. It was important that I speak directly to them. Because I was the guy who they were entrusting with their lives to get them home safely.

After we hit the mine, we ran out of fuel. We stayed a few days at anchor, performing our helicopter mine-clearing mission. Then we were ordered to Bahrain for repairs. The cracks were growing. There was a lot of fear that the damage was beginning to expand.

Our minesweeping group completed sweeping that channel just before G-Day. The battleship *Missouri* moved in and began shelling the Kuwait coast as the ground offensive started. That was extremely effective. Because that continued to freeze thousands of Iraqi forces on the coast. They could not ignore the amphibious threat from the sea. It grabbed their attention long enough to allow the U.S. Marines to quickly move into Kuwait City with so few casualties.

Once we got a clear path out of the mine field, we transferred some of our helicopters to the *LaSalle*. And the rest of our equipment was transferred to our sister ship, the *New Orleans*. She assumed a stand-in role for us during the ground war.

While we were in Bahrain completing our mine damage repair, my crew was watching CNN. They saw all the Welcome Home ceremonies and the tremendous emotion that was taking place around the United States.

I had to remind them that we were not going home after our repairs were completed. But return up north and complete another three to six months of minesweeping operations before we go home. They were very depressed and had a melancholy attitude.

I told them, "I asked the Navy Historical Center to do some research for me. They found that the *Tripoli* was the first U.S. warship since 1865 to suffer major mine damage and still continue her mission. We weren't towed out of the Gulf. We came out under our own power."

Their attitude changed. Not only because they accomplished something special. But because they knew that the American people would not forget them if we stayed at sea for another few months.

This group of young men was exposed to the most serious challenge of their lives. Not all of them were America's finest. Some came from broken homes and not the most ideal backgrounds. They may not have known that they were capable of rising to the occasion like they did. But now, whether those young men make the Navy a career or go back to the civilian community, American society has a group of young men who have tremendous pride in their ability. Not because they're "warriors." But because they have self-esteem.

PREPARING THE BATTLEFIELD

COLONEL LAYTON DUNBAR

SAUDI ARABIA 1990–91
GROUP COMMANDER
4TH PSYCHOLOGICAL OPERATIONS GROUP

Planning the invasion of Kuwait, the worst fear of allied commanders, whose forces were greatly outnumbered, was the potential for massive casualties. As a result, a multifaceted psychological campaign was created to break the fighting spirit of the Iraqi troops and to encourage their surrender.

There is a dictum, "You win your battles before the fighting begins." And if you've really done it right, the fighting won't start. The objective of Psychological Operations is to convince enemy soldiers to cease to resist.

We use the term "psychological preparation" of the battlefield. The same way that artillery prepares the battlefield for an infantry assault, there is an intelligence preparation. To be effective, you need to begin before the war starts.

I went to Saudi Arabia in October 1990 to prepare to take command of the 4th Psyop Group, the only such group in the U.S. Department of Defense. In Desert Storm, we gave support to the Marines, as well as Army combat units. We also supported some of the Arab Coalition forces. Because they didn't have any Psyop units.

By the time an Army officer is assigned to me, he has gone through two years of extensive training: graduate level schooling, foreign language studies, and several courses at the John F. Kennedy Special Warfare Center at Fort Bragg.

Psychological operations along the Saudi/Kuwait border began in late December or early January, a couple of weeks before the air war started. We used special operations airplanes to drop leaflets to Iraqi units along the border. They flew twenty to thirty miles inside of Saudi airspace, outside of Iraqi air-defense range. They went up to 25,000 feet, tailgate down, dropping millions of leaflets. The higher we got, the farther the leaflets would blow into Kuwait.

My higher headquarters was General Schwarzkopf's Central Command. As a matter of habit, I would take all products to the CENTCOM J3 [Operations and Planning officer] in Riyadh to make absolutely sure that our operations were ethical and legal. We have our own lawyer in the 4th Psyops Group. But for the more complicated elements of international law issues, we would refer to the senior lawyer on CENTCOM staff.

New operations ideas were always submitted to General Schwarzkopf for approval. He came up with a number of ideas on his own. Not only because he was a specialist in the region, but because he was an experienced soldier.

Through December, the Saudis were reluctant to approve the use of Psyop leaflets. In fact, many of us didn't think that a war was inevitable. There was a concern that dropping leaflets over Iraqi soldiers in Kuwait might further upset Saddam Hussein, and hinder negotiations that might get under way.

As the January 15 deadline approached, the Saudis were persuaded that the use of leaflets across the border was probably a good thing. It became a multinational psyop effort. We had Saudi people, Kuwaitis, Brits, and some Egyptians who worked with us. The 4th Group handled coordination. It was tricky to get all of these national groups to agree on what the message ought to be.

The leaflets started out quite mild and benign. The initial theme was "Arab Brotherhood," and "Muslim Brotherhood." There were pictures of Saudi and Iraqi soldiers arm in arm, saying, "We are Muslim brothers. Why are we fighting each other?"

We moved on from those appeals to sharper messages. To

make sure that the Iraqi soldiers knew that a January 15 deadline had been established [to withdraw from Kuwait] by the United Nations: "You have until then to get out of Kuwait. If not, the consequences could be very severe."

From those, we moved to more intimidating leaflets that highlighted our technological superiority. That this was a multinational coalition: the whole world was against the Iraqi army.

By the time the air war started, we began highlighting firepower of Coalition forces. And the fact that the Iraqi soldiers were totally isolated on the battlefield. After the air war began, F-16s armed with leaflet bombs would drop 120,000 leaflets per mission. F/A-18s and B-52s also delivered leaflets.

The day that the air war started, we initiated a radio network, the Voice of the Gulf. It broadcast in Arabic to Iraqi soldiers, using Kuwaiti announcers. We broadcasted on several AM frequencies and a couple of FM. Whatever type of pocket radio the Iraqi soldiers had, they could tune us in, eighteen hours a day.

We mostly broadcasted news in Arabic, using wire service reports. We mixed in Psyops messages, which were mostly accurate information. We told the Iraqi soldiers exactly how the war was going. They certainly weren't getting that information from their command. And the Kuwaiti underground movements took great heart in listening to those broadcasts.

A couple weeks after the air war started, General Schwarzkopf called me in. He said, "Our campaigns aren't causing as many defectors and deserters as we had hoped. Why don't you tell them that we're going to bomb the hell out of them?"

A good Psyops man needs to know what it's like to be a soldier on the ground. When you know how a soldier thinks, then you can communicate with him. During the Vietnam War, General Schwarzkopf was caught by accident in a B-52 strike. He knew how terrifying that could be—the psychological impact that has on a soldier. He said, "Let's maximize that psychological impact. Let them think about it. We'll give them the opportunity to flee and save their lives."

So we came up with a plan to drop leaflets on a particular Iraqi division along the front lines: "We control the skies. We can bomb you whenever we like. We advise you that in twenty-four hours the B-52s are going to bomb your division." We dropped about one million leaflets over that division to make sure they got the word. And we broadcast that message over our radio network. The next day, precisely as promised, the B-52s flew over that unit and carpet-bombed.

The following day we dropped more leaflets and another radio message: "We told you we were going to bomb and we did. You have one more chance to defect. Because we are going to bomb again tomorrow." And we did.

The Air Force was reluctant to notify Iraqi troops about B-52 missions in advance. But General Schwarzkopf made a good case about why it was important to do so.

We found by interrogating prisoners after the war that leaflets and our radio broadcasts were highly effective. By bombing we proved that we told the truth. That enhanced our credibility, and gained a big audience for our radio broadcasts. They all started tuning in to find out who was going to get bombed the next day.

Some of the intelligence we gathered was that many of the Iraqi soldiers didn't know where they were. They didn't know what direction to go. How far. We transmitted messages that said, "All you have to do is walk toward Mecca for three hours." Every Muslim knows where Mecca is. Because they pray in that direction five times a day.

We asked for volunteers among defectors to go on the radio. We were very sensitive about this, because of the way Saddam had exploited American prisoners and the hostages. Had we coerced anyone or given the appearance of coercing a false statement, it would have had awful retaliation on American prisoners.

We would ask for volunteers, and put a microphone in front of them. We asked, "What would you like to say to your comrades on the other side of the border?" And we let them talk.

On February 24, the ground war began. Army and Marine infantry and armor battalions were accompanied by sixty-six Psyop loudspeaker teams across the border. My guys hump with the infantry guys, carrying the same gear the infantrymen do, plus a loudspeaker on their backs that can weigh forty or fifty pounds. Helicopters also broadcast Psyop messages to encourage surrenders.

More than 98 percent of Iraqi defectors and prisoners questioned had in their possession or had seen our Psyop leaflets. Around seventy percent did what the leaflets told them to do—abandon their equipment.

And over half the prisoners interviewed said that they had heard the Voice of the Gulf radio broadcasts, with most of

those saying it influenced their decision to surrender peacefully. That saved a lot of lives. Every Iraqi soldier that surrendered or defected was one fewer that our soldiers had to
confront in a foxhole.

KNIGHT STRIKE

COLONEL RANDOLPH HOUSE

SAUDI ARABIA 1990–91
BRIGADE COMMANDER
1ST CAVALRY DIVISION

*On February 20, four days before the ground campaign of
Desert Storm was launched, the "Black Jack" Brigade of the
1st Cavalry Division made a daring daylight raid into the Iraqi
side of Wadi Al Batin, a wide gully that runs along Kuwait's
western border.*

*This dangerous feint had a dual purpose. First was as a "re-
connaissance in force" to draw out Iraqi forces in the area for
U.S. artillery and air power to attack, and also to prevent an
Iraqi strike on the nearby logistics headquarters of the U.S.
Army VII Corps.*

*More important, it would draw in Iraqi forces facing along
the Saudi border from the interiors of Kuwait and Iraq. This,
along with the Marine amphibious deception, would clear
Iraqi forces away from central Kuwait, thus opening the door
for allied ground forces to break through the Iraqi obstacle
barriers and advance on Kuwait City.*

*And with the Iraqi leadership focused on the wadi, the
"Knight Strike" would provide tactical cover for the U.S. Army
VII Corps and XVIII Airborne Corps to secretly swing west,
behind the 1st Cavalry. This was a primary reason for their
successful performance of General Schwarzkopf's "Hail
Mary" sweep across the Iraqi desert.*

I never intended to make the Army a career. In 1968, I graduated from Texas A&M University. My brother had been in

Vietnam, so I decided I had to do that. My intention was that as soon as I came back from the war, I would get out of the military and go back to school to get my veterinary certification. I still think of going back to veterinary school. I've got two daughters, one is in college and the other is a high school junior. But I've been committed to my job as a commander.

Before we departed for Saudi Arabia, I told my soldiers that we were going to make history. What was different from the last time I went to war in 1970 was that the soldiers now had the support of the American people. We knew it from the minute we left Fort Hood [Texas] in a convoy from Houston and Beaumont. The people of Texas were lining the streets and roads as we drove through little towns.

In my brigade, only one officer beside myself and a few of my senior NCOs had fought in Vietnam. No one else in the brigade had an appreciation for the carnage of war ... like having an eighteen-year-old die in your arms. I made an effort to talk to all of my company commanders and lieutenants. I said, "You have to continue to be a leader, even after you've experienced the shock of battle for the first time."

In Saudi Arabia, we learned that the division's role in the ground war was to be both a deception force and a reserve force. Like being the middle linebacker in football, we had to be prepared to go in any direction on short notice. The division had developed ten contingency plans. And I developed another for my brigade that we called "Knight Strike."

Knight Strike was a power move right up the Wadi a Batin, the gully that forms the tri-border area of Saudi Arabia, Kuwait, and Iraq. In Arabic, "wadi" means *dry riverbed*.

The Wadi al Batin was formed by glacier movements thousands of years ago. The eastern side is fairly rugged with some steep areas. The western side is a gradual incline back to the level of the desert. It runs toward the Euphrates River in Iraq to the north, and to King Khalid Military City [Saudi Arabia] 100 miles to our south. That is where General Schwarzkopf put the 1st Cavalry in early January, to begin the deception that the main allied attack would come up the wadi.

General Schwarzkopf's plan was to keep the Marines on ships off the Kuwait coast to tie down numerous Iraqi divisions. If the 1st Cav moved up to the border on the traditional invasion route, that would make sense to Iraqi generals.

After the air war started, the enemy's intelligence-gathering resources were limited. Our armored division moved right to the border, doing recon patrols and shooting MLRs [Multiple-Launch Rocket System rockets] across the border, to hold the Iraqis' attention. We had some artillery duels and helicopter raids. They took our fake, hook, line, and sinker. They moved in additional infantry divisions and a whole corps of artillery.

They believed that the main allied invasion would come straight up the wadi, then turn right toward the center of Kuwait en route to the sea. They put mines and obstacles in the wadi. And they dug elaborate "fire trenches."

On Tuesday, February 19, one month into the air war, we had no idea that G-Day was only five days away. It was just another day in the life of a soldier. Our division commander got a message from Army Command: "Tomorrow you send a major mounted force up the wadi."

Our division commander, Major General John Tilelli called me. He asked, "Can you execute Knight Strike tomorrow at noon?" I said, "Yes, sir."

The next morning we moved up to the border. At noon, our lead unit to cross into Iraq was the 1st Battalion/5th Cavalry (Task Force 1/5). I had the brigade's other two battalions stay back in reserve. I went in with 1/5, which had two tank companies (28 tanks), two Bradley vehicle companies (28 Bradleys), we had some mobile air-defense weapons and Bravo Company of the 8th Engineers. Our objective was to find the Iraqi positions and test their response. We were not to attack them decisively or risk heavy casualties. We called it, "Reconnaissance in force."

I rode in with the lead company of 1/5. This was the first time that my brigade was going into close combat. I believed it was my place to be up front, if for no other reason, to be a calming effect when the shooting started. And to read the ground and see the battlefield. The maps we had made the area look flat, like a bowling alley or a desktop. But there are indentations and ripples everywhere.

Our diamond formation had scouts forward. Behind them was a mechanized infantry company in Bradley fighting vehicles. On the wings were two tank companies. And in the back of the diamond were two more mech infantry companies. The Bradleys have TOW antitank missiles.

My Command Group was three vehicles: my command "track" [armored personnel carrier], a communications track, and a tank as my overwatch. My commo track had my Air

Force guy to coordinate air support. I also used it as a backup vehicle in case my track got hit.

Before the mission, I ordered, "We're not going to fire on anybody unless we're fired on." With that kind of rule, you prevent people from having happy triggers. We were all loaded and ready. But we went in very conscious of the fact that we didn't want to mistakenly shoot our own people.

We were without air cover. All available attack helicopters were involved in another operation. As we moved forward, we passed through some mine fields. We had tanks with mounted plows lead the way, rooting out mines to clear a path. Everybody shifted to a file formation behind the plow, moving at around ten miles per hour.

As soon as we were through the mine field, we spread back into our attack diamond. About ten kilometers up the wadi, our scouts in Bradley vehicles started receiving fire from dug-in Iraqi bunkers on a small ridge. I could see the scout platoon leader's vehicle. Machine-gun bullets were bouncing off his track. He was as cool as a cucumber for a young lieutenant.

The scouts were trained that when they came under fire, to peel to the wings and let the lead company come forward firing. Around a hundred Iraqi artillery guns began shooting at us. I had my own artillery on the Saudi side of the border. Within seconds, we had a lot of artillery support fire coming down on the Iraqis.

The first bunkers that our scouts encountered were on our side of the ridge. But as Alpha Company swept through those bunkers, they went over a small crest that did not appear on any map, and you couldn't see until you were upon it. The Iraqis had constructed a beautiful reverse-slope defense, exactly like in Russian army manuals. This reverse slope had mine fields and obstacles in depth. Their bunkers faced in from the next upslope. Coming over the ridge, we were trapped within the kill zone of their mortars, artillery, and direct fire. And we were too close to call in our long distance fire support.

Coming over the top, two of our tanks hit mines. The explosions were huge—one occurred within 100 meters of me—the entire tank was engulfed in black smoke that billowed up several hundred feet. We were near an Iraqi communications tower. I watched the smoke almost cover the top of the tower. Amazingly, none of the soldiers inside the tank were injured. But shrapnel hit some of my engineers who were riding on top of their vehicles.

One of the tank drivers didn't know what happened. There was so much shooting going on and explosions from artillery that the driver didn't realize that he hit a mine.

From my position near the front, I could see the flow of the battle. My artillery observer was in my track talking on the radio to call in fire. The usual safe distance to bring it is within 1,000 meters. But on two occasions, I brought it within 400 meters to knock out an Iraqi observation post that was calling their artillery on us.

Unfortunately, my track had five antennas, which attracted enemy fire. In my other command track I had an Air Force major, Mike Hart. I could listen in on his radio frequency talking to Air Force A-10 "Warthog" airplanes that came in to give us fire support. We were the only fight in Iraq. Every A-10 in the Theater wanted to get in on the act.

They were flying so low over us that we could read "U.S. Air Force" on their wings. Maybe 500 feet above us. They initially fired on Iraqi tanks with rockets. Then they swooped in firing their Gatling guns right over our heads. We weren't exactly sure where these A-10s were from. But my soldiers were sure happy to have them around.

The A-10 air controller overhead contacted us by radio and said, "You've got twelve artillery pieces shooting at you." A few minutes later, "twenty-six" . . . then, "forty-five." It kept going up. Finally, one A-10 pilot said, "I've stopped counting at a hundred."

We watched the A-10s roll in with missiles to take the artillery out. The Iraqis were firing a lot of SAM missiles at the airplanes to protect their artillery. So the A-10s kept at a higher elevation and used their missiles.

Artillery kept exploding all around us. I watched a young soldier named Ardon B. Cooper administer first aid to a wounded soldier. Mortar and artillery rounds were impacting all around him. He threw his body over the wounded kid. His back got peppered with shrapnel.

I watched him get up. His helmet had been blown off. Blood gushed out of his mouth and he collapsed. A medic from 1/5 rushed over and worked on him for three or four hours on the battlefield. We put him in a helicopter to try to stabilize him. He was full of holes. We later learned that he died that night. But the guy Cooper shielded did live.

Iraqi artillery gunners were accurate enough to put their artillery into our diamond formation. I could gauge the skill of their gunners because in Vietnam I was under mortar attacks a bunch, and under artillery attack on the DMZ a couple of times.

I got on the radio with the Commanding General and said, "They're shooting a lot of artillery at us. But it's not very well-aimed." They were walking it in. So we maneuvered around it. Sometimes they'd shoot behind us. Sometimes right next to us. A couple of times, the impact blew sand on me and shrapnel flew between my radio antennas.

My Command Group had a tactic we called the "Texas Two Step." Every time the explosions got too close, I'd call on the radio, "Let's do the Two Step." And we'd all maneuver around a bit. We trained hard enough to coordinate without becoming targets for friendly forces.

The 1st Cavalry had no incidents of "friendly fire" casualties in Desert Storm. That was due to training in the desert for months. And there was some luck involved. To coordinate with the A-10s, all of us had orange panels—standard aircraft marking panels—on the backs of our vehicles.

At one point, when the fighting was very fierce, I was listening to a lot of different radio conversations simultaneously. I observed the battle through my vehicle's open hatch. Or I used binoculars . . . standing on top of my vehicle. I would move to a place with a little cover, then when artillery would hit all around us, I'd move to another spot. Iraqi hand held weapons were fired against my track and the Vulcan air defense track behind me.

We fought into a bunker complex. The Iraqis had an AT-12 antitank battery hidden on our flank. We were moving forward, the Vulcan 200 meters behind me. That AT-12 obviously saw my five antennas, and the air defense weapon. Iraqi Doctrine is the same as ours: Take out Command and Control and air defenses. The AT-12 opened fire with their 100mm cannons, just missing my track. But their next shot hit the Vulcan. The round penetrated the turret and a soldier was decapitated.

I couldn't let the deaths I saw in the heat of battle effect my concentration on the radios and to coordinate our firepower. I had seen so much carnage in Vietnam . . . I had men die in my arms. People who I had been very close with. So maybe I got a little bit hardened. But my overriding concern in battle was for the men in the 1/5 Battalion. Their battalion commander had never been in war before. I was later told that my remarks over the radio were very calming to the commanders. I just told everybody to settle down.

Once the A-10s were rolling in to take out the artillery, our mission was complete. We had found the enemy and had drawn them out of their positions by eliciting one hell of a response. I had three tracks hit; three soldiers dead; and fourteen wounded.

We went into the teeth of the Iraqi army and overran their initial defense belt. We could see no enemy left alive in that infantry battalion supported by tanks. We took only around fifteen prisoners. They didn't give up until after we had overrun their positions and started throwing hand grenades into their bunkers and clearing trenches. We didn't see any white flags. It was very different from how the Iraqis acted later.

Around 1500 [three P.M.] General Tilelli radioed, "I want you back into Saudi Arabia by dark." So we pulled back. U.S. forces continued to hit the Iraqi positions with MLRs and B-52 strikes. And the next four days our artillery pounded the area.

SEAL MISSION

CAPTAIN TIMOTHY HOLDEN

SAUDI ARABIA 1990–91
SPECIAL OPERATIONS TASK FORCE COMMANDER
SEAL TASK FORCE MIKE

During the Gulf War, Navy SEALs were involved in some 270 special operations missions. Among the most critical to the success of Desert Storm was the performance of a small platoon that, under the cover of darkness, swam to the Kuwaiti just before the main ground attack commenced. Their mission was to plant and detonate explosive charges along the beach to convince the Iraqis that the Marine amphibious force was preparing to attack. This artful deception by a handful of young special operators helped to tie down some 80,000 Iraqi soldiers along the coast, as the Marine ground attack swept in behind them. The SEAL officer responsible for coastal operations was Captain Timothy Holden.

In December, when President Bush called up another 200,000 forces to the Gulf, planning began for the Desert Storm offensive. At that time, I was named Commander of Task Force Mike, just south of the Kuwait border at Ra's al Mish'ab. We were responsible for SEAL coastal operations. That included cross-border search and rescue for downed pilots using our special operations [armed dune-buggy] vehicles.

And my staff started working with General Walt Boomer's MARCENT [Marines CENTCOM] staff to plan the amphibious deception operation to tie up large numbers of Iraqi forces along the coast. We discussed doing recon from the sea onto the beach near Kuwait City.

We didn't have combat veterans. So our leadership wanted to ease into this. Not put our people into the middle of combat without a buildup. The initial plan called for: first, reconnaissance probes from high speed boats to test the Iraqi reaction. If no reaction, launch our rubber boats and go within 200 yards from the beach, to test them again.

Then, launch swimmer scouts from rubber boats to swim to the shoreline and report on Iraqi defense positions. We made extensive use of our handheld video cameras, to film whatever the scouts could see.

In my opinion, the biggest breakthrough for our operations was the GPS [Global Positioning System] for navigation. Our tactic is to bring a high-speed boat off the coast and launch a rubber boat from it. Then the rubber boat has to navigate ten or fifteen miles to the beach. In a desert shoreline environment there is absolutely no visual references. There's no mountains, there's no rivers, or landscape features to know if you're in the right location. With a GPS in every boat, a guy could drive to a point and know that he was exactly on the mark. Then navigate around and come right back to the point he was assigned.

To withdraw and recover, the rubber boats would maneuver, north or south, so the high-speed boat wouldn't repeat its pattern and be seen returning to the same area. The GPS could rendezvous the two boats right on the money. And if the scouts see something new somewhere, they can report back, "I saw it at point X on my GPS." The next night they could go back and find it.

Fortunately, we were located with the Marine Corps' RPV [remotely piloted (air) vehicle] company. They coordinated with us to fly their cameras over specific beach areas. Our goal was to find an uninhabited beach large enough for a Marine amphibious assault. Through a series of recon missions, we determined and proposed a site for General Schwarzkopf's amphibious deception operation. Our objective was to preoccupy large numbers of Iraqi troops while land-based Marines attacked across the Kuwait border.

The SEALs were tasked to swim in and plant explosive charges to make a lot of noise to get the Iraqis' attention. We later added naval gunfire support and air strikes into the same area to give the diversion more credibility as a preparation for an amphibious landing. If it wasn't credible, the Iraqis wouldn't be sucked into it.

SEAL teams' platoons tend to reflect the personality of their commander. Each platoon has completely different personalities. I knew which SEALs would be best for various aspects of the mission. I was also trying for each platoon to have the opportunity to do reconnaissance. And then come back to debrief everyone. In doing that, the Group found what works best and then developed standard ways of doing things.

A SEAL platoon leader has got a lot of supermotivated, hard-charging guys, who run down the road at ninety miles an hour. The challenge isn't to keep them running, but divert them over to the track you want them to stay on.

I emphasized to my young officers, "I will back you one hundred-percent for making smart aggressive moves. Take a risk, if it's a smart risk. But if you cut corners on a safety procedure, or try to cheat or work your way around a problem, I'll have your ass."

Some people miss the fact that special operations people are not only physically fit, but also very quick-witted. If you give a very detailed list of "don't do this, don't do that," it's going to get screwed up. Because a platoon leader, operating in a small group behind enemy lines, never knows what is going to happen.

As a commander you have to give him good general guidance. And spend enough time talking with him about the mission so that he understands what you want him to do, without you telling him how to do it. So that he can adapt to the situation: blend in with his environment, avoid contact with the enemy, not return fire.

To accomplish your mission and protect your people, you need to constantly think about two steps downstream from where you are now. Have alternative contingencies to fall back on if things don't work according to plan.

As a commander of a tight-knit unit, I knew my people well and what they do best. I know their wives and kids. When I sent them into dangerous situations in the Gulf, I did think about the risk factor quite a bit. When I took over as commander of Special Warfare Task Unit Mike, I gathered everybody together. I told them, "My number-one goal in being your commander is to take you all back to San Diego and have a beer with you after this whole thing is over."

Nobody ever came up to me and said, "Your comments made a big difference to me." Or, "That eased my mind." But that was something I was committed to deliver on.

We didn't have a lot of time to practice the amphibious deception mission. The actual mission took place on the night the ground offensive began. It was pretty straightforward: swim in to the beach and blow things up. To make the Iraqis think that a Marine amphibious landing was about to begin.

We had lots of problems getting intelligence and getting good premission imagery. The air campaign and planning for the air campaign was sucking in all the resource intelligence, and directing it toward strategic targets. We needed more tactical information in border areas, and up and down the coast. Tactical intelligence is always a problem. You never know who will move into an area since the last time you photographed it. Unless you have people right there to monitor and communicate.

We relied primarily on Marine RPVs to look at various beach areas. They were located at Ra's al Mish'ab with us. If we had a request that was really hot, we would have a video that same day or night analyzed.

The beaches that the Iraqis believed most likely for an amphibious assault were located on the coast of Kuwait City, just above our deception operation. In the water they had a three-strand stack of concertina [barbed] wire. Right at the beach edge another three-strand stack. Five yards further onto the beach they had a strand of barbed wire, shin high. After that— what I found most amazing—was a five-yard-deep, basket-weave pattern of concertina wire, just about ankle high.

In the holes between the wire were land mines . . . as far as you could see in either direction. And beyond that were bunkers every twenty-five to fifty yards, with chain-link fences in front to deflect any antitank weapons Marines use.

The idea was to trap our Marines in the wire and use automatic weapons from the bunkers to cut them down. The bunkers created overlapping fields of fire.

I chose the sixteen-man platoon that I thought would be best suited for the operation. My staff discussed the general plan. The platoon then discussed among themselves their approach. They then brought it to my staff and we worked out the details. I believe it is important that the platoon be involved in preparing the operation.

After doing repeated recons of the coast, we chose a spot. The plan was to create a stir there. Because it wasn't heavily defended, Iraqi units from all over the area would come to reinforce it. It was close enough to Saudi Arabia to draw in troops from along the border, just four hours before the Marines would kick off the ground offensive.

BEHIND ENEMY LINES

CHIEF WARRANT OFFICER 2 RICHARD BALWANZ

SAUDI ARABIA 1990–91
A-TEAM LEADER
5TH SPECIAL FORCES GROUP

On the night of February 23, 1991, as the ground war was about to begin, an eight-man Special Forces reconnaissance team led by Chief Warrant Officer 2 Richard Balwanz was lifted by helicopter deep into Iraq to monitor any enemy reinforcements moving on Highway 8 toward the battle area.

Balwanz, thirty-nine, a native of southern Ohio and father of two, is nicknamed "Bulldog" by his peers because of his powerful compact build. He had been in Special Forces since he was a young sergeant in 1978. However, neither he nor any member of his team had ever experienced actual combat. Unknown to them, they were in for a "mother" of all first "real-world" tests.

You don't do things real fast with the Arabs. When we arrived in Saudi Arabia at the end of August, some A-teams were sent to work with Pan-Arab forces on the Kuwait border. But the Saudis wanted nothing to do with them. They sent the teams back.

More negotiations went on before we sent a couple of people to their headquarters. It took another month before they realized, "Yeah, these guys have something to offer." As the training went on, the American advisors became invaluable to the Coalition. Because of the coordination we did with U.S. Air Force support.

I can speak just enough Arabic for basic conversation. Just, "How are you doing . . . You're looking good today . . . Time to eat." But once in the field, I picked up a few words every day. Before long, I found myself talking Arabic to people, having little conversations. I'd walk away and think, "Did I do that?"

During Desert Shield, my ten-member A-team manned a patrol station on the Kuwait border. We patroled at night and did observation during the day with twenty-four-man Saudi A-teams. We lived with them, ate with them, slept with them. Each combined team patrolled a border sector of around thirty-five miles.

After the air war started, Special Forces were pulled off the border and U.S. Marines took over that mission. I left the border in December to take command of another A-team. During the ground war, we were assigned deep recon into Iraq.

There really is no place to hide in the desert. So we did a lot of research and development for digging hide-site recon positions. We carried camouflage netting to cover our hiding holes. We had some aerial photographs and imagery, but a recurrent problem is that intelligence for special operations is not routinely gathered. We lacked information on things like soil composition for digging hide sites or parachuting, and how civilians would react if they see us.

The local people living in our operations area in Iraq were primarily nomadic bedouins and Arab rural people. In the military we do a real good job on enemy battalions and companies. But we don't do a real good job on civilians. We need to know their patterns of behavior and how they live day to day. In Desert Storm we didn't have that information.

On the night prior to the start of the ground war, we went into Iraq. We flew in special operations Blackhawk helicopters of the Army's Task Force 160 Aviation unit. We flew over the desert at 140 knots, at very low altitude. They were flying so low, at one point we hit a sand dune. The pilot pulled up at the very last second. The ground tore the rear wheel off. That scared the heck out of me. But it didn't seem to effect the pilot at all.

I said, "What's going on?" he said, "Oh, we hit a sand dune. Don't worry about it. We're going to get you there." To them it was like stubbing your toe. That gave me a lot of confidence. When we arrived at our target area, they hovered as we got off. Then they departed.

My eight-man team was dropped near a little village north of the Euphrates River, between Baghdad and the town of Nasaria. Shwasgas was the little village near the Shadarif River, a tributary of the Euphrates.

We were surrounded by farmers' fields. A flat open area similar to Kansas. You could see forever, like a grassy table-top. The clay soil composition was much different than Saudi where we practiced digging our hide sites in sand. We tried to get Iraqi soil composition for training, but we couldn't find any. So we brought small shovels, but no picks or any tools for hard earth. Each guy was already carrying 150 pounds of equipment on his back. A lot of it was communications equipment, and the hide-site kit that is prefabricated camouflage materials. And each man carried five gallons of water.

In addition, our ammunition and weapons systems included M-16 rifles and two or three grenade launchers. Two of us carried silenced 9mm pistols, which proved worthless in a desert firefight. We had nothing to counter armor.

Our mission was reconnaissance, just hide and not look for a fight. In the premission analysis we found no reason to expect problems. There were some Iraqi units to the south, but nothing in our area except local militia and civilians.

When the helicopters dropped us off, it was real quiet. We moved through the canals to hide our footprints. The canal water was anywhere from knee deep to chest deep, around two meters at its widest point. With nobody around, we could walk all over the place. We had on our night vision goggles and could see no movement.

Our mission was to watch the highway and report back to the 18th Airborne Corps [in Saudi] what the enemy was doing after the ground war kicked off. Would they send reinforcements? Would they withdraw? What types of equipment would they send down the road?

My team dug into our positions along the canals, which are used to catch water during rainstorms. It had rained recently. That made the ground a problem to dig into, sticky and muddy. We dug our underground hide sites that night. We had two sites, four men in each position, within 300 meters of the road. Close enough to identify armored vehicles and different Iraqi units.

We got up at daylight, around six A.M. We began to realize there might be problems. The fields began to come alive with people. It was like a recreation area. People were wandering everywhere. Men were herding cattle and sheep. Women were picking up firewood. Children playing. The main village area was probably one or two kilometers away, but there were some homes just off the side of the road. We were discovered by children.

No matter how good a soldier you are at camouflage, you don't get perfect. We were totally covered except for a corner that we used to view from. We were totally quiet except for our hearts thumping.

There were three kids: two girls and a boy, maybe five to seven years old. The kids came up so close that we could hear them talk and breathe. They were playing and carrying on. And they noticed that something didn't look right. They came up, poking at our cover material, and peeked into our hide site. They saw guys with camouflage paint on our faces.

Startled, the kids started running off. My team reflexively jumped into the canal. We had the silenced automatic pistols. The guys were looking to me like, "Should we waste these people?"

I snapped back, "No."

It's easier to set back and say, "If somebody came upon me, I'd just blow him away. That way I wouldn't compromise my team." But I have children of my own. I looked at those kids and thought, "It's not their war." It might have been the wrong decision. But I said, "No, we're not going to shoot children. Or unarmed civilians. I'm sorry, but that is not going to happen."

I had to assume that our position was compromised. That the kids were running to tell the village people. They were screaming and there were people all over the place. We were set up on either side of the canal in the middle of an open field where you could see for a mile. So I pulled my teams out of the hide sites and got on the SATCOM [satellite communication] radio. I told our headquarters, "We probably need to be exfiltrated [by helicopter] because we have been caught."

We backed away from the road, up the canal, and started looking around. None of the civilians gave any indication that we were there. So I called back on the radio and cancelled my exfil bird. I said, "I don't think the kids told anybody. They may have thought we are Iraqi soldiers."

I made the decision, "We are going to carry on the mission from this ditch." We were about chest deep and continued to watch the road. We could still see lots of people walking around, herding their sheep and goats and cattle, and some women gathering wood.

At noon that day, we reported back to the 18th Airborne Corps headquarters about the traffic. Right after that—around twelve-thirty—we got caught again. Children . . . this time with an adult. They looked right down at us. I spoke to the guy in Arabic, *"Salaam Aleikum,"* which is a greeting, "Peace be upon you." They just took off without saying anything. We saw the guy take off back to the village. So I gathered my team and we moved further away from the road, up the canal. It didn't take very long to see what was going on.

Probably twenty minutes later, here come the bedouins, armed. They were coming up along the canal. They had long rifles, probably semiautomatic SKS models. Shortly thereafter, they had contacted the local militia, and here comes four deuce-and-a-half trucks, a bus, and a Toyota landcruiser-type vehicle. Approximately a company of Iraqi soldiers unload. I said, "Uh-oh, we're in trouble now."

I radioed for an exfiltration. Headquarters said, "Okay, we're going to get some close air support for you first." I said, "Contact them now. We are gonna be in a fight in just a minute."

I made a decision to destroy all of our classified equipment, except for one radio to talk to the aircraft and a SatCom radio to talk with 18th Airborne Corps. We took off our rucksacks. We had trained for this type of contingency in training for the mission, so we had survival gear. But we weren't prepared for the shock of going into combat. We had one guy who had been in Grenada. Everyone else—including myself—had never experienced combat before.

We stuck explosives and one-minute time fuses into the classified radios. We activated the time fuses and started to move away while the Iraqis were moving in. They had a plan to maneuver. They sent a platoon into the canal to move on our right flank, and another platoon on our left flank in the canal. The other two platoons were on the high ground. They were so close that by the time the one-minute fuses went off, they were on top of the rucksacks. We came under a heavy volume of fire from our flanks and behind us.

I moved my guys into a defensive position at an L-shaped elbow in the canal. The Iraqis were bearing down on us, screaming Arab war yells and running with their guns firing. I ordered my M203 [grenade] gunners to fire into the flanks, where they were running at us in groups of four or five. A grenade would explode and only one guy would still be running. That stopped the assault. But our close air support was still twenty minutes away. With a company of Iraqis coming at us, our survival chances weren't too good.

At one point, I turned around and saw two of my guys actually waving good-bye to each other in the ditch. They thought, "This is it." I gave a command that nobody was to shoot on automatic, "Pick out a target, take your time and squeeze off a round." Because we didn't have the ammunition for sustained combat. That's the thing that really saved us—my guys' marksmanship.

Every time a gun fired, an Iraqi dropped. We probably shot forty people in the first five to ten minutes of the attack. It slowed things down to a firefight. Nobody was charging us anymore. Of course, they were taking shots at us. They were shooting with their AKs. The most effective fire came from the bedouins with their long barrels. We were just real lucky, really fortunate. Perhaps God was looking out for us, also. Because rounds were impacting in the dirt within inches of our heads.

People on the road were waving down more military vehicles, "Hey, we've got some Americans here." Another group of maybe thirty people and a dozen vehicles were lining up on the road, when the first F-16 airplanes flew over. We tried to use the SATCOM radio, and LST-5 [multi-purpose radio] that has a small satellite dish and an antenna to talk to airplanes. Well, we lost that antenna. We could hear him. But there I was in the ditch and couldn't talk to him.

Some of my guys tried to point the dish in his direction. Our radio call sign was Guard. We could hear him say, "I heard Guard down there. But I can't hear him anymore. If we don't hear anything within the next few minutes, we'll just hit the communication site." A mile to our south was a big Iraqi communication complex. A few minutes later the bombs started dropping down there.

That got the civilians out of the area. It was reminiscent of an old Civil War battle where local people would come out to observe. Women and children standing along. But when the bombs started dropping at a distance, they left. One of the guys I was with happened to carry a small survival radio. He started calling for help. An AWAC aircraft responded. The AWAC got a hold of our close air support. In the meantime, the Iraqi militia was along the road getting ready for another assault.

The first air strike we called in was against the thirty people along the road and their vehicles. The F-16s dove in with their cluster munitions. The bombs hit about a kilometer away from us. I decided to hit that target first. That paid off. Because when we called back the aircraft to give him a BDA [bomb damage assessment], there were a lot of secondary explosions. The fuel tanks on the vehicles were blowing. The pilot responded, "I don't need a BDA on that."

After that, when Iraqi vehicles came down the road and militia tried to flag them down, they said, "No, no." Then we started calling in cluster munitions dangerously close on our flanks. The F-16s dropped 2,000-pound bombs and cluster bombs within 200 meters of us.

We were trapped in that ditch for around six hours. When the aircraft would leave to refuel, the Iraqis still tried to get together. There were three distinct attacks. The last two came between the flights of the F-16s coming in. We found out later that Saddam had come on the radio: "The war has started and we are kicking the Americans' asses. Everybody take up arms."

All the local people were excited, taking up arms and coming out to hunt us. The thing that worried me the most was the canal, because it wasn't straight—it was snaked. I called an air strike right into the canal. So me and Sergeant 1st Class Robbie Gardner went further down the canal to adjust the air strike. We moved shoulder to shoulder. In my line of thinking, we'd catch the lead Iraqi assault element by surprise—they didn't expect us to attack.

Within a few hundred meters we came around the corner and were face-to-face, within fifteen to twenty feet, of their three-man point element. They were still hunkered down in the ditch from the air strike. It was like an old-fashioned show-down at the O.K. Corral. This time we did shoot on automatic. We killed all three.

We continued forward. The rest of the Iraqis turned and fled down the ditch. We chased them all the way to where we had blown up our gear to make sure that the classified equipment was destroyed.

We gathered up what personal gear was left in the ruck-sacks. We took that and the captured weapons back to our defensive position. Meanwhile, another truck pulled up with a squad of fifteen soldiers jumping into the ditch. So we called in another air strike.

By now it was getting dark, which posed a serious problem for the F-16s to discriminate our position from the enemy. During daylight we used signal mirrors. But we hadn't carried smoke grenades, which was a big mistake.

As the sun got lower and night set in, pilots were asking, "Where are you at?" Well, the sun and the moon were in the sky at the same time. Sergeant 1st Class DeGraff was on the survival radio. He told them, "This might sound silly. But you fly from the sun toward the moon. When you're directly over me, I'll let you know." It worked. The pilots were able to see the faint glint from our signal mirror and continue the close air support.

The bombs were hitting so close that we were stunned by shock waves and dirt from explosions of 2,000-pound bombs. We laid flat. When the bombs impacted, the ground felt like a bowl of Jell-O. The earth would roll.

When night fell, I thought, "The Iraqis are really going to hit us now. Because we can't get effective close air support." So we waited until a half hour after darkness. We were fortunate to have night vision goggles. I said, "We have to get out of this ditch."

So we crawled for 300 meters across the open field to a berm. The F-16s were in contact with us the entire time. They said, "Your search and rescue helicopter will be here in about twelve minutes." Even though they held their fire, just the sound of jets circling overhead kept the Iraqis at bay. Out of the initial one hundred militia and soldiers who attacked us, we observed maybe twenty still on the battlefield. There were a lot of dead. My team probably shot forty of them with small arms. The cluster munitions and 2,000-pound bombs took care of the rest who tried to Sneaky Pete around our flanks.

The helicopter came on the radio. It was the same Blackhawk crew from the Army's 160th Aviation that inserted us. They said, "We're coming in." I told them, "We haven't taken any fire in forty-five minutes, since it got dark." They said, "Give us your exact location."

After we'd been moving around so much, we didn't know our exact location. Our GPS had been destroyed, broken up in the fighting. But we had our old PRC-90 survival radio. A pilot said, "Turn it on." It kept beeping enough for the pilots to sweep right in on top of us. We climbed on board in an instant. We were very fortunate that nobody got killed. We didn't even have anybody wounded. And we got out of there.

That we all came out alive was most important. I remember thinking in the first hour of the battle, "If I get killed, I hope that I'm one of the first. Because I don't want to sit here and watch my team get shot up."

I can't give enough credit to the F-16s and the Task Force 160 pilots. I later spoke to some of the F-16 pilots that flew on the mission. They were Reservists from South Carolina.

THE BEACH

BRIGADIER GENERAL JOHN ADMIRE

SAUDI ARABIA 1990–91
REGIMENT COMMANDER
3RD MARINE REGIMENT, TASK FORCE TARO

Aided by the deception operations that tied down Iraqi forces on the coast and along the Wadi al Batin, General Norman Schwarzkopf called the Marines breach of the Iraqi mine fields a "classic" military operation. Task Force Taro, designated as a heliborne force to leap over the obstacle zone, received surprise orders as the ground war approached. They would do a secret breach of the mine field—on foot and with little more than their bare hands.

On February 19, we received orders to move from the coastal area, ninety miles west, to join our parent division. And we received orders to change from our role as a heliborne force. Our main mission was going to be a secret infiltration force into Kuwait before the main ground attack began.

That was a psychological shock to us. We had trained for a quick strike north, including clearing trench lines and breaching obstacle barriers. Now we had a mission we had not anticipated ... within seventy-two hours.

I tried to turn that into a positive. I addressed my troops, "Let's be proud that General Myatt has confidence in us." Our mission was to protect the division's flank from Iraqi counterattack.

I think the change happened for a couple of reasons. We had worked with the Arab Coalition forces since September. They were going to attack up the coast on the right flank of the division. Since we were known to the Coalition, we would attack between them and the rest of the U.S. forces.

Breaching the barriers was going to be a formidable task. Absolutely no doubt about it. We had practiced it with armor, with tank plows, with explosive devices, with engineers' mechanical gear. Now, all of a sudden, our orders state, "You will breach without any tanks, with only a few light mechanized vehicles. There will only be a platoon of engineers, but no explosives. This is to be done in a secret clandestine manner."

We had to go on foot, at night. Carrying only our rifles with a bayonet attached. The old World War I style: on your hands and knees probing for mines. If you hear the clink of metal, you move to the side and continue to carefully crawl your way through the mine field.

We crossed the border into Kuwait on the night of February 22. We moved cautiously around fourteen kilometers, to within six kilometers of the first barrier. The desert is pretty damned flat, but there are undulations. We were able to literally hide my regiment of around 3,000 Marines in the small indentations of the terrain. The Iraqis never knew we were there. We dug in and during daylight hours tried to use the terrain to our advantage.

We waited until a couple of hours past dark on the evening of February 23. Our infiltration was planned for around eight P.M. We knew that our division's ground attack was going to kick off at six A.M. the following morning.

It would take us all night to carefully move through the barriers and establish our fighting positions. But we were uncertain that the offensive would happen. There were last minute political negotiations conducted by the U.S. and the Soviets. Late in the day we received an order to delay our operation. The clock went to nine P.M., ten P.M. . . . I was getting concerned. Because I didn't want to go through the mine fields any faster than we planned. It had to be a slow and deliberate process.

I communicated with General Myatt over the radio. We worked out an agreement, "Initiate your movement toward the infiltration. But don't do anything irreversible." If there was a diplomatic solution, we were not to prematurely trigger a conflict. It was difficult for me to explain to my Marines what the hell "irreversible" means. It wasn't up to me if the Iraqis would open fire.

To our advantage, smoke from oil wells that Iraqis had sabotaged made the night pitch-dark, providing better cover for our movement. Late that night we got the word: "Go."

The first obstacle was a barbed-wire fence that identified the mine field, which was 100 to 150 meters in depth. Then there was a more formidable fence—triple strand or concertina wire. Behind that was the earthen berms. Behind that were antitank ditches and traps that they attempted to flood with oil to set on fire when tanks approached. That didn't work very well because most of the oil sunk into the sand.

We had three battalions: my 1st Battalion was detached from us to execute a helicopter-borne raid into the Burgan oil fields to lengthen security on the division's right flank. I had 3rd Battalion do the initial infiltration. I kept 2nd Battalion south, because intelligence estimates of Iraqi forces in the Al Wafra oil field was sketchy. We figured on anything from a reinforced Iraqi battalion to a reinforced brigade. I didn't want to leave our artillery and combat support vulnerable.

We couldn't take for granted that the Iraqis wouldn't fight. We knew they had been beaten down by the air war. But we were particularly concerned about chemical warfare.

All of my Marines went across the border in full protective clothing. But we carried our gas masks because we needed good visibility crossing the mine field. We could put our masks on in a hurry if we got hit with gas.

We all knew that our fundamental mission was to get through that barrier or else the entire division might fail. We carefully probed for land mines the old-fashioned way—with bayonets.

There were thousands of mines. The wind whipping the sand exposed some. But we didn't know if that could be a trap, with others buried deeper. Some Marines took initiative, "These antitank mines are going to take 4,000 pounds to set them off. I can hop from one to the other." And I'll be damned if they didn't do that. It was amazing.

All of my Marines made it through the barrier zone without casualties. We set up fighting positions behind enemy lines, and radioed our progress to General Myatt.

All the Task Force Commanders on the radio heard my reports. Colonel Fulford, the commander of Task Force Ripper that co-led the main attack into Kuwait [along with Task Force Papa Bear], later told me, "When the news of your infiltration spread through my forces, everyone's morale went sky high." His Marines said, "If they can cross the barrier with bayonets, we've got armor and mechanized vehicles and breaching devices. Hell, we can make it, too."

We figured the first barrier would be defended lightly. Between the two barriers was our most vulnerable period. We would be massed and exposed in an open-bracketed artillery fire zone. And our flanks were exposed to Iraqi armor.

Being heavily outgunned, our key support was Marine air. The ground campaign was planned around having a period of five good days of weather so air support would be a factor. Wouldn't you know it, the night we attacked it rained. And the Iraqis had exploded 600 oil wells in the area. So the smoke pollution was unbelievable. At ten o'clock in the morning it looked like midnight. Visibility on the ground was less than 1,000 meters. On the ground it was hard to distinguish friend from foe, much less at 10,000 feet from the air.

Without air support we were trapped. Our two Marine divisions were against an estimated eleven Iraqi divisions. The Iraqis had far more armor, mechanized personnel carriers, and artillery than we had. Iraqi forces began to gather for a mass counterattack. They were ready to come at us.

At that time of year the winds traditionally blow down from the mountain ranges of Iraq from the north down toward the Gulf. That made us very vulnerable to Iraqi chemical weapons.

But around noon, it was Divine intervention . . . the wind suddenly shifted. It started blowing from behind our backs. And it blew north for the next five days. It was almost like

Moses in the Red Sea . . . the skies opened for aircraft of all services who loitered over the battlefield hoping for a break in the clouds. The Iraqi forces were almost completely destroyed.

I'm an infantryman. But I'm the first to admit that the U.S. Air Force, naval air, Marine air, and Army helicopter gunships combined to save a lot of Marines' lives.

It seemed that the Iraqis were most afraid of air. When we captured prisoners, we would use a vehicle to lead the Iraqis back to a PW [prisoner of war] holding area. We didn't require them to walk with their hands over their heads in single file. We told them, "If you get unruly and start any problems whatsoever for this Marine in the Humvee, he's just going to take off and leave you." That's the thing they feared most. Because they knew as long as they were with us, and we had markings on the vehicle for aircraft to recognize us as friendly, they were safe.

I used a Humvee as my mobile Command Post. It had two radios. I used one to communicate with the generals at higher headquarters, and with the other I could talk to my own battalions.

I was also tied into the division tactical radio net. So I could monitor what was going on with the other Marine regiments. My regiment was spread across a pretty broad front—twenty to thirty kilometers. I kept track of everyone by plotting units on maps. But for a commander, it's a natural habit to picture the battlefield in your mind's eye. And I was normally touching base with the battalion commanders.

One of the big transitions that a combat officer has to make as he proceeds up through the ranks is to accept that you can't be in the thick of the fight with the lead unit.

As a senior commander, you have to put yourself a little further back behind your lead elements. I would usually put a battalion up front, my command group next, then the other two battalions. So I put myself up as far as I could. In all fairness to my subordinate commanders, if I got too far forward I would be preempting the battalion commander. He'd be wondering, "Why is he supervising or looking over my shoulder?"

From the time that we crossed the first barrier to the time that we secured the airfield, Task Force Taro did not have a Marine or sailor wounded. Phenomenal. In our entire division, some 20,000 Marines, we had six Marines killed and forty-five wounded.

Hell, if we went to a combined arms exercise at Twenty-nine Palms, California, with that number of forces and fired the same amount of ammunition, we'd have more people hurt in that peacetime environment. But we had trained intensively for six months. When we crossed into Kuwait, everyone was very conscious and alert.

POINT-BLANK

FIRST SERGEANT ANTHONY MCPIKE

SAUDIA ARABIA 1990–91
TANK LEADER
C COMPANY, 1ST TANK BATTALION,
1ST MARINE DIVISION

If a Marine tells me that he is never afraid, there is something wrong with him. That's the type of person you want to stay away from. Yes, I was scared. Because I knew that the officers in my unit had no combat experience. In fact, I was the only staff NCO in the whole company that had combat experience.

I knew beforehand that as a tank leader if I acted overly heroic, like, "This stuff doesn't bother me," then the troops would pick this attitude up and start doing something stupid. In combat, if I go in with one hundred men, I want to come back with all of them.

Before the ground war, I used to get up at night and walk around the compound to check the security watchers on the tanks. I'd check others. Especially those who would jump when a bomb went off in the distance. I didn't ridicule them. I let their fear subside. Then I would calm them.

At our area of the Saudi-Kuwait border, we could hear airplanes overhead every hour of the night flying to and from combat missions. And when Marine mobile artillery conducted raids, the self-propelled artillery sounded like tanks. That plays on your mind. Because you might think that enemy vehicles are in our maneuver area. But after a while those initial scares helped the troops and calmed them down when the real fighting began.

When we got the word that we were moving to the assembly area, I had a talk with the troops. I told them point-blank, "The time for talk is over. I've tried my best to pass on my knowledge and experience about our tanks, as it was taught to me. Apparently some of y'all listened, and some of you didn't. Those of you who didn't listen are going to pay the ultimate price. The worst thing in the world is to get into a battle against another armored vehicle, and your tank stops running. Because you failed to do what you were supposed to do. The only thing I will do after the fact is to come around and bag you and tag your body. All you are going to be is a memory in somebody's mind."

When I said that, eyes opened wide. Not only among my troops, but with officers. They could not believe that I would say something like that to the troops. I told the captain, "You can say anything you want about my comments. But you've got to realize one thing. My ultimate responsibility is to make sure that these troops take care of these vehicles so they can fight and survive." We went into battle with seventeen tanks. And we came back with seventeen tanks.

In one incident, I was on road security. With us were two captains and a warrant officer, a gunny, a master sergeant, and a 1st sergeant. We found some EPWs [enemy prisoners of war] who surrendered. These two captains did one of the stupidest things I've ever seen.

Without even securing the area, one captain tried to order some troops that were flanking alongside the EPWs, which they were doing correctly. But this captain grabs a rifle and runs across the field. He didn't even know what was in front of him. Me and the other 1st sergeant saw that and just shook our heads. We went back to our Humvees and sat there.

You can't talk with people like that captain. When it was over, the Marines thought it was funny. They came up to us and asked, "Is that what you're supposed to do?"

Something else that I felt important to keep in check was that a lot of troops wanted to open fire. The 1st sergeant and I talked to a lot of them. We said, "Y'all don't understand. The minute you pull that trigger and kill somebody, your life is changed forever. That's a feeling you'll never get rid of.

"You might think it's funny now. But it's not. You might take the life of another human being that is not even offering a threat to you. I can understand if a man is running at you with his weapon blazing or with a fixed bayonet. But if he's standing there with his hands on top of his head, don't tell me you're just going to take him out."

They said, "Hell, Top, he's the enemy." I said, "That's right. But you've got to realize that 'enemy' should be treated humanely. You are an American fighter. You are not a paid killer. How about if somebody did that to your child?"

They said, "Wow, Top, we didn't think of it like that."

In Saudi Arabia, a chaplain gave us a class on combat leadership. I think that his class should be mandatory. He said, "There is a fine line between reality and fantasy. Once you cross that line, all the psychiatrists in the world will do nothing but get wealthy on you."

Under the stress of combat, anyone can cross that [psychological] line without realizing it. You need a squad leader, a platoon sergeant or a seasoned platoon commander—a young lieutenant is not prepared—to see that in a troop before he is too far gone.

The leader should call that young man aside and say, "Hey, you and I need to get together and talk about this." Or smack him over the head or do whatever it takes to bring him back to reality, as quickly as possible. If that young man is allowed to mess up, you defeat yourself. Because it affects the whole platoon. And once a leader loses the respect of his troops, he'll never get it back.

AIR ASSAULT

BRIGADIER GENERAL JAMES HILL

SAUDI ARABIA 1990–91
BRIGADE COMMANDER
101ST AIRBORNE DIVISION (AIR ASSAULT)

An essential component to the "Hail Mary" sweep was a massive helicopter air assault by the 101st Division—the largest since the Vietnam War—into the Tigris and Euphrates river valley. Their mission was to set up a forward fuel and ammunition base for advancing ground and air forces. In addition they were to shut off any Iraqi reinforcements moving to battle areas, to guarantee the swift encirclement of Iraqi forces in Kuwait. Colonel James Hill was tasked to lead the heliborne air assault into Iraq.

Central to General Schwarzkopf's "Hail Mary" operation was to cut off Iraqi reinforcements who might head toward Kuwait. During the planning for our air assault into Iraq, my division commander, General Peay, said to me, "Here's your mission objective. Tell the division what you need to accomplish it."

I decided that to mass combat power ninety miles inside of Iraq, I would take three of my infantry battalions, plus a battalion from another brigade and my artillery battalion. And I also took the larger part of the Aviation Brigade, that included sixty-five Blackhawk [transport] helicopters.

I spent the night before the air assault working in my TOC [tactical operations center]. I slept a few hours on the floor, leaned up against my rucksack.

When I was in Vietnam, I participated in more than seventy combat air assaults. When I walked to my helicopter on the morning of February 24 to go into Iraq, I expected to feel some degree of fear. Just as I had felt when I was a platoon leader. But I guess the fact that I had done it so much, especially the training in Saudi ... I felt tremendous exhilaration.

None of my battalion or company commanders had previous

combat experience. They were surprisingly poised. I found some soldiers who were scared to death—and they should have been. When those young soldiers climbed into their helicopters at six-thirty that morning and crossed the border into Iraq, none of us knew what was going to happen. They had to overcome the same fears as American soldiers of any other war.

For the air assault into Iraq, I set up three TOCs to coordinate communications. One was at the big assembly area in Saudi Arabia. Then, I put myself in a Command and Control helicopter, integrated into the troops' flight. The third TOC I had put in at the Cobra site, as the main assault landed. I sent my S3 [Operations officer] in with a team to set up on the ground, so that I could immediately talk with somebody in Iraq. That man was my command sergeant major, Robert Nichols.

Cobra was a huge area, ten-by-twenty kilometers. It was essential to have people there directing units as they landed. Sergeant Major Nichols had to coordinate our places on the ground, with the help of some motorcycle scouts. Then he had to lead them out fifteen kilometers into hostile territory.

I talked with Sergeant Major Nichols when he first came aboard a few months before Desert Shield, "I want you to help me and the Army define the role of a sergeant major in combat." I used him differently than anyone else uses their sergeant major. I had tremendous trust in him. And that boosted the esprit of my entire NCO corps.

Before we went into LZ Cobra, I pulled in a bunch of scouts on motorcycles. I told Nichols, "Sergeant Major, these scouts belong to you. I want you to mark the positions where we're going to bring the support units inside Cobra. As soon as you do that, go outside the perimeter around fifteen kilometers south. You are the link-up man to meet the brigade XO [executive officer] who is bringing up a 700-vehicle convoy." The action was essential to the entire operation, to set up a refueling station for aviation units.

FIRE BASE COBRA

COMMAND SERGEANT MAJOR
ROBERT NICHOLS

SAUDI ARABIA 1990–91
BRIGADE SERGEANT MAJOR
101ST AIRBORNE DIVISION (AIR ASSAULT)

The evening before we flew into Iraq, all the chaplains held services, which were widely attended by soldiers who made peace with themselves before going into combat.

On the morning of February 24, I was in the third helicopter of the initial air assault into Iraq. After we crossed over the border escarpment, our Blackhawks flew around ten feet over the desert. I looked out the bird; as far as the eye could see to our left, right, and rear, more than 300 helicopters were flying north into Iraq.

Within a short time, we overflew a logistics convoy of friendly troops. Pilots had to lift up to avoid hitting Humvee antennas. Our ground units' attack path was one hundred miles into Iraq in wheeled vehicles. As we crossed over, the ground soldiers were screaming, yelling, cheering us on. It was a wonderful feeling.

We dropped back down to ten feet above the deck and flew for another hour at 150 to 170 miles per hour, just as hard and as fast as those Blackhawks would go.

As we flew closer to our touchdown point, we were given "fifteen minutes . . . ten minutes . . . five minutes . . ." We could see the horizon, black with smoke from explosions. Our Apache attack helicopters were attacking an Iraqi battalion in the target sector. Fears, hopes, and dreams flash through a soldier's mind within moments of combat.

We touched down. Instantly, 2,000 soldiers assembled in their units, ready to fight. To secure the base, we had four infantry battalion—three from our brigade and one from the 2nd Brigade. By the time the second airlift got on the ground, our

3rd and 1st battalions were in contact [fighting] with the dug-in Iraqis. Trenches. Bunkers. A-10 aircraft circling overhead, dropping bombs.

Our Apaches had gone back for refueling and rearming. So our Cobra helicopter battalion was now doing the dirty work. The Iraqis were being hit from all sides with bombs, gunships, ground forces, and artillery.

Our 320th Artillery Battery are some of the unsung heroes. Initially, their rounds did not have the distance to reach the Iraqi positions. They had to move forward more than four kilometers. By this time, our ground infantrymen were charging uphill toward the Iraqi trenches like Gettysburg. The artillery people mounted up, loaded and unloaded ammunition, and were ready to shoot within twenty-four minutes. That is unheard of, even under the best training conditions. But they did it that day. Their airbursts over the bunkers and trenches helped to turn the tide. The Iraqis ceased to fight.

When we attacked, luckily, the Iraqis were facing the opposite way, toward French forces making the "Hail Mary" sweep further west. The Iraqi battalion commander expected to fight the French in two or three days. The speed of our airlift from the opposite direction surprised them. The Iraqis didn't like it because we "cheated." And they chose not to fight. It looked like they all were issued handkerchiefs to surrender. Because everybody had a white piece of cloth. By the third hour, we were taking hundreds of prisoners.

While that fight was going on, I and eight motorcycle scouts had as difficult a job as I could ever have imagined. Thirty minutes behind our flight were lift helicopters in-bound with giant fuel bags. Our job was to secure and clear the ground of all bomblets and land mines. Because if the fuel bags blew up, we would lose the ability to complete the air assault. There were Iraqi munitions and U.S. Air Force cluster bomblets scattered all over the place. We had thirty minutes to clean an area larger than two football fields.

We accomplished that. And marked the location as "Clear" as the helicopters appeared on the horizon. About that time, the brigade's operations officer called me. He said, "Sergeant Major, we've got a problem.

"First and 3rd battalions' scouts are under fire. Both battalions are fighting a battle. Our supply convoy is by themselves. You've got to link up with them and guide them into Cobra.

"The success or failure of the division's mission will be determined when the ground convoy linkup is complete, and getting the convoy's forty-five fuel trucks unloaded into the fuel pod."

I was in my Humvee, carrying a load of ammunition. Young Staff Sergeant Argo, a Ranger, was able to take part of the scout team. Into the night, guided by a GSP "Slugger," we navigated through the desert to locate the supply convoy. We found them twenty miles out and guided them into the defense line. Refuel and rearmament facilities were set up in time for incoming helicopters to complete the division's mission along the Euphrates valley, to cut off Iraqi reinforcements.

THE ULTIMATE WEAPON

BRIGADIER GENERAL THOMAS DRAUDE

SAUDI ARABIA 1990–91
ASSISTANT COMMANDING GENERAL
1ST MARINE DIVISION

I was shocked by the speed of the Iraqi Collapse. There were Iraqis who fought. But the number of prisoners is a tribute to the discipline of young Marines. They had to make the decision on who was going to live and who would die.

In debriefings, Iraqi prisoners said they had been told by their leaders, "Marines have to kill a member of their family to be allowed into the Corps. They cut off prisoners' arms."

We had one group of prisoners who were real unhappy when they found that they had been captured by American Marines. We were moving forward rapidly and couldn't take them to the rear. So we took them with us.

When night came, the Iraqis saw Marines digging [foxholes]. They started wailing and begging for mercy, thinking that these were their graves. We had sergeants yelling, "Tell those guys to shut up." Young Marines said, "We tried. They won't stop."

So a gunny said, "Okay, I'll shut them up." He used the ultimate weapon . . . The *Sports Illustrated* "swim-wear" edition.

When he showed the Iraqis that magazine, the look on their faces was, "We might be going to Allah. But have you ever seen this much skin in your life?"

HIGHWAY OF DEATH

COLONEL JOHN SYLVESTER

Saudi Arabia 1990-91
Brigade Commander
Tiger Brigade, 2nd Armor Division

On the third day of the ground war the Iraqi army in and around Kuwait City embarked in a biblical-sized convoy, loaded with stolen loot and whatever weapons they could carry. There was only one main highway—the Jahra Road—that stretched from the city to the Iraq border. Colonel John Sylvester's Tiger Brigade was given the mission to take the high ground overlooking the main intersection of the road. And to intercept the massive exodus on what became known as the "highway of death."

Our Tiger Brigade Mission was to cut off the Iraqis' rear exit from Kuwait City. The 1st Marine Division was heading to the Kuwait Airport. The 2nd Marine Division was to hold the shoulder of Kuwait City, so the Arab Coalition could come into the city without worrying about their flank.

There were oil fields all around a series of six roads that ring around Kuwait City. My mission was to block the Jahra Road—the main route north to Iraq—and all the high ground around it. The objective was to trap Iraqi forces escaping from Kuwait City.

I put the 1/67 Battalion against the east-west Atraf Road, to close off that ring. And sent the 3/67 Battalion further north against the Objective Colorado, which was the Jahra Road. Above it, the Mutlah Ridge was 300 feet elevation.

At the rear base of the ridge was a huge mine field exactly

like at the Saudi border. The Iraqis wound up blowing up a hell of a lot of their own people who tried to go through that mine field when our airplanes targeted the Jahra Road.

The 3/67 Battalion took the high ground in front of the Ali Al Salem air base and positioned themselves on the ridge. The visibility was very poor, even with thermal sites. So they had to come to a lower elevation to make sure that no escape route was available. The problem wasn't only the oil-field smoke. There were probably several thousand vehicles, bumper to bumper, that had been burned and destroyed by air power. Yet the Iraqis were still pushing passage.

My 3/67 Battalion had to knock out a bunch of Iraqi vehicles. That added to the smoke and fire. So they came down the back of the ridge, through that mine field at night, under fire. A couple of our kids earned the Silver Star for courage. They were in the lead tanks plowing a path through the mine field. Bouncing Betty mines were laced all over that area. They climbed down the front of their tanks, grabbed the wires with their hands and cut the trigger wires.

By the end of the first night, we had well over 1,000 prisoners in two or three different compounds. It quickly became obvious that we didn't want to be slowed by tending to them. So we made sure they were disarmed, pointed them south, gave them food and water, and told them, "Keep moving." I instructed my combat support people to police them up.

My bigger concern was to prevent my own people from shooting each other with our ground fire systems. The way we essentially handled that was twofold: first, a great measure of luck. The other was an extraordinary effort by soldiers, sometimes putting themselves at risk, to make absolutely sure that they were seeing bad guys.

Every company had different-colored taillights. Alpha Company was all blue, another was all green, etc. We also had a lot of colored smoke. We would throw the smoke as a marker, so we wouldn't shoot any vehicles in front of the colored smoke. But the main way we averted fratricide was the teamwork we developed from intensive training. As a result, we suffered no cases of fratricide. But there were some close calls.

For example, we had just finished knocking out a bunch of Iraqi tanks. All of a sudden there's two brand new hot spots on our thermal sites. Very fortunately, my young gunner said, "Something doesn't look right," and held their fire. Possibly hazarding themselves. But they saved the lives of two Bradley vehicles full of scouts.

I stopped calling for artillery after a while. Because it was obvious we could kill their armor at ranges beyond which we could kill us. And every time we killed their armor, 150 guys would come out of holes in the ground to surrender. And you can't surrender to an artillery piece.

The problem was, we'd go for three kilometers and see nothing but white flags and hands in the air. Suddenly you'd find tanks dug in, ready to do you dirt. Or there'd be a bunch of guys, in a bunker or a building, ready to die for Allah. You never knew. So my instructions were very clear, "Knock out every single mechanical piece of equipment you see—every truck, every tank. But the only soldiers on the ground I want anybody to kill are those fighting. Otherwise give them a chance to give up."

It's hard to tell what is a mistake and what isn't a mistake in the heat of battle. My canceling artillery may have had consequences. I lost a top-notch sergeant to a bunch of Iraqis hiding in a bunker. The Battalion Command was moving through the center of the battle on the Mutlah Ridge. They went by the bunker and Iraqis popped up, started shooting. The master gunner of the battalion, Sergeant 1st Class Harold Witzke, grabbed a machine gun and rushed the bunker. He got killed.

Had I started shooting artillery again, I might've taken those guys out. But I also might have killed 200 guys waving white flags, too. And I didn't want to do that.

When the Iraqis began their retreat from Kuwait City, they put any vehicles that could run on the Jahra Road. They had already been hit massively from the air. When we rolled in, they had no idea that we were there.

You cannot imagine the carnage that was on the ground that night. I have never seen anything like it in my worst imagination . . . Smoking pits with pieces of people, everywhere you looked. Bodies stacked up everywhere. Charred and melted vehicles. I'm not being melodramatic. It was a scene right out of Hell.

Along the highway that was later called the Death Highway, there were a hell of a bunch of Iraqis still fighting. Especially the guys who holed up in a police post overlooking the highway. It was a multistory concrete cinder-block building. They had barricaded the windows and set up a bunch of bunkers up in the hillside. I guess somebody had told them to hold that road.

I suspect that they were Republican Guard elite special forces. They had camouflage uniforms, wore bloused boots and looked like disciplined soldiers.

I had an infantry company attack that building. The fight went all through the night and into the next morning. That's where my infantrymen earned their money, fighting room to room. The Iraqis had AK-47 rifles and rocket-propelled grenades. They sprayed a lot of bullets around. Finally, twenty-eight Iraqis in the building surrendered. The other fifty-two died.

On the highway, among the dead were Iraqi soldiers of every conceivable uniform and unit. It was a mass attempt to loot the city.

When I first drove up to that scene and looked, the very first thing that caught my eye was a bus. It had a great big red crescent on the side and two blue lights on top that were flashing. I thought, "My God, we've blown up a bunch of ambulances." I started investigating. I looked in hundreds of vehicles. Every one was full of loot: household goods, jewelry, brand new racks of clothes out of stores, stereos, motorcycles . . . unbelievable. And every vehicle also had weapons and gas masks and military paraphernalia. These soldiers had flat looted that city of everything that they could get.

I felt bad, as any soldier does, in taking life. But there was a point where I didn't feel that we were killing soldiers. They were criminals. But I guarantee you, my soldiers never shot anybody who wasn't armed and fighting back. There were all kinds of dismounted Iraqis running around. Because of the possibility of Kuwaiti refugees being mixed in, I told my troops, "You don't shoot at anybody unless they have something that appears to be an antitank weapon."

Nearby there was a mosque and some barracks buildings called the Freedom Rest Center. It was full of bad guys who had come out of that long gaggle of shot-up vehicles. But inside the mosque were several Iraqi doctors and nurses. And a number of wounded and refugees, and maybe forty-five women and children. We went in and set up an aid station right outside of the mosque. We had to be careful. Because earlier, when we thought the Iraqis had no fight left in them, up popped the guy who kills Sergeant Witzke. That took place less than a half-mile from the mosque.

OPERATION PROVIDE COMFORT

LIEUTENANT COLONEL JAMES ZUMWALT

SAUDI ARABIA, KUWAIT, IRAQ 1990–91
DETACHMENT COMMANDER
4TH CIVIL AFFAIRS GROUP, MARINE CORPS RESERVES

Within three weeks after the "100-hour" ground war of Desert Storm concluded, a rebellion by the long-oppressed Kurdish minority in northern Iraq was crushed by Saddam Hussein's forces. Tens of thousands of desperate Kurdish refugee families fled to neighboring Turkey. Unwanted, they faced starvation, sickness, and continued attack by the Iraqi army.

A United Nations effort was mobilized to stop the slaughter and return refugees safely to their homes. American military specialists joined the Kurdish relief program. Among them was Lt. Colonel James Zumwalt, a Washington D.C. area lawyer, and Marine Corps Reserve civil affairs expert.

At the end of April, we returned to Saudi Arabia from Kuwait. I informed my group commander, Colonel John Easton, that I would like to volunteer to assist the Kurdish refugee effort in northern Iraq.

So while the rest of my unit returned to the States, Captain Jeff Higgins and I boarded a giant C-5 transport airplane to southern Turkey. Then, on May 5, along with a full load of marines and soldiers, we crammed into a CH-53E Sea Stallion helicopter departing Turkey for Zhaku, Iraq. We sat on benches with our sea bags and other gear stacked tightly in the aisle between us. We were told that three army troops had been wounded in Zhaku, one seriously—both legs blown off and one eye lost—when they stepped on a land mine. And three Kurds died as a result of tripping a mine the day before.

Flying over northern Iraq, I was surprised by the sharp contrast to the flat desert in Kuwait and Saudi Arabia. The Zhaku area is surrounded by beautiful green mountains, covered with grass and trees. Saddam Hussein had a summer or winter palace not far away, in Al Almadiyah, at round 7,000 feet.

Upon my arrival in Zhaku, I immediately went to work for Colonel James Jones, Commander of the 24th MEU [Marine Expeditionary Unit] as his Marine Corps consultant for civil affairs. Additional expertise was provided by the Army's 431st Civil Affairs Company which was attached to the 24th MEU. The 431st is a reservist unit from Arkansas, commanded by Lt. Colonel Sam Gibson. We developed an outstanding working relationship.

Colonel Jones explained the game plan for resettling the Kurds: We were to set up a triangular safe haven for them, formed by three cities: Zhaku, Al Almadiyah—which had just been secured by Coalition forces—and Dahuk, a city of 500,000, was still occupied by Iraqi forces who were looting as they withdrew.

The compound occupied by the 24th MEU at Zhaku was a former Iraqi army divisional headquarters in an area surrounded on three sides by mountains. The compound was similar to the broken-wall adobe structures in the old Clint Eastwood "spaghetti" westerns. Across the road from our position was a former PLO [Palestine Liberation Organization] terrorist training compound. A painting of Saddam Hussein was on a wall.

In our compound, I admired a plot of beautiful rosebushes. The beauty of the roses posed a stark contrast to the brutality of Iraqi soldiers against the Kurds in this compound just a few days earlier. One day while digging defensive positions near the bushes, we began to smell a horrendous odor. We discovered that we had uncovered some human body parts.

We asked the local people about this. They told us that seventy Kurds had been arrested, killed, and buried right there. The Iraqis evidently planted flowers over them, sadistically using the bodies as fertilizer.

I was assigned to go into Dahuk along with the lead coalition elements to conduct a civil affairs assessment of the city—focusing on medical needs, electricity, water, and food resources. Upon completion of the assessment, we were to coordinate with the U.S. Army and various international agencies to ensure that all civil affairs requirements were met for a very large

Kurdish population expected to return to the city. We began putting together a team of medical people, combat engineers, Seabees, and Army Special Forces to assist with the effort. Meanwhile, several hundred thousand refugees waited in camps in the mountains along the Iraq-Turkey border.

As our assessment team of around thirty drove into the city, every piece of high ground along the route was occupied by Iraqi troops who stood armed, glaring down at us. To see thousands of battle-hardened Iraqis around our small group was a much different feeling than being surrounded by friendly Coalition troops in the desert of Saudi Arabia and Kuwait. These Iraqi soldiers had been held back in reserve by Saddam and had been slaughtering Kurds up to the time we arrived.

We gained a little comfort as we gazed skyward and saw dozens of Army and Marine Corps attack helicopters and fixed-wing aircraft. Their low-level flights over the high ground sent a clear message.

Our reception by the people of Dahuk was very enthusiastic. Quickly indentifying us as Americans, people immediately waved. Children warmly shouted "Hi, mister!" or "Thank you, mister!" People came out of their homes to offer us food and drink.

Within days, thousands of refugees began returning. As we assisted them, they reciprocated by opening their homes to us, begging us to maintain a presence in the city.

I examined two small residential areas that had been destroyed. We discovered that the Iraqis had apparently destroyed blocks of homes prior to our arrival, in retaliation for the Kurdish resistance. And before departing, they placed mines all around the city.

A French soldier stepped on one such mine just outside of Dahuk which killed him and injured two other Frenchmen. In a separate incident, a U.S. Army soldier stepped on a mine which blew off both his legs and injured a nearby Marine. The Marine is credited with saving the soldier's life by his quick action to apply tourniquets.

Our EOD [explosive ordnance] people made a grisly discovery while going through some of the destroyed houses—the rubble had been booby-trapped as well. It was set up so that when Kurds returned to their demolished homes and began to pick up the debris, a box full of plastic explosives would detonate.

EOD began taking all the ordnance they found, and depositing it in an isolated location on the outskirts of the city. One evening, as we assembled for our daily six-thirty P.M. meeting, smoke was observed coming from this area. We rushed out to find some Kurdish children had started a fire. Fortunately, we were able to put it out before it reached any of the explosives.

Being a parent made me much more sensitive in the work I was doing with the Kurds. I thought about my children quite a bit when I was in Saudi and Kuwait, but I saw very few children. The absence of children allowed me to get totally wrapped up in my job. But in northern Iraq, working with Kurdish children . . . hearing reports at our daily briefing of children being lost, due to disease, starvation, or stepping on mines—made me think about my own kids and how devastated I'd be if something happened to them.

I carried a small football with me in Dahuk. Every place we stopped I'd throw it around with local kids. Sometimes a couple hundred kids would gather excitedly, yelling, "Mister, mister!" Wanting me to throw them the ball.

One very touching moment for me involved an absolutely beautiful child six or seven years old. Captain Higgins stopped our vehicle and got out. We were approached by this small girl who came up and grabbed my hand. She looked up at me, squeezed my hand and said in English, "Thank you, mister, thank you,"—and walked away.

By June 2, the Kurds had observed Coalition forces pulling out of Dahuk in small numbers. This really upset them. I awoke before dawn that day at four A.M. The temperature hit close to 100 degrees. Little did I realize that day would get hot in more ways than one before it was over.

In the late afternoon, scores of Kurds started a demonstration downtown. The number of participants continued to grow, to about 80,000. Initially, the march was organized and peaceful. Banners written in Arabic, Kurdish, and English called for: (1) fair treatment by the Iraqi government, (2) a continued presence of Coalition forces plus the extension of the safe haven to other cities further south, and (3) removal of Iraqi secret police from Dahuk who, it was alleged, had secretly reentered their city in large numbers. Shooting soon erupted.

The Iraqi civil police claimed that the Kurds had stormed the police station, so they opened fire, killing several demonstrators. The Kurdish Pesh Merga [a political organization] leaders who were trying to control the crowd, claimed the Iraqi police fired without warning.

When the shooting started, we had just finished briefing a meeting attended by both military and civilian NGOs [nongovernmental organizations] such as CARE and other charitable groups, who were to take over our operations.

We rushed to put on flak jackets and helmets. We could see several RPG [rocket-propelled grenade] rounds being fired. Using the three-foot-high balcony wall for cover, we took up defensive positions to prepare for any possible attack against the hotel compound. We could see smoke and flames rising from burning police cars, as well as from the police headquarters. Mortar rounds soon exploded.

I observed someone moving behind this balcony wall, perpendicular to my location. I saw a head pop up to carefully scan the horizon. Then a hand, then an arm, and finally a naked torso. The hand stretches upward and seizes its objective—a set of uniform trousers and shirt dangling from a laundry line. This soldier, wearing only his shorts, had obviously been caught "with his pants down."

Shooting in the city lasted about an hour. As darkness fell, the last flames from the burning cars and buildings could be seen. It provided the only light in the city, as electricity had now been disrupted. Watching this scene, I was hit with a sudden emptiness—for I felt that everything we had worked so hard for, to get this city back on its feet and resettled, would be lost.

Later that evening, the United Nations representative came to the front gate of our hotel compound, accompanied by a group of Pesh Merga leaders. Like the Afghan rebels, the Pesh Merga are extremely factionalized. Each Pesh Merga leader had his bodyguards with him.

The lights were out in the hotel. A lantern was lit and placed on a table with all the meeting participants sitting around it. The Pesh Merga sat down, the light reflecting off their rugged faces, and told their version of the evening's events. They ended their discussion by alleging such violence was likely to continue unless Coalition forces remained.

The next morning at four-thirty A.M. I was eager to make a firsthand assessment of what damage had been done in the city. Temperatures already reached over 100 degrees. Driving through the streets of Dahuk, however, one could not tell that a brief battle had been fought only hours earlier. The marketplaces were bustling.

Upon reaching the battle zone, the evidence was clear that

death and destruction had taken their toll. The gutted and blackened skeletons of brand new police cars and those driven by the secret police cluttered the road.

Later that day, I said farewell to my Army counterparts who like myself, were preparing to leave Dahuk. I departed by helicopter for Zhaku on the first leg of my trip home. As I watched the mountains of Dahuk disappear in the background, I knew I would never see that city again.

I couldn't help but wonder, of the nearly 200,000 refugees we helped resettle there, how many would still be alive in the months ahead.

HOMECOMINGS

COMMAND SERGEANT MAJOR JOSEPH GARRETT

VIETNAM 1967–68; SAUDI ARABIA 1991
BATTALION SERGEANT MAJOR
19TH COMBAT ENGINEER BATTALION

After the war, there were planes leaving Saudi with some open seats. Some high-ranking person came up with the bright idea, "Let's send six or eight of our guys home on these planes." I got hot. I said, "We came here together. We go home together." I raised hell, threatened to quit. Did whatever I could to get my way.

My story to all the young soldiers, including the officers—who were also young—was, "You don't realize right now what this will mean to you. Don't say, 'I'll do anything. Just let me go home today.' Because you really don't know what you're talking about. Talk to me twenty years from now when you think back on this." That goes back to my experience when I was young.

I came into the Army in 1967, right out of high school. On my seventeenth birthday I was sitting at the Reception Station at Fort Leonard Wood, Missouri.

I was one of those guys who never questioned going to war in Vietnam. I felt, "Hey, this is what I've got to do. We've got to do right because *my country* wants me to do these things."

Less than six months later I was in Vietnam with the 101st Airborne Division, where I was eventually promoted as a Specialist 5 to senior demolition team leader. About ten months into that tour I blew myself up while destroying an enemy bunker. Both of my wrists were broken by debris flying through the air. I was evacuated to an Army hospital in Japan.

I can remember going home from the hospital in July 1968, with casts on both arms. My folks lived in Ann Arbor, Michigan. I got into a cab at Wayne County Airport. The driver had his call-radio on. The Students for a Democratic Society [the radical SDS] were having demonstrations against the war. A cab somewhere ahead of us hit a demonstrator by accident. Now the students were rioting and rocking that cab. And that driver was telling all the other cabs over the radio, "Don't go into this area."

My cab driver turned to me and says, "Buddy, you got to get out." I said, "What are you talking about?" He said, "I don't want you to be in my cab when these people see me." I said, "Look, mister, don't make me get out of this cab. I'll tell you what I'll do. I'll take my Army jacket off. You stop right here, while I go into a store to buy a shirt."

The man stopped the cab. I went into a store and paid forty-two dollars, which was big money in 1968, and bought one of those double-knit, real pretty "I'm a gigolo" type shirts. Put it on over the casts on my arms. And he drove me home. With my green trousers and low-quarter shoes underneath. I'll never forget that as long as I live.

As a Vietnam vet in the Gulf, I was ready to fall on my sword for my battalion to come back together as a team. And we did come home together. To a parade here in Louisville. Folks were cheering at the airport when we flew in. We had a police escort to Fort Knox. Our wives and kids were there for us.

I don't think that every soldier understands the importance of the reception we received. But later on they will.

PART V

Visions

COMING HOME

BRIGADIER GENERAL
JAMES HILL

SAUDI ARABIA 1990–91
BRIGADE COMMANDER
101ST AIRBORNE DIVISION (AIR ASSAULT)

Coming home from the Gulf War, Vietnam veterans among the victorious American forces were emotionally moved by the "Welcome Home" parades and spontaneous celebration. However, there was a quiet sobriety expressed by most senior military people. The greatest challenge they faced was to prevent their troops and young officers from becoming overconfident and resting on their laurels.

I had a harder time coming home from Desert Storm and adjusting to this environment than I did coming out of Vietnam. Even though I was actually spit on in Los Angeles airport the first day I was back from Vietnam.

I was walking down a hallway and three guys came from the opposite direction. They called me a "murderer" and spit on me. I told them, "If you do that again, I'll prove your accusation."

It was very difficult to understand this country when I came home from the Gulf and stepped off the airplane a conquering hero. I am very uncomfortable when I am asked to stand up in a crowd and get applauded.

Senior officers immediately started telling young soldiers not to let the Gulf War get to their heads. The bigger issue we have to deal with is the expectations that many people will have based on the last war. Both in the military community and in the civilian community.

That we won the ground war in a hundred hours is wonderful. But war is an unpredictable thing. We can fight that same enemy tomorrow and take greater casualties, and take a lot longer to win the war. Yet still be as good in what we do.

OVERCONFIDENCE

FIRST SERGEANT ANTHONY MCPIKE

SAUDI ARABIA 1990–91
TANK LEADER
COMPANY C, 1ST TANK BATTALION,
1ST MARINE DIVISION

My wife asked me, "Why haven't we taken advantage of some of the honors that people are offering Desert Shield and Desert Storm veterans?" I looked at her and said, "Because people are patronizing us. They think that we did so much. I don't feel that we are anymore of conquering heroes than the troops who came back from Korea or from Vietnam." If the Iraqis had put up any kind of resistance, it could have been a much different picture.

We went into Iraqi supply containers and found brand new chemical protective gear, brand new gas masks, brand new rifles, brand new ammunition. If we had gone up against any measurable amount of resistance, the war would have lasted much longer. My question is: If that was the case, would we have been welcomed back with open arms like conquering heroes?

I told my wife, "If you want to go to a parade, go ahead. If you want to go to some celebration event, take the kids and go. But I feel that I've done my time. I've been through two conflicts. I'm alive and I'm healthy. That's enough."

The Gulf War was a limited stress environment. It was enough to test our character and put theory into practice and test how well our team could function. But it didn't put us under the stress of seeing a lot of friends being killed. We didn't have one intense firefight after another for weeks or months. The next time might not be so easy.

I told my men, "You have not been in a war. This only

lasted a hundred hours. You need to put into perspective that you fought a skirmish."

Hopefully, at the training centers people will keep things in perspective. The problem is that people might let all of the parades and honors get to their heads. With budget cutbacks, some people might think, "Why do you need so much training, we have the greatest military force in the world?"

People might become overconfident by what just happened in the Gulf. They might get taken by surprise in a future deployment while they dwell on past laurels.

Training needs more emphasis on what our troops need to do, instead of prepare with, "This is what we did in Grenada." Or, "This is what we did in Vietnam . . . or Kuwait."

You cannot go through life with what worked for you in the past. Something that might work perfectly in a desert environment might not work in a forest.

For example, a lieutenant was given a Bronze Star with a Combat V for leading his platoon through a mine field—by stepping on antitank mines.

Maybe the situation called for him to do that. The problem now is that members of his platoon may automatically assume in a future crisis, "Hey, we ran across a mine field before, stepping on mines. Didn't none blow up. We're good to go." As a result, maybe a whole platoon or a whole company will get wiped out. Maybe that lieutenant becomes a battalion commander and issues the same orders and wipes out a whole unit. He might say, "I don't understand, it worked for me in Kuwait."

NINTENDO WAR

GENERAL CHARLES HORNER

SAUDI ARABIA 1990–91
COMMANDING GENERAL
CENTRAL COMMAND AIR FORCES & U.S. 9TH AIR
FORCE

Some people's attitude toward Desert Storm troubles me deeply. They call it the "Nintendo War." The idea that it was a bloodless mechanical thing—computer against bunker, or bombs against trucks. It loses sight that there is great suffering and death in war.

I sometimes worry about the generation of leaders who came into the service after the Vietnam War. Because they haven't experienced the type of adversity that bonds my generation of senior leadership.

I've heard people say about commanders, either, "You get too much credit," or "You don't get enough credit." My opinion is that anybody who starts getting a big head is a fool. Especially with all the parades and public speaking after the war, I try to be careful not to get a Napoleonic complex. [He laughs.] My wife makes me stay pretty honest, too. To her I'm still "Chuckie," overweight and getting older.

One thing I got from the war is a much deeper appreciation for my family. My kids are all grown now. When we first got married, I told my wife, "Flying comes first, you come second. As long as you understand that, we'll have no problems." She said, "I accept that."

To show how I've changed my priorities: last week I was supposed to get a big award in Washington. I'd have loved to stand in front of my peers and accept that tremendous honor. But instead, I flew cross-country to see my grandson. I believe that is healthy.

Being in the service of this nation puts many demands on a

person. When I think about Vietnam, the outcome of that war was not as important as the intent in which we served.

I don't believe we have to go through another Vietnam. We can learn from the Vietnam experience. If we do get involved in war, we have to make sure that we don't politicize it to the point of dividing the country. And that the American people stay committed. During the Vietnam War, it seemed that American society was at war with itself.

If we learn anything from Desert Storm, it's that we should never use war as a solution to anything, other than as a last resort. And based on its result, hopefully, any aggressor in the world will think twice before he engages us in war.

WARRIORS

MASTER SERGEANT JAMES GRAHAM

SAUDI ARABIA 1990–91
TANK LEADER
COMPANY C, 1ST TANK BATTALION,
1ST MARINE DIVISION

I can't tell you what makes a warrior. Looking back at the conflicts I have participated in, I spent two tours in Vietnam, Beirut in 1982–83; and in the Gulf War, you can see a significant difference in the style of leadership.

Vietnam was such an ugly thing. Many people in the military were not terribly excited about fighting that war. People thought more about surviving and getting home than about winning. The leaders had a lot more challenges to motivate their people.

In Vietnam, my senior NCOs were World War II and Korean War veterans. My 1st sergeant was on his third tour of Vietnam. When those guys talked, it was like E.F. Hutton— you listen. The key lesson they told us was not to worry about the politics of the war. We fight if our political leaders tell us to. "A warrior is a warrior. We fight because *that* is what we do." And they were right.

In the Gulf, all of the military that I observed were supportive and willing to do what was necessary to win. We had a mandate. Iraq had invaded Kuwait and we believed that Saddam was a bad guy. This overshadowed the fact that all Middle Eastern countries are basically screwed up.

There is absolutely no doubt in my mind that this whole Middle Eastern thing will fall apart morally. Because of all the undemocratic things the Kuwaiti leaders do. And lack of human rights. In ten years we'll look back and say, "I can't believe we fought for these guys. Because they're a bunch of assholes, too."

We'll probably never know the real reason why we ever went to Kuwait. We rely on people who make policy to have their motives together so that when they send us somewhere, we have clear directions about what needs to be done. We hope that is always the case. But we all know better . . .

It's kind of funny. Because of all we saw in the media, trying to convince everybody that this was such a great cause. When you're in a mine field at two o'clock in the morning and Iraqis have their guns trained on you, you're not thinking about patriotism and the goodness and moral right of our invasion. You're fighting to not let your buddy down. And to get your fellow Marines through the mine field—to survive.

Colonels and generals don't win wars, it's the sergeants and below. The commanders may have a great battle plan. But it's the guys on the ground who have to execute.

It's not the "oorah-oorah" guys. Charismatic leaders are the guys with heart. It's all the same, whether we're on the battlefield in Kuwait or here at the tank range. You get a couple of good natural leaders in a company, who are the fighters, and the motivation spreads.

SNAKE HEAD

LIEUTENANT COLONEL
JAMES ZUMWALT

SAUDI ARABIA/KUWAIT/IRAQ 1990–91
DETACHMENT COMMANDER
4TH CIVIL AFFAIRS GROUP, MARINE CORPS RESERVE

"Lessons learned" can often be the most important legacy of battle. Sometimes the most profound lessons can be gained by listening to the insights of our adversaries.

After the ground war ended, I was asked by my commanding officer to head a team to interrogate senior Iraqi prisoners. Our mission was to compile a list of "lessons learned" for historical purposes. Among the points I noted:

- Many said that they were led to believe that Saddam was going to work out a political solution. As a result, they were totally unprepared when the air war began.
- Some wondered why U.S. ground forces didn't attack earlier as Iraqis were simply waiting to surrender. The comment was also made, that had the air war continued without a ground war for much longer, the Iraqi army would have sued for peace due to the devastating loss of its supplies and equipment.
- On their failure to take any offensive action, they commented, "If we moved, we feared that we would be attacked by air."
- A counterattack plan was not initiated when the U.S. ground attack started as Coalition forces came across at several points. The Iraqis wanted the attack to stabilize before launching a counterattack. While they waited, U.S. forces drove north so quickly, the Iraqis could not respond.
- "Saddam is a snake. You don't kill a snake by beating its

337

back and leaving its head alone. The U.S. should have chopped off the snake's head."

STRANGE BEDFELLOWS

CHIEF WARRANT OFFICER 2 RICHARD BALWANZ

FORT CAMPBELL, KENTUCKY 1991–93
INTELLIGENCE
5TH SPECIAL FORCES GROUP

I came home from the desert in the middle of March, not long after we got out of Kuwait City. The entire 5th Special Forces Group was back by mid-April. Now it's kind of like the operation never happened. It's a memory.

One of the main things we were concerned about is that we can't rest on our laurels. We've got to keep moving forward to new missions. The Middle East is still the Group's area of responsibility. We'll have teams moving there to help rebuild the Kuwait army.

We can never preguess our missions. Ironically, we'd been going to Jordan for years and years. But when the war kicked off, Jordan was one of the countries that backed Iraq. And now, again, we're preparing to go back to [work with] Jordan. That shows how politics makes strange bedfellows.

BALANCE OF FORCE

BRIGADIER GENERAL
JAMES HILL

FORT CAMPBELL, KENTUCKY 1991–93
CHIEF OF STAFF
101ST AIRBORNE DIVISION (AIR ASSAULT)

After Desert Storm, some pundits claimed that, "We only need to keep our armored and heavy mechanized forces." I disagree.

If anything, the 101st Division's Eagle Flight in Desert Storm proved that an air assault division can move large forces of people behind enemy lines. This is especially important when the weather or terrain prohibits an armored or parachute assault.

There are other scenarios more conducive to Marine Corps amphibious assault. For example, Haiti. But if we went into Peru's mountainous cocaine-growing terrain, heavy tanks wouldn't do any good. Nor would soldiers on foot. We'd have to be able to quickly move forces from mountaintop to mountaintop. You need helicopters.

What if we took our same Desert Storm forces and plop them down in Peru or Colombia or Burma for the drug war? We'd have a different set of circumstances in dealing with the local people, the guerrillas, the terrain, resupply, and the media.

Within five to seven years, almost all Vietnam veterans will be retired. Few people will have the experience of fighting guerrillas in populated areas. Those of us who stuck around after Vietnam to rebuild, took our army into the desert and proved it was a great fighting force. That was the vindication of a life's work. The hardest job now is to draw it down without reducing the cohesiveness, readiness, and leadership edge.

The analogy between the post-Vietnam period and today is not all that different. We came out of Vietnam and were struggling as an army for an identity. Because we didn't have a mission. So we latched on to NATO. Fortunately it was there.

Right now, as the Soviet threat in Europe disintegrates, an identity crisis is emerging for the Army: Why do we exist? What is our role? What are we here to protect? Morale in the Army can deteriorate and public opinion can turn against us in a heartbeat.

SPEED, SURPRISE, AND MASS

LIEUTENANT GENERAL BUSTER GLOSSON

THE PENTAGON 1991–93
DEPUTY CHIEF OF STAFF
U.S. AIR FORCE

Since Clausewitz [a widely studied nineteenth century Prussian army officer and theorist], some things haven't changed in warfare: speed, surprise, and mass. The Gulf War redefined *mass* and it reinitiated the importance of *surprise*. We have overwhelming power. The unfortunate part is that when you use that power, many times you pay for it in terms of lives. So in planning the air war, we strived to use as much surprise as we could, in order to have minimum loss of lives.

We've always thought of *mass* as tonnage of bombs. That's no longer true. Mass is synonymous with lethality. Precision weapons in the F-117 and F-111 airplanes provide a lot of lethality at a precise point. We don't need thousands of bombs like in previous wars.

In the 1960s when I was flying in Vietnam, we had to fly numerous sorties over a target to knock out a bridge or whatever. In World War II, we used about 9,000 bombs to get one bomb inside a target area approximately 100 by 30 feet. In Korea and Vietnam we used about 400 bombs to do the same thing. In Desert Storm, we used one bomb to hit one corner of a 100-by-30-foot target. From a logistics standpoint, that greatly diminishes the amount of support materials and manpower to support a war effort.

I don't want to give the impression that "unguided" or "dumb" bombs are not needed in modern warfare. Nothing could be further from the truth. The psychological impact of the B-52s dropping those bombs on the Republican Guards and Iraqi army twenty-four hours a day was mind-boggling.

That's why Iraqi divisions that originally numbered between 8,000 to 12,000 soldiers were down to 3,000. It wasn't because of a precision way that we bombed that army . . . it was the devastating psychological impact of having that much tonnage dropped on you twenty-four hours a day continuously.

Our future Air Force is going to need a balance of weapons technology. We pay about ten dollars a pound for an unguided weapon. And $200 a pound for a guided weapon. It would be cost-prohibitive to attack a land army for psychological impact with B-52s using precision weapons.

We have to be ready to fight the next war, not the last one. There's no question about the advantage that precision weapons give. It doesn't matter if the next war is in the Pacific, the Middle East, or the European scenario. The principles of speed, surprise, and mass are not going to change. But we must ensure that they are used correctly.

Any war where you are trying to destroy targets that may result in civilian casualties and collateral damage, you need precision weapons. That is straightforward. Thank goodness, our nation cannot—and will not—tolerate needless death. It doesn't make a difference if that death is American or people in a country we are fighting.

Now that we have the technology to do things with almost unbelievable low loss of life, that will be expected. I just hope that we didn't create false expectations in Iraq. Because there is always a chance that we will be asked to perform future missions that are more difficult. That may result in a greater loss of life than we would predict. Then we'll hear that "somebody did something wrong." Not necessarily. The conditions are different.

COMPETITION

COLONEL LEONARD SCOTT

Carlisle, Pennsylvania 1990-92
Director of Military Strategy,
Plans and Operations
& Faculty Instructor
U.S. Army War College

During a draw down of forces, it's very difficult in a unit for a colonel or a young captain to see good people leaving. Automatically they might assume, "It's all going to hell in a hand basket."

I saw that happen in the 1970s when we drew down from Vietnam. But we didn't fall on our face. All we did was get better. Because we had so many good officers stay.

Right now, we have a wealth of good young officers throughout the Army. We've trained them up from ROTC or West Point. And the Army, with its emphasis on what I call "real" training at places like the National Training Center [at Fort Irwin, California] and the Joint Warfare Center, creates a pretty close replication to conditions of war. We proved that in Desert Storm, where most of the units with no combat experience did so well.

In the draw down, the Army leadership will cut the force size, but they want to keep a high emphasis on quality training. That keeps the soldiers focused and motivated. And can prevent us from losing a lot of good soldiers for lack of a challenge.

Frontline units must be ready in case of war. The problem I see in these units is that young officers and NCOs only train in their profession [specialty] for a very short period of time. Because our system requires having to move people all the time to get their "tickets punched" for promotion. Usually after three years they transfer out.

For example, every light infantryman wants to go into the

82nd Airborne Division. A young guy gets to do that for three years. He's the happiest guy in the world. Boom. He gets orders to be company commander or an executive officer in a training company at Fort Benning, Georgia. Then he has to go to school at Fort Leavenworth, Kansas. So he's gone from the infantry for five or six years.

When a bunch of these good infantry officers transfer out, their morale and focus drops. They start looking at the reality: "The Army is getting smaller. If I'm not good enough, I can't stay in. It's going to be a long time before I might get back to a good unit. I'm not going to be able to stay in the Army because it's too competitive. I'm going to be lost."

In that interim process to qualify for a higher rank, some will make the decision, "I don't need this. I can't stand this competitive business. I did good in my unit, and now I'm having to retest all over again. I've had enough."

We lose some good young people. But on the other hand, the process of trying to qualify for a higher rank is also a means of competitiveness and elimination. That results in even better officers that eventually return to infantry units. We're going to hold on to quality young officers who believe they're going to make it.

Older people like myself will have to leave. Because there are far fewer senior command positions available. Five or ten years ago I would have probably gotten command of a brigade with no problem. I did not get a brigade because there are now only seventeen brigades available. And there are 3,000 qualified officers vying for those seventeen brigades.

I was Commander of the Airborne School at Fort Benning, Georgia. That is under Training Command. Not one single lieutenant colonel who commanded a training battalion was selected for brigade command, during the past three or four years. When you appear on a list for a frontline battalion command, you are thrilled, flying high. But it's the opposite to see your name on another list that says, "You've been selected for training battalion command." That automatically means that you will never get a brigade. And that is the facts of life right now. Is it fair? In terms of "fairness," probably not. But in terms of the overall good of the Army, the answer is yes.

You'd want to have a colonel command a brigade who has led a line battalion, and has done all the training and preparation for war. That is more fair to the Army's needs. I don't *like* that. But I agree with it.

Still, it's very difficult to swallow if you want to stay in the Army and become a general. For a lieutenant colonel, when you get the word in black and white regarding battalion command, you know that your dream is over.

ROLES AND MISSIONS

SECRETARY JAMES WEBB

THE PENTAGON 1984–88
ASSISTANT SECRETARY OF DEFENSE
SECRETARY OF THE NAVY

Almost everything going on now with the downsizing of the armed forces was predictable when I was Assistant Secretary of Defense and then Secretary of the Navy in 1984-88. I began calling for a reduction of U.S. forces in NATO Europe in late 1984.

In American history, only since the end of World War II has the United States placed large forces in local defense of other countries. In 1949 we reinserted our forces to Europe in what was called a "temporary measure" to allow these other countries to redevelop their economies and provide for their defense against Soviet threat.

In 1984–87, as an Assistant Secretary of Defense, my main responsibilities related to transitioning the American military from a peacetime to wartime footing in a variety of scenarios. I discovered that we had at least 50,000 more troops in Europe than we did at the end of the Vietnam War. It became clear to me that we were being used by our NATO allies, but willingly by American planners who wanted a "holding tank" for force structure. By 1986, we had 65,000 more Army people in Germany alone than Great Britain had in its entire worldwide army. And Britain had 91,000 people in its entire air force. While we had 88,000 Air Force people in Germany and England.

When I resigned as Secretary of the Navy, some people thought that I was protesting cuts in the overall Defense budget. Instead, I was asking whether we had a national strategy on which to build and shape our forces.

I was trying to get people to focus on how to clearly redefine our national security strategy: What do we want to be able to do around the world? Once we have defined that, then you go to the military services and rearticulate the roles and missions that we want the different services to perform.

The last time there was a real debate on the roles and missions issue was in 1947–48, after World War II, when the Department of Defense was created by combining the old Department of War and the Department of the Navy. There were huge fights in trying to downsize. These debates culminated in a series of meetings which were canonized in Department of Defense as the "Functions Papers." From those documents there has been only marginal variance for more than forty years.

What we need to do now, in my view, after a redefinition of strategy, is to ask: How big an Army or Marine Corps do we want? What do we want them to do? Where do we want them to be? Are we still a maritime nation? Does that matter anymore? The Air Force argues that we are now an air and space nation. We really need to have a cat fight—the likes we have not seen in forty years—to define our services' roles and missions.

I believe that the smartest way to shape the U.S. military is to, first, keep a strong Navy. We are by necessity a maritime nation. We conduct our business overseas very largely through our sea trade routes. There are still maritime threats from other countries. Not only in the sea lanes of the Middle East, but for instance, with the emergence of the Chinese, who are now trying to obtain aircraft carriers. Navies are versatile. They don't require bases on foreign soil to operate. Ultimately, navies don't fight navies . . . countries fight countries. The best way to avoid war is to clearly identify our national interests and to protect them.

The second vital need is to develop maneuverable forces. I would like to see the military forces in NATO eventually become "regional" forces, in the same sense that our Marine Corps division in Okinawa is a deployable crisis-response force. Instead of having them tied down to specific "local" defenses along the edge of a battle area—like the Cold War defense of Germany—have them be highly deployable the way that they were in the Gulf. But these forces will need enough bulk to be able to fight a sustained war. The trick is to develop a sizable enough force to hold in place while you mobilize necessary reinforcements behind them.

In downsizing military manpower, there is always a tendency to lose highly capable combat leaders who are ambitious and restless. They want to try other professions during peacetime. But at the same time, the military has always been able to keep a cadre of quality leaders who believe that their function in life is to rise to the top. They offset the numbers of quality people who leave the service. The farthest down the modern American military has been was right before World War II. The Army was gutted down to 136,000 people. Yet they were able to produce leaders like Eisenhower, MacArthur, and Patton.

With space, nuclear forces, aviation, we need continued R&D [research and development] to stay on the forward edge of technology. Typically, we spend ten percent of the defense budget on forward-looking R&D. Those are the crown jewels.

TECHNOLOGICAL EDGE

GENERAL RONALD YATES

WRIGHT-PATTERSON AIR BASE, OHIO 1992–93
COMMANDING GENERAL
AIR FORCE MATÉRIEL COMMAND

In early 1992, as part of its post-Cold War structural reorganization, the Air Force integrated its Logistics (supply and maintenance) and Systems (technology and weapons development and production, including aerospace development) commands into its largest organization. The new Matériel Command, with 130,000 military and civilian employees and an annual budget of some $32 billion (almost half of the Air Force's total budget) would rank in the top five of Fortune 500 corporations, if listed.

Headquartered at Wright-Patterson Air Force Base in Dayton, Ohio, the Matériel Command's 1992 research and production network included thirteen air bases, five logistics centers, four production centers with associated "super laboratories," and three test centers nationwide.

Its first overall commander, General Ronald Yates, a fifty-four-year-old Tennessee native, is only the second four-star general to have graduated from the Air Force Academy. The former fighter pilot and test pilot who dreamed of becoming an astronaut, now has responsibility to oversee the research and development of a significant portion of the nation's future air defense and space technology.

People ask, "What's wrong with defense management?" They say things like, "There's too much congressional meddling . . . There's no budget certainty . . . The requirement issues are uncertain." And I say, "That's the definition of the job."

In this command position, my responsibility involves numerous laboratories and production sites spread across the United States. It's impossible to micromanage every project. The most basic requirement is that I need good, well-trained people in the right jobs. If you've got the wrong guy in a job, he can make more dumb decisions than you can fix. It's not a narrow type of business situation where I can say, "Here's what I want you to do. Here are your operating limitations. If you have any further questions, check with me before you do anything."

And with our budget being cut back, on-site quality management becomes all the more important to maximize available resources. That is the key, not only for the military, but for private industry.

From the late 1970s to the mid-1980s, during my work in the field, I learned quite a bit in directing the F-15 and F-16 aircraft development programs. You can't know how an airplane will perform until you are in the testing phase. Your obligation is to try to find out as much as possible before you get to that final stage. To prevent major performance problems and cost overruns, you need to set up risk-reduction milestones all the way through the process.

After I was assigned to Air Force Systems Command in 1990, I made a major emphasis on how to more effectively apply science and technology. I encouraged our laboratory people to consult very closely with the war-fighting community. They don't know for certain who the future enemy might be. But our fighter pilots have the best sense of what will give them the best flexibility for any threat level.

In the past, we've kept the war fighters insulated from science and technology. It's like a wall with a sliding door. The airplane operator is kept on one side of the wall and the developer is on the other. Occasionally, we raise the sliding door and we show the operator a technological device and say, "What do you think about that?" He may say, "I don't like it." So you close the door. A little while later, we open the door again and stick another item out.

We can no longer afford to operate like that. Starting around 1990, we started to get the users involved in the development process. That meant bringing squadron and wing commanders to meet with scientists.

When we first did this, I said, "We will have the scientists present their projects to the operators." So we got the scientists to stand up and talk to these war-fighting guys. And they explained about new metal alloys or electronic components. The war fighters said, "Hey, this is neat. But what the hell does it mean to me? How can I use it?" And the scientists said, "I don't know. I haven't thought about that yet."

Both groups of people said, "Time out. We're not ready." And they went their separate ways. The war fighters made an effort to find out about what science and technology means. The scientists said to each other, "If we want to keep our programs funded, we'd better think about practical uses for our research." After a while, I brought these people back together for some very useful dialogue. As a result, the process has become very therapeutic to both sides.

The operators really aren't interested in materials. They're interested in capabilities. The scientists are interested in keeping their projects funded. So they try to figure out, "How many different kinds of military applications can I find for this project that I'm inventing?"

As a result, for the first time, we have operational pull on the laboratory process. A war fighter can explain to scientists, "If I had this capability, I could turn the tide of battle." And the command will consider putting more funding into that specific development.

The types of innovation by our research-and-development people during Desert Storm really didn't relate to basic science and technology. You can't have a scientist in a university who is thinking about a theory or an equation, have something produced immediately for the battlefield.

However, we did have operators in Desert Storm who had problems, and we found people in laboratories who helped to find quick solutions. But those were solutions based on adapting technologies that already existed. For example: the satellite Global Positioning Navigation System brought space technologies into the infantry trenches.

The GPU-28 laser-guided weapon went from a concept to operational use as a deep hard-target [concrete bunkers] penetrator in under six weeks. Less than five hours after arriving in Theater, the first GPU-28 was flown into combat.

After Desert Storm, the problem we face is taking a budget ax and lopping off up to ten percent from Science and Technology. We may eliminate the seed technology of tomorrow's key weapons system.

A scientist doesn't know when they discover something in a laboratory what the end result or application will be twenty years later. We shouldn't pressure them by saying, "If you don't tell me right now what it's going to be used for, we're going to cut your funding off."

For example, thirty-five years ago at the Wright Lab we had people working on a fusillary project. They talked about some unusual characteristic that came out of this work. That's how we discovered "composites"—the seed to stealth technology.

After this discovery became known, pilots started saying, "That could give me a fighter able to go through enemy air defenses undetected. Instead of sitting on my own side of the battle line, waiting for attacking airplanes and fighting over my own airfield, I could go attack his airplanes over his field. That could change the nature of air warfare." But it took about twenty years until we flew the first experimental Stealth airplane.

The F-117 Stealths are able to go after highly defended targets. They were able to knock out the Iraqis' Command and Control for its nationwide air defense network. That meant better protection for our less stealthy fighters and bombers, which prevented a lot of airplanes from getting shot down. That not only saved the pilots' lives, but saved the American taxpayers billions of dollars worth of airplanes. That is the long-term cost effectiveness of our investment in stealth technology. The F-117 airplanes are expensive. But in the long run you save a tremendous amount of money and lives.

In a decreasing budget environment, we first must maintain our Science and Technology base. Then we have to decide on weapons systems that are going to provide us with the most flexibility.

Our aim is to not have to drop another "dumb" bomb off a fighter. Because if we're going to put a fighter pilot in harm's way to attack a target, we want the bomb to hit the target. In the Gulf War, we didn't have any all-weather precision munitions. They were either electro-optical or laser, for which you need certain climatic conditions. We want to be able to drop precision munitions in any kind of weather. And we want to make it cheap enough that we can put the technology on every bomb.

We're not talking about inventing new bombs. We're talking about putting a kit on every 2,000-pound bomb we own, that assures that every one of them will come very close to the target.

It also means that a B-52, which carries a lot of 2,000-pound bombs, can open its bomb bay and the bombs will go to eight or ten different targets, each bomb separately programmed. This is not "magic." These will not have the precision of laser-guided bombs, but they will be a hell of a lot better than the dumb bombs.

We'll still need precision bombs to attack special targets. We'll have to balance the cost of the cheap bombs with how many times we'll have to use the "golden beebees." And when we cut back the number of airplanes, as mandated by the draw down, we need to have smarter bombs to prevent attrition on our limited number of pilots.

Tomorrow's war is unlikely to be a Desert Storm. Saddam made the mistake of using his playbook from his last war. He thought we'd do the same. Our next adversary won't make the same mistake. They'll know what we used in the desert and how we used it. And they'll work hard to defeat us. So we've gone back to our workbench to exploit new technologies to be able to give our war-fighting commands the weapons systems they'll need to fulfill the Air Force's global reach.

We're not lacking for matériel challenges. Desert Storm identified several: We need long-range Stealth; all-weather precision-guided munitions; improved ability to destroy enemy missiles on the ground or intercept them while they are still over enemy territory. We need highly competent near-real-time bomb-damage assessments that can be sent directly to battle planners from target areas. We need enhanced surveillance and communications.

Our industrial base has changed over the years. In the Second World War, the P-47 Thunderbolt airplane was built at the

Fairchild facility on Long Island. It took eight days to construct an airplane. Today it takes three *years* to construct a fighter airplane.

It's tough to perceive what the threat will be with the world changing so quickly. There is no satisfactory answer. We look at computerized intelligence estimates. However, intuition should not be denigrated. A lot of why this nation became great is because certain leaders said, "My gut tells me that this is the right way to move."

RIVERS AND GULLIES

COLONEL MICHAEL ANDREWS

SAUDI ARABIA 1992–93
CHIEF, TRAINING AND OPERATIONS DIVISION
SAUDI ARABIAN NATIONAL GUARD MODERNIZATION
PROGRAM

History is replete with examples of soldiers surviving desperate situations and winning when they theoretically shouldn't. I disagree with the computer games that predict victory or defeat based upon a tally of organizations and equipment. Soldiering is about heart. The whole business of war is about moral supremacy. Throughout history, smart leaders have capitalized on their soldiers believing in a just war. That instills a sense of purpose and values greater than self-preservation.

As we train for the future, in an era of declining budgets, we risk becoming impersonal and mechanistic. We have a lot of war games that are computer-based. The average young officer may begin to view war as a board game, like chess. There is a real danger in that.

I'm not ashamed to say that there have been times during a war game, two or three o'clock in the morning, when I have cried while manning a board exercise. Because I have imagined the board symbols in that war game as real people.

God help us if we detach ourselves. As a commander, I have

to make my junior officers realize that. One of my favorite quotes is from Stephen St. Vincent Benet's "John Brown's Body":

If you take a flat map and move wooden blocks on it, they behave as they should. The science of war is moving live men like blocks. Getting wooden squares into position at the right time. But it takes time to mold men into blocks. Flat maps turn into rivers and gullies, and you can't pick them up in your hand to move them.

It's all so clear on the map: Blocks curling around other blocks and crunching them up . . . But men get tired and orders are slow. You move too slowly and take too long. It's not like it was on the map. And soldiers die . . .

Regardless of the technological advancements, we have to give credence to the human dimension of combat. I talk with my young officers about a particular incident:

I was a green lieutenant in Vietnam. My unit was hit with some small arms and automatic weapons fire, a couple of RPGs [rocket-propelled grenades]. I had a brave platoon sergeant, who I had a lot of respect for. I ran over to him and grabbed his elbow. I said, "I want you to take two squads and swing around, so the enemy doesn't flank us."

I looked at him. He was frozen. He was in a catatonic seizure—he couldn't move and he couldn't talk. He had never done that before. But that's how his nervous system reacted at that particular moment.

The intense firepower that we bring to bear today can have a profound impact on the psyche of soldiers under sustained combat. Perhaps we saw an inkling of it from the Iraqi trenches in Kuwait. After a month of conventional air strikes, they didn't want any more. Imagine two armies going toe to toe with equal conviction and firepower.

The American performance in the Gulf War was a product of intensive training. In Stateside duty we try to impress on our soldiers that they are doing a dress rehearsal in case it ever becomes real. Our training system over the past ten years has been one of our strongest areas. We have to be very careful as we downsize the Army's budget. And as we congratulate ourselves about the Gulf victory, we can't be overconfident. We've got to continue the things we have been doing right.

I look at my lieutenants today and feel some concern. When our young guys go out to maneuver, on a big exercise once a year, they have all kinds of people with clipboards looking over their shoulders.

In contrast, as a young lieutenant in Vietnam, I maneuvered my unit every day, eight to ten hours. We went with the contours of the land, operating in radio silence. After three or four months you get the feel of it and do it real well. Lieutenants today never get that opportunity. We go to the field once or twice a year for maneuvers, and the young officers are never alone.

We need to allow young leaders to go out by themselves to work it out. And we need to eliminate their fear of failure. We shouldn't produce timid or hesitant leaders who are worried about screwing up. We need audacious, risk-taking, tenacious warriors. Young guys who are full of piss and vinegar who are risk takers. And you can't grow them by creating training environments where we are constantly looking over their shoulders.

There is no question that the average soldier today is easier to train and to motivate than we had in the draftee army. Lower-quality guys have gotten out. The entry standards are high.

The hardest problem is to keep these good young guys all fired up. If they're not challenged, we'll have good people leave the Army because they don't feel a sense of mission/ purpose/vision. One of the problems in the future is to keep young leaders challenged and growing.

The downsizing of the Army is a worrisome time. We need the "peace dividend," we need to be smaller, there's no question. We need to do things more cost-effectively. But if we move to get smaller too quickly, we may sacrifice some fundamental training that we have benefited from in recent years. Especially if there should suddenly be another substantial conflict. Or simultaneous battles in two or three directions.

With the worldwide availability of high technology and the possibility of tinhorn despots having nukes and chemical weapons, the world is perhaps more dangerous than ever. Throughout history, unforeseen momentous events have occurred when countries have let down their guard.

Our business is about deterrence. We helped to prevent a war in Europe by presenting a strong, professional appearance and being well-trained. Bullies pick on weaklings. Our potential enemies are watching. As the world becomes more complex and the potential results of war become even more horrible, we need to send a constant unwavering signal. That we're a strong, professional military force that they don't want to tangle with.

SHOULDER PATCH

COLONEL JOHN SYLVESTER

FORT KNOX, KENTUCKY 1992–93
DIRECTOR
ARMOR TRAINING SCHOOL

Coming back from the Gulf, I told all my subordinate leaders in the Tiger Brigade that they needed to work very hard to prevent a letdown. And, "Make training as interesting and challenging as you possibly can." There was a very prevalent attitude that, "We've been to war. We had met the elephant. We won." But although we did a lot of things well, there wasn't enough attention to detail that we should've had. Some guys think that because we won, attention to detail is not required.

That is the challenge to leaders now. I tell soldiers, "The only thing your combat shoulder patch does, is give you the right to say that training works."

One thing that I heard over and over from soldiers was, "Wow, sir, it was just like training." A tanker drives along the desert and sees three tanks out there. The TC [tank commander] says, "Gunner: Sable [missile], three tanks. Left tank!" BOOM. "Target, right tank!" BOOM. "Target, center tank!" BOOM. And it's over. The same as we do on the practice range.

I tell them, "Now you have the bragging rights to tell younger guys without the combat shoulder patch: train. Because when you go to war you want it to be 'just like training.' "

CHAOS

COLONEL MICHAEL WYLY

Quantico, Virginia 1988–91
Vice-President
U.S. Marine Corps University

What is an infantry officer going to need in the future? We must train people well enough to have self-restraint and the coolness of judgment necessary to operate in chaotic and unpredictable situations, as often happen in combat.

Senior leadership still sometimes has the desire to take the chaos out, to make the world orderly. Some people stay in the military because they want to live in an orderly world. They like to live on bases with traffic moving slowly and all the grass cut. So there is often a desire to reject all chaos and try to make war orderly. What we realistically need is a unique organization that can thrive and do its best job in a chaotic situation.

In an emergency or crisis, the Marine Corps' job is to go into a situation that we are not familiar with. Field commanders need to be flexible enough to assess who and what we're up against, and how to be able to outthink them.

The American Revolutionary Army of George Washington was adept at small unit and commando tactics against conventional British forces. Independent thinking is part of our heritage. Although we sometimes neglect that part of our heritage in military tactical doctrine. I tried to bring it back by placing an emphasis on field skills and maneuver. The negative response I got was, "After all, the American field commander can call upon attack aviation, smart bombs, artillery, and the M-1 tank."

My question is, "What if he is up against a guerrilla army like in Vietnam and he doesn't have heavy fire support available?" Possibly because the terrain and weather limit or prevent armor or air support. Or if there is a political situation, near a populated area, where he can't use fire support? That is where independent thought of a junior commander can save lives.

THE GATEKEEPER

COLONEL WESLEY FOX

QUANTICO, VIRGINIA 1989–92
COMMANDER
MARINE CORPS OFFICER CANDIDATE SCHOOL

For some three years, no young Marine became an officer without first passing the scrutiny of Colonel Wes Fox, Commander of the Officer Candidate School. A Korea and Vietnam war veteran and Medal of Honor recipient, the powerfully built, square-jawed Fox remained a role model until he retired in mid-1992.

In OCS [Officer Candidate School] my mission is to screen candidates for leadership potential. OCS is elevation and screening. Young officers get their training at the Basic School. And the Infantry Officer Course hones a young lieutenant into a leader of a Marine rifle platoon.

When a young person comes through my door with the desire to be an officer, I look at sincerity, integrity—which is a hard one to get a feel for in a six-week program. On Day One I inform them, "Don't come before me with a question on your integrity. If you do, you're out of here."

A lot of our evaluation is subjective. We can grade their academic tests and physical fitness. But when it comes to the way he performs in leadership exercises, a lot of that is the way his peers rate and respond to him. And we watch his performance in his training squad, how he contributes and helps the next guy.

I'm a pretty good judge of character. In Vietnam three lieutenants joined me at the same time. One, Bill Christmas, impressed me immediately as my kind of leader. I gave him a rifle platoon, and he was always involved with his Marines. Not standing around giving orders with his hands on his hips, but clearing fields of fire with a machete. I never failed to find him sitting beside some new rifleman to instruct him on what needed to be done. He was respected by his Marines.

Another lieutenant thought everything was a big joke. I gave him my mortar platoon and kept him nearby to observe him. He turned out to be a big bullshitter, sitting around at night swapping tall tales with Marines about girlfriends they had in high school.

After a while I was required to make that lieutenant a rifle platoon commander. I sent him on a patrol with a squad. He got himself in trouble and I had to send a corporal to bail him out. The corporal had been on that same area earlier in the day, and correctly kept his patrol off the trail. His point man observed an NVA gunner who was setting ambush. The corporal's squad assaulted the ambush site from behind and waxed all the NVA. One Marine was slightly wounded.

The lieutenant walked right down the same trail. He was ambushed in the same spot and got on the radio screaming for help. So I sent the corporal with a squad to pull his butt out.

I don't believe, from an OCS perspective, that we do anything more different today than was done twenty or thirty years ago. We just have more time to do it. And because of the draw down of the force, we can be a little more fussy. We keep only the better-thinking and better-qualified individuals.

Today, Marine recruits have to be high school graduates. An eighth grade dropout, like I was forty years ago, would have a rough time getting in. At colleges, Marine Corps Selection Officers only send us those students who they think are the best. And we weed out 36 percent of those.

Today, because of General Al Gray's "Warrior Training," young Marines are much better skilled in combat. We teach more of the important things throughout our schooling system of how Marines need to think and plan for war.

For instance, during the last week of OCS we have the Battle Fitness Test. That is a nine-mile movement, wearing full combat gear, over different obstacles at a forced-march pace. The time of completion is part of the score. And at the end of it, the candidate is given a mental test. That's a new approach: exhaust him and then see how he responds mentally. The test is basically a map reading and compass problem. His sweat is dripping all over his map. You give him two minutes to complete the question. Some of these young guys get all flustered. Others are cool and collected.

And we've got a Reaction Course that requires people to lead and make choices. There are twenty-eight stations on it, each is a difficult task. Students lead four-man teams. He has to delegate tasks to team members, and provide guidance and supervise as they move through it. They have to discover for themselves that they can't complete everything in the allotted time.

It's not important that they perform every task. It's how they prioritize their tasks, and perform as leaders. We weed out those who can't think. Even though I have all college graduates, we still reject more than a third.

In combat, often things may not go according to plan. You have to improvise and find ways to keep your people alive and accomplish your mission. There's a whole lot of schools in the country that teach management. But there's no place that teaches you how to motivate young people to reach down inside themselves like we teach Marine Corps leaders at the Basic School. That starts a learning process that continues throughout a Marine's career.

A combat leader has to face the time when he will have to ask young people under his command to put their lives in a precarious situation for reasons they may not understand. That's a heavy responsibility. But it's made easier if you really love those young men and know that what you're doing has to be done.

Your Marines need to know that your first thought has been to consider their well-being. They will then charge up the enemy's gun barrel for you in a moment's notice and never ask why. Marines volunteer to put on the uniform knowing that moment may come. They aren't saying, "Hands off, don't get me killed." They're saying, "Don't waste me." That's a term that was used quite often in Vietnam: "He got wasted . . ." "We wasted a bunch . . ." I can't think of any worse thing that can be said of a leader than, "He wasted some Marines."

With all the new sophisticated weapons, we need a more thinking, more capable individual behind the weapon. But he still has to be taught and motivated by good leaders. If we ever go to war with a major military power, a lot of our sophisticated electronics may jam and computers may malfunction. Then it's back to an individual using common sense to solving problems. That's why we have a Reaction Course to teach young leaders to expect the unexpected, prioritize their problems and organize people to help each other. That's leadership.

BE YOURSELF

MAJOR GENERAL
ROYAL MOORE, JR.

EL TORO, CALIFORNIA 1989-92
AIRCRAFT WING COMMANDER
3RD MARINE AIRCRAFT WING

I don't think there are any "born leaders." I think today's top leaders are people who have grown into those positions. But younger people, because of their pride, are afraid to look around.

I try to encourage them, "Steal leadership traits that you admire in others. Modify it, change it around to make it work for you. That doesn't mean I want you to be phony. Take those traits that seem natural for you."

When I made general, a lot of old generals tried to tell me how to play the role. A lot of great mythical things. But one wise old Marine told me, "Just be yourself. Because you'll louse it up trying to be a phony."

There isn't a great deal of difference between inside the military and the outside community. Other than the haircuts and we have a little more discipline. What goes on in the Marine Corps and what goes on at a major corporation isn't all that different. In fact, some civilian business executives attend the National War College and other advanced military schools. And military officers attending the War Colleges visit corporations as part of their curriculum.

Recently, the Westin Corporation asked me to give a guest lecture on the military theories of Sun Tzu and von Clausewitz. I asked why. They said, "We want to apply the military theories of war-fighting to our business practices. And most importantly, to talk about leadership."

I don't emphasize any one trait of leadership. Except, taking care of my people. If you are going to ask your Marines to do impossible things for you, they've got to know in the pits of their stomachs that you're behind them 100 percent. To include concern for their dependent families.

The last thing I say to my new squadron commanders is, "Take care of my Marines." They know that if they don't, I'll destroy them. I instill that fear in them.

THE LIBRARY

GENERAL ALFRED GRAY

THE PENTAGON 1987–91
COMMANDANT
U.S. MARINE CORPS

As Commandant of the Marine Corps, General Al Gray will be remembered for reviving the idea that "all Marines are infantrymen" and the transition to a Maneuver war-fighting doctrine. However, Gray believes that an equally important aspect of his legacy was the institutionalization of the Marine Corps University.

The Marine Corps University is not necessarily a new idea. We recommended it in a 1968 study at Quantico. It didn't come about, because one of the requirements to be a War College-level university is you need a bigger library. I always had that in the back of my mind. When I became commandant, I said, "We need an amphibious warfare library." I changed the word to "facility," so I could get it through Congress. That would be the heart and soul of the Marine Corps University.

I also wanted to reach out to improve all the enlisted schools, the Staff NCO Academy, and I wanted NCO training standardized, which hadn't been done before. As a former enlisted man, I felt very strongly about that. I'm an educational maverick in my own right. In the 1950s and 1960s, I got a lot of education on my own by reading.

I patterned the Marine Corps University on the "University Without Walls" approach. I knew all about the Open University at the University of Maryland. I visited the Open University in England, when I was Commander of the Fleet Marine Force in Europe. At the time, people didn't understand why I wanted to visit that place. But that idea became the model of the Marine Corps University.

And I was a student at the Syracuse University independent master's degree program. One of the reasons I did that was to learn how the program worked. I talked with professors about applying it in the Marine Corps. They said, "Yes, you can."

We had to get $15 million in the Marine Corps budget to start construction. The rest is being raised through private donations. The library is now under construction at Quantico. It was thrilling to watch the first steel girders going up.

SERGEANT'S TIME

COMMAND SERGEANT MAJOR WILLIAM MCBRIDE

FORT BRAGG, NORTH CAROLINA 1984–91
DIVISION SERGEANT MAJOR
82ND AIRBORNE DIVISION

The 82nd Airborne is listed in nineteen different contingency plans for rapid response to crises. We have to be ready to go to Southwest Asia, the Caribbean, Latin America, wherever we're needed. When you have a sense of purpose that you may be at war tomorrow, within eighteen hours notice, you take your job seriously.

Out of my more than thirty-four years in the Army, twenty-six have been in the 82nd. All of our people are volunteers twice—into the Army and into airborne. I was a battalion sergeant major in the division in 1977, when women first started arriving, mostly in a support battalion as parachute riggers. They were forced on us. The division's position is that when we parachute into a target area, everybody is a combatant. Everyone has to be prepared to fight—clerks, cooks, mechanics, whoever.

We now have around 287 females in the division, including

nineteen officers. Everybody must be able to run four miles in thirty-six minutes. Everybody must be able to do a twelve-mile road march in three hours or less, wearing a thirty-five-pound rucksack and combat gear. Support troops must do this quarterly, combat units every month. Regardless of sex or age.

I've had some serious injuries in the past few years. I've broken both ankles in jumps. I've broken my tailbone, my collarbone. Every battalion in this division has forty-year-old sergeants major who must complete the four-mile run every month. And we have an emphasis on marksmanship and weapons training. The nature of our business—jumping into combat with all of our equipment on—requires that we stay physically fit. And leaders have to get out in front and do it.

When I first came into this division in 1957, as a young soldier, paratroopers had a reputation of being hard-drinking, hard-loving, hard-fighting. It was acceptable to get drunk, get in a fight and not show up. They punished a guy, but it was a more forgiving army than it is today. A guy could be busted and then promoted two months later. We had guys who were great soldiers for twenty-seven days. The first three days after payday, he was out getting drunk, gambling, whatever. But the rest of the month he was super. You can't do that today. This is an unforgiving army.

When I took this job, my boss said, "Sergeant Major McBride, if you get a DWI [driving while intoxicated], I expect you to retire." So when I was out drinking, I made sure somebody else was driving. Now I drink Diet Coke or Diet 7-UP. I walk around with a glass full of soda.

During my first tours with the 82nd, in the 1950s and '60s, a lot of our people hadn't finished high school. They were a bit rougher around the edges when they came into the Army. I quit school in the tenth grade in Philadelphia. I went to work for a construction company. Got laid off and decided to come into the Army. I turned eighteen in October 1956. There wasn't a lot of construction work in the winter months. So in January, I told a buddy, "Let's join the Army." This is where I got my high school diploma.

In those days, some of our best soldiers came out of the draft. The company clerks and the guys with the high aptitude scores were college graduates or people with two to three years of college. But as we went into Vietnam, the Army started drafting anybody. Standards were lowered. Judges would put guys in the Army rather than in jail. So we got some real trash through the draft, too. Every unit suffered from this.

Today the Army practically requires that young people who enlist have a high school diploma. It's not that these kids are necessarily more intelligent than others. But the fact that they completed school is an indicator of success.

I haven't seen anything today that we use in the infantry that I couldn't have mastered when I was a private. But we see more and more systems come on board that require continual study and training to master. The satellite GPS navigation systems that we work with have computers. And it takes a little mathematical mastery to work the TOW and Dragon antitank systems. It's no longer, "Pick this up and pull the trigger."

We were fortunate that the Iraqis had no ability to interfere with our satellites. It goes further than that. I'm concerned about mortarmen who rely on their mortar ballistic computer rather than being able to manually compute firing. If those guys lose their computer or it breaks, they may not have the ability to manually compute. Because they've been trained on their little box.

Soldiers will always need to know how to use the old-fashioned compass. Because satellite navigation aids sometimes aren't accurate enough to call in artillery fire. Supposedly they tell you where you are to the meter. But in reality, unless they're calibrated exactly right, you'll have some deviations. And when you call in artillery, you don't want it to land on you.

In part, the Army's strict attitude is a response to the breakdown in discipline during the 1970s. The Army's leadership has always imposed those higher-conduct expectations on the officers. It was not acceptable for an officer to be drunk outside of his Officers Club or his fraternity. But now—and I'm a little leery of this—we have very little difference in standards between officers and NCOs. An NCO's career can be ruined by a DWI. He will never be promoted. I'm not sure if that is right or wrong.

Despite the changes in the Army during my thirty-five years, the means by which NCOs lead people hasn't changed. I don't think the leaders' tools have changed.

The hardest job in the Army is to be a young sergeant. Because you feel that everybody is challenging your authority. So you overcompensate and become a disciplinarian. With the approach, "Goddammit, you do it because I say so."

We build leaders day by day, little by little. There's no magic formula. You have to give a young sergeant things to do that will build his confidence. You've got to let him drill troops and give physical training. You've got to let him give classes and instructions. You've got to rehearse him, to let him develop his self-confidence.

My approach was to use the Army's system of formal schooling. Making sure you get the right guy in school at the right time. If a guy is a squad leader and he hasn't been to the relevant school, you give him a priority to attend that course.

The second things I had were unit programs to foster leadership. Every time a brigade is on post duty they run a basic leadership course. We also work on making sure soldiers continue their education whenever possible in civilian education programs. We give a quota to units on post support that they have to send 125 people to improve their math and reading skills. And we have psychology training and counseling.

But I think we're making some mistakes. I'm concerned that NCOs are starting to worry about the wrong things. We've got too many NCOs today who are worried about managing their careers. They worry about becoming a drill sergeant and other assignments because it looks good on their record. Getting their "ticket punched." And take certain assignments not for the right reasons.

I still believe that sergeants should keep their minds on getting the job done and taking care of their soldiers. If they do the job right, their boss and the system should promote them.

FATHERLY IMAGE

COMMAND SERGEANT MAJOR WILLIAM EARL MCCUNE

FORT HOOD, TEXAS 1991–93
BRIGADE SERGEANT MAJOR
1ST CAVALRY DIVISION

After twenty-six years of active duty, I still like being around young soldiers. I've seen so many changes during my career.

I'm not proud of all the changes we had to go through to get here.

When I was in Germany in 1974–75 there were some violent clashes—blacks against whites. Five black guys standing on a corner, and MPs would come break it up. If you didn't have a basketball, you had to disperse. [He laughs.] Guys were hanging lieutenants and captains out of windows.

In Saudi Arabia we never had any of that business. I think that it's the maturity of the type of folks we're getting. We don't get militant-type folks into the Army today. Those folks are not volunteering because they know that it's too much of a controlled society with our drug testing and disciplined lifestyle. Soldiers we get today have graduated from high school with good home values.

Things deteriorated in the early 1970s because the cycle started in 1966 where guys with nonleadership ability other than to walk point in combat made NCO. I am one of the few guys to survive that period because I had an old platoon sergeant, Sergeant 1st Class Davis, who took care of me. So I didn't mind working for him. He was like my father.

We don't have the "father image" guys anymore. We don't have the old guys who would kick your butt and who disciplined his own soldiers. You aren't permitted to do that now. You can give soldiers extra training, but you can't discipline them in a fatherly manner.

Most of today's platoon sergeants are not old. They're young E7s, around thirty years old. That's not a fatherly image to soldiers who come into the army in their early to mid-twenties.

THE COCKPIT

REAR ADMIRAL RILEY MIXSON

THE PENTAGON 1991–93
DEPUTY ASSISTANT CHIEF OF STAFF
OF NAVAL OPERATIONS
FOR AIR WARFARE

Air-to-air engagements are historically brief. They don't last long. But you have to be able to function with split-second reflexes despite the physical stress. The ability for any fighter pilot should be sorted out in training exercises. Those who can't measure up, shouldn't fly.

I tell groups of young officers, "You never know when you are going to war. When you go, you have to be able to use your weapons systems to the utmost advantage." That takes a hell of a lot of hard work.

For example, the F/A-18 Hornet strike fighter has incredible capability. You have to train very hard to become proficient in using its avionics and weapons systems. When you achieve that level of proficiency, then you can perform like the pilots who switched from ground attack to shoot down two Iraqi MiGs. And then switched back to ground attack to hit their targets.

In addition, you are given all the information from your radar and your ECM [electronic countermeasure] systems. Translating all of that into situational awareness requires a lot of dedication, study, and training.

I don't think that women flying in combat will adversely affect our capabilities. Women have shown that they can fly airplanes. There's one regime, however, that is very physically demanding. That is a dog-fight—air-to-air combat. Because of the prolonged physical stress on the body. I don't believe we have tested very many women in that regime over a very long period of time. It will take a certain type of female who keeps herself in extraordinary strength conditioning.

In flying, a g is pressure equal to your body weight. Resistance to moving your head from side to side. In combat you pull five to six g's. The effect is that your head wants to slump down, your chin is pulled down toward your chest. It takes a fair amount of strength in your neck muscles. Not only to hold your head up, but to be able to twist your head from side to side and keep situational awareness of what is going on around you.

We didn't see much of that in the last war because there was no prolonged air-to-air combat. That is the only area where I would have some concern about female fighter pilots' endurance. The stress is both mental and physical.

PHANTOMS

COLONEL GENE "NEAL" PATTON

GEORGE AIR FORCE BASE, CALIFORNIA 1989–92
DEPUTY COMMANDER FOR OPERATIONS
35TH TACTICAL FIGHTER WING

As part of the reorganization and streamlining of the Air Force, by 1995 more than 1,000 fighter airplanes are scheduled to be cut. Although some of the aircraft will go to reserve units, many experienced pilots will no longer have a place. And there will be far fewer opportunities to fly for aspiring young recruits. Through the Desert Storm era, the Air Force had thirty-six air wings, each made up exclusively of one type of aircraft. In the new plan, there are scheduled to be fewer than twenty "composite" fighter wings, made up of a mixture of aircrafts. Among the wings being dismantled is the 35th Tactical Fighter Wing—the venerable F-4G "Wild Weasels."

With the budget cutbacks, air bases are being closed down. Very experienced pilots will be told, "We don't need you anymore." Younger guys are being encouraged to get out through the Early Release programs.

They are getting rid of the "Wild Weasels." The F-4G airplanes are going to the National Guard and out of active duty.

The Air Force is looking ahead. It's finding ways to put the HARM missile on other airplanes. But those aircraft may not have the capability of the F-4G Phantoms. Because the thing that makes it such an excellent weapons system is the interface between the HARM and our APR-47 computer which pinpointed threats so very well in the Gulf War. The support that we gave people was proven very necessary. The only U.S. airplanes lost to SAMs [surface-to-air missiles] were when the F-4Gs weren't around.

I'm real proud of the old F-4 Phantom. After all these years, still being a war horse. That's a tribute to the young men that flew it. And the young men and women who maintained it.

In retrospect, I hope that the Air Force is not naive enough to rest on our collective laurels and say, "We did so well in the Gulf, we found all the solutions for ever and ever."

We shouldn't forget that the Iraqi air force failed to show up. The ground threat was troublesome: lots of guns, lots of bullets, lots of SAMs. But their intercept aircraft could've given us fits if they were aggressively flown.

I don't know that younger guys who flew in the air campaign have gotten overconfident. Sure, fighter pilots are cocky. But guys flying fighters are always cocky. They think they're invincible, God's gift to the ladies and everything else. [He laughs.] I don't know if that's true or not.

I'm in charge of closing the wing down. I have no idea where I'll be going from here. I've got to close this base down and figure out what I'm going to do.

After twenty-five years of flying, I still enjoy every time I fly. I guess some things become routine after a while. But I truly enjoy it. Most of the guys are eager to fly anytime they can.

I took a week's vacation recently to catch up with a lot of odds and ends. When I got back to flying yesterday, it was like, "Jeez, I'm back where I belong."

SHOWING THE FLAG

REAR ADMIRAL WILLIAM FOGARTY

PERSIAN GULF 1989–91
COMMANDER
JOINT MIDDLE EAST TASK FORCE

In 1993 the Navy announced plans to lose close to one-third of its fleet. From a high of 545 ships during Desert Storm down to around 350. Senior officers, like Rear Admiral William Fogarty, remember the 1970s, when an under manned Navy had to deal with a number of unforeseen crises. The extended time at sea for a limited number of ships placed tremendous stress on naval crews, and demoralized the institution.

In the downsizing of the Navy, some strong leadership is required to deal with the cutback of the number of ships. I'm not a proponent of the theory that less ships with high technology can make up the difference.

Throughout my career I have seen that you must have enough ships and forces to be able to be a credible deterrent. For example, an intercept force or any kind of blockade or naval quarantine, where you are planning to set up a defensive barrier, takes a number of ships.

We can say to ourselves, "The worldwide threat of conflict has gone away. We can concentrate on a reduced number of ships in a limited number of places where the next war may start." That would be wonderful if we could look in the crystal ball that way. I'm not sure we can do that. Especially with the amount of sophisticated military technology that is being sold all over the world.

China's navy is getting bigger and their technology is getting stronger. They are shopping for an aircraft carrier. And they're getting a new port at Hong Kong within this decade. India has expanded its naval forces. Iran is trying to purchase submarines. And we ultimately don't know how things will develop in the Soviet Union.

Another interesting problem: What if the mission of the Navy in the future is not only to provide a deterrent force in the Third World, but also to police contraband goods that are moving on international waters? A kind of broad interdiction program to stop the transfer of illegal weapons, technology or drugs.

Let's say, for a matter of discussion, that the Soviet Union in their quest to get money, offers to ship missiles to a Third World country. Or China sends missiles to Iran, as they did during the Iran-Iraq War. To have a quarantine or blockade or interdiction force on the open seas takes a lot of ships. We may get all the countries of the world together to help like during Desert Storm. However, we may have to do it on our own. That may not require aircraft carriers. It will require ships that have enough room on board for helicopters, to be able to stop and search merchant ships.

The way that my little crystal ball sees the future, is more little bonfires in the Third World to put out. For example, in the Middle East, to deploy some 8,000 miles from the United States requires a number of ships because of logistics requirements and time away from home. The further you are away from home, the more people and more ships it takes to rotate. Unless you want to keep your people at sea nine or ten months a year, send them home for a couple of months, and then back out to sea. The burn-out that creates is counterproductive.

At any given time, because of wear and tear, a third of our ships are down for maintenance. Another third are in training, because after maintenance you can't just get up and go. You need some time to get the ship ready, not only for proficiency in combat, but for safety of the crew. You need damage-control training and overboard training, and helicopter- or airplane-crash training.

Another number of ships are needed for U.S. coastal defense. So we can't have more than one interdiction operation going on at a time. It's a numbers problem.

We may want to show the flag in South America, Europe or wherever. Without an adequate physical presence, some people may be tempted to act aggressively. As a result, we would have to respond with a much larger force into a situation out of control. There's a big difference between people seeing your ships patrolling off their coast rather than hearing, "We can be there in three days if something should happen."

I'd much rather have three frigates patrolling an area where they can intercept more ships, as opposed to one ship with an awful lot of high-tech firepower.

On the other hand, I think we showed during the Iraq war that the technology of smart weapons, seeing in the dark, instant communications, and other new innovations are important. All of the research and development that we did years ago paid off.

We need to stay technologically ahead of the game. On the other hand, we have to keep enough numbers of ships. So if things happen in the world, we don't have to rely on somebody else. Like we did for countermine warfare in the Gulf. Or count on other services like the Army or Air Force, who may not get to a crisis area because there is no place to land.

The Iraq war was a little bit special because American forces had access to bases in Saudi Arabia and the United Arab Emirates and Bahrain and Qatar. That may not be the case in the future. There may be a situation where we can only get there by water. Then you have to stay twelve miles away because of the sovereign waters of countries. The only service that can do that is the Navy.

The Navy gives our government diplomatic capabilities. In dealing with Third World crises or terrorist incidents, you may need diplomatic time. We can have a ship off the beach far enough to be seen but not on sovereign territory. We can get under way with the warning, "The carriers are coming," and give diplomacy time to work.

That's different from sending the Air Force. Because once they take off, they can't linger over a target area or they'll run out of fuel. With the speed at which they operate, there is little time for a diplomatic process to resolve a dispute. When the 82nd Airborne jumps from airplanes, they are on the ground and in combat. And the Marines are most effectively transported by ship.

With less ships, you will have to use violent force more frequently. For example, if you are doing an intercept operation with one ship covering a vast area, vessels may try to run the blockade simultaneously. The only choice you have is to either let dangerous contraband go through or use your weapons to knock them out. In such a case, which may be politically explosive, you lose diplomatic leverage and deterrence. With less ships you are forced to take a more offensive posture.

In the Intercept program in the Gulf, if we didn't have sufficient maritime assets to vocally warn a merchant ship and send a search team on board, the only choices would have been to sink it or let it go by. Because of the political sensibilities, the orders from Washington or the United Nations may have been, "Let it go through." The ship may have been carrying nuclear triggers for Saddam's weapons of mass destruction or some type of bacteria for his germ warfare munitions. Or transporting a terrorist group.

Most of the dope runners in the world, and those people who deal in the black market and arms sales to Third World countries, will be delighted to know that the United States is decreasing its number of ships.

MOTHBALLS

REAR ADMIRAL DAVID BILL

The Pentagon 1991–93
Director
Surface Combat Systems Division
U.S. Navy Headquarters

Battleships are being retired because of the cost to sustain 1,600 crew on board. We do have the ability to take the ships out of mothballs to be made battle-ready. However, the time it would take to put its machinery and guns into operating condition is another story.

Shaking a ship down and training its crew takes time. For a battleship it would take a good six months with everybody working hard. And with the technology and speed of modern warfare, six months might be too late. And to build a new ship takes between seven to ten years from design to launching.

The battleship represents two unique capabilities. The Navy doesn't have any other guns that can replicate the sixteen-inch gun's ability to support Marines ashore. The other capability is a "presence" role. A battleship is an awesome warship. Its presence offshore can deter an aggressor.

"Forward presence" is very much a part of the Navy's role and mission. The only ship comparable in winning friends and influencing people is an aircraft carrier.

The next largest surface naval weapon we have is a five-inch gun carried by a number of ships. That has less range than a sixteen-inch gun and less punch. And its range puts a ship closer to shore, increasing danger to the crew. But due to the fiscal climate, we have no other choice right now. Even in limited crises we will have to use aircraft, which requires an entire carrier battle group and puts pilots at risk.

Missile systems on cruisers and destroyers won't fill the role of the sixteen-inch guns. Tomahawk missiles, the strike weapons carried by those ships, are strategic target weapons. They are a lot more expensive than a sixteen-inch round, and used for pinpoint accuracy or fixed targets at great ranges. You would not fire a bunch of those into an area to suppress artillery or moving armor targets.

We are living in a very dynamic period of history. We cannot forget that the decisions we make today will effect sailors ten or fifteen years from now. They have to be prepared to meet the uncertainties and potential crises and actual combat that may take place.

There is certainly no navy in the world today that comes close to the capability that our navy has. But what will be the effect when we eliminate one-fourth to one-third of our ships, as is called for, in the next five years? It depends on which ships are taken out. And whether we have the resources to keep our ships ready, our people trained, and our weapons current with worldwide technology developments.

COUNTERMEASURES

CAPTAIN BRUCE MCEWEN

THE PENTAGON 1991–93
HEAD
CARRIER ACQUISITIONS PROGRAM
U.S. NAVY HEADQUARTERS

The important present and future role of the Navy is to keep the sea lanes open. Mines are low-tech and inexpensive weapons. Any country or terrorist group can produce them to block the flow of international shipping.

Looking at the history of modern naval warfare, the United States has made the same mistakes with mine countermeasures over and over again: we get involved in an armed conflict, and mines become an important issue. We respond to it with ingenuity. And then we forget about it. We allow our capability to atrophy for several years until we need to do it again.

Today, we need to focus on minesweeping and low-tech challenges. The challenges we'll likely be facing in coming years will likely be more Third World situations. We're going to be dealing with low-tech. Small regional areas. Hopefully, it won't involve armed conflict. But simply our resolve to support the United Nations. However, Third World countries are investing in a lot of state-of-the-art weapons.

One of the best things that Navy carrier task forces have been able to do over the years is to provide a forward presence. I wish I could count the number of crises that were averted because the U.S. Navy was nearby. Somebody thought twice about imposing their will on a neighboring country.

We routinely deploy amphibious-ready groups throughout the world, without carrier battle groups in support. Because the amphibious groups carry their own attack helicopters, and they have Harrier jump jets. But mines can deny the U.S. the ability to conduct a Marine amphibious assault.

As a reduced naval force, in future operations, our amphibious assault ships are going to have to support mine counter-measures.

COUNTERTERROR

LIEUTENANT COLONEL ANDREW GEMBARA

WASHINGTON, D.C. 1988–89
ASSISTANT DEVELOPER
U.S. SPECIAL OPERATIONS COMMAND OFFICE

Special operations is one area of the military whose numbers and budget appears to be holding firm in the "downsizing" period. However, many career Special Forces people are concerned that the new emphasis on unconventional warfare may attract a number of conventional people who are simply looking to extend their military careers.

On paper, it appears that a lot has happened with Special Operations. The command has grown. More money was put into projects like Army Rangers, more aircraft on the Air Force side. A lot of people got on the bandwagon. They see this as a place to get promotions. Take the number of officers at SOCOM [Special Operations Command] and look at their records to see how many are special-operations qualified.

There was a tremendous problem before 1980 because we weren't ready for counterterrorism. During the Reagan years, there was a big knee-jerk reaction to correct that, by throwing a lot of money at it.

The problem we have in the post–Desert Storm period is that although lots of money has been given, because it's been a "black" [secret] project, no one talks about the units. And there's been very little accounting. People might be very surprised if they saw where that capability actually is.

With psyops people, you'll find language problems. We don't have enough people who can speak foreign languages.

And if you look at the melting pot that the United States has become, and you relate that to the parts of the world we have an interest in—Latin America, the Middle East, and Asia—you shake your head and ask, "How many Hispanics have been recruited?" There are plenty of Hispanics in the military. But how many are in Special Forces? How many blacks are in Special Forces? Especially with a new Special Forces 3rd Group created for Africa. There hasn't been a realistic effort to recruit American citizens whose roots are in those places. There still is too much "good ol' boy" business.

Our special operations revitalization has become consumed by the conventional military structure. During the past eight years, proportionally, a lot of money has gone into special operations compared to what we had. But it's still under one percent of the defense budget.

Most of it has gone into aircraft and C-130 airplanes. You talk to the A-Teams and they still do not have the type of equipment they need—the lightweight portable stuff that you have to hump on your back into dangerous areas. They still don't have enough radios and communications equipment that they need. The SEALS are still unable to come up with the right types of underwater vehicles.

If we are going to correct this, we may need a separate Special Operations Agency. Still under the Defense Department, but autonomous. Not necessarily beholden to the Army, Navy or Air Force. But answering to the national leadership. Similar to what the OSS [Office of Strategic Services] was during World War II.

When OSS was disbanded after the war, the new CIA carried out the paramilitary role for a while. But there's been a gap and a void ever since the close of the OSS. No one really speaks exclusively to the paramilitary and the unconventional. Once military people cross over to this unit during their careers, that's where they should stay.

The use of special operations is more of a political tool than anything. That is why OSS was closer to the Washington political leadership. Conventional military leaders see that as a threat to their control.

If the Russians or Chinese or Middle Eastern belligerents are not in a position to make conventional trouble, the problems we will face will be small-scale, unconventional and dangerous. In order for us to deal with these problems effectively, we need a military force that understands the cultures and languages. And can operate in countries in any region of the world in a low-key, behind-the-scenes role.

If we had to do a Vietnam-type of intervention over again—and we may in someplace or another—I hope we avoid the introduction of major U.S. ground force units. In Vietnam we weren't prepared to understand the culture, the ways of the people. Everyone was a "gook," an enemy: "If you don't kill them, they'll kill you." We became a bigger part of the problem.

Our advisory teams have done a better job in Central America. It was Congress who limited the number of troops we could have there. Which became a good thing. I was in the Pentagon during 1980-82 in the Security Assistance Office. I had the Middle East. The guys next to me had Central and South America. I remember them pushing for more forces for El Salvador, but they didn't have the legislation. So they made do with what they had. It was amazing that our Special Forces could do the mission with so few resources and personnel. The quality of our advisory teams just had to be better.

After the 1992 cease-fire in El Salvador, both warring sides have requested that U.S. Special Forces remain. The guerrillas trust the Special Forces people to be honest brokers to monitor and mediate the peace agreement. This is a true example of the high rapport that Special Forces has established with the local people throughout the country.

With the Communist world breaking apart, and the Chinese unable to do more than sell weapons, the narcotraffickers are becoming the patrons of regional rebel groups. And as Fidel Castro gets discredited in Cuba, homespun groups like the "Shining Path" in Peru become role models for the region.

The trend for these terror groups is decentralized quasi-Marxist networks financed by drugs. That's harder to fight. And a place like Peru is three times larger than Vietnam. If we get overly involved, it will become a quagmire. That's why we have to look at the harder long-term issues. It's not just military alone.

The State Department has a role in this, too. In a number of countries where we have special operations teams on training assistance missions, Special Forces people come under the leadership of the local U.S. Embassy. The downside of that is you could have a political appointee as ambassador who doesn't know anything about the country or special operations work. Or he can be heavily influenced by other U.S. agencies.

There is also a problem created by the changes in Eastern Europe. American officials are doing a lot of back-patting about what a good job they've done. But they don't deal with any long-term plan in Third World countries, or deal well with problems.

We should go beyond the political/military to include civil affairs. That's how Special Forces was originally conceived. Kind of a Peace Corps that can survive in a dangerous situation.

In some places, like the Andes, cocaine may be the only cash crop for the mountain people. The only involvement they have with any authority figures is the drug traffickers. The central government hasn't done anything for them. The narcobarons are a quasigovernment structure. They provide medical care, food, and the basic needs. They have schools built. Then suddenly we come in to try to kill these guys, without a larger plan. That's very dangerous. Unless you replace the cocaine crop with something better.

Short-term plans are not the answer. Crop substitution takes three to five years before anything will begin to bring benefits to communities and people can begin to change their lives. That costs more and is a harder effort. And it's further complicated by our military commanders who are promoted after short tours—just two years. Obviously, commanders will want to make a mark for themselves in that short time. That's how decision-making becomes jaded. We need continuity of command, and a promotion system that incorporates that process.

Often without shooting, Special Forces soldiers can teach others to defend themselves and use developmental equipment to be able to provide for their people. Community development is an important part of the job. It's not "Rambo" going in and blowing away hundreds of people. That type of fantasy sells movies and television. But it misportrays the real role of Special Forces.

HONOR CODE

BRIGADIER GENERAL
DAVID BARATTO

FORT BRAGG, NORTH CAROLINA 1989–92
COMMANDING GENERAL
JOHN F. KENNEDY SPECIAL WARFARE CENTER &
SCHOOL

The role of special operations in the post–Cold War takes on increasing important dimensions: preventing the spread of regional "brushfire" wars, counterterrorism, and in interdicting the international drug and illegal weapons trade. The John F. Kennedy Special Warfare Center & School at Fort Bragg is the American military's premier education center for special operations.

The post–Cold War era presents a complex international environment. And the military is not in the policy lead. The State Department is in control.

The "National Strategy" written by the White House National Security Council now mentions "peacetime engagements." I had no idea what National Strategy was as a battalion commander. Today we are careful to make sure that our special operations doctrine lines up and supports the National Strategy. We are much more conscientious in trying to stay abreast of geopolitical changes.

The root of a conflict may be described as "the guerrillas out there." But it may not be guerrillas at all. It may be that the population is disaffected. It may be that the economy is disrupted. A Special Forces soldier has to put the *whole* picture in perspective.

Today's battlefield is increasingly dominated by the human mind. Not weapons systems or tonnage of bombs. Special Forces got a lot of publicity in the Gulf War. But a lot of what we do is not seen by the public.

I've been to remote outposts in a place like El Salvador to visit a sergeant 1st class who is advising a Salvadoran army brigade and has real problems with an insurgency. I've seen a brigade commander put his arm around the Special Forces sergeant and tell me what an important contribution he has been to the unit, and tears start coming down his face. That is all the gratification and reward I need. A successful FID [foreign internal defense or advisory] mission may prevent conventional U.S. forces from getting involved.

A young soldier may be in a country where, because of the culture or political system, it is easy to be corrupted or compromised, without even realizing it. He may think that he's establishing rapport or friendships, but he's falling into a trap. Once he falls outside of basic integrity, he's compromised himself. He loses credibility and ultimately will not be able to accomplish his mission.

As a cadet at West Point, I was vice-chairman of the Honor Committee. I developed a very defined set of values about integrity in the simplest sense: no lying, cheating, or stealing. If a soldier maintains inviolable codes on those three traits, the rest will follow.

I tell people coming into the Special Warfare School, "Once you fracture your integrity by violating any one of those three things, trust vanishes. No matter how many appeals you make. If you have betrayed my trust, how do I know you won't fracture it again?

"Adhering to those three traits, you may lose some battles. But you won't place yourself in a compromised position. Each of you represents the entire Special Forces community. People may forget a face, but they never forget the green beret."

OPERATION SAFE PASSAGE

COLONEL KENNETH BOWRA

FORT CAMPBELL, KENTUCKY 1991–93
GROUP COMMANDER
5TH SPECIAL FORCES GROUP

After Desert Storm some people said, "We can put the Vietnam experience behind us." To the contrary, there's a lot of good lessons that we need to retain.

After a year at the Army War College, I was promoted to full colonel and given command of the 5th Special Forces Group. I looked back at my experiences in Vietnam and Cambodia that I believed valuable, and how I could apply those as a Group commander.

In addition, Desert Storm showed us that in the post–Cold War era, the trend is for coalition warfare. Our Special Forces people trained the Arabs across hundreds of miles. My Group engineer was on the Kuwait border showing the Arab Coalition how to use equipment to breach Iraqi defensive barriers. And a Special Forces artillery forward observer was also involved.

I've got fifty-four A-teams in 5th Group now. We can train fifty-four indigenous battalions. During Desert Storm, 5th Group soldiers trained, advised, led, and worked with 109 Arab maneuver battalions and brigades combined. Like the original Kennedy-era Special Forces, we speak the languages. We understand the customs. That's why we excel in perform-training assistance better than anyone else. We can gain the trust and confidence of the people.

An example of our mission: I was a battalion commander in 5th Group in November 1989. We were on an exercise in the Horn of Africa when we got the call to proceed to Pakistan by January to participate in Operations Safe Passage. We were part of a United Nations team. Our mission was to teach Afghan refugees living in Pakistan's northwest frontier how to deactivate the millions of mines that the Soviets had planted in Afghanistan. Hence the name "Operation Safe Passage." The refugee camps were in absolutely barren mountainous terrain near the Khyber Pass.

I deployed one company and kept two-thirds of my battalion back at Fort Campbell. We went through the entire U.S. Department of Defense community looking for mine-clearing expertise. We found that there were really no experts. Everybody had bits and pieces of information.

My Alpha Company went ahead to Pakistan under United Nations colors. We developed the training program that was adopted by the United Nations for their other training teams: British, Italian, French, Turkish, even Thais who brought mine-detecting dogs that can sniff explosives.

I rotated my companies on a six-month basis. Eventually all three of my companies participated in the program. The number of Afghan people we trained was amazing. We also initiated a Master Trainer Program.

Our goal was to train local people to take over our job.

I would go there periodically to inspect the program. Of all the eight to twelve countries of the United Nations that participated, almost all of their personnel were engineers by branch. Our contingent was the only special operations unit. What set us apart was like working with the Montagnard tribes in Vietnam, we understood the customs of the people. We spoke the languages: Farsi, Urdu, and Pushtu. The Afghans could relate well to our guys.

During free time, our Special Forces people were invited back to the camps for dinners and weddings. That's what separates Special Forces people from other branches—we understand the customs. It wasn't a nine-to-five job, like with other participants. Our guys lived and stayed with the local people.

We heard about a Soviet mine device that we had not seen before that was being used in Afghanistan. It was a mine-field control device which could remotely trigger a single mine in a given area. And it can differentiate between an animal and a human, by seismic reading. We wanted to become familiar with this device.

We sat down with some Afghans and asked them about these devices. A short time later, early in the morning, my team walked out of their house. On their doorstep was a device we were asking about. The Afghans went into the field and brought one back in. It was to their benefit to educate us, so that we could figure out how to train them to deactivate the devices.

During the entire two years of the operation, we did not lose one soldier. In the process, we actually became experts. We put together some publications, documenting everything we found and learned. We distributed them in the Army community. The John F. Kennedy Special Warfare Center at Fort Bragg put together a publication that we shared with other services.

By the time the two-year United Nations program ended, we trained 50,000 Afghans in mine-clearing. In other mine-awareness classes civilians were given cloths with pictures of mines and instructions about what to do if you are caught in a mine field.

SEA ANGELS

SERGEANT MAJOR JOSEPH CELESTINE

BANGLADESH 1991
BRIGADE SERGEANT MAJOR
5TH MARINE EXPEDITIONARY BRIGADE

A growing role for U.S. forces in the post–Cold War period is to provide humanitarian assistance after international conflicts or natural disasters. One of the first missions was after the Persian Gulf War. The 5th Marine Expeditionary Brigade was diverted to Bangladesh, one of the poorest countries in the world, to distribute food, water, and medicine after a calamitous typhoon had destroyed much of the country.

On the way home from the Gulf War, our 5th MEB [Marine Expeditionary Brigade] was assigned to provide disaster relief to Bangladesh after the typhoon. Around 150,000 people had perished in flooding, millions were homeless. The entire country is situated below sea level. It's like a huge swamp. The people there were living poorly already. To have a disaster was devastating.

We were assigned to help the poorest of the poor. Those

who the Bangladesh government had a problem getting emergency supplies to. We reached them by helicopter, by small boats, by landing crafts. There were a lot of waterways that went inland, with flood water still moving quite swiftly. The crafts we put in the water needed some power to maneuver against the strong current. Where we couldn't take a craft we used helicopters into the most remote areas.

When we first arrived, we went into an area where flood waters had receded. Right in the middle of a dirt-poor village, five or six miles from the coast, sat two or three huge boats that had been washed in by the flood. It beat the hell out of me how they were going to get those boats back to the ocean.

Villages use little duck ponds for human wastes and use another small pond for drinking water. The flooding meshed them both together. So there was no safe drinking water. Probably the best thing we did was to bring in units to make potable drinking water.

I involved 80 percent of my Marines in the MEB in the relief effort. We tried to send only the number of people ashore who needed to be there, because of the danger of diseases like typhoid. We were worried about them coming back to the ship and infecting others. So we ran a careful program to immunize and then disinfect the crews before they came back in contact with everyone.

I took a helicopter over the area to survey the situation. Villagers were huddled wherever they could find high ground, like little islands. Some of the lowlands were still submerged. When they saw the helicopters, people panicked and ran toward us. So there was danger in airlifting food. We had to send security teams to control the people for orderly distribution.

Food supplies were being donated in huge bulk sacks from various countries. Staple foods like flour and rice. Our job was to move them from the ship to survivors. My Marines felt good about helping. They could see the immediate results—the looks on people's faces.

We also had frustration. Women were reluctant to drink potable water. It had a taste of chlorine. And there is something in their religion about not taking foreign substances into the body. They went back to drinking infested water. They washed in the good clean water and drank the dirty water. It took a major effort by Bangladesh officials to persuade them that there is nothing wrong with chlorinated water.

We changed our unit's name to "The Angels of the Sea."

That's what the people called us, "You are like angels coming from the sea." One of the things that impressed me most was that we had more equipment and medical supplies on board our ships to sustain life than this whole country did. That not only told us how poor that country is. It also told us how fortunate the United States is.

It would be a great opportunity for every Marine to do a relief operation like this early in their career—even if it was in the United States. Going to an impoverished place like West Virginia and building a water system for coal miners. Anything to get an appreciation for how fortunate we are. To realize that we not only have the ability to deal with combat when we are called upon, but we can also build something for people, too.

A lot of Marines in 5th MEB were frustrated after sitting for so many months aboard ship in the Gulf War during the "Deception" operation. And then the war didn't last for very long. They trained so hard and wanted to be involved. But those same kids got to see their training and equipment used for life sustaining work in Bangladesh. It made me feel good to see the smile on my Marines' faces. And how hard they were willing to work.

SOMALIA

COLONEL KENNETH BOWRA

SOMALIA 1992
GROUP COMMANDER
5TH SPECIAL FORCES GROUP

The 5th Special Forces Group operates in the CENTCOM area of operations—the Persian Gulf and the Horn of Africa. In August 1992, we were assigned by CENTCOM to support a limited U.S. emergency mission into Somalia. Four months later, more than 20,000 U.S. troops were authorized by the United Nations. In the months before the Joint U.S. Task Force arrived, the CENTCOM operation was titled Provide Relief.

Brigadier General Labuti put the mission together on very short notice.

We provided a battalion headquarters and one company. I sent Alpha Company of my 2nd Battalion under Major Kent Listoe. He had six A-Detachments [Teams], around 72 people. Each 12-man A-Team has experts in engineering, communications, weapons, medicine and intelligence. More importantly, our Group has operational expertise in the geographic area.

The 5th Group had conducted training missions in Somalia in 1987 and 1988. Some of our senior NCOs were involved, and had a good feel for the place. Our other soldiers had the advantage of knowing the region and could anticipate the environment we would have to operate in.

Each day, we assigned an A-Team to be an airborne [inflight] reaction force and another A-Team as a reaction force on the ground, out of Mombassa, Kenya. Their mission was to provide security for all U.S. humanitarian flights into Somalia. They would fly in on C-130 transport airplanes, ready to respond to any type of emergency. Each team had two desert mobility vehicles on board [armed jeep-like vehicles], which mount a 40mm grenade launcher and a .50-caliber machine-gun. We could move in and evacuate an airfield or provide emergency medical care for any type of crisis.

Between August and November, there were eighteen to twenty U.S. supply flights per day into Somalia. The most dangerous risk to the crews was during the down-loading of food in remote Somali airfields. Gunfire by Somali bandits was an almost everyday occurrence. Two aircrafts were actually struck by small arms fire.

Our soldiers also supported Task Force combat controllers by going into airfields to do a risk-analysis prior to any U.S. flights coming in. They would radio to in-coming flights to warn of any danger. It was inherently dangerous because of armed Somali bandit gangs and the state of anarchy. However, our reaction force had a capability to pull air crews and any other people out of a no-win situation.

In a desperate situation it takes a very mature individual to make a critical decision. The average A-Team member is thirty-two years old. And in special forces we specialize in language and customs of our operational region. At various airfields our guys were able to talk with armed individuals or gangs, rather than going in and making poor decisions that may have resulted in firefights.

The Provide Relief airlift under General Labuti flew more than 1,400 sorties, a quarter-million tons of food and critically needed relief supplies. This was all accomplished before President Bush's decision in late-November 1992 to send [Army and Marine infantry] troops under Operation Restore Hope. In early December, when the operation changed our special forces skills gave additional depth and flexibility to the Joint Task Force. We continued our field mission by providing support [in part, through reconnaissance patrols] for conventional ground units.

In November, I flew into Somalia on a relief flight with one of my teams. We went into a barren remote region. Absolutely bare—no trees at all. What I saw was absolutely anarchy.

We attempted to fly into one field. Around fifteen minutes after we became airborne, we received word from our people on the ground that a firefight had broken out between Somali factions who were located on opposite sides of the airfield. So we had to abort and go to an alternate landing site, which was a dirt strip in another area of the country.

As we helped off-load the airplane, an ancient-looking Somali man came by. He was wearing an old Soviet tanker helmet. We walked up to him—we were not in military uniform, as requested by relief organizations. The old man looked at us, popped to attention, and saluted.

At other off-loadings we saw organized gangs that were hired as security by various relief organizations. They didn't have armed vehicles, but some pickup trucks. It appeared to me that the Operation was just a temporary partial solution. The initial U.S. commitment was clearly needed to get food into desperately needy people's hands. But the situation in the region is rough. It will take quite a long-term commitment by the United Nations to provide any long-term stability or solutions.

SHAPING THE FUTURE

GENERAL ALFRED GRAY

The Pentagon 1987-91
Commandant
U.S. Marine Corps

One of the great lessons not lost on Vietnam was, "We ain't fighting again unless somebody declares war." That was apparent in Desert Storm. We got a mandate at the United Nations. And the mandate of the American people through the Congress. We learned from Vietnam that we have to have the American people with us.

This trend will continue. Unfortunately, the end of the Cold War has not resulted in a world at peace. The collapse of the bipolar balance of power and the shift to a multipolar world has resulted in a less stable and more complex world. Regional powers are attempting to achieve dominant roles. Instability in any region of the world can have a severe negative effect on the global economy. And in the Third World, dramatic increases in population, coupled with the growing gap between rich and poor, will continue to be a major cause of revolutions, insurgencies, and regional wars.

We need a well-thought-out strategy to include consequences of all actions. In areas of crisis, the U.S. ambassadors and country teams at the embassies, and the unified military commanders, need to put some real time on specific problems. While I was Commandant of the Marine Corps, the Panama crisis was an example.

For a couple of years people kept saying, "We've got to do something about Panama. We've got to do something about Noriega. We've got to take him out."

I said, "We could go down there and take him out. But what do you want to have happen in Panama?"

Nobody wanted to talk about the consequences of shaping the future. For those two years before Operation Just Cause, I said, "Do you want to make Panama the fifty-first state? The fifty-ninth territory? What the hell do you want to have happen? I'm not afraid of anything. But, I'm sorry, I have a problem with this."

Trying to shape the consequences, you're not going to have all the answers. You can't foretell all the problems. But for instance, in planning Desert Storm, surely somebody should have been aware of the challenges in southern Iraq from the Shiites. And the Kurdish issue came to the fore as we began to examine the regional dynamics. People are too comfortable with making decisions today and letting the guy on the next watch worry about the consequences.

LICS

COLONEL LEONARD SCOTT

CARLISLE, PENNSYLVANIA 1990–92
DIRECTOR OF MILITARY STRATEGY,
PLANS AND OPERATIONS
& FACULTY INSTRUCTOR
U.S. ARMY WAR COLLEGE

In the post–Cold War, unconventional conflicts involving ethnic and religious rivalries, guerrilla insurgencies, anarchy and narcoterrorism threaten regional stability and world peace. These low intensity conflicts or LICs challenge conventional military doctrines.

Right after the Gulf War ended, we had a guest speaker at the War College who talked about how great the United States' forces did. After he was done, one ally stood up, an officer from India.

He said, "Very interesting presentation. You talked of your lessons learned. But you must understand that Saddam Hussein and the Third World also has lessons learned. They learned not to take on the United States or any other major force in conventional warfare."

They learned that any attempt to take on the United States on a conventional basis, tank-to-tank or weapon-to-weapon, is going to fail. But nonconventional warfare has defeated the United States. The lessons of Vietnam are relevant. Beirut . . . And look at South America right now, the drug war is still unresolved. It doesn't take a rocket scientist to realize that the way you defeat a large nation is through the will of its people. And the way to defeat the will of the people is through time—you grind a conflict out. Unconventional warfare is the way to go.

I don't think we'll have whole armies going overseas to fight anymore. We talk in terms of a corps with two to three divisions for our next battle. I believe that the next one will likely be nonconventional warfare. Are we strong in nonconventional warfare? Our line units are not.

Our Special Forces has always done their job. But our line units like the 82nd Airborne are trained for basic conventional war. Not for anything like the Vietnam-type conflict. We do very little training on LIC [low-intensity conflict] environment. Because nobody can put their hands around it yet. This includes "nation building."

A nineteen-year-old soldier carrying an M-16 rifle is not trained to be a nation builder. He is trained for basic infantry tactics. He's not trained to sit around and guard airfields, or build schools and dams. That is not an easy transition, especially in a hostile environment. That was one of our problems in Vietnam.

The War College is the last formal military schooling that any officer receives. We teach at an operational and strategic level of warfare. We touch on LIC at the strategic level. But the exercises are not very effective. Because the strategic level requires political decisions outside of the U.S. Army. Decisions by State Department and a variety of government agencies must be tied together. The amazing thing is that here at the War College we do not sit with State Department to do exercises on LIC. That tells me that it would be screwed up if we go into that type of situation.

We always say in the Army that, "We have to train as we are going to fight." LIC is coalition warfare—an internal coalition of the White House and government agencies with the military. Yet, we never get together in an exercise scenario where we learn what each other does.

I taught a course on LIC at the War College for a couple of sessions. There were times I thought, "Wait a minute. The

State Department ought to be teaching this part of the course." They don't provide us any instructors. They do have one representative here, but he doesn't teach classes.

The post–Cold War geopolitical situation is increasingly explosive. There are so many ethnic and border conflicts that could escalate into something larger. There is a need for us to put time into looking at the possibility of having to go into low intensity or uncertain political crises.

From the military side, our leadership—particularly General Colin Powell—has articulated our concerns to the President and the Secretary of Defense. That was especially apparent when President Bush explained to the public why American soldiers couldn't intervene into Bosnia. It would take thousands of soldiers to go into a situation like that—it would be a quagmire.

He got that information from Colin Powell and other military leaders who know exactly how we screwed up in Vietnam. We went in with our eyes closed and didn't know what logistical line and security and all other related factors would entail. We have studied our mistakes. We've learned from them. And we have a good knowledge of what it means to commit American forces.

In a few years the Vietnam veterans will be gone from active duty. But we are teaching the next generation of leaders what it means to commit the American army. They will be able to say, "This is what it will cost you, Mr. President, if you decide to do that."

I'm worried about the other agencies. We have a real problem with State Department and others who don't have an understanding of what the implications are in bringing in the Army. They have to realize that you just don't bring in the 82nd Airborne Division. The 82nd cannot survive on the ground by themselves for more than three or four days without support. You must also bring in their resupply, logistics, medical services, engineers.

Before long, instead of one division, you've got the equivalent of two corps on the ground. And you've got to protect all of those people. Which means that you bring in another corps for security. So rather than 20,000 soldiers, you end up sending more than 100,000 people.

I don't know that State and the other agencies understand what our limitations are. I don't believe they are trained for that. With the all-volunteer force of the past two decades, fewer and fewer people in other agencies have military experience. And there is no school similar to the War College for them. There needs to be some way of getting the military and all government agencies to work together in some type of simulated LIC environment scenarios.

When I was teaching LIC, I was very upset with the scenarios I was given. For example, if we had to work on the border of Mexico, the U.S. Army would not be the key player. We have to work with another agency. However, the Army works on a Campaign Plan system. In other words, the commander comes up with a campaign plan. He gives his guidance, which is his vision of how he wants to accomplish the mission. From there he spells out the phases that he wants it in. And then he says, "Execute." His forces then look at the leader's guidance and come up with complementary tasks and missions.

The State Department has been unable to write a campaign plan for us. They don't know how to give us the vision. Or how to spell out pertinent things for us. So the Army has to ask them ten or twenty times. Then when you find out what their structure is, they don't have a staff to support it. They don't know what the hell we're talking about. So, in a crisis, there is a very high probability of misunderstanding and failure.

We've all got to read from the same sheet of music. My God, in the drug war there are forty-some agencies involved. The Army is just a subordinate. The lead agency needs to know our capabilities, to be able to communicate what they need. Whoever is the leader—from whatever agency—needs to be like Schwarzkopf. He has to provide the direction, the campaign plan. If nobody knows what the campaign plan is, how can we execute?

POLICY DECISIONS

SECRETARY JAMES WEBB
SECRETARY OF THE NAVY

THE PENTAGON 1987–88

Lessons were learned from Vietnam and the Gulf War. But they may not apply in formulating effective policy for a crisis like Bosnia. For every military engagement we have to redefine the circumstances in which we will use force, how we use it, and the size and duration of forces deployed. The decision process changes every time we have new personalities in executive positions.

During the Gulf War, there was a very cordial relationship between President Bush, Secretary of Defense Cheney, and Joint Chiefs Chairman Colin Powell. But the Gulf War was a very unique set of circumstances. Politically, it was based on very simple facts on which to develop a military structure. Saddam Hussein put a lot of his army in one flat desert area, dug in, and dared the United States to do something about it. That enabled U.S. policy makers to develop a clear-cut response and precise objective—to evict Iraqi forces from Kuwait. I don't know of another circumstance today that is as clean militarily.

Once the President and Congress decided to use military force, it was very simple to turn to military leaders and say: "Define a force to take out this specific military target." In other situations like Beirut, Vietnam, Bosnia, or even Somalia, the military aspects of the problem are threaded into complex political negotiations. In Vietnam, much of the terrain was mountainous or densely forested. The enemy used deliberate tactics to turn populated areas into battlefields, and uncontrolled borders allowed for hostile resupply and reinforcements.

In 1962, Bernard Fall (a French journalist/historian on Indochina) warned that if we did not understand the very specific nature of the deliberate political violence that was being conducted by the Vietnamese Communists, we would never win. And until the end, U.S. policy makers never fully comprehended that it was a war of political violence.

In the Balkans, we could be faced with similar military and political problems. Gradual military escalation with the hope of driving the Serbs to the bargaining table, without clearly defined political and military objectives, could expand the conflict.

When I look at a crisis like the Balkans, it reminds me of the problems I saw as a journalist in Beirut in 1983.* Our marines were sent into Beirut supposedly to separate warring factions, with the guarantee that we weren't on any particular side. But when you get in the middle of a five-sided argument, if you give any hint that you are listening to one side, the other four attack you. In Beirut, after we signalled that we were supporting the Lebanese army in the battle of Sukalgar, our neutrality was over.

Looking at Bosnia, I ask, "Which side is so compatible with what we believe or is so vital to our national interests that we should put young American lives on the line?" Are we on the Serb side, the Croat side, the Muslim side? No matter how strongly we may feel about people being raped and brutalized, we have to clearly define what we are defending. And what will we do if the defenses we try don't succeed? Because once we commit troops, while politicians and commentators analyze events from Washington, young soldiers are putting their bodies in front of bullets. That is reality in war.

Because of unpredictability in the personality-driven relationship between our chief political and military leaders, and the unpredictable international climate caused by instability in the former Soviet Union, the Congress should have a major role in determining when and where we use military force. During the Cold War, the executive branch accrued greater powers to order troops into combat because the threat from the Soviet bloc was clear and required the ability to respond immediately. In the post–Cold War era the political tensions are more vague and the nature of the response requires more consideration and debate. In situations where our country or military forces do not face direct attack, we should carefully

---

*Webb's coverage of Beirut for "The MacNeil-Lehrer News Hour" received an Emmy Award.

weigh our options and return to the original intention of the Constitution to give the Congress a much greater role.

I resigned as Secretary of the Navy in 1988 because I did not believe that strategic considerations were driving the reductions in force structure. Those questions become paramount today with the extensive downsizing of our forces and overseas deployment bases. We need to redefine our role away from static defense of NATO and possibly Korea, and maintain strong maneuver forces capable of crisis intervention or full-scale combat deployment from these reduced forward bases.

I disagree with the philosophy that, "You should only fight wars you are sure you can win." I know a number of incidents in world history where if people had that attitude, the world would have been changed for the worst. In the confusion of the post–Cold War era, we should ask which of these crises are essential to what we believe and to our interests. Then define a clear approach that will bring these conflicts to a conclusion. But we need to remember that military force is not always the right answer. If force is used imprecisely or out of frustration, the situation could be made worse.

For example, the debate over Balkan intervention seems to be a microcosm of a very large problem that goes beyond Bosnia. If we go in support of the Muslims, beyond a certain point we antagonize not only the Russians, but also the Greeks. That could widen the war. Ancient antagonisms in the region include hostilities between Slavic peoples and Muslims. And between the Greeks and Turks, which was a big problem in trying to keep NATO together and remains a delicate balance. Both of those countries are fired up about the fighting among their neighbors. We have to clearly weigh how an American military intervention would effect our role as a political mediator in that entire region.

National security policy shouldn't be emotionally driven by seeing people suffering on the TV screen. When we use an American military force overseas, it is either in support of an ally, or with a coalition of allies for a specific reason. However, something may be so important that we go in alone for our own reasons. If American interests define that we support a particular side, we may want to use our forces as "multipliers" in the role of trainers or fighting along side the people we are defending, like we have done in South Korea. And if we determine that, "this is a place where we have to be," we must get involved in a wholehearted way and with clearly defined objectives.

During the ill-fated mission to Beirut in 1983 we only had 1,200 Marines on the ground. But when the Marines successfully intervened in 1958, they had 12,000 who took control of the hills surrounding Beirut, secured the entire area and sorted things out, then got the hell out of there. In 1983, after Vietnam, if we had sent in any more Marines the media would have screamed. So our Marines were put in an impossible situation. Once we tilted our hand toward the Lebanese army and became targets of the other factions, we should have either put more Marines in or got those few Marines out. The final result was a lot of people killed when the Marine barracks was bombed.

Our country was founded on a set of ideals, and our national character is that Americans love to be loved. An example is our air drops of supplies into Bosnia. Our European allies are much more capable of doing that job because it is the region where they live. But they all politely told us, "That is very nice," and declined to do anything themselves. So our forces were reluctantly directed to do the job with a lot of caution. As a result, dropping the bundles of food from high altitude had mixed results, and initially made some of the people it was intended for sniper targets.

In defining national security policy, the Joint Chiefs, particularly the Chairman, has the responsibility to make sure that the President has heard every option available and the gains and losses involved before making a policy decision. It's a tough call for a military leader to determine when to lay out those options privately, and when it is necessary to voice them publicly. The big difference with the generation of military leaders from the Vietnam era is that they are more comfortable stating publicly the down side of certain policy options.

However, within a few years all Vietnam veterans will be retired from active duty. And there is a noticeable change happening in the attitude of senior military people. Right after the Gulf War, they had confidence in their relationship with the President to publicly weigh policy options for situations like the Balkans. However, the first months of the Clinton Administration produced noticeable tension and instability in the relationship between military and civilian leaders. As during the Vietnam era, senior military people expressed concern about not being allowed into executive offices to give counsel when policies were being determined.

During the Vietnam War, the Joint Chiefs had a weak structure. They went to the President as a corporate body, with divergent opinions. Presidents Kennedy and Johnson, often authorized policy through the Secretary of Defense to the U.S. Commander in Vietnam, irrespective of the advice of the Joint Chiefs.

As we became deeper embroiled in Vietnam, President Johnson, who was a political compromiser, tried to apply that style of policy without making a clear decision one way or the other on how we should conduct the war. And the Chiefs were frozen out of the process.

Today, the Goldwater-Nichols law gives the Chairman of the Joint Chiefs of Staff centralized authority as the principal military advisor to the Secretary of Defense and the President. That relationship is personality-driven as well. Each President will put his own stamp on how he wants to do business. And the President will create his own operational model.

I'm also concerned about a cycle of history that has been repeated after every American war, the Gulf War being no exception. The further downsizing of the military appears to be driven by the "Desert Storm Equivalent" theory formulated by Secretary of Defense Les Aspin when he was still in Congress. But there will probably never be another war as simple as that. And to judge other nations' military capabilities on Iraq's military force numbers can lead to the types of Vietnam era problems caused by President Johnson's statistics-oriented Secretary of Defense Robert McNamara [whose staff included Les Aspin]. Every army in the world has different qualities of people behind the machines. Different qualities of leadership, different mindsets. And unlike the Iraqis in Kuwait, other armies will fight tenaciously if they have the right reasons.

There is a danger in becoming over-confident. A vulnerability in our armed forces is that we now have a more political officer corps that can have a negative effect. I say this having been around military people from the time I was born. An example is how the Tailhook Scandal [a September 1991 post–Desert Storm incident of sexual abuse by a group of naval aviators] went out of control. One of the reasons was that after the incident was reported, political-minded officers tried to determine how to play their cards rather than fix the problem.

I don't mean to personalize this. But if I was Secretary of

the Navy, and heard about the incident, I would've called the senior military officer present and said, "Fix that now. You've got thirty seconds to start an investigation, or you are retired. I want the people who are guilty of battery or abuse out of the Navy. And separate the people who were simply there but are innocent of any wrong doing." If they had done that, when the Congress made inquiries, the Navy could have said, "We dealt with the people. We don't tolerate that behavior. It doesn't represent the culture of the Navy." No more than people getting out of hand at a fraternity party speaks for the culture of a university.

However, leaders originally assigned to deal with this put their own self-preservation over the good of the military. And when public attention to the incident became feverish when the Congress got involved, the Navy didn't support innocent people. For example, after the incident a Rear Admiral helped his former female aide write her complaint then put his own cover letter on it and personally handed it to the Chief of Naval Aviation urging an investigation. He was known as a superb officer and had received honors as the Navy's fighter pilot of the year and commander of its outstanding fighter squadron. However, he was summarily relieved of his command, without being allowed to present his own case, when he was mistakenly accused of not having assisted his aide.

A difficult period could develop if the Executive Branch imposes social policies without an understanding of military culture. The President ultimately chooses the Joint Chiefs of Staff and Commanders of each military theater and every senior officer of four-stars and above. Emphasis on social issues may require that senior military leaders, in order to be promoted, must support political policies that have not been properly planned and do not yet exist. What will that say about the types of people being promoted?

If there is a dangerous political/military crisis that could involve thousands of lives, will the President have military leaders that will give him pragmatic unvarnished advice? Or will they be yes-men? How will they separate politics from sound military reservation? The majority of people I know at senior levels will try to find a way to give honest advice. But that doesn't rule out a President looking to promote people who won't.

After Vietnam, when the military was struggling, the Carter Administration tried to impose a lot of social theories as policy. They put a priority on women's issues. They were not winning on passing the Equal Rights Amendment through Congress. And the military can become a very convenient social laboratory. So the Administration decided that they were going to end all restrictions on women in combat. The civilian leaders ordered the Joint Chiefs of Staff to testify before Congress in favor of women in combat.

Marine Commandant Bob Barrow first told the Secretary of the Navy and the Deputy Secretary of Defense he did not believe that was a legal order. The military has a duty to support any existing policy. But you cannot order a military leader to give you the advice that you want to hear. Whether or not women should have a role in combat, it was the height of arrogance for civilian leaders to order the military to support a policy that does not exist. This is different than if the Congress had already voted that all restrictions should be lifted. In that case the Commandant must comply, or be bounced. But if the Commandant and the other Chiefs are being asked for their advice, their responsibility is to give an honest opinion.

Barrow told the Secretaries that he was going to check with his legal counsel to determine whether that was a legal order. But if he was to obey the order, he was also going to tell Congress the circumstances under which he was testifying. As a result, the Secretaries backed off. In my opinion, that was one of the key events in the military regaining self-confidence to take care of itself after Vietnam.

The question today is how many senior people will make compromises on certain issues for the benefit of their own promotion. What will the civilian leadership do to find people who will implement the social experiments that they want? It's a two-way street. A combination of radical downsizing and experimental social policies can destroy the integrity of what was rebuilt after Vietnam.

The intangible ingredients of a competent force are spirit, morale, and leadership by example. When discipline and self-respect breaks down, that usually starts at the top. If the senior leadership becomes a hierarchy of compromise, when it comes time to make life or death decisions, troops won't believe that their superiors are looking out for their best interest. And as a result, they won't perform very well.

A lot of what makes a leader is personality-driven. In our military there will always be people who have the courage to stand up for their convictions. The question is will they be re-

tired as colonels. Or whether they will be allowed to make
their way to the top.

THE CIRCLE

BRIGADIER GENERAL
JOSEPH "KEITH" KELLOGG

STUTTGART, GERMANY 1992–94
COMMANDING GENERAL
SPECIAL OPERATIONS COMMAND, EUROPE

I spoke with then-Colonel Kellogg in his 82nd Airborne Division office at Fort Bragg. He placed his wallet on the table and pulled out a piece of plain white paper, folded into a four-inch square. He told me that he obtained it at the Vietnam Veterans Memorial in Washington, D.C. It was a computer printout of the hometown and date of birth of a young sergeant who perished during Kellogg's first platoon command.

Coming home from the Gulf War was very emotional. On April 1, 1991, I got aboard a chartered United Airlines flight in Saudi Arabia. The airplane was decorated with red, white, and blue balloons, American flags and banners. A couple of the senior stewardesses had flown as young women on charter flights for American soldiers to and from Vietnam. We reminisced about that. We said, "This sure isn't like twenty years ago."

I told my young troopers, "Really enjoy this."

I first began to feel the *closure* with the Vietnam era when we got up to the Euphrates River in Iraq. I said to myself, "We've closed the door on Vietnam. We've done it. The circle is complete."

I started to get a sense of the impact when we got back to Saudi Arabia and I was able to watch CNN. We were stunned by some of the Homecoming celebrations.

I went to the parades in Washington, D.C., and New York

City. In Washington I felt the circle had been closed from twenty-four years ago, when I first came into the Army.

When we were marching down the street in Washington, I thought, "This is the parade that should have been held twenty-four years ago." It was frustrating because there were a lot of very brave acts by brave men in Vietnam that have never been recognized.

After the parade, I went to the "Wall" [Vietnam Veterans Memorial] as part of my personal closure. At the memorial, people help you find the name of the person you lost in the war. I was looking for the name of one of my squad leaders from my recon platoon in the 101st Airborne Division who was killed in action. The memorial people give you a piece of paper so that when you find his name engraved on the Wall, you place the paper over it and rub it with a pencil to get a stenciled copy.

I knew that his full name was Harold D. Stanton, and that he died on January 16, 1968. But I didn't know he was from Jonesboro, Illinois. And I didn't know when he was born. He was one of the first people I ever lost.

It happened two weeks before the infamous Tet Offensive. Our recon platoon was in War Zone D, near the Cambodian border, leading the battalion. We walked into a hellacious firefight.

We didn't realize that we had hit an entire North Vietnamese regiment that was moving from Cambodia to attack Saigon. We had a tiger by the tail. They began to fight a rearguard action against my thirty-three men. We stayed on them. It was a bloody mess. Sergeant Stanton was killed during the fighting.

Those guys who were in my first platoon in Vietnam stay with me. The years have faded, and the memories have faded. But I still remember what they did.

The young sergeants took care of me when I was a green lieutenant. They taught me the right things about how to stay alive in combat.

After the big Gulf War parade ended, I walked over to the Vietnam Veterans Memorial to talk to Sergeant Stanton. I told him and all my other soldiers who perished, "Closure complete. The lessons learned in Vietnam were good ones. We did the job in the Gulf." I didn't break faith with my guys.

The genesis of the victory in the Gulf was Vietnam. That's where it started. The commitment of the commanders in the

Gulf were people who years ago said, "Never again. I will not let that happen to this army again."

What we learned in Vietnam we brought forward with us. If that saved the lives of thousands of Americans, and allied and Iraqi civilians, then the 58,000 who perished in Vietnam didn't die for nothing.

GLOSSARY

ARVN: South Vietnamese army
ATO: air tasking order
AWACS: the Airborne Warning and Control System aircraft
BDA: bomb damage assessment
CINCLANT: Commander in Chief, Atlantic
CINCEUR: Commander in Chief, Europe
CINCPAC: Commander in Chief, Pacific
CENTCOM: Central Command; area of authority, Southwest Asia, Horn of Africa, Persian Gulf
CORPS, THE: Marine Corps
CP: Command Post
CSAR: combat search and rescue
DELTA FORCE: top-secret, antiterrorist unit
DEPMEDS: deployable medical systems
D.I.: drill instructor
DOCTRINE: military battle-fighting philosophy
ECM: electronic countermeasure
EOD: explosive ordnance disposal
FAC: forward air controller
FID: foreign internal defense
FLIR: forward-looking infrared
FMLN: Farabundo Marti National Liberation Front; a coalition of Communist and revolutionary organizations in El Salvador
GPS: Global positioning satellite navigation system
G3: Division Operations & Planning officer
GUNNY: gunnery sergeant
HARM: high-speed antiradiation missile
HUEY: transport helicopter

HUMVEE: or Hmmwv; High-mobility multipurpose wheeled vehicle

J3: Operations & Planning officer on a Joint Command Staff

KIA: killed in action

KHMER ROUGE (KR): quasi-Maoist Cambodian Communist movement

LANTIRN: Low-Altitude Navigation and Targeting Infrared System for Night

LAW: light antitank weapon; shoulder-fired

LIC: low-intensity conflict

LZ: landing zone

MEDEVAC: medical evacuation

MEU: Marine Expeditionary Unit

MIA: missing in action

MLRS: Multiple Launch Rocket System

MP: military police

M113: armored personnel carrier

MTT: military training team

NCO: noncommissioned officer

NVA: North Vietnamese army

OCS: Officer Candidate School

PAVE LOW: Air Force MH-53J electronic warfare helicopter

PDF: Popular Defense Forces; in Noriega's Panama

PSYOPS: Psychological Operations

RPG: rocket-propelled grenade

RPV: remotely powered vehicle

RULES OF ENGAGEMENT: military rules for conducting hostilities

SAM: surface-to-air missile

SOCCENT: Special Operations, Central Command

SOCOM: Special Operations Command

SOG: Studies & Observation Group

SOUTHCOM: Southern Command; area of authority, Latin America

SPECIAL FORCES (SF): U.S. Army special operations forces

S2: Intelligence officer

TAC AIR: jet fighter bombers

TACC: Tactical Air Control Center

THEATER: area of war operations

TLAM: Tomahawk land attack missile

TOC: Tactical Operations Center

TOT: time on target

TOW MISSILES: Targeted on wire antitank missiles
TRIPLE-A: antiaircraft artillery
USSOCOM: U.S. Special Operations Command
VC: Viet Cong
WIA: wounded in action

INDEX

AL SANTOLI

* * *

Published by Ballantine Books.
Available in your local bookstore.